the rockies

Project Editors: Diana Ackland and Janie Freeburg
Field Editor: Sriyani Tidball
Directed and Designed by Hans Johannes Hoefer

APA PRODUCTIONS

Insight Guides

THE INSIGHT GUIDES SERIES RECEIVED SPECIAL AWARDS FOR EXCELLENCE FROM THE PACIFIC AREA TRAVEL ASSOCIATION IN 1980 AND 1982.

THE ROCKIES

First Edition Published by
©APA PRODUCTIONS (HK) LTD, 1985
All rights reserved ISBN 9971-982-22-6
Printed in Singapore by Singapore National Printer Pte. Ltd.
Color Separation In Singapore by Colourscan Pte Ltd

U.S. and	British Isles edition:	Australia and
Canadian Edition:	HARRAP LTD	New Zealand edition:
PRENTICE-HALL INC.	ISBN 0245-54292-2	LANSDOWNE PRESS
ISBN 013-782277-4		ISBN 0-7018-1942-1

APA PRODUCTIONS

Publisher and Managing Director: Hans Johannes Hoefer
Executive Director Marketing: Yvan Van Outrive
Executive Editors: Adam Liptak
Jay Itzkowitz
Financial Controller: Henry Lee
Administrative Manager: Alice Ng
Editor: Stuart Ridsdale
Assistant Editor: Vivien Loo
Production Coordinator: Nancy Yap

Contributing Editors

Ravindralal Anthonis, Jon Carroll, Virginia Hopkins, Jay Itzkowitz, Phil Jarratt, Tracy Johnston, Ben Kalb, Wilhelm Klein, Saul Lockhart, Sylvia Mayuga, Gordon McLauchlan, Kal Müller, Eric M. Oey, Daniel P. Reid, Kim Robinson, Ronn Ronck, Rolf Steinberg, Desmond Tate, Lisa Van Gruisen, Made Wijaya.

Contributing Writers

A.D. Aird, Ruth Armstrong, T. Terence Barrow, F. Lisa Beebe, Bruce Berger, Dor Bahadur Bista, Clinton V. Black, Star Black, Frena Bloomfield, John Borthwick, Roger Boschman, Tom Brosnahan, Linda Carlock, Jerry Carroll, Tom Chaffin, Nedra Chung, Tom Cole, Orman Day, Kunda Dixit, Richard Erdöes, Guillermo Garcia-Oropeza, Ted Giannoulas, Barbara Gloudon, Harka Gurung, Sharifah Hamzah, Willard A. Hanna, Elizabeth Hawley, Sir Edmund Hillary, Tony Hillerman, Jerry Hopkins, Peter Hutton, Neil Jameson, Michael King, Michele Kort, Thomas Lucey, Leonard Lueras, Michael E. Macmillan, Derek Maitland, Buddy Mays, Craig McGregor, Reinhold Messner, Julie Michaels, Barbara Mintz, M.R. Priya Rangsit, Al Read, Elizabeth V. Reyes, Victor Stafford Reid, Harry Rolnick, E.R. Sarachchandra, Uli Schmetzer, lisa Sharp, Norman Sibley, Leslie Marmon Silko, Peter Spiro, Harold Stephens, Keith Stevens, Michael Stone, Colin Taylor, Deanna L. Thompson, Randy Udall, James Wade, Mallika Wanigasundara, William Warren, Cynthia Wee, Tony Wheeler, Linda White, H. Taft Wireback, Alfred A. Yuson, Paul Zach.

Contributing Photographers

Carole Allen, Roland Ammon, Ping Amranand, Walter D. Andreae, Ray Cranbourne, Rennie Ellis, Alain Evrard, Ricardo Ferro, Lee Foster, Manfred Gottschalk, Allen Grazer, Werner Hahn, Dallas and John Heaton, Brent Hesselyn, Dennis Lane, Max Lawrence, Bud Lee, Philip Little, R. Ian Lloyd, Bret Reed Lundberg, Kal Müller, Ronni Pinsler, Günter Pfannmuller, G.P. Reichelt, Dan Rocovits, David Ryan, Frank Salmoiraghi, Thomas Schöllhammer, Blair Seitz, David Stahl, Tom Tidball, Paul Van Riel, Rolf Verres, Joseph F. Viesti, Paul Von Stroheim, Bill Wassman, Jan Whiting, Rendo Yap, Hisham Youssef.

While contributions to Insight Guides are very welcome, the publisher cannot assume responsibility for the care and return of unsolicited manuscripts or photographs. Return postage and/or a self-addressed envelope must accompany unsolicited material if it is to be returned. Please address all editorial contributions to Apa Productions, P.O. Box 219, Orchard Point Post Office, Singapore 9123.

MARKETING, SALES AND ADVERTISING

Insight Guides are available through the international book trade in 30 countries around the world as single copies or as complete collectors sets at discounts. Visit your nearest bookshop. Should any of the Insight Guides listed below be unavailable or out of stock, please refer to the ISBN numbers when ordering through the bookshop or direct through these distributors.

Distributors:
Australia: Lansdowne Press, 176 South Creek Road, Dee Why, N.S.W. 2099, AUSTRALIA **Benelux:** Uitgeverij Cambium, Naarderstraat 11, 1251 Aw Laren, The Netherlands. **Denmark:** Copenhagen Book Centre Aps, Roskildeveji 338, DK-2630 Tastrup, Denmark **France:** Librairie Armand Colin 103 Boulevard St. Michael 75005 Paris France. **Germany:** Nelles Verlag, Schleissheimer Str. 371b, 8000 Munich 45. **Hawaii:** Pacific Trade Group Inc., P.O. Box 1227, Kailua, Oahu, Hawaii 96734, U.S.A. **Hong Kong:** Far East Media Ltd., Vita Tower, 7th Floor, Block B, 29 Wong Chuk Hang Road, Hong Kong. **India and Nepal:** India Book Distributors, 107/108 Arcadia Building, 195 Narima Point, Bombay-400-021, India. **Indonesia:** P T Jaeng, Jalan Patiunus 47, Pekalongan Jateng, Indonesia. **Italy:** Zanfi Editori srl-Via Ganaceto, 121-41100 Modena, Italy. **Jamaica:** Kingston Publishers, 1-A Norwood Avenue, Kingston 5, Jamaica. **Japan:** Charles E. Tuttle Co. Inc., 2-6 Suido 1-Chome, Bunkyo-ku, Tokyo, Japan. **Kenya:** Camerapix, Press Centre, Chester House, P.O. Box 45048, Nairobi, Kenya. **Korea:** Korea Britannica Corporation, C.P.O. Box 690, Seoul 100, Korea, 162-1, 2-ga, Jangchung-dong, Jung-gu, Seoul, Korea. **Mexico:** Distribuidora Britannica S.A., Rio Volga 93, Col Cuauhtemoc, 06500 Mexico 5 D.F. Mexico. **New Zealand:** Lansdowne Rigby, Unit 3, 3 Marken Place, Glenfield, Auckland. **Pakistan:** Liberty Book Stall, Inverarity Road, Karachi 03, Pakistan. **Philippines:** National Book Store, Inc., 701 Rizal Avenue, Manila, Philippines. **Singapore and Malaysia:** MPH Distributors (S) Pte. Ltd., 601 Sims Drive #03-21 Pan-I Warehouse and Office Complex, Singapore 1438. **Sri Lanka:** K.V.G. de Silva & Sons (Colombo) Ltd., 415 Galle Road, Colombo 4, Sri Lanka. **Spain:** Altair, Riera Alta 8, Barcelona 1, Spain. **Sweden:** Esselte Kartcentrum, Vasagatan 16, S-111 20 Stockholm, Sweden. **Switzerland:** MPA Ch. du Bochet 68, Ch-1025 St. Sulpice, Switzerland. **Taiwan:** Caves Books Ltd., 103 Chungshan N. Road, Sec. 2, Taipei, Taiwan, Republic of China. **Thailand:** Apa Productions (Pte) Ltd., 5, Lengkong Satu, Singapore 1441. **United Kingdom:** Harrap Ltd., 19-23 Ludgate Hill, London EC4M 7PD, England, United Kingdom. **Mainland United States and Canada:** Prentice-Hall Inc., Englewood Cliffs, New Jersey 07632. U.S.A.

German editions: Nelles Verlag GmbH, Schleissheimerstrasse 371b, 8000 Munich 45, West Germany. **French editions:** Les Editions Errance, 11 rue de l'Arsenal, 75004 Paris, France Distributor: Librairie Armand Colin, 103 Boulevard St. Michael, 75005 Paris, France. **Italian editions:** Zanfi Editori srl-Via Ganaceto, 121-41100 Modena, Italy.

Advertising and Special Sales Representatives

Advertising carried in Insight Guides gives readers direct access to quality merchandise and travel-related services. These advertisements are inserted in the Guide in Brief section of each book. Advertisers are requested to contact their nearest representatives, listed below.

Special sales, for promotional and educational purposes within the international travel industry, are also available. Interested parties can contact marketing director Yvan Van Outrive directly at Apa Productions (HK) Ltd., P.O. Box 219, Orchard Point Post Office, Singapore 9123.

APA PHOTO AGENCY PTE LTD

General Manager: Sylvia Muttom
Together with our associate, Tony Stone Worldwide, the APA Photo Agency represents the work of many leading photographers for publication rights. More than 150,000 original colour transparencies are in our files and available in SE Asia and throughout the world for advertising, editorial, cultural and educational uses.

Singapore: Apa Photo Agency Pte Ltd 5 Lengkong Satu Singapore 1441. **London:** Tony Stone Worldwide 28 Finchley Road St John's Wood London NW8 6ES. **Paris:** Fotogram-Stone Agence Photographique 45 rue de Richelieu 75001 Paris France **Barcelona:** Fototeca Torre dels Pardals 7 Barcelona 08026 Spain **Johannesburg:** Color Library (Pty) Ltd P O Box 1659 Johannesburg South Africa 2000 **Sydney:** The Photographic Library of Australia Pty Ltd 7 Ridge Street North Sydney New South Wales 2060 Australia **Tokyo:** Orion Press 55-1 Kanda Jimbocho Chiyoda-ku Tokyo 101 Japan.

CARTOGRAPHY

To complement **Insight Guides** and bring readers a more complete package of travel information, Apa Productions — in cooperation with cartographer Gunter Nelles of Munich, West Germany — has begun publication of a series of detailed maps on selected travel destinations. Initial maps cover Asian countries and cities:

WESTERN INDONESIA   BALI   MALAYSIA   NEPAL   PHILIPPINES
SRI LANKA   THAILAND

Joining the growing number of American titles in Apa Productions' *Insight Guide* series is this guide to the Middle Rockies, stretching through the five states of Colorado, Utah, Wyoming, Idaho and Montana. Years ago it was fortune, fame and freedom that drew enterprising travellers westwards and now, *Insight Guide: The Rockies* leads the way in the same enterprising spirit.

Apa Productions is a Singapore-based publishing house whose innovative approach to creating travel chronicles has been honored throughout the world. Since publisher **Hans**

Hoefer

Ackland

Freeburg

Hoefer established Apa in 1970, the *Insight Guide* series has won worldwide recognition for its sensitive cultural portrayal of leading travel destinations. Having studied printing, book production, design and photography in Krefeld, West Germany, Hoefer is a disciple of the Bauhaus tradition of graphic arts.

Heading the *Insight Guide: The Rockies* project were two California-based editors, **Diana Ackland** and **Janie Freeburg**, who coordinated each stage of the massive project from concept to finished product. They organized field editors, writers, photographers and shaped the book carefully during its nine months of production.

Diana Ackland's editorial background started in New York where she was an editor in the Features and Articles Department of *Good Housekeeping* magazine. From there she moved on to Los Angeles where she became Promotion Manager for the *Los Angeles Times* Syndicate. Now she serves as Vice-President of Sequoia Communications, the Santa Barbara company Ackland and her husband Donald run. Ackland was educated at Pine Manor and Dickinson Colleges on the U.S. east coast where she studied English and Art History. She fell in love with the Rockies during her first visit there in the summer in 1984. The Wapiti Valley between Cody (Wyoming) and Yellowstone Park is particularly close to her heart.

Janie Freeburg, managing editor of Sequoia Communications, brings a variety of experience to her editorial work. She has planned, edited and designed a number of publications in eight years as a public relations specialist. Her work has covered such diverse topics as surgical advancement, women's studies and musical arrangement for the celtic harp. Freeburg graduated from the University of California, Irvine, with a degree in Comparative Cultures, followed by studies in commercial art and graphic design—a combination that she says makes her a good conversationalist who loves to produce books.

In addition to the California project editors, Field Editor **Sriyani Tidball** was indispensable to the project. Tidball gathered a strong group of writers from the Rockies area, helped develop the editorial format, met multiple deadlines, worked on the preselection of her husband's photos and wrote several pieces herself—including the massive *Guide in Brief* section in the back of this book. Tidball's previous experience with Apa Productions included work on the *Insight Guide: Sri Lanka*. A Sri Lankan herself, Tidball was educated at the University of Sri Lanka, the Royal Institute of British Architecture and the University of Nebraska. She holds a degree in Architecture and has been a director of the Sri Lankan branch of Grant Kenyon and Ekhart, Foremost Productions (publishing), and is also a partner in her husband's photographic company. Her work has been published in several Asian magazines inflight airline magazines. Even though Tidball is the mother of three, she still finds time for her favorite cause—the Community Concern Society in Colombo for Sri Lanka's poor.

Tom Tidball, who wrote the National Parks section and contributed the majority of the beautiful photography for this book, runs the Tidball Photographic Company in Sri Lanka. Born and raised in Lincoln, Nebraska, Tidball studied at the University of Nebraska and received a degree in education. He taught pre-school and public school and then switched to free-lance photography in Asia. He now produces publications and audio visuals. Tidball came back to America specifically to work on *Insight Guide: The*

Rockies. He and his wife and children travelled throughout the five Middle Rockies states during the summer of 1984 shooting approximately 4,000 slides of Rockies landscapes, festivals, people and their lifestyles. His photographic archive was invaluable to this book.

The Tidballs wish to extend special thanks to Richard Grant, Dr. Maryanne Parthum, the Denver and Colorado Conventions and Visitors Bureau, the Aspen Chamber of Commerce, the Salt Lake City Visitors Bureau, the Wyoming Travel Commission, Montana Travel Promotion, the Idaho Travel Committee and the Shoshone Bannock Tribal Council—all of whom assisted with their Rockies trip and research.

Photographer **Joe Viesti**, based in New York City, went to the Rockies on special assignment to shoot winter scenes, activities and ski resorts in a vast winter wonderland. Viesti has combined his profession, photography, with his love of travel, his fascination with other cultures, and his desire to focus on positive and colorful images of man. His work has previously been represented in the *Insight Guides* to *Florida, Southern California, American Southwest, New England, Continental Europe* and *Texas*. He has shot for American Express, National Geographic Society, TWA Airlines and several travel corporations. His work has also appeared in publications such as, *Geo, Stern,* and *Pacific*. For the past eight years, Viesti has specialized in photographing celebrations around the world; in 1984, his colorful collection was tapped for the UNICEF *Engagement Calendar*, marking the first time the work of a single artist has been featured solo.

Barbara Fifer who wrote "Rocky Mountain Highs and Lows" and "Bozeman, Montana" is the assistant editor of *Montana Magazine* in Helena, MT. Born and raised in Ohio with a B.A. from Ohio University, Fifer has been a speech and press writer for the AFL-CIO of Montana and an editor for the Montana Historical Society and Brodart, Inc. Her work has been published in *Southwest Art, Montana, the Magazine of Western History, Sphere Magazine* (Ohio Univ.) and the *Sidney (Ohio) Daily News*.

Linda Zuick, author of the Rockies history section and the "Jackson Hole, Wyoming" piece, is from Lincoln, Nebraska and she holds a B.S. in microbiology and chemistry from the University of Nebraska plus a "half completed" masters degree in English. Zuick knows the Rockies like the back of her hand since she spent many summer vacations and winter ski trips there as a child. Other travels include "too many summers with five children in Northern Minnesota and two weeks worth of London too long ago!"

Virginia Hopkins did an outstanding job writing four major pieces for this book: "Rocky Mountain People," "The Front Range of Colorado," "Colorado Mountain Towns" and "The Aspen Mystique." Hopkins knows North America well having lived in Aspen, Colorado and in New York City after her graduation from Yale University, Connecticut. Her vast knowledge of the Southwest United States formerly won her the role of project editor for Apa's *Insight Guide: American Southwest*. Her Rockies experiences made her an indispensable contributor to

S. Tidball   T. Tidball

Zuick   Hopkins   Jones

this new book. Hopkins' qualifications include editing *Aspen Magazine* and writing for publications as varied as *Life* and *Outside* magazines.

Professional rodeo barrel racer, **Patty Jones**, was the perfect choice for the "Blazing Saddles: Cowboys, Ranchers and Farmers" feature. Jones, as part of an armed services family, travelled all over the United States and Europe, but she considers the American West her home. Jones studied at the University of Colorado at Colorado Springs, and she now lives and works at the Dickinson Livestock Marketing ranch where she is advertising manager. Her first love, however, is the rodeo and she serves as president of the Colorado Chapter of the Womens' Professional Rodeo Association. Jones' writing has appeared in the *Texas Longhorn Journal, Western Horsemen, Pro Rodeo Sports News, High Plains Journal* and many other periodicals.

Betty Stevens, author of "Indians Then and Now" and "Canyon Country," is a reporter for the *Lincoln, Nebraska Journal* and the *Durango (Colorado) Herald*. She has also worked with Prentice-Hall, Washington, D.C. since 1968. Her articles have appeared in a wide variety of religious and Sunday supplement newspaper magazines. Perhaps her most interesting assignment was a series of articles written from Wounded Knee, South Dakota, during the American Indian Movement takeover in the spring of 1973. There she got an inside look at modern Indian life by participating in an all-night peyote rite with the Native American church and an Indian sweat-lodge purification rite. She has reported on Indian interests since 1971.

Viesti   *Fifer*

Stevens   *Hara*

Pamela Stenmark, as a ski expert and author of the book *Skiing for Women*, was the perfect writer to tackle the "Outdoor Rush" and "Ski Resorts" pieces. Stenmark lives in one of the most glamorous Rockies ski resorts— Vail, Colorado—and she serves as public relations manager there for Vail Associates, Inc. Formerly, she was director of the Copper Mountain (Colorado) Institute and an instructor in the Vail Ski School for eight years. Stenmark studied at the University of Colorado at Boulder and is widely travelled.

Sheila Andren's western roots go way back to her grandfather, Jim Corder, who came to Wyoming from Kentucky in a covered wagon. Andren was raised in Cody, Wyoming, and is now director of public relations there at the prestigious Buffalo Bill Historical Center. Andren studied at Montana University in Bozeman and lived and worked in Billings, MT, before returning to Cody. Her experience includes advertising copywriting, media planning and agency ownership. Through her work at the Historical Center she has been widely published in national and international magazines and newspapers. Her piece on "Cody, Wyoming" gives a glimpse of her special world in Cody.

Historical consultant, **Anthony Godfrey**, author of the "Salt Lake City, Utah" piece heads his own agency, Godfrey and Associates. He was educated at S.U.N.Y. in New York and the University of Utah where he is currently majoring in Western and native American history. He has travelled throughout the Rocky Mountains since 1972, and as an "outsider" to Salt Lake City he has seen it grow and change extensively like much of the new American West. Godfrey's writing has also appeared in *Arizona and the West* magazine.

The author of "Utah, North of Great Salt Lake" and "Mormons: A Chosen People" is **John R. Alley, Jr.**, editor of Howe Brothers Book Publishers in Salt Lake City. Alley was raised in the Salt Lake area and studied history at the University of Utah. He is currently a Ph.D. candidate in history at the University of California, Santa Barbara. Alley has been published in the *Utah Historical Quarterly* and in the following books: *Handbook of North American Indians, Vol. II Great Basin* (Washington: Smithsonian Press); *A Utah Navajo History* and *The Las Vegas Paiutes: A Short History*.

Photographer **Hara** wrote the special sidebar on "Taking Good Photographs" for *Insight Guide* travellers who want to capture memorable images of their visit. Hara is a Texas girl who moved to California to study photography at the Brooks Institute of Santa Barbara. In 1980, she received a grant from Chevron to do a three-year nature photographic project on California's Channel Islands. She has also done projects for the National Park Service and the Smithsonian Institution. Her work has appeared in *National Geographic's Traveler, Better Homes and Gardens, Smithsonian Magazine, Mademoiselle, Glamour, Seventeen* and *Esquire* among others, plus books, such as *A Visit to the Queen Mary and Spruce Goose*, the *Official Hearst Castle Photo Tour Guide, Vintage Valley: Santa Barbara Wine Country* and *Scenic Highway One*.

Others who assisted in putting the book to bed are: **Bruce Bernstein**, a graduate student at Princeton University, who photographed many of the historical reproductions in this book; the **Princeton University Library** which was generous to open its fine collection to Apa's cause; editorial critiquers **Adam Liptak** and **John Beckman** whose advises and comments were invaluable; Apa's assistant editor **Vivien Loo** who guided every step of the book development process assisting in editorial ideas, layouts, photo gathering, copyediting, typeset and paste-up; and production staff **Nancy Yap** and **Rafie Sain**.

—Apa Productions

TABLE OF CONTENTS

TABLE OF CONTENTS

WELCOME TO THE ROCKIES

Your first encounter with the Rockies is one of life's magical moments. You will be treated to a breathtaking panorama of some of America's most awe-inspiring natural beauty: sweeping colorful vistas, towering mountains, charming mountain villages nestled in valleys and mountainsides, sprawling ranches with farmlands that stretch as far as the eye can see, and the occasional, unexpected metropolitan cities that surprise the visitor with their very existence after endless natural splendor.

The Rockies present a wealth of unsurpassed virgin beauty— what former United States President Theodore Roosevelt called "scenery that bankrupts the English language." Shimmering blue lakes, scenic roadways, parks, forests, recreation areas and wondrous rock formations are free for all to enjoy. And, as if this were not enough, there is also the added thrill of the rodeo, skiing on choice mountain slopes, ballooning over snowpeaked mountains, and whitewater rafting down a rushing river. . . not to mention the abundant fishing, sailing, camping and backpacking on hand at every turn.

The air here is really fresher, the water clearer, the sky bigger than any place you will ever see. The clean, crisp atmosphere penetrates the senses. A combination of adventure, natural beauty, wildlife, sports, history and art is to be found in all five middle Rocky states: Colorado, Idaho, Montana, Utah and Wyoming.

The Rockies today are as unchanged as when the first pathfinders, Lewis and Clark, unlocked the American West. They were followed by mountain men, fur traders, gold and silver prospectors, land and cattle barons, cowboys and ranchers, copper kings, countless visionaries, and today, those in search of the robust life.

Welcome, then, to the Rockies. Enjoy everything they have to offer: the varied recreational activities, the scenery, the wildlife and the history. Memorable adventures await you here. . . .

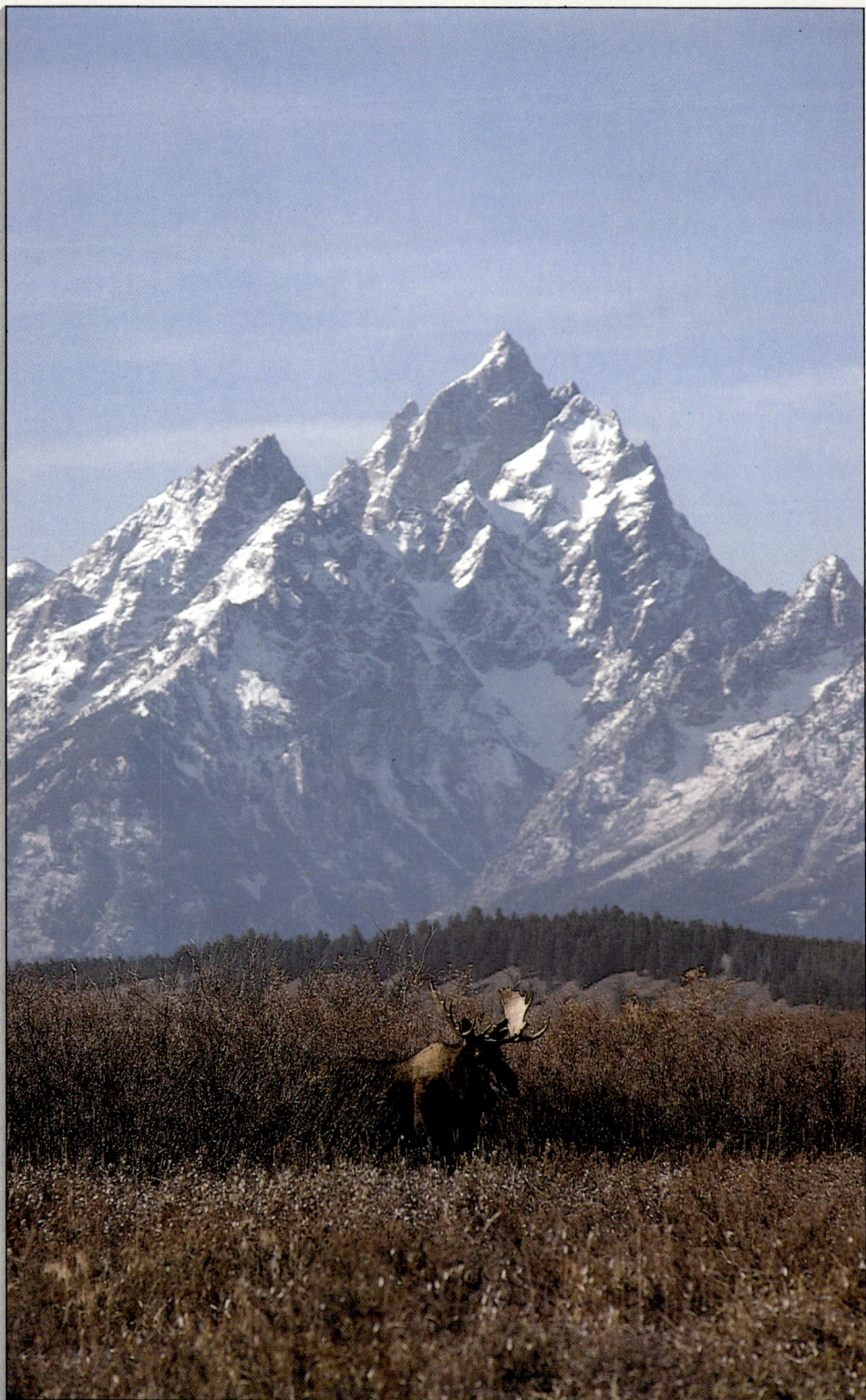

ROCKY MOUNTAIN HIGHS AND LOWS

Because of their many perpetually snow-capped peaks, the Rocky Mountains were called the "Shining Mountains" by the Indians who lived or travelled within sight of them. That poetic name was recorded by the Verendrye brothers, French explorers who were the first whites to see the Rockies, in what are now Montana and Wyoming, in 1742-43.

Plains Indians, such as the Cheyenne, who lived east of the Rockies in the flat country of the High Plains, considered the mountains a place where only spirits could safely go and humans dared not venture—a place to hold in awe, but not one to explore.

When Europeans began to come into this area, they pragmatically called the range filled with bare-rock crests the "Stony," and then the Rocky Mountains. These ranges were, to them, not a forbidden place, but a barrier to be challenged. The mountains slowed, but could not stop, the westward push of the United States population. The first whites in this area were fur trappers who lived in isolation; then, wagon trains heading for the lush Pacific Northwest forests and the California gold fields found advantageous passes that let them through the barrier.

The land of the Rockies still hasn't been conquered, however. Populations in the five Rocky Mountain states are among the lowest in density in the United States today. For example, the western half of Colorado is in the mountainous portion of the state. Of the 34 counties there, 11 have from five to 20 residents per sq mile (two sq km), 12 have two to five, and the remaining 11 have fewer than two people per sq mile of land.

Much of the land in these five states is owned by governments, state or federal. In order of amount, the federal shares are:

Montana, 30 percent; Colorado, 36 percent; Wyoming, 48 percent; Idaho, 64 percent; and Utah, 66 percent. Mineral extraction and forestry, as well as recreational uses of such land is carefully controlled by the government. Among these publicly owned lands are "wilderness areas," portions protected even more completely where, by law, humans may only visit.

The concept of "wilderness area" continues to be hotly debated in the United States. At one extreme are those who believe that the mineral and timber resources

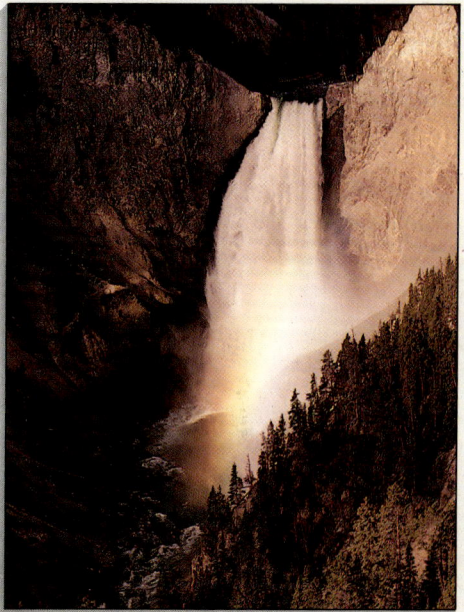

"locked away" there should be fully utilized. At the other extreme are those who believe that not only current wilderness areas cannot be opened to development, but that still more land should be added to the system. Most U.S. citizens, naturally, fall between these two viewpoints, and seek a compromise solution. While acknowledging the nation's and the world's need for resources located in the Rockies, they believe that preserving these remaining true wilderness areas are worthy goals. They are aware that, besides providing a home for wildlife, these pristine mountain forests benefit human ecology and supply one of the west's most precious resources: water.

And so, today's Rocky Mountains are no

Preceding pages, aspens in Rocky Mountain National Park; a future bronco buster straddles his horse trailer; springtime snowmelt near Medicine Bow; yellowing aspens signal an end to summer; participants in the Avon Balloon Race rise to the occasion; a sea of mountain wildflowers near the West Teton foothills; and a charming Queen Anne style Colorado home. Left, bull moose are common sights in the Grand Teton National Park; and right, dramatic Yellowstone Falls sets a rainbow in motion.

longer the abode of mysterious spirits, or a great wall separating one part of the nation from the other. They are settled lands—if lightly populated—clustered around intact wildernesses. Their future is a point of national concern, but for now people who come to live or vacation in this area seek spiritual and physical refreshment among the beauties of the Shining Mountains.

Grand Mountains and Great Rivers

Travelling through the Rockies gives a sense of seeing earth's geology at work, as a wide range of conditions vividly illustrates this planet's shaping forces. In Wyoming, Grand Teton Mountain abruptly rises to 13,737 feet (4,100 meters), towering 7,000

wise sweet air. A plume of steam at the edge of a cold stream alerts the visitor to a hot spring emptying into the icy, melted-snow water.

Mighty rivers rising in these mountains leave their mark, too, as they carve paths downward and outward. North America's deepest gorge is Hells Canyon in Idaho—it's one mile (1.6 km) deep, cut through rock by the coiling, well-named Snake River. In Colorado, the Arkansas River has cut more than 1,100 feet (335 meters) through granite to form Royal Gorge; from its headwaters, the Arkansas drops 6,600 feet (2,000 meters) in elevation within only 150 miles (240 km) before reaching flat land.

The entire Rocky Mountain chain of mountain ranges extends for 3,000 miles

feet (2,100 meters) above the fertile valley named Jackson Hole. Around the valley that holds Salt Lake City, Utah, and the Great Salt Lake, the Wasatch Range rises 6,000 feet (1,800 meters) above the valley floor. These mountains without foothills show how the tremendous forces of colliding continental plates uplifted the Rocky Mountains.

While mountains may seem to show the thickness of the earth's surface crust, Yellowstone National Park in Wyoming demonstrates how comparatively thin this crust is and what forces are constantly at work beneath it. Here, geysers periodically spout boiling water from the depths. "Mudpots," or rock basins filled with constantly boiling mud, spew their sulfur smells into the other-

(4,800 km) from Alberta and British Columbia, Canada, into Mexico, and at most points is several hundred miles wide. The highest peak in this entire cordillera is Mt. Elbert in Colorado, which stands at 14,431 feet (4,400 meters). Because of different climate and geographical conditions, the Rockies' ranges are conveniently divided into the Northern, Middle, and Southern Rockies. The states covered within this book are within the Middle Rockies, which includes the Wyoming Basin—the desert-like "hole in the mountains" used as a wagon train passage by the Mormon, Overland, and Oregon Trails of the 19th Century.

The Rocky Mountains are young ones on the North American continent, formed as what was once the western coastal edge of the great Canadian Shield tectonic plate pushed westward—butting against the eastern edge of the eastward-moving Pacific plate. The result of this powerfully grinding but gradual "collision" was the upward thrust of the Rockies. Land that had been at sea level rose so that today the *base* of the Rockies is about one mile (1.6 km) above sea level.

Slow and Steady Sculpture

Glaciers of the later Ice Ages sculpted these uplifted mountains, and inland seas of their melting waters filled mountain valleys as the last Ice Age closed. Major volcanic action further shaped some mountains,

most are small tremors causing little or no damage—usually unsensed by people. A half-century ago, though, throughout the year of 1935, a series of earthquakes damaged buildings in Wyoming and Montana.

High Country and Climate

The landscape of the Rockies further demonstrates the youth of these ranges. Its soil is thin and stony because fewer eons of erosion have gone into its creation. In this shorter time period (60 million years), fewer species of trees have evolved to survive here than in the Appalachian chain (225 million years old) that parallels the eastern U.S. coast.

Vegetation in this high country is as much

building upon the upthrust rock masses, as in the San Juan Mountains of Colorado.

Although most geologic changes occur too slowly for humans to witness, an event in 1959 demonstrated that the block faulting which built the Rockies does indeed continue. At Hebgen Lake in Yellowstone National Park, one August night, the lake bottom tipped 20 feet towards the northeast, and a massive landslide tragically buried 50 campers before they could flee. Earthquakes are common throughout the Rockies, but

An aerial view of the Rocky Mountain peaks and valleys in Wyoming, left; and elements of time take their toll on rock formations at Capitol Reef (Utah), right.

a product of altitude as of longitude and latitude. In fact, the higher peaks rise well above "timberline," the point after which trees can no longer grow. The western side of the mountains receives more moisture than the eastern, as clouds cool when rising over the land mass and their moisture condenses to fall as rain—or, in greater quantity, as snow. Tall and dense fir woods characterize the lower elevations on the wetter westward side, with pine forests on the drier east, and spruces braving the higher slopes towards timberline.

Climate throughout the Rockies is generally dry, making for clear skies that enhance the ability to see for long distances. Nights are much cooler than days in summer (and much *colder* in winter). Because snow forms the greater proportion of annual precipitation than rain, "snowpack" throughout the area is carefully monitored. This is each winter's snow accumulation, whose melt feeds rivers supplying the region's comparatively scarce water. Where the coolness of altitude is too great for snowpack to melt in the summer sun, glaciers form.

From April into June each year, springtime in the Rockies means the flooding "run-off" season as snow melt runs into streams, whose mergers form the headwaters of several major rivers. The Arkansas, North and South Platte, Rio Grande, Missouri, and Colorado Rivers all rise in the Rockies. The Continental Divide, which generally follows the crest of the mountains,

bearing animals; mined precious and then basic metals (and more recently, radioactive ores); cut the forests (originally "clear-cutting," or removing all trees without replanting, a practice no longer followed).

Agriculture began as mining camps sprang into being, but in these dry lands before irrigation was introduced, cattle and sheep ranching predominated. In "open range" days, this meant letting the herds of cattle or flocks of sheep graze where they chose, taking the natural grasses. It is only in the 20th Century that tourism became a major "industry" for the Rockies, affecting delicate ecosystems in some locations, but not permanently removing resources.

Because this land is rough to travel and ungenerous in agricultural soils and water

is the great watershed of North America. Precipitation falling, or melting down, the east side of the Continental Divide flows ultimately into the Atlantic Ocean; that falling to the west of the Divide flows to the Pacific. Of the major rivers mentioned, only the Colorado flows to the Pacific.

Hearty Lifestyles

In the Middle Rockies, the rugged land and climate dictate what major industries can flourish—or even exist. After the native people, who lived off the land's wildlife and its natural crops, those who came and stayed participated in what are called extractive industries. They harvested the pelts of fur-

supplies, major cities have not developed in the Rockies. The two metropolitan centers of the Middle Rockies, Denver and Salt Lake City, are much like cities of their size elsewhere in the U.S.—but not representative of the smaller settlements that characterize the region.

A Friendly Place

A "small town" friendliness and casualness pervades life throughout these five states (even in Denver and Salt Lake City). Manners are less formal and dress answers as much to practicality and comfort adapted to weather conditions as it does to fashion. The lack of pretension may be a legacy of the frontier heritage, when all were equal in scrabbling for a living in a tough land. (Contrary to the images of western movies, many well-educated people joined the mining rushes, but dared not "put on airs," or flaunt their training or former social stations on the frontier.) Besides frontier memories, perhaps the grandeur and majesty of the mountains tends to dwarf human customs, leading residents unconsciously into simplifying their ways.

If there is a hint of a class structure here, it is the mild and unstructured one of pride in being a native resident; that is, non-Indians who were born here, or who can trace their families back as residents over three or four generations, take pride in the fact. This demonstrates how recent European settlement is in the Rockies.

People who live here are proud, also, of the beauties of the land, and are pleased to share them with visitors. If their hearty openness with strangers offends, it should be remembered that the friendliness is intended as a compliment.

Wild animals abound in the Middle Rockies, both in the "wilderness areas" where no humans may live, and in the national parks with their thousands of visitors each year. Some species delicately coexist with human settlements—deer, antelope, and even elk.

By far the two most spectacular animals to be seen here are the grizzly bear and the buffalo (American bison). They are the rarest, largest, and most dangerous animals found in today's Rockies.

Although a few buffalo are privately owned (and experiments continue in crossbreeding them with cattle to produce "beefalo" meat), the only two herds remaining in the United States are in Yellowstone National Park and at the National Wildlife Refuge at Moiese, Montana.

Visitors to Yellowstone in summer and winter will see buffalo grazing stolidly. The

adult male stands up to seven feet (two meters) tall and weighs up to 2,000 pounds (900 kg). When stampeded, these massive animals can outrun humans; when frightened, they will defend themselves by goring with their short curved horns. They are not to be approached on foot—or surrounded by a group.

Grizzly bears do their best to avoid humans, but backpackers in wilderness areas may encounter these huge omnivores. Grizzlies have poor sight and hearing, and may move towards the unknown in order to understand it. They will try to flee from humans unless in pain, or feeling trapped, or unless someone comes between a sow and her cubs. The best advice, of course, is to

Left, herds of bison at home on the range in Wyoming just as they were in the days of the Indians; and right, fascinating formations in Arches National Park in famous Monument Valley.

keep your distance.

Adult females weigh from 350 to 450 pounds (150 to 200 kg) and males range from 800 to 1,000 pounds (360 to 450 kg). Their coloring ranges from dark brown to straw-colored blonde with silvery tips to the hairs, giving the grizzled look for which they are named. A noticeable hump at the shoulders and an indented face above the snout distinguish them from their bear cousins. Fewer than 800 grizzlies are thought to exist in the United States outside of Alaska, with half of those in Glacier and Yellowstone National Parks and their continguous wilderness areas.

Black bears present more danger to people, because more of them exist and because they have become less afraid of the human

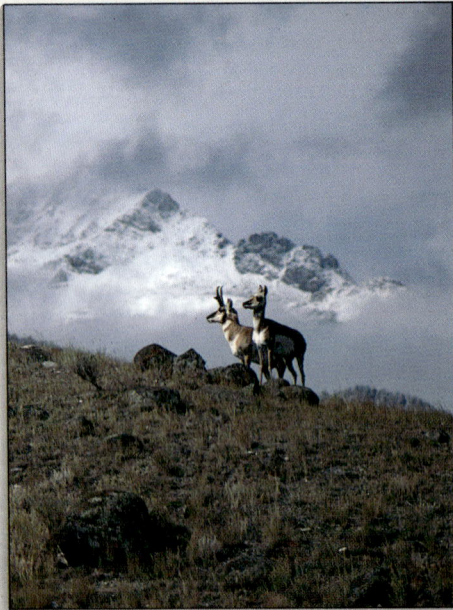

presence. In the national parks, some even adapted quite happily to foraging garbage dumps and "begging" for food at campsites or by the roadsides. Modern management policies helped alleviate this harmful adaptation, but human encounters with black bears are a constant concern of park rangers.

This bear may be brown or reddish ("cinnamon") in color, as well as black, but usually has a brown face and a white blaze on the chest. Adults are five to six feet tall (about two meters) and weigh from 200 to 500 pounds (90 to 230 kg).

Four members of the deer family are common to the Rockies, including the moose, the largest deer ever to have existed. Although fossils show that the moose

was once larger, today's bull moose weighs from 1,000 to 1,400 pounds (450 to 630 kg); he stands about six feet (1.8 meters) high at the shoulder. Their antlers are the largest grown by any mammal, with five to seven prongs spreading out from solid "shovels" nearer the head. Record antler widths from prong to prong begin at five feet (1½ meters). Moose are fond of marshy areas and the grasses that grow along river banks. They are strong swimmers and will even take to open waters.

The slightly smaller elk also carries large antlers, in this case, open prongs sweeping upward and back from the head, nearly as large as the moose's. The elk's "rack," or set of antlers, may weigh 50 pounds (23 kg). When fattened by summer forage, a bull elk weighs from 500 to 700 pounds (225 to 300 kg), with a shoulder height of about five feet (1½ meters). Elk range through the lower-elevation forests and onto the plains.

Where the Deer and Antelope Play

Mule deer and white-tail deer, smaller relatives of the moose and elk, live wherever human populations are thin enough in the Middle Rockies. The mule deer is recognizable because of its long ears and stiff-kneed, springing manner of running. The white-tail is named for its "warning flag" tail, white on the underside, which snaps upright when the animal is frightened.

Residents of the Rockies call the slight pronghorn an "antelope" even though it is unrelated to Old World antelopes. The animal's delicate appearance—weighs only about 100 pounds (45 kg)—belies a strong constitution designed for survival by flight. Antelope eyesight has been compared to humans using seven-power binoculars, and the animals also have enlarged lungs and windpipes. Thus, they range freely in open country, sensing danger and running from it. Herds of antelope can be seen in open grasslands, even along busy roads.

Visiting the Middle Rockies means enjoying a great variety of spectacular scenery, having opportunities to view many types of wild animals, small as well as large, and being warmly welcomed by the people. It is a land of extremes in climate and geography, but the hardness of the land has bred a robust people who are happy to share the rugged beauties around them.

Left, clear mountain air and unusual wildlife are common in the Rockies; and right, a rare close-up view of a Rockies Bighorn Ram—now an endangered species.

EVOLUTION OF A MOUNTAIN

Billions of years of heat and movement formed the rock base upon which the Rocky Mountains were built. There is geological evidence that at one time they lay at the bottom of a sea; then this rock base slowly but steadily broke apart and pushed upward. It was eroded by rivers, blown by winds, heated by volcanoes, shaken by earthquakes frozen by glaciers.

These centuries of incredible fluctuation and the constant pressure from beneath the earth's surface with the semiliquid land bubbling up like porridge, were essential to the formation of the Rocky Mountains as we know them today. The rock rose, fractured and cracked, pushing ever upward to form cliffs thousands of feet high.

In Colorado, these mountains take up an area more than six times the size of the Swiss Alps—with 53 snowy peaks towering more than 14,000 feet (4,260 meters) above sea level and a total of 1,143 mountains rising to altitudes of 10,000 feet (3,040 meters) or more.

In Idaho, the landscape gaps between the mountains were depressed and filled by lava flows and carved by the violent Snake River itself. The lava plains here are second in size only to the Columbia River Plateau of Oregon and Washington. Craters of the Moon National Monument at the north edge of these lava fields preserve their breathtaking volcanic features.

Evidence of the ancient rock layers bending and turning upward can be found everywhere in the Rocky Mountains. Lifted, folded, mangled, crushed and broken rock formations created today's magnificent scenic features. The vast mineral wealth there, concentrated deep in the earth's cracks and crevices, has challenged man for 100 years to make a living from the resources before him.

The concept of the movement of the earth is difficult to grasp as the infinitely slow uplift of great landmasses brings forth the mountain peaks and valleys. The uplift goes on too slowly for the human eye to perceive.

But today, landslips occur occasionally as if to remind us that the eternal hills are still changing. In 1959, an earthquake in western Yellowstone Park terrified 20,000 tourists. In 1925 near Jackson Hole, Wyoming, a cowboy outran a mile-and-a-half long rain-soaked avalanche of hillside while six of his cattle died.

Ancient Cliff Dwellings Reveal Past Secrets

One of the natural wonders of the world, the Rocky Mountain range today still shares

CLIFF DWELLINGS SOUTHERN COLORADO.

its ancient secrets. The sides of these mountains reveal ancient marine life fossils, fascinating dinosaur remains and rocks formed in the hot interior of the earth—invaluable links to our planet's history.

Near the southwest corner of Colorado is a green tableland 15 miles (24 km) long and eight miles (13 km) wide rising 1,500 feet (455 meters) from the surrounding valleys. Tribes of peace loving Indians lived in homes on these tablelands or mesas until about 700 A.D. They were followed by another group of Indians, the Anasazi (or ancient ones), who inhabited pueblos on the mesa and later built sheltered caves in the walls of the canyons that supported it until

Preceding pages, ancient Indian petroglyphs remain on this rock slab from Arches National Park. Left, erosion has created incredible formations in Bryce Canyon National Park (Utah); and right, remnants of ancient Indian civilization remain in these cliff dwellings in southern Colorado.

about 1300 A.D. The Navajo and Ute Indians lived for many years on the lands surrounding the mesa but stayed away from the cliff dwellings that were abandoned about 600 years ago. These present-day Indians believed the dwellings were inhabited by departed spirits.

"Far View House," is a well-preserved pueblo dwelling, which gives some clues about the lives of the Indians who lived there. Living rooms were rectangular and larger circular rooms, called "kivas," were thought to be ceremonial halls. Fireplaces, pottery, utensils and grinding stones were found in the living rooms and were most likely used by the Indian women for their daily household chores.

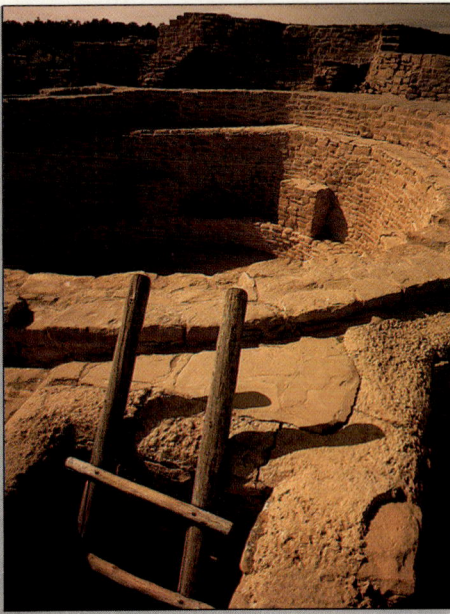

Mesa Verde National Park

More of these Anasazi structures were found in 1888, when two cowboys hunting cattle, stopped to rest their ponies and discovered a group of ancient dwellings in a huge cave about 50 feet (15 meters) below the rim of the mesa. They found what is now called "Cliff Palace." This structure with its 200 living rooms is thought to be the largest group of dwellings of its kind. The four-storey rooms have walls decorated with red and white primitive art designs. There is a 30-foot (nine-meter) tower in the Palace, most impressive because each of the stones which contributes· to the curvature of the tower has been shaped with the crudest

tools. Grinding bowls and storage bins for corn were found in the Palace, and there may have been a spring to furnish water for the ancient Indian population, estimated to have been about 400.

In 1906 by an act of Congress, the archeological ruins were set aside as a national park. That portion of the mesa which contains the cliff dwellings is now known as Mesa Verde National Park and can be easily visited today.

Little else is known about the Rockies history until the 16th Century when white men ventured into the southern part of the mountain area. Francisco Coronado set out from Mexico City in New Spain in 1540 searching for the Seven Cities of Cibola to the north. Rumors were rampant that the seven cities were stocked with gold and gems. The Spaniards were so angry when they discovered that Cibola was nothing more than a collection of pueblos and caves, that they ransacked the place from kiva to kiva killing the male Indians and raping the women. Thus they provided the Indians with a sample of what was to come for the next 300 years.

Coronado nevertheless continued north and no one is sure where he concluded his fruitless search. He returned to Mexico City with the members of his unfortunate expedition having accomplished two things. He had destroyed forever the myth of great golden cities to the north, and he had given the Indians a deep and bitter hatred of the Spanish.

Expedition north, however, continued for various reasons: some of the explorers wanted to convert the Indians to Christianity and others were interested in elevating their family's social status.

But the Spanish, continually harassed by the hostile Indians in their attempts to conquer the frontier to the north, were ultimately defeated by the French when Napoleon took the Louisiana Territory from Charles IV of Spain. Thus the Louisiana Territory, which had passed from French to British to Spanish hands, reverted to France in 1802. It did not remain so, for long, however, for Napoleon sold the entire territory, also known as the Louisiana Purchase, to the Americans the next year.

Ladders connected the multilevels of the Anasazi Indian cliff dwellings, left. Right, the famous Cliff House in the Canon de Chelly.

EXPLORERS, TRAPPERS AND TRADERS IN THE 19TH CENTURY

The Louisiana Purchase occupies some 827,987 sq miles (2,150,000 sq km) of land between the Mississippi River and the Rocky Mountains, stretching from the Gulf of Mexico to the Canadian border. The purchase took place in 1803 during President Thomas Jefferson's first administration. The price was $15,000,000, making it the greatest land bargain in the history of the United States.

Within weeks of the purchase, President Jefferson sent his private secretary, Captain Meriwether Lewis, and Lewis's friend William Clark off on a mission to gather information about this newly acquired territory. They were to investigate the plants and animals, the Indian culture and trade, and the possibility of discovering a passable route over the mighty mountains to the Pacific.

The Lewis and Clark Expedition

Lewis and Clark set out from a spot near St. Louis on May 14, 1804, with a party of 45 men, most of them rugged frontier men whom they recruited and trained themselves. The records of Lewis and Clark tell of an 8,000-mile (13,000-km) round trip to the Pacific Ocean.

A French Canadian trapper named Toussaint Charbonneau and his family joined the group in North Dakota. He and his pregnant wife, Sacagawea, were to serve as interpreters and horse traders for the party as they travelled through the Shoshoni Indian country.

The Lewis and Clark expedition set out from Fort Mandan for the west in the spring of 1805. They fought the Missouri's currents, struggled through deep canyons, and learned from the Indians as they went. Across the Continental Divide, and down the Columbia River they travelled until they finally saw the Pacific Ocean on November 17, 1805. They spent the winter and started back the way they had come. The party divided there with Lewis going north and Clark following the Yellowstone River east. In August of 1806, they were reunited and the expedition was complete, having brought to the nation a real sense of pride and the first glimpse of understanding about the northern reaches of its territory.

Before Lewis and Clark had returned, President Jefferson sent Thomas Freeman with a second party to the south portion of the Louisiana Territory. Although his expedition didn't cause quite the stir that the Lewis and Clark expedition did, it provided valuable information about the extent of Spanish military operations in the area and the appropriate waterway to the Rocky Mountain country.

That waterway was the Arkansas River and Captain Zebulon Pike was selected to explore it. In 1806, while making a map of the Arkansas and Red rivers east of the Rockies, he followed the Arkansas into Colorado

and discovered the peak which carries his name. He noted it on his map as "Highest Peak" and it was officially named "James Peak" after the first man who scaled it. But trappers and hunters persisted in calling it "Pike's Peak" and in 1835, "Pike's Peak" it became. Zebulon Pike's notes on his exploration were of a military intelligence nature, as he was an army officer at heart and not so concerned with the possibilities of the development of the territory.

In 1818, Congress ordered an expedition to continue Pike's work and to investigate animal, vegetable and mineral life and trade with the Indians, as well. Major Stephen H. Long was to be in charge of the expedition. Like Pike, Long named the first mountain he observed in the Front Range of the Rockies, "Highest Peak." That peak is the highest summit in Rocky Mountain National Park and is now known as "Long's Peak." Otherwise the group contributed little toward the knowledge of the region.

By 1841, proof of the riches of the West were filtering back and exploration began anew. Always the travellers were at the mercy of the Indians, especially the seven fierce Ute tribes. John C. Frémont made five expeditions across the mountains mainly for the purpose of publicizing the West.

route proved futile for a variety of reasons (not the least of which was the vicious Rocky Mountain winter). The man who did find it was John Gunnison. Marauding Indians were as much a problem for Gunnison as the weather had been for Frémont. Gunnison in fact, died when he was struck by an arrow as he was trying to explain to an Indian that he was an explorer not a settler. The Gunnison expedition brought the United States government to the realization that any further explorers would have to be military men.

The history of the real pathfinders can be

THE NEW WEST

AS IT WAS.

SCALE OF MILES
0   100   200   300   400   500

Until this time, an artist was sent along with each expedition to sketch significant scenery, but Frémont was the first explorer to make use of the new invention, the camera. In addition, he was distinguished by his determination to find a central route to California as there was increasing talk of a railroad being built through to the Pacific Ocean.

Frémont's attempts to find the central

traced in the story of the Rocky Mountain fur traders. From Lewis and Clark's expedition until the middle 1840s, commerce in the west was controlled by the fur trade. The employees of the fur trading companies and the free trappers (who sold furs they trapped themselves) were the first real explorers of the West. Unfortunately, they left few records of their discoveries behind. These mountain men didn't write, but they read trails and tracks and weather signs. Trusting their instincts and sense of direction, they carried a more complete map of the Rocky Mountain country in their heads than any expedition hired by the government was able to put together.

Beaver was the fur that lured men to the

Preceding pages: *The Fireboat*—a rendition by western artist Charles Russell to depict the uneasy coexistence between early settlers and Indians. Left, early explorers became great leaders of the West; and right, "The New West" in the 19th Century.

West. The skins were used for hats and muffs, coats and linings and collars. Two hundred thousand pelts a year were sent to China alone during this period for the Emporer's garments. The demand for the pelts nearly killed off the beaver, but a change in fashion saved them from extinction in the nick of time.

The men who trapped the beaver loved their life. Clad in their buckskin suits and coonskin caps, they lived entirely in the open with their Indian wives and families. They met other trappers at the annual "rendezvous" where white men and Indians gathered to drink, trade and gamble. The heads of fur companies met their employees, paid them for their furs and gave them supplies for the year. The free trappers

William H. Ashley was the owner of one of these fur-trading companies, the Rocky Mountain Fur Company. He employed some of the West's most famous mountain men: Jedediah Smith, the tough Methodist who went west with a gun in one hand and a Bible in the other; David Jackson, who gave his name to Jackson Hole; William Sublette, one of two brothers who trapped; Thomas Fitzpatrick, "Broken Hand" as he was called by the Indians who both feared and admired him; and Old Jim Bridger whose prowess as a storyteller was almost as great as his skill with a rifle. All of the mountain men in one way or another had a profound influence on the history of the Rockies.

Besides these mountain men, pioneers seeking a way West on wagon trains were

JAMES BRIDGER—See following page.

brought their furs and the Indians came to gamble and trade. The business transactions at a rendezvous usually took about a week. The furs were graded and bargained for and this was followed by two to three weeks of carousing. Gunpowder and whiskey were the medium of exchange and more than one trapper went back to the wilds with nothing to show for a year's work but a bad headache. The owners of the fur-trading companies were the ones who profited, not the trappers. The trappers looked forward to exchanging tall tales around the campfire and discussing new trails and passes. Racing, wrestling and boxing matches, target practice and a variety of other competitive sports went on as the whiskey flowed freely.

the next settlers. William Sublette proved that wagon wheels could negotiate the mountain passes and this opened the trails for them in the 1830s. In addition to supplies, the wagon trains brought tourists and journalists who talked and wrote about the Rocky Mountain country and its wonders, one of which was the warm and versatile buffalo robe. This, in turn, produced increased demands on the fur business and necessitated the cooperation of the Indians who could slaughter great herds of buffalo.

Forts and trading posts started to replace the annual rendezvous. Fort Laramie, the midway point between the Missouri and Salt Lake on the Overland Trail, was built on the site of a rendezvous in 1834. It operated as a private trading establishment until 1849 when the government bought it to use as a holding place for their troops that protected the gold rush caravans. There were 12 buildings surrounded by a four-foot-thick (120-cm) adobe wall that was 20 feet (six meters) high. It could corral 200 animals if need be and 40 men were employed there by Sublette's fur company as traders, tailors and buffalo hunters. Fort Laramie was the capital of the Rocky Mountain country until the discovery of gold.

One explorer, Jedediah Smith, was determined to travel west from New York State. He was 25 years old and came from a family who had provided him with extensive schooling and a firm devotion to the Bible. He credited his Bible as much as his knife

It wasn't the danger of his work that led Smith to give up the trade but the fact that the beavers were over trapped and fashions had changed. The pack of furs he delivered to St. Louis in 1830 was his last and he sold his holdings in the company and set his sights on the Sante Fe trade. From the start he encountered trouble with the weather and the Indians. Finally, Smith was killed by a band of Indians before he ever reached Sante Fe, no doubt with his gun in one hand and his Bible in the other.

Kit Carson was another hunter and trapper with a vast knowledge of the Rocky Mountain country that he shared with exploring parties and military expeditions. Soon his name was famous throughout the Rocky Mountain range. He was known and

and rifle for carrying him through incredible dangers. Smith, Sublette and David Jackson bought the Rocky Mountain Fur Company from Ashley and trapped up and down the Rocky Mountain territory. Smith enjoyed the dangerous life of the trapper. He met a grizzly bear in the Black Hills and was so badly chewed that he nearly died, but was sewn up with a needle and trapped on.

Far left, Jim Bridger—early explorer and mountain man; and left, holding on for dear life on the Colorado River. Above, turn-of-the-century Sioux Indian moccasins fashioned from porcupine quills; and far right, covered wagons hauled freight through the Ute Pass.

feared by the Indians and envied and respected by the other trappers and mountain men during his eight years as a buffalo hunter. His second wife was Josepha Jamarillo, the sister of Charles Bent's wife. Josepha Carson was one of the members of the Bent family that witnessed Charles Bent's murder by the Indians when he was the governor of New Mexico. With the Indians and whites no longer trusting each other and the chaos created by Bent's death and the start of the gold rush, the day of the mountain man was drawing to a close. Kit Carson died in 1868 having outlived the last act of the mountain man drama.

Thomas Fitzpatrick, called "Broken Hand" (after his new rifle exploded in his hand maiming several of his fingers), was a trapper and hunter who became the first federal Indian Agent in the Rocky Mountain country.

The practical experience he gained dealing with the Indians while he was trapping was to come in handy 20 years later when the government was formulating the official Indian policy in the Rockies. With the buffalo disappearing and the hunting grounds of the Indians being devastated, Fitzpatrick urged the Indians to turn to agriculture and tried to persuade the government to start a program to equip them for that agricultural life. Under his leadership, the first great treaty between the whites and the Indians was drawn up with 10,000 Indians present at the meetings at Fort Laramie in 1851. It could

of the tales he told there are still repeated in the West; that he'd come West so long ago that "Pike's Peak" was nothing but a hole in the ground at the time is one among them.

Tom Tobin, one of the last of the mountain men, exemplified the real attributes of courage and freedom from fear. All during the summer of 1863, the daring and violent Espinoza brothers terrorized the southern region of the Rockies, killing, raping and thieving. The commander of one of the military units in the area hired Tom Tobin to solve the problem. Tobin knew the mountains in the area as well as any man alive and set out in search of the brothers. He found the culprits when he spotted crows circling over them in a canyon and there he killed them both single handedly. Not wanting to

truly be said that Thomas Fitzpatrick set a firm foundation for trust and understanding between the two peoples.

James Bridger, a hunter, trapper, fur trader and guide was one of the mountain men who bought into the Rocky Mountain Fur Company in 1830. He was one of the first white men to see the area that was to become Yellowstone National Park and he may have also discovered the Great Salt Lake. In 1843, when the fur trade declined, he built Fort Bridger in southwest Wyoming, a way station to supply immigrants on the Oregon Trail. By 1850, the fort had been taken over by the Mormons and Jim Bridger was among many old trappers and mountain men who went to live at Fort Laramie. Many

waste gunpowder, Tobin merely wounded the two, then cut off their heads with his knife. Tobin needed proof of his kill to collect his pay. The bodies were too cumbersome to haul across the mountains, so he threw the heads in a sack and returned to Fort Garland and deposited his bloody trophies at Colonel Tappan's feet. When he died in 1904, he had outlived by nearly 50 years the other legendary mountain men he'd known.

Squabbles with Mexico

Explorations to the Rockies were interrupted by the Mexican War of 1846. The squabbles between Mexico and the United

States were 20 years old. Idle mountain men were harassing Mexican wagon trains and the United States was worried about the Mexicans exciting the Utes and Apaches. At Taos, Mexicans and Pueblo Indians raged into the home of Charles Bent, the military governor of New Mexico, scalped him in front of his family and rode off with his scalp tacked to a board. To achieve peace and extend its frontiers, the United States became involved in what many historians felt was an unnecessary attack on a weaker nation. By the treaty of Guadalupe Hidalgo, the United States acquired California, Nevada and Utah and parts of Arizona and New Mexico, Colorado and Wyoming.

William Gilpin was appointed as the first governor of the new Colorado Territory in New Mexico had an inordinate number of secessionists in their midst. So a Southerner on the side of the Union (Gilpin) didn't waste any time squelching the secessionist idea before it had a chance to take hold.

The Confederates swept north up the Rio Grande intending to seize the Colorado gold fields in 1862 but were forced to retreat. Even as the Civil War was won in the Rockies for the Union, another war was started with the Indians.

The Indian War

The War Department had withdrawn most of the weapons and regulars from the Rocky Mountains and sent them east to fight the Southerners. The Indian tribes all

1861. Having visited the Rocky Mountain country in the days of the Mexican War, he must have been astonished as he rode into Denver on a stagecoach. What had once been a favorite camping ground had turned into a bustling city of several thousand people with hotels and restaurants.

There was a method to President Lincoln's madness when he offered Gilpin the post of Governor of the territory. Colorado with its gold rush was important to the economy of the Union. But Colorado and

Left, Buffalo Bill Cody triumphs over the Indians; and right, Mormon pioneers make peace with the Indians during their travels.

through the western mountains, realizing that the white man was at a disadvantage. were tired of being confined to various uninhabitable reservations. For 10 years they had suffered in silence and now they were intent on moving to more bountiful hunting grounds as had been their custom. Their revenge was swift as they overtook anything from stage routes to isolated settlers.

Indian war parties on the rampage in 1863 and 1864 continued their destruction despite vigorous United States military operations. Colonel Chivington, who had won the Civil War for the Union in the Rockies, took over the handling of the Indians. Governor Evans who had replaced Gilpin, felt things were headed for a truce when Colonel Chivington and his 600 men marched into a camp at Sandy Creek and methodically shot every Indian man, woman and child there.

News of his treachery reached the other tribes around Fort Laramie and the Indians began a full scale war led by Sitting Bull. Communication between Denver and the East became non-existent and settlements were pillaged and burned. The economy was in ruins and the whole territory was on the verge of starvation. Chivington was reprimanded and the Massacre at Sandy Creek was denounced as the most unjustifiable crime in American history, but the war with the whites didn't end until the Battle of the Little Big Horn in 1876.

Heeding the 'Call'

Religion was one the reasons that settlers first undertook the trip West across the Rocky Mountain Country. Once William Sublette proved to them that wagon trains could cross the mountains, missionaries felt sure that they possessed the time, energy and courage to move their households West. Marcus Whitman was such a missionary; commissioned in 1835 by the Presbyterian and Congregational Churches, Whitman was to go West and report back to them on the feasibility of setting up missions. He reported that not only could women and wagons cross the Rockies but that milk cows could be herded, guaranteeing a solid agricultural foundation. In 1836, a missionary party of six set out to take the overland journey through the Rocky Mountain country and on to the Pacific, two of the six being the first women to make such a trip.

While Whitman and his group were settling in Oregon, other men were looking to another part of the West as their Promised Land. The Mormons were being persecuted for their beliefs which at first were much like the beliefs of any other religion (later Mormonism came to include the doctrine of polygamy.) The Mormon Church was founded by Joseph Smith who left his home in New York State about 1830 seeking the New Jerusalem he'd been told of in a "revelation." He teamed up with Brigham Young in Independence, Missouri, and the Mormon Church grew by leaps and bounds alienating people as it went. Smith's "revelation" on plural wives caused an explosion that resulted in his death and Brigham Young took his place as head of the church.

Young organized the Mormons for a journey West in 1846 to a remote New Jerusalem where they would be safe. There was no-thing haphazard about the Mormon migration—they knew exactly where they were going. Wagons, horses, seeds for crops, cows, oxen, men, women and children travelled west in military formation and rarely had trouble with the Indians. They ran across mountain men in the Rockies who scoffed at the idea that they could grow corn in the dry Great Basin to which they headed, but they didn't know Brigham Young had studied irrigation.

In July 1947, they reached the valley of the Great Salt Lake and went to work planting crops, building irrigation ditches and planning their city. Some of the original 150 settlers went back east for their families and soon there was a long line of Mormons winding through the Platte Valley, over the sand hills, past Fort Laramie, across South Pass down to the valley. By October, they were 4,000 strong, and they had indeed found their New Jerusalem.

The Oregon Trail

Except for Captain B.E. Bonneville's dress rehearsal with a train of 20 covered wagons headed west in 1832 and the Mormon's pilgrimage, it wasn't until the discovery of gold in 1848 that the covered wagon mass migration started. One observer in the spring of 1849 estimated that there were 12,000 wagons in the Rocky Mountain country headed for California. Fifty five thousand travellers were said to have stopped at Fort Laramie in the summer of 1850 alone.

The Oregon Trail was the longest of the overland routes used in westward expansion. Ruts left by wagon wheels can still be seen today along the trail. Families travelled up the Platte River to Fort Laramie, Wyoming; and along the North Platte to its Sweetwater branch; across the South Pass in the Rocky Mountains to the Green River Valley at Fort Bridger, Wyoming; through the Snake River area and on to Idaho; across the Blue Mountains to Marcus Whitman's mission and down the Columbia River to Fort Vancouver, Oregon. Settlers dealt with flooded rivers, Indian attacks on their wagons, cholera and scarcities of food, water and wood. The journey took six months and was a severe test of endurance and strength.

Courageous pioneers settled the West in *The Homesteaders*, by artist John Clymer.

SACAGAWEA, THE INDIAN HEROINE

Of the many characters in American history, few are as idealized as Sacagawea, the Shoshoni Indian girl who was the famed guide and interpreter for the Lewis and Clark expedition to the Pacific Northwest in 1804-1806.

Sacagawea, whose name means "bird woman" was kidnapped when she was a young girl by the Hidatsas Minatarees tribe in Atsina country, and taken to North Dakota. She was sold as a slave to a French Canadian trapper Toussaint Charbonneau who subsequently married her. It was about this time that Lewis and Clark and their party were spending a winter in Mandan North Dakota waiting for the spring to start their expedition. Two French Canadian interpreters were employed by Lewis and Clark so they could intercede with the Indians for the expedition. One was Toussaint Charbonneau who came with his 16-year-old pregnant wife, Sacagawea. Both captains were delighted when she joined the group, for they thought she could help them bargain with the Indians for the horses they needed to make the mountain crossing. That February Sacagawea gave birth to a little son who was named Jean Baptiste and called "Little Pomp" meaning "First Born" in Shoshoni. The little boy at two months was carried by Sacagawea on her cradle board on this 3000-mile (4800-km) adventure. He was loved by all and especially by Captain Clark. Throughout the journey Sacagawea proved to be very resourceful as she guided the group through the wilderness, showing them what berries and roots could be eaten. Great courage and good temperament were her attributes and Meriwether Lewis wrote of her "... if she had enough to eat and a few trinkets to wear I believe she would be perfectly content anywhere."

Once when one of the boats almost turned over, she calmly recovered all the valuable articles from the water. Her amiable disposition made her one of the most popular persons on the expedition next to "Little Pomp."

Sacagawea helped tremendously when the expedition reached her native tribe, the Shoshonis, at Beaver Head Valley, Montana. Their Chief Cameahwait turned out to be Sacagawea's brother whom she had not seen since she was kidnapped. When she realized this she threw her blanket over him "... weeping profusely. The chief himself was moved not in the same degree. After some conversation between them, she resumed her seat, and attempted to interpret for us, but her new situation seemed to overpower her, and she was frequently interrupted to tears." Clark wrote.

That First Winter

In two weeks time the explorers were ready to proceed. Sacagawea helped bargain with the Shoshonis for 21 horses and two guides. This next part of the journey took almost a month as the party travelled through the rugged Bitterroot Mountains. The winter set in and they struggled with freezing rain, sleet, heavy snowfall and some frost-bitten feet. On top of this there was a terrible food shortage. They ate unfamiliar boiled yams, bear grease and candles which resulted in many digestive problems.

During the entire adventure the warm-hearted Captain Clark was devoted to "Little Pomp." He tried to persuade his parents to let him bring the boy up as his own son with a proper education. On the return journey, he named a 190-foot (60-meter) rock column pillar "Pompy's Pillar" along the Yellowstone River, which is still located about 25 miles (40 km) from Billings, Montana. In August 1806, the party returned to Fort Mandan where Charbonneau, Sacagawea and Jean Baptiste left the expedition.

When Jean Baptiste was six years old, Charbonneau took another wife—a total of three wives for "the polygamous old interpreter." Charbonneau was a constant pursuer of young Indian girls and even at the age of 80 he married an Assiniboine girl of 14. Sacagawea later left him and moved to St. Louis. There William Clark educated and cared for "Little Pomp."

There are two versions to Sacagawea's life at this point. Some records indicate that she died in her twenties in South Dakota. Indian tradition and other records say she had a long life.

The Lost Woman

These other accounts say that later on she lived with the Comanche Indians in Oklahoma marrying an Indian man named Jerk Meat. She lived harmoniously here giving birth to two (some records say five) children. Jerk Meat was killed in battle and Sacagawea began wandering again. The Comanches not knowing her whereabouts called her "Wadze-wipe" (Lost Woman). She did spend time in Fort Bridger where she lived with Jim Bridger's wife. Jim Bridger was one of the most respected and well known mountain men of the Rockies. Bridger married three times, each time to an Indian woman from a different tribe. First to a Flathead, then to a Ute and his third wife was a Shoshone, like Sacagawea. In 1871, Sacagawea moved to the Wind River Reservation where she decided to live with her own tribe.

Sacagawea was the first woman to speak in tribal councils. She introduced "sundance" to her tribe. "Sundance" is an event that takes place four days and nights in which the dedicated participants fast and seek a vision or fulfill a vow. Due to her good relationship with the whites, she was instrumental in keeping her tribe from getting involved in the terrible Indian wars as the Shoshones and their Chief Washakie served as scouts for the U.S. army.

The Burial Site

Sacagawea died when she was nearly 100 years old, and was buried in the Wind River Reservation. Her grave can be visited today. It is located west of Fort Washakie across from the Wind River Valley, where "she sleeps with her face towards the sunnyside of the Rocky Mountains." Beside her grave is the grave of Brazil, her adopted son according to Shoshone customs, who was the orphan of her dead sister. He lived and died with her on the reservation.

It is remarkable that Sacagawea's son, Jean Baptiste, who was educated in the court of a European Prince returned to the Rockies to try for a career as a mountain man. At the end of his life he went home to his mother's people, the Northern Shoshonis, to die in the Wyoming country of the Wind River Mountains.

Today Sacagawea is considered one of the six most important women in American history. She travelled from Missouri to the Pacific Coast, and it was her contribution that made the Lewis and Clark expedition a success. Her services as an interpreter, horse trader and a native to the wilderness cannot be overestimated. The Shoshoni girl from the Rocky Mountains left an enduring image in a very literal sense. There are said to be more statues erected in her honor than any other woman in the history of the United States.

Indian heroine Sacagawea, sculpted by Harry Jackson, 1980.

PONY EXPRESS

CHANGE OF
TIME!
REDUCED
RATES!

EFFECTIVE JULY 1st, 1861

10 Days to San Francisco!

LETTERS

WILL BE RECEIVED AT THE

OFFICE, 84 BROADWAY,

NEW YORK,

Up to **4** P. M. every TUESDAY,

AND

Up to **2½** P. M. every SATURDAY,

Which will be forwarded to connect with the PONY EXPRESS leaving ST. JOSEPH, Missouri, the following SATURDAY and WEDNESDAY, respectively, at 11:00 P.M.

TELEGRAMS

Sent to Fort Kearney on the mornings of MONDAY and FRIDAY, will connect with PONY leaving St. Joseph, WEDNESDAYS and SATURDAYS.

EXPRESS CHARGES.

LETTERS weighing half ounce or under *(reduced from $5.00)* $1.00
For every additional half ounce or fraction of an ounce $1.00

In all cases Express CHARGES are to be Pre-paid.

RIDERS WANTED

Young, skinny, wiry fellows. Anxious for adventure and chance to see our great WEST. Must be expert riders, willing to risk death daily. Orphans preferred. $60 PER MONTH and keep. Apply at above address.

RAILROADS, ROUNDUPS AND TOURISTS DURING MID-19TH TO 20TH CENTURY

Transportation to the West improved with the emergence of the stagecoach in the mid-1850s, 10 years before the Pacific railway was finished. Stagecoaches were to travel in the 1800s what the airplane is to travel today. The stage drivers solved the problem of the need for speedy mail and passenger service. Ben Holladay, a well-known character in the saga of the lusty stagecoach days, was a driver-turned-owner of his own firm. He knew first-hand that the success of the coach company lay in the hands of the drivers, and he is credited with immortalizing their role. Ben Holladay sold out to Wells, Fargo, and Company in 1865 after a series of disasters, not the least of which were attacks by Indians. The stagecoach disappeared almost completely with the coming of the railroad. It was soon relegated to the fundamental business of freighting over the back roads of the Rocky Mountain country that the railroads couldn't reach.

An even faster method of transportation was the Pony Express. Galloping through the central Rockies, its primary purpose was speed. The riders changed ponies frequently, and in the 18 months that it was in operation, the riders raced the clock and the Indians as well. Some of the greatest stories of the old West come out of the courage and endurance of the Pony Express riders.

How the Rails Began

The opening of the Rocky Mountain country for rails begun in 1853. A man named Grenville Dodge was to ultimately decide what route it should take. President Lincoln called on Dodge, upon the conclusion of the Civil War and made men and materials available for the project. The big question was a matter of only a few hundred miles, the route from Julesburg over the Continental Divide. Trappers and traders had told Dodge of a way through the Continental Divide that was below South Pass (which had been the wagon-stagecoach route), but it wasn't until he was accidentally led by a group of Indians through an outlet to the West, that the Granite Canyon route

Left, an early help wanted ad for the Pony Express reveals the dangers of the job; and right, the Gold Boom region near Pikes Peak, Colorado.

was complete.

Dodge went to work recruiting thousands of young men recently discharged from the Union and Confederate armies, and the operation for the completion of the lines ran with military precision. By 1867, 250 miles (310 km) were laid and the Continental Divide had been crossed. On May 10, 1869, the Union Pacific tracklayers met the Central Pacific tracklayers and drove a golden spike to mark the railroad's completion at Promontory Point in Utah. The Pacific trails chapter was complete and the Rocky Moun-

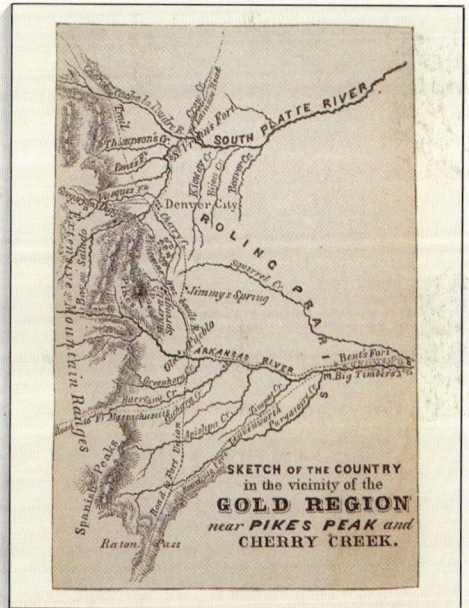

SKETCH OF THE COUNTRY in the vicinity of the GOLD REGION near PIKES PEAK and CHERRY CREEK.

tain country was a real part of the United States at last.

Cattle and Sheep Feuds

When the railroads extended their tracks West, ranchmen looked West likewise for new pastures. Hesitant about taking their cattle into the mountains, the ranchers were worried about the weather and the altitude. After years of reluctance, they started moving into the mountain valleys and found them more than agreeable for their livestock. The water was abundant and the grass nutritious. The cattlemen came to believe that their pastures produced the best grades of beef.

The men who raised cattle and those who raised sheep were in real competition for the best pastures on the government-owned lands of the West. They actually killed each other's livestock when they were found in forbidden territory. Each group felt that the other was making life impossble for them and their families. Many a gun battle was fought between rivals until the government established national forests and assigned pastures to various ranchmen.

Most ranchmen held two roundups each year. In the fall, the cowboys gathered the cattle together and separated them according to their brands and selected the marketable beef to be driven to the nearest shipping center. In spring, another roundup was held to brand the calves. Early roundups were

model farming community in the late 1860s. Many Easterners went along with his scheme and during the spring of 1870, 400 families went West by train to set up their Utopian-like colonies. When the colonists turned toward capitalism, Meeker reapplied his puritan agrarian ideas to the Ute Indians on the reservation in northwestern Colorado. He won neither the respect nor the confidence of the Indians and he and 11 of his employees were killed in a massacre. Colorado's outrage over the hideous atrocity drove the Utes forever out of their beloved Rocky Mountains.

When gold was discovered in California, adventurers started scurrying through the Rocky Mountains on their way to the Pacific Coast. Some camped by promising looking

great social occasions with bronco busting, horse racing and all kinds of contests, much like a modern day rodeo.

Many settlers took advantage of the Homestead Acts to start farming the mountain country and selected places near the streams in the Rocky Mountain country where water was readily available and the valley lowlands were more fertile for farming. Nathan Meeker was the patron saint of these Rocky Mountain agriculturalists.

A Model Farming Community

With the success of irrigation and the beginnings of the cattle industry, Meeker was consumed with the idea of establishing a

streams on their way West and never left the Rocky Mountain country. Others remembered it and returned when they failed to make their fortune in California. However, when they got there by 1860, there were hundreds of men looking for "pay dirt" in the mountain streams. They were followed by thousands more prospectors looking for mineral wealth.

There are endless stories carried around in the heads of the old timers in the mountains. One of them is the "lost-cabin-mine" theory. The versions vary, but basically the story is that a Spanish explorer found gold in the Rockies, built a cabin and carried all that he could along with a map to show where his claim was. After he died, one of his descendents searched for the cabin and the mine and when he couldn't find it, he sold the map to an American prospector. The possibilities of the map changing hand were as numerous as the gullible prospectors who believed the story.

A party of men in 1858 heard that some Cherokee Indians had found gold in the streams near "Pikes Peak." These nine men did indeed find a decent little deposit, but it was nothing compared to the rumor that spread like wild fire of the quantity of gold around "Pikes Peak." Thousands of people loaded up their wagons and headed West with "Pikes Peak or Bust" painted garishly on the side. Many went limping back a few months later with "Busted" labeling their wagons this time.

needed to be built so the ores could be treated and the resulting concentrates taken to the smelters in Denver or Pueblo.

Meyer Guggenheim and his seven sons had phenomenal success in the smelting and refining business and they established the Guggenheim Foundation to support research and the arts.

Virginia City, Nevada, grew up on the site of a lode. The Comstock Lode was made up of several rich veins of silver and gold. One part alone was rumored to produce 200 million dollars' worth of ore. Ethan and Hosea Grosh discovered silver at the sight in 1856 and died before they could develop their claim. It was rediscovered in 1859, and the stampede that was to be called the Comstock Lode began.

MAMMOTH HOT SPRINGS — MAIN TERRACE.

Mining is Big Business

Cripple Creek appeared on the mining maps upon discovery by W.S. Stratton. With a blowpipe (a tube to blow air or gas on a flame to increase the heat), he found an ore called telluride not known to miners in the 1890s, but it was to make the Cripple Creek region one of the most famous mining centers in the world. These finds in the Cripple Creek region in the early 90s proved the necessity for large scale lode mining. Mills

Probably the mining city with the most sensational career is Leadville. In 1877, there were 200 people in the whole Leadville region and three years later there were over 14,000 in the city itself. The boom at Leadville began in 1878 and the story was a familiar one. Two relatively inexperienced fellows struck it rich and the roaring mining camp took off. Saloons, dance and gambling halls grew like mushrooms and fortunes were made and lost. Not only gold, but silver was found in the hills around Leadville ($9,000,000 in one year alone).

Of all the fantastic things happened in Leadville at this time, one of the most spectacular ws the opening of the Crystal Castle. It was a ballroom, skating rink,

Left, *Post Office in Cow Country*—a painting by Remington; and right, early tourists at Mammoth Hot Springs, Yellowstone Park.

dining hall and riding gallery and was composed almost entirely of blocks of ice. The rooms were heated and lit by electricity with massive pillars and towers throughout the building.

Horace Tabor's personal story is at least as fantastic as that of the Crystal Palace. He backed the two men responsible for the claim that set Leadville awhirl. The mines he bought and sold brought him great fortunes and he was free with his money. He built a bank and an opera house and gave freely to philanthropic institutions. He kept his mistress, Elizabeth McCourt Doe, well-situated in a suite in the Clarendon Hotel in Leadville. Once he set his sights on becoming the U.S. Senator from Colorado, he divorced his wife. He wanted to marry Elizabeth,

ROCK CUT, NEAR ASPEN.

"Baby Doe," in Washington, so he bought himself a senate position which did little to popularize him with either his colleagues in Washington or his constituency at home. Tabor and his new wife were never really accepted in society, and when the silver market collapsed, their happy days came to an end. Tabor's debts mounted faster than he could add them up and he gave up everything. Tabor died a pauper and when he was buried a great part of Colorado's past went with him. "Baby Doe" live another 35 years and never gave up hope that the price of silver would revive itself.

Ups and downs in the mining business were common. Ghost towns exists in all the old mining districts. When the streams were emptied of gold, one by one the miners and their families moved away. The last to leave was usually an old prospector whose hopes were not so easily crushed.

20th Century Tourists

With the 20th Century and the advent of the family vacation, the Rocky Mountains portion of the United States became known to millions of people. Every grade of accommodation was available: from campgrounds in the national parks where only water was provided; to chateaus in the mountains with every modern convenience. Dude camps with pack animals and old-fashioned ranches took in boarders who wanted a peek at life a hundred years ago. Providing recreation and inspiration, the tourist business probably brought more money into the Rocky Mountain country than all the mineral wealth taken out of it.

During Teddy Roosevelt's presidency, preservation of the national parks, monuments and primitive areas that attract tourism was nourished. That meant alienating the ranchers in the Rocky Mountain country who had been grazing their livestock on public lands. The fight was bitter and long but the fireworks were confined to Congress—not a shootout as might have occurred in the old days.

The time between the First and Second World Wars was, for the Rockies, one of uncertain change. The depression that was death to shock investors and the railroads brought a flicker of life back to the mining industry. The cleanup operations in the mines were boasted in 1934 when President Franklin Roosevelt devalued the dollar. Gold prices leaped from $20.67 an ounce to $36 an ounce. It wasn't a true resurgence, though. Actually mining just shifted its course to copper, lead, zinc and other minerals. Improvements attributed to the War turned surviving mines into giants.

The Second World War slowed the tourism stampede. Afterward, it came back stronger than ever. Towns overwhelmed by the crowds rebuilt themselves to look as they had in the past. Today the great Rockies range with its rich history still calls to the nation. Its spectacular beauty, one of our great national heritages, awaits the contemporary explorer.

Left, early train routes cut paths through the Rockies; and right, palace car life on the Pacific Railroad in the 19th Century.

PALACE-CAR LIFE ON THE PACIFIC RAILROAD.

Looking toward Ophir

Jack Stern
1982

PEOPLE

The history of the Rockies tells the tale of many outdoor lovers who came to unlock the beauty of the mountains. Fur trappers like John Colter and Jim Bridger; mountain men like Jedediah Smith and Kit Carson; explorers like Lewis and Clark; all were enthralled by the opportunity for adventure in this land. And even long before they arrived, Indian tribes including the Arapahoe, Bannock, Shoshone, Crow, Nez Perce, Paiute and Ute inhabited this mountainous country.

The rich resources of the Rockies have rewarded many fortune seekers with gold, silver, copper, timber, furs, cattle, oil and coal. All have had their heyday and some are still prospering. The Rockies was the land of the Spanish explorer, the cliff dweller, the Oregon Trail, the Mormon Trail and the gold rush. Today, the gold that lures people to the Rockies is the clean crisp, invigorating and sparkling air. The "rush" is still on! Backpackers, campers, mountain climbers, whitewater rafters, river-runners, fishermen, balloonists, skiers, hunters, windsurfers and hang gliders all flock to this year-round playground to enjoy unlimited outdoor adventures.

There is more to the Rockies than its breathtaking vista points, national parks and famous museums. The Rockies today means diverse people—cowboys, cattle barons, shepherds, ranchers, miners, fruit farmers, park rangers, naturalists. . . Most of the people who live here reflect the environment. Names like Big Horn, Wind River, Medicine Bow, conjure pictures of more than mountain ranges—they bring to mind images of real people: the Mexican vaqueros, whose families inherited generations of ranching expertise; native Indian families on vacation in a resort on a Colorado reservation; the first settlers who originally came to the American West from Europe in search of a place to call "home," where they could work and worship freely. All these people and even the thousands of outdoor lovers who now live in the Rockies are all tied by birth or choice to the Rocky Mountains—a part of the country in which might lie the very soul of America.

ROCKY MOUNTAIN PEOPLE

There's no doubt in the minds of those who live in the Rockies that they are a breed apart, whether their families have been here for three generations, or whether they came for a year off from college and never left.

The mountain men who ventured into the unexplored and nearly impenetrable wilderness of these mountains were the first whites to come under the spell of the Rockies. For men like Jim Bridger and Jedediah Smith, it was more than the money they earned for beaver pelts, for that was usually spent on whiskey, women and gambling at the annual rendezvous, and on supplies for the next year. When the demand for beaver pelts died out, the mountain men became guides and scouts for the wagon trains heading west. A relatively small handful of people heading west in wagon trains stopped at the eastern plains and foothills of the Rockies and became farmers and cattle ranchers.

The next group to invade the Rockies were the miners, and though most of them followed the siren call of big strikes and easy riches from valley to valley or mountain range to mountain range, many stayed even after the silver had played out. The first white men to settle in the lush and spectacularly beautiful Estes Park area in northern Colorado were Joel Estes and his son Milton, who built a cabin in the grassy meadows at the bottom of the valley in 1859. They later sold their property to the Earl of Dunraven, who wanted to turn it into a game preserve.

Joe Shipler was among the first to stake out claims in the Never Summer Mountains at the headwaters of the Colorado River in 1879. Though he never got much silver out of Shipler Mountain, he and his family lived in the Kawuneeche Valley until 1914.

Though the 100,000 people who headed west for Colorado in 1859 were ostensibly on their way to make a fortune panning gold in the mountains, they were spurred by a depression, and by the promise of new beginnings. Only half of them made it, and very few stayed on. The 5,000 or so that were left

Preceding pages: a western landscape adorns a street wall in Silverton (Colorado); Miss Coors, Shelly Burmeister, and her trusty steed; and a cigar chomping farmer on his Rockies ranch. Left, "old friends" enjoy a stroll through the aspens; and right, a park ranger shows the valley's natural beauty.

a year later were a determined, hardy bunch.

There was "Uncle Dick" Wooton, who opened the first tent saloon in Denver. He arrived on Christmas Eve with a wagonload full of groceries, and 10 kegs of Taos Lightning whiskey. In the spirit of Christmas, he put one of the kegs out in front of his tent, cracked it open with an axe, and handed out free drinks—reputedly the first big drunk in the new town. Wooton was a native Virginian who had first come to Colorado by way of Bent's Fort, where he met Kit Carson and hunted with him. He later made his fortune by hacking out a 27-mile (43-km) road over Raton Pass, on the New Mexico border, then charging a hefty toll to those who wanted to cross it. He wisely let the Indians pass without charging them, probably to save his own skin, but also perhaps out of a sense of justice, considering that the Indians had been using the route long before the white man appeared on the scene. When the Santa Fe railroad wanted to use his pass, Wooton sold his rights to them, and helped build the graded track.

The freewheeling atmosphere of new mining towns spawned or attracted many a character, male and female. One of them was Poker Alice, a widow in her early twenties, who ended up in Denver after the Civil War. When she was unable to find a "respectable" way to make a living, she took a job dealing cards in a saloon, and found she had a talent for gambling. Like most gamblers, Poker Alice made the circuit of mining towns, earning a reputation along the way for toughness. She packed a gun, smoked long, fat cigars and is said to have shot a few men who tried to cross her. When she tired of the itinerant life of the gambler, she opened a bordello.

Women in the old West were divided into two categories, good and bad. However, the "hurdy gurdy" girls, as saloon waitresses and prostitutes were called, often ended up marrying, and with the scarcity of women in the West, they were usually in a position to

himself elected sheriff of Bannack and Virginia City. After years of being terrorized by "The Innocents," a group of citizens calling themselves the "Vigilantes," led by John X. Beidler, took the matter into their own hands. Eventually Sheriff Plummer was given away by one of his men, exposed as the leader of the notorious band and hung.

There was a great fascination with the early West not only back East, but in Europe as well. Oscar Wilde toured the mining camps of the Rockies, and said the miners were the best audience he'd ever had. Silver bricks were laid in Leadville for the visit of President Grant. Dukes, lords, barons and other dignitaries from Europe came to invest in the mines and hunt grizzlies. Susan B. Anthony and Elizabeth Cady

be choosy. The "good" girls were almost by definition married or had parents who were wealthy enough to support them until they found a husband.

While most mining towns established law and order within a matter of months, there were also those that remained lawless, spawning legends of gunfighters and outlaws. Henry Plummer was one of the "baddest" of the Montana outlaws, but as handsome and charismatic as he was, he literally "got away with murder" for years. At the height of his checkered career, Plummer led a band of more than 100 men, calling themselves "The Innocents." They robbed stagecoaches and mines in Montana—and at the same time somehow managed to get

Stanton spent months among the women of the Rockies, lobbying for women's rights. In the late 1800s and early 1900s, celebrities flocked to the health spas and hot springs of the Rockies in much the same way they flock to the ski slopes today.

Town Origins

Throughout the Rockies, the pattern of settlement was similar. Mining towns sprang up overnight and disappeared just as quickly when the silver or gold failed to live up to its promise. Those towns that survived and grew, such as Helena, Montana and Boise, Idaho, were favorably located along roads or railways. Nearly every town in the Rockies has its origins in mining—the ranchers, farmers and merchants followed the miners. Some towns continued to flourish because ores such as copper, coal and uranium were found. Others such as Glenwood Springs, Colorado Springs and Idaho Springs became health spas. Jackson, Wyoming, grew because it borders on Yellowstone. Today there are towns that exist solely because of their ski mountains—Vail and Beaver Creek are two prime examples. Aspen was almost a ghost town when the skiing craze hit and revived it, as were Steamboat Springs and Breckenridge.

Mining is still a major industry in the Rockies, from the massive open pit copper mines of Montana and the Climax molybdenum mine near Leadville, Colorado, to small gold and silver mines that are privately owned. Mining is very much a way of life among the hardy prospectors who continue to tunnel into the sides of mountains. Without the backing of a large company, their equipment isn't radically different from what their predecessors used a century ago. The hours are long, the pay is low, the work is hard and dirty, but for some it's the only life they know, and the life they choose.

The promise of wide open spaces, freedom and opportunity inspired a variety of religious and utopian groups to settle in the Rockies, of which the Mormons were the largest and most successful. Greeley, Colorado, was founded as a cooperative agricultural colony that sold its goods to the mining towns. The original members were religious and conservative, banning drinking and gambling, encouraging church socials, libraries and schools. Other towns along the Front Range of Colorado, such as Longmont, Fort Collins and Colorado Springs, became thriving towns in the same manner. Though they soon ceased to be communally owned they were very successful, and established a tradition of conservatism that survives to this day.

Tourists began flocking to the Rockies within a few decades after the miners arrived, to gaze at the splendor of the snow-capped peaks; to hunt for elk, bear and mountain lions; to fish for trout in the streams; to cure illnesses in the hot springs; or to play cowboy at the dude ranches. One narrow gauge railway that followed a creek bed survived by catering to trout fishermen, who were dropped off at likely looking spots

Left, western artist Micky McGuire at his easel; and right, a young rodeo contestant says his prayers before entering the ring.

along the way. Colorado Springs became a famous health resort for the wealthy, beginning a tradition of sumptuous grande dame hotels in the middle of nowhere, many of which still stand.

The Skiing Boom

Throughout the early and mid-20th Century, the Rockies remained somewhat obscure. Denver, Cheyenne and Helena were little more than sprawling cow towns, hanging on for their economic life to mining, agriculture and ranching through booms and busts, droughts and depressions. Tourists continued to trek west in the summers, but the winters found most towns semi-deserted and economically impoverished. It was

skiing that finally made the Rockies a year-round tourist attraction. What began after World War II as a somewhat eccentric industry catering to a select group of wealthy clients, has done nothing but mushroom ever since. The birth of the ski industry created a mini-boom of immigrants in the mountain towns, who were willing to forego the convenience and money of the cities for the easy going lifestyle and beauty of the ski resorts—not to mention the opportunity to spend a good part of the winter on downhill skis.

The growth of the ski industry in the sixties coincided with the era of the hippies, the flower children who, at least for awhile, rejected the values of their parents in favor of a simpler, less ambitious lifestyle. Of the thousands who moved to the mountains, most were eventually absorbed into the mainstream of the mining, ranching and resort towns, but there are still plenty of holdouts who live in log cabins with no electricity or running water and lead a largely self-sufficient lifestyle. Bearded and long-haired mountain men and their female counterparts are still a relatively common sight in the mountain towns of the Rockies. For these people, the Rockies represent the same things they did to the first immigrants—the space, freedom and opportunity to live their lives as they choose.

The ski bums who came and never left are a similar group in ski towns. They came on vacations, or during a year off from college.

doctors, lawyers, businessmen, managers and entrepreneurs with them. Typical would be the successful New York City advertising executive who made a lot of money, got fed up with the frenetic lifestyle, took his life savings out of the bank, moved to a resort town and opened up a shop, a real estate office, or a lodge. Many of these immigrants also brought with them a firm commitment to preserving the beauty of the mountains. Thousands of young people have moved to the Front Range of Colorado where, they believe, they have the best of both worlds—the sophistication and excitement of a metropolis, with the recreational playground and pristine wilderness of the mountains only a few miles away. The Front Range has attracted many hi-tech industries in the past

They fell in love with the thrill and adrenalin of downhill skiing and with the mountains. When the idyllic summers came, they couldn't bear to leave, and they put down roots. Their first few years in town are usually spent washing the dishes, cleaning the hotel rooms, running the ski lifts, waiting on tables, and performing all the other services so vital to a resort town. An equal number only stay for a season. Most ski resorts have an ample supply of young transients who are willing to do menial labor in exchange for skiing.

The seventies saw an even larger wave of young immigrants in the cities and the mountain towns. Many were hippies-turned-professionals who brought their skills as

decade, creating its own Silicon Valley and lucrative jobs for young professionals.

Outdoor Attractions

If there're one easy generalization to make about those who live in the Rockies, it's that they love the outdoors. Health and physical fitness is virtually a regional obsession. It often seems that everyone under the age of 40 is involved in jogging, bicycling, aerobics, athletic clubs or exercise classes of some sort. The goal is not only staying thin and fit, but excelling in one or more of the many mountain sports, from riding clunker bikes over mountain passes to skiing, hiking, rock climbing, kayaking and backpacking. If those sports are too taxing, there're always trout fishing, ice fishing, bird watching, gardening, horseback riding, jeeping, snowmobiling, ballooning, and golf—the point is getting outdoors, enjoying the wilderness, the scenery, the crisp air and the blue skies.

For every sport in the Rockies, there are races, contests, celebrations and festivals, from marathons to rodeos, that are well and enthusiastically attended. Summers are all too fleeting in the Rockies, so they're approached with gusto, with a sense of now-or-never, take-it-while-you-can. When hunting season arrives in the autumn, hunters flock to the mountains by the thousands—many say it's as much an excuse to get out into the wilderness before winter sets in as it is a desire to shoot a deer or an elk. And

musicians of the Telluride Jazz Festival. Acting troupes, filmmakers, classical musicians, craftspeople, painters and sculptors flock to the mountains where, it seems, their creative juices flow like nowhere else. To celebrate these artists, every resort town has its concerts, festivals, fairs and shows.

Every resort town also has its part-time resident celebrities—some come for the skiing, some for the cultural events, some simply for some peace, quiet and mountain air. Former President Ford prefers Vail. Jack Nicholson, John Denver and a host of others like Aspen. Billy Kidd swears by Steamboat Springs, and others prefer Jackson Hole, or Park City, Utah. Writers seek the solitude and big horizons of Montana and Wyoming, painters look for Victorian

even with the long winters, there never seems to be time to get in enough skiing—there's always one more run to make, or one more turn to carve out of the powder.

Arts and Culture in the Mountains

Though the Rockies are something of a cultural wasteland in the winter—with the exception of the big cities—the idyllic summers attract artists of every kind, from the dancers of Ballet Aspen to the top notch

Boulder (Colorado) cheerleaders in motion, left; and all eyes are on this bronco bustin' cowboy at the rodeo, right.

towns, weatherbeaten cowboys and vistas of snowcapped peaks. There aren't any logical reasons for these choices, but once made, people tend to be chauvinistic about the character, charm and beauty of their favorite mountain town.

The Rockies Melting Pot

The Rockies have always been an Anglo melting pot, with heavy German and Slavic populations in the mountains. Other ethnic groups, such as blacks, Chinese and Hispanics, tend to be concentrated along the Front Range, in urban settings. Blacks played a large part in the settling of the West—the Museum of the Black Cowboy in Denver covers this history in fascinating detail. The Chinese came to build the railroads in the late 1800s, and many settled in Denver. Southern Colorado is a part of the Southwest that has been settled by Hispanics for centuries, and there has been a natural migration to the cities. In some of the small, isolated Hispanic villages in the San Juan mountains of southern Colorado, English is a second language, and the cultural milieu is much the same as it has been since the 1500s. Adobe houses, strings of red chilis hanging in the sun, and the cadence of Spanish mark these villages. In Denver, Hispanics are by far the dominant ethnic group. Over half of the population of the Denver public school system is Hispanic, and the Hispanic community is playing an increasingly important

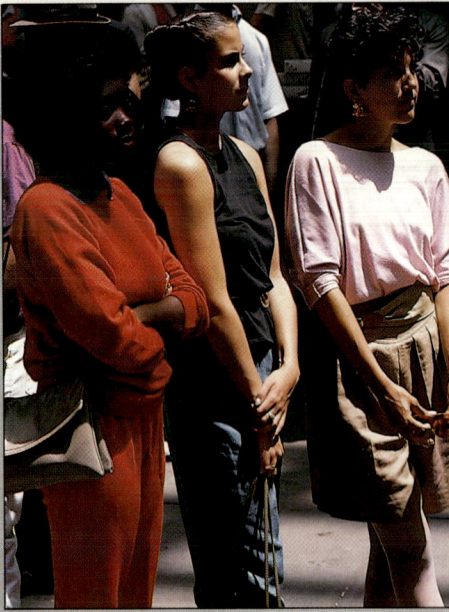

role in the politics of the city.

In contrast to the large reservations in the Southwest, there are relatively small Ute, Cheyenne, Crow, Shoshone, Bannock and Arapahoe reservations scattered about the Rockies. Each tribe has its own celebrations and ceremonials, but they aren't widely publicized off the reservation, so the best way to find them is to stop and ask. The Plains and Mountain Indians tended to be more warlike than their Pueblo neighbors to the south, and their land was more valuable to white settlers. As a result, they were nearly wiped out by the late 1900s, and have slowly made a comeback both in terms of population and in preserving their cultural heritage.

Another unusual and disappearing group of people in the Rockies are the Basque sheepherders. It was only a little more than a decade ago that large herds of sheep created traffic jams on the streets of Aspen and other Rocky Mountain towns in the spring and fall. Overgrazing and the competition of large ranches spelled the demise of the independent Basque sheepherder, but many can be found working for large ranches, living a simple life in primitive trailers.

The Role of the Ranger

Travellers who venture into the national parks, forests and wilderness areas of the Rockies are more than likely to meet a ranger working for one of the numerous government agencies that maintain, regulate and watch over them. Being a forest ranger isn't just a matter of looking for fires and building trails these days. Most have degrees that make them experts in the conservation, management, identification and preservation of the plants and animals of the Rockies. Their job description may include giving nature talks and walks, keeping the peace at crowded campgrounds, picking up litter and looking for lost backpackers. It can also include spending weeks at a time alone in the wilderness on foot or horseback, maintaining trails and signs, cataloguing flora and fauna, weathering violent thunderstorms on high peaks, and enjoying the peace and solitude of the wilderness.

Winter visitors to the Rockies are more than likely to meet another group whose jobs entail more than meets the eye—ski instructors and the ski patrol. Competition is stiff for these jobs and those who make it are highly qualified and certified. On any given day, a member of the ski patrol may have set off an avalanche with dynamite, marked a dangerous spot on the ski slope, put a broken leg in a temporary splint and hauled the injured party off the mountain in a sled, and gone on an out-of-bounds search looking for a missing skier.

The people of the Rockies are much like people anywhere else in the United States, but there is a certain exuberance, a *joie de vivre*, a keen appreciation among those who have fallen under the spell of the blue skies and snowcapped peaks. It's right there in the eyes and the hearts of the people, and it can be contagious!

Left, three lovely ladies represent Denver's ethnic mix; and right, the ultimate Fourth of July costume on a modern Uncle Sam.

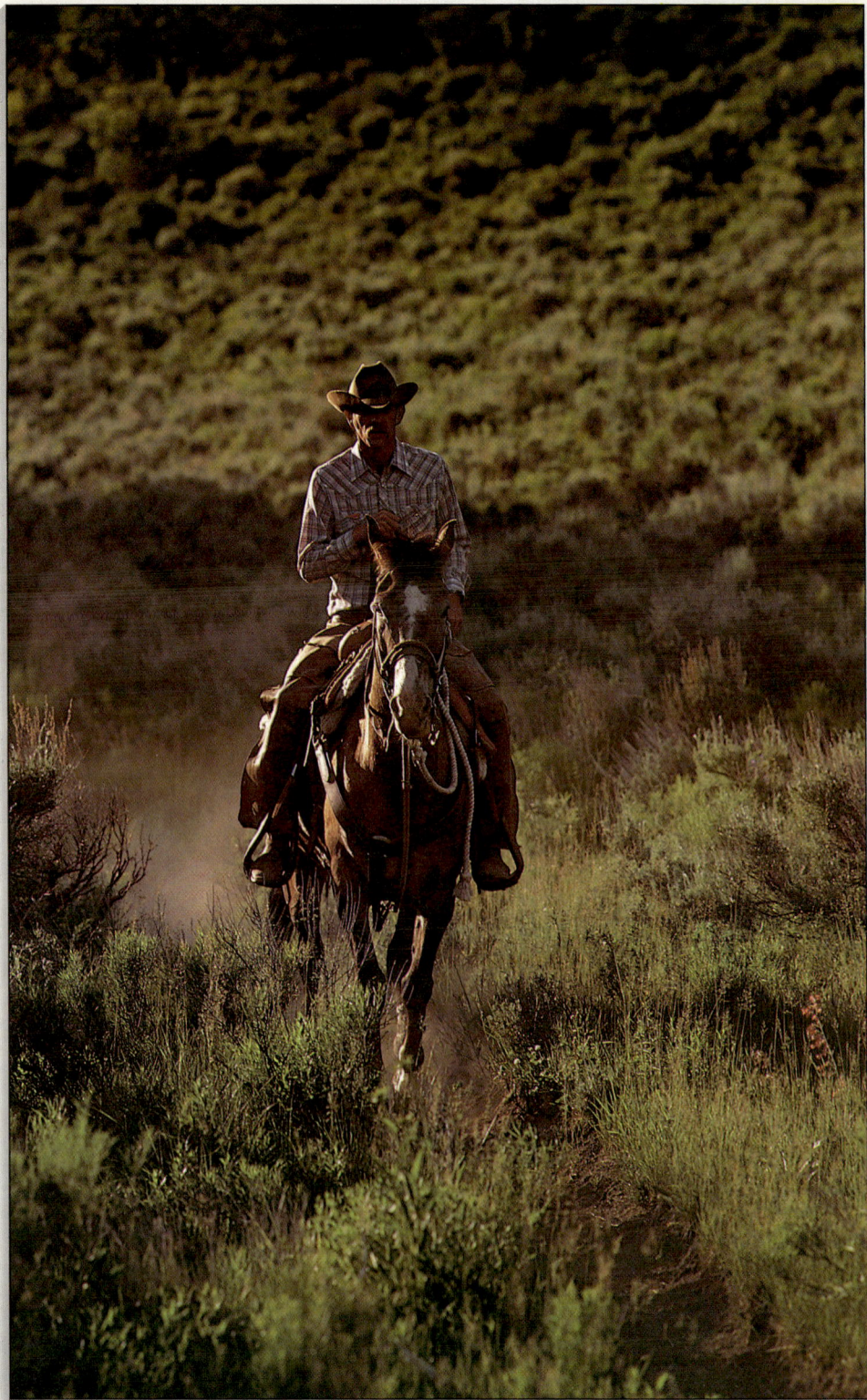

BLAZING SADDLES

Western Cowboys, Ranches and Farmers

Cowboys, a vanishing breed? Only time will tell, and it will be a long time before the Rocky Mountain cowboys vanish. Working cowboys (cowpunchers), rodeo cowboys, cattle and sheep ranchers, even farmers, in this western region are collectively referred to as cowboys.

Cowboys still wear their well-known traditional outfits: broad brimmed cowboy hats, pointed, high-heeled boots, rawhide belts with fancy buckles, denim jeans, shirts that snap all the way down, and sometimes neckerchiefs that protect them from dust and wind when pulled up "bank-robber style." You'll be sure to hear a cowboy at a distance because his spurs "jingle-jangle" as he walks.

Some have skin that's as weathered and wrinkled as the clothes they wear, some sport shirts of flashing, bright colors and wear smiles that are just as "shiny." You won't see all of them whirling a rope, or with a "chaw" of tobacco tucked inside a cheek. Rarely will you see a cowboy shed tears or be unkind to the opposite sex.

There are cowboys working daily with machinery over acres and acres of crops. Some are seen horseback "moseying along" with their cowherd or sheep flock, and some are noticed caring for fruit orchards.

Traditionally the cowboy promoted his image astride a horse, handling it with respect (and affection when no one was looking), the same way he handled lady friends. Well, almost the same, cowboys were known for "treating their horses, a mite better than their ladies."

A cowboy's life is a lonely one, his best friend is sometimes his horse or his own company, and it hasn't changed much over the past hundred years.

The "old cowboy lifestyle" may be a dying way of life today. Modernization has moved in over the past century. From a time when

Preceding pages: an exotic belly dancer at the Colorado Renaissance Festival; a Crow Indian in clown costume; and calming the roped steer as the dust settles on this Wyoming ranch. Left, horse and rider hit the lonesome Western trail; and right, a specially bred longhorn steer at the Dickinson Ranch.

fence lines didn't even exist to present-day barbed wire, electric fences, truck power, and modern equipment; the cowboy may soon be put on the endangered species list.

Some say, "As long as people are eating beef, we'll have cowboys." We all know that cowboys "won the West." Now, it seems, they're just trying to keep from losing it.

A cattle rancher used to be called a cattle baron or a cattle king, depending upon the number of cattle he owned.

A man of few words, known for his endurance of Mother Nature's ever-blowing wind,

burning sun and freezing snow, a cattle rancher never used the word "quit."

It wasn't unusual to own a ranch covering more than 1,000 sq miles (2,500 sq km) teeming with cattle and a few cowboys to tend the herds.

Cattle ranches today are few and far between compared to those operating in years past. But, travelling across the golden plains of Colorado and Wyoming into the mountain regions, you can see a little history come to life.

From Herefords to Texas Longhorns, every breed with beef on its sides can be found grazing the endless grasslands. If you keep your eyes open, you might also notice antelope or deer, even a hawk or an eagle. You won't have to look hard to find jack rabbits, but you may strain yourself in an attempt to avoid hitting one as they frequently insist on jumping in front of unsuspecting drivers.

Woolly America

Heading north from colorful Colorado into the great Wyoming range area, you'll notice that cattle decline and sheep begin to appear. Wyoming, originally known as "cow country," is now a heavily populated, wool-producing state.

Range wars between sheep and cattle ranchers during the 19th Century became a major theme in Wyoming's history. It was the cattlemen in Wyoming who claimed first-

maining cattlemen, and sheepfeuding ceased to exist. As a result, wool became the state's leading industry in the early 20th Century.

Cowboy Farmers

Pioneers made their way west, blazing the trails for the crowds who followed them. Those same pioneers soon became farmers. miners, ranchers, cowpunchers or gunmen. "Go West Young Man," stated Greeley, a Colorado farmer — and they did, literally by the thousands.

Farmers flocked into vastly populated areas to feed miners attracted by the gold rush, cattlemen drawn by Federal land grants, and other pioneers. Sheep ranchers followed, giving the farmers one more

" CUTTING OUT."

come, first-serve rights to the land. However, as sheep vied for space, the conflict grew violent.

In one skirmish, more than 150 masked men attacked a sheep ranch killing at least 2,000 sheep and a number of sheepherders, who tried in vain to protect their woolly charges.

These range wars, otherwise known as sheep slaughters, continued until the Wyoming Wool Growers' Association was organized. The organization attracted many members who eventually put a stop to the bloodshed.

In reality, sheep were more profitable than cattle. Sensing this fact, cattlemen became sheepherders, outnumbering the re-

reason to cultivate crops.

When the miners and traders moved on, the farmers and ranchers stayed behind to settle the states of Idaho, Wyoming and Colorado. These hardworking men and women, standing firm against adverse weather conditions, possessed an undying love for their land that made possible the Rocky Mountain cowboy farmer of the 20th Century. You'll find those farmers today harvesting everything from potatoes to wheat to fruit orchards.

Rocky Mountain Crops

Ask any American where potatoes are grown and he'll say Idaho. Although potatoes are grown across the United States, the largest crop is cultivated in Idaho, mainly in the irrigated Snake River area.

Luther Burbank is known as the "Father of the russet burbank potato," developed in 1872 and still the leading potato variety grown in the state. Burbank accidentally found a seed pod in his New England garden and transferred it to Idaho. Then, Joe Marshall, the legendary "Idaho Potato King," developed the potato to its present value.

Marshall had such a love for "his" potatoes that any employee he observed handling them carelessly or bruising them was instantly fired. Thanks to Marshall, Idaho is the number one producing potato state in the United States.

alternately planted. A crop is raised in one field one year and another the next year, enabling the fallow fields to rest to enhance the quality of future crops.

Wheat farmers are always gambling on weather conditions, losing when a hail storm or drought ruins the crop and waiting until the next year for another chance to win.

Two-thirds of the Colorado wheat is shipped to other countries, a blessed excess that feeds hundreds of million abroad. In turn, income from the fields feeds the farmers' families and their state taxes pay for schools, roads, parks and other systems — a boon to the state's economy.

As the Rocky Mountain regions in the United States evolved, cowboys found fu-

The tall, amber-colored wheat grain seen all over Colorado's Rocky Mountain plains is the state's chief field crop, producing a record high of 117 million bushels in 1983.

Successful wheat farming in Colorado began in 1876, the same year Colorado reached statehood. Cowboy pioneers learned to cultivate their land for this golden crop, opening the door for the wheat raising families of today.

Long, hard hours are spent planting, tending and harvesting a wheat crop. Fields are

Left, roping and herding steer in the old days was called "cutting out"; and right, herds roam the plains of a Wyoming Ranch.

tures in what their soil would produce. Riches were made in potatoes, in wheat and some in mouth watering, taste-tempting fruit.

Pounds of Peaches

Peaches, peaches and more peaches are produced each year in Colorado, mostly in the Grand Valley near Mesa County. In fact, the town of "Fruita" is named for the massive amount of peaches grown in its vicinity. More than 7 million pounds were produced in Mesa County in 1983. In April the western slopes of the Rockies are covered with the beautiful colors and smells of peach blossoms. About 400,000 peach trees are scattered over 2,700 acres (1090 hectares) bearing fruit from July through September.

The soil of the western mountain valleys is the most fertile in the nation, and the land west of the Continental Divide gets more than two-thirds of the state's surface water from rain and snow run-off. The dry, warm climate is ideal for growing fruit. In addition to peach trees; orchards full of cherries, pears and apricots dot the countryside.

Local roadside stands, farmers' markets and grocery stores make fruit easily available to tourists at very reasonable prices. Plan your Colorado vacation during the summer months, and drive through this fruit-full area for sights, scents and tastes you'll never forget.

Texas Longhorns were the first cattle in

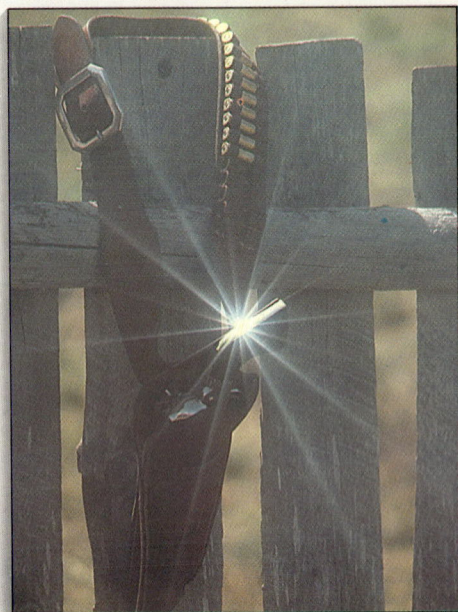

the Americas, hunted as wild animals in larger herds than the buffalo and eventually becoming more endangered. Without the Texas Longhorn, all the romantic legends about cowboys and their adventures wouldn't exist.

In 1493, Christopher Columbus brought Spanish cattle to this continent, and 200 years later, descendants of those cattle were grazing the Mexican ranges. In 1690, about 200 head of cattle were driven north to a mission near the Sabine River, land that would soon be known as Texas.

By the Civil War, nearly 300 years after setting hoof in America, millions of Longhorns ranged the southwestern plains. In the next quarter century, 10 million head were

herded north as far as Colorado, Wyoming and Montana.

Charles Goodnight and Oliver Loving in 1860 created the famous Goodnight-Loving trail, driving several hundred Longhorns into Denver City for the Colorado goldminers. Around the same time, Lovell and Reed, a well-known firm of Texas cattlemen, brought in another herd, thereby starting the range cattle industry in a country now called Colorado.

The Longhorns could travel nearly 100 miles (160 km) without water, surviving on prairie or mountain grasses no other animal would even look at. Their calves stood up right after birth and travelled side-by-side with the mother. Longhorns were feisty, rangy animals, adept at protecting their young from natural predators, such as the coyote.

At the turn of the century, in less than 40 years, an overwhelming demand from Europe for American beef imports brought the Longhorn closer to extinction than the buffalo. The federal government then intervened and established two wildlife refuges in 1927 for the preservation of the Texas cattle.

In 1964, when the Texas Longhorn Breeders' Association was formed, less than 1,500 head of Texas Longhorns existed. Three years later, Darol Dickinson bought a few Longhorns, the first step in developing a Texas Longhorn empire.

Dickinson Ranch today comprises 40,000 acres (16,200 hectares) on nine separate ranches in Colorado and one in Canada. Running 1,500 head of Texas Longhorn cattle and operating the largest private embryo transfer operation in existence, Dickinson's net worth today is $6.5 million. His enterprise has been solely supported by the sale of Texas Longhorn cattle for 18 years.

Darol Dickinson and his Dickinson Ranch have claimed a spot in the history of tomorrow's Texas Longhorn by ensuring their popularity and survival in today's industry. Visitors are encouraged to "stop in," as they have for the past 18 years. Here is a good place to surround oneself in western lore. Those traditions are still alive on this busy, working ranch, located in the heart of Colorado's plains, just a few minutes east of Colorado Springs on State Highway 94. At the crossroads of Ellicott, just look for the "long horns" — and the cowboys.

Left, the sun highlights a symbol of the old West—the pistol; and right, a thoughtful Wyoming ranch hand represents the outdoor life.

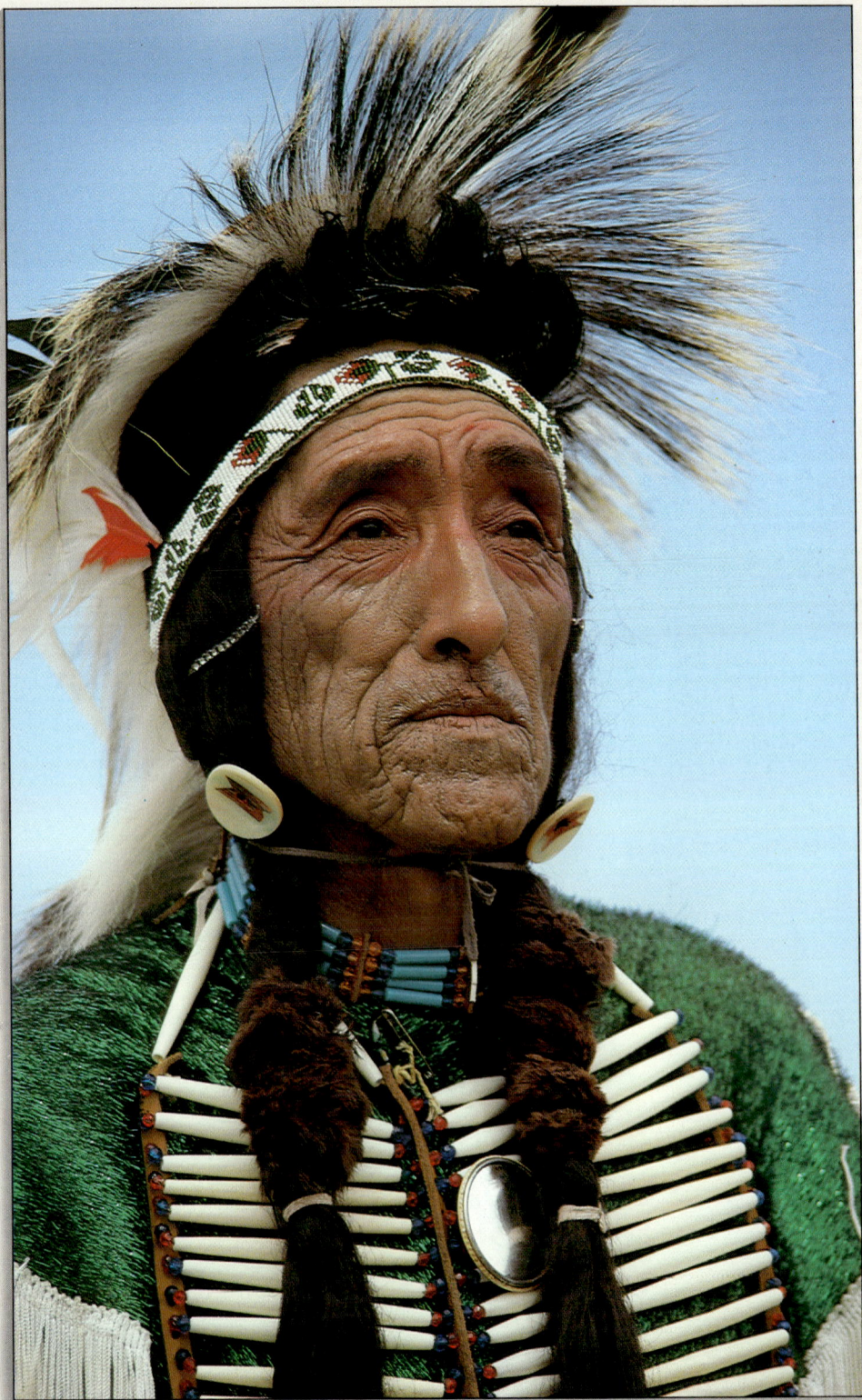

INDIANS THEN AND NOW

He rises from his pallet inside the Sundance corral. It is just before sunup on the ritual's third day. The Sundance participants have been without food and water since Friday evening. It is now Monday and they have been "standing thirsty" in a spiritual quest that will hopefully include renewal and rededication through individual visions. Outsiders have gathered in the morning darkness to seek a blessing at this high-holy moment of sunrise.

Leonard Burch, immediate past chairman of the Southern Ute Tribe, takes the flute made from the bone of a turkey leg and the haunting notes he creates seem to pipe the sun out from under its mauve coverlet, over the mountain top. Burch's only garb is a bright red breech clout.

Two days later, dressed in a three-piece business suit, Burch has jetted to Washington D.C., where he is explaining to the U.S. Congress the importance, to Indian and Anglo alike, of damming up the river waters of the State of Colorado before they flow into New Mexico and Southern California.

In just 48 hours, Burch has passed from the old way to the new.

The Call of the Mountains

The Utes are just one tribe (with several bands) of Indians who called the Rocky Mountains home. Their neighbors were the Crow, Flathead, Blackfeet, Bannock, Shoshone, Crees, Nez Perce, Arapahoe and Cheyenne. Some of those tribes, like the Arapahoe and Cheyenne, were Plains Indians who moved West to escape the encroaching white settlers. The Cheyenne came to the Big Horn Mountains after the defeat of General George Custer at the battle of the Little Big Horn in 1876.

They were unique as tribes, but had some things in common. The Utes were known for their horsemanship. The Comanches had a reputation for their skill in warring, the Blackfeet for their cunning in dealing with the white aggressors.

As they intermingled, they learned from each others. It was from the Shoshones that

Preceding pages, a dramatic Shoshone Indian chief in full traditional garb. Left, the well-worn face of a Crow Indian.

the Utes learned the Sundance. The Sundance is the most sacred religious observance of Plains Indians. It includes fasting and dancing in an enclosed area, always facing the sun or some other sacred object such as a buffalo head on a pole in the center of the corral. The object is spiritual growth through a vision quest. Some tribes pierced their flesh as a sign they would fulfill their vows. The U.S. government banned the Sundance for that reason, but it has been making a comeback since the 1960s as tribes recapture their culture. The Shoshones obviously learned the Sundance from either the Arapahoes or Cheyennes.

The Shoshones called themselves "the people" and except for the latecomers, if they were asked where they came from, they said they had been there forever. Rock art substantiates a very old history of the people whose lives were shaped by their geography. They followed the game to high country in the summer and to the valleys in winter. Before they were introduced to the horse, they used buffalo products for everything— food, shelter, clothing, tools and ceremony.

Indian Legends

The Shoshones knew the ways of both animals and plants and respected them even as they used them. They had a universal belief that animals, like humans, had souls that survived death. Their respect for animals stemmed from that belief. They thought animal souls reported to living animals how they were killed, butchered and consumed. Living game refused to allow their bodies to be slain by an unkind hunter, who thereafter found hunting more and more difficult.

When Indians saw an eclipse, they believed an animal was trying to swallow the sun or the moon. Many of their original legends and stories give human properties to animals like the coyote, the lizard, the eagle and the mountain lion.

Most tribes had taboos concerning pregnancy, birth, menstruation and going to war. Some tribes isolated the expectant mother immediately before birth and for 30 days thereafter. Isolation from the tribe was common for women who were menstruating and such women were barred from tribal rites such as the sweat lodge. In some tribes, preparation for war included dancing, fasting and isolation to insure abstinence from sexual activity.

Indian medicine was a mix of religion, magic and herbalism. In most nonliterate cultures, marriage was a contract between kin rather than between two individuals. It was widely celebrated and served as a way to regulate sexual activity.

The Indians made beautiful works of art, such as beadwork, tanned leather, bone and teeth breastplates and other adornments. They often wore furs in their hair or as a decorative part of their clothing.

Arrival of the White Men

The functions of Indian societies were clearly defined, and these groups were a far cry from the "savage nomad" myth pro-

Peter and Paul Mallet are credited with being the first men to have reached the Rockies by crossing the plains in 1739. The Spanish priests Dominguez and Escalante, exploring for Spain, got into the Rocky Mountains as they searched for a trail from New Mexico to California. When Lewis and Clark came west in an attempt to find a commercially feasible land route across the continent, their contact with the Rocky Mountain Indians was the Shoshones who were riding Spanish horses through their trade with the Utes and Comanches.

It was the introduction of the horse into tribal society that brought drastic change. Mounted, the tribe members could pursue both game and enemies over far greater areas. In their exchanges with neighboring

moted by the white aggressors.

What happened to these early tribal societies is that they were made to trade the lands they called home for the most uninhabitable acreage their white oppressors could force upon them. They were beaten by disease, such as small pox, to which they had no immunity; superior and unethical military attacks; and a U.S. government that did not honor its treaties.

Indians in the Southern Rockies probably encountered their first white men when the Spanish colonization of the Pueblos began about 1600. Contact with those Spanish invaders and Mexican explorers into the Rocky Mountain region is reflected in the Ute language.

tribes, they picked up new ways of warring and celebrating.

Miners, Traders & Broken Treaties

From 1795 to 1822, the U.S. government operated trading posts. Indians' contact with traders was mostly friendly. Traders wanted the beaver and buffalo pelts that the Indians could supply, and the Indians wanted the cooking utensils, guns, ammunition, beads, fabric and liquor that traders could offer in exchange.

The first treaty the U.S. signed was with the East Coast Delaware Tribe in 1778. From then until 1849, when the Bureau of Indian Affairs was moved out of the U.S.

War Department to the Department of the Interior, all Indian agents were military officers charged with protecting the interests of the fur traders, missionaries, miners and finally the settlers. No one was charged with protecting the interests of the Indian.

It was the California gold rush in the middle of the 19th Century which alerted the Indians to the fact that the resources on which they depended were finite and that the white invaders had little respect for either the land or the animals.

They began to fight back with attacks on forts, wagon trains and settlements. This encouraged the white invader to annihilate "the savages."

The miners who poured into the area for the Pike's Peak gold rush not only drove out timber lands. Feeding railroad workmen further reduced the buffalo herds and for the majority of whites who favored exterminating the Indians, killing buffalo became a means to that end as they realized the Indians' dependence on the shaggy beasts.

As Indians killed and looted in a vain attempt to protect their resources, the U.S. government shored up its resolve to conquer the natives by force.

Every tribe faced its military "Waterloo." Weakened by a plague of small pox, the Shoshones and Bannocks had gathered on the Bear River in 1863. A military attack took the lives of 400 people. By the next year, 20,000 whites had entered Idaho's richest mining area.

buffalo and other game but wantonly killed without utilizing their kill. That practice was an affront to the Indian and made it harder and harder to supply meat to their tribes.

On the heels of the miners came the trans-continental railroad. The venture not only appropriated vast amounts of land to the railroad and its right-of-way, but decimated forests and buffalo herds. Twenty-five hundred railroad ties per mile stripped

Left, a modern Zuni Indian jewel made of shell and turquoise at the Museum of Mesa Verde National Park; and right, buffalo was the main food and clothing source for the Indians seen here in *Buffalo Hunt*, by Frederic Remington.

In 1854, the Utes were called to a peace conference held in Taos, New Mexico. Blankets were given to the Indians as gifts and every person who received a blanket contracted small pox. Even now, many Utes believe that plague was deliberately introduced by the whites who came to talk peace. With more and more settlers coming into their territory, the Utes joined the Apaches to drive the whites from the country around Fort Carson, Colorado.

Gaining entrance to Fort Carson on Christmas Day, the Indians staged an uprising killing all but one man and taking the one woman in the fort and her two children captives. Kit Carson led the defensive military attack against the Utes, defeating them.

The Sand Creek Slaughter

Colorado Governor John Evans ordered the Cheyennes and Arapahoes to lay down their arms and report to Fort Lyons. Indian agent Colonel John Chivington believed only a harsh lesson would persuade those two bands of warriors to behave. With the Cheyennes and Arapahoes encamped at Sand Creek, Chivington followed them there with 900 "military" men, most of whom were miners who had enlisted in the cause of exterminating the "savages."

More than half the Indians killed at Sand Creek were women and children. Soldiers also disemboweled several pregnant Indian women. The event was termed "The foulest and most unjustifiable crime in the annals of

what they were signing. In a U.S. Supreme Court Case in 1945, U.S versus Shoshone, Chief Justice Black wrote, "Ownership meant no more to them (Indians) than to roam the land as a great common and to possess and enjoy it the same way they possess and enjoyed the sunlight, the west wind and the feel of spring in the air."

Whether or not they understood mattered little as almost every treaty they made with the U.S. was broken before the ink was dry.

Mediator or Traitor, a Matter of Interpretation

The treaty with the Utes is a typical example. That treaty was signed in 1868 by Chief Ouray. It designated the land on which the

America." It plunged Colorado into a state of emergency, martial law and economic crisis because of the whites who protested such brutality.

The Blackfeet, too, were suffering from a plague of small pox in 1870. When they saw soldiers approaching their encampment on the Marias River, Chief Heavy Runner went out to meet the soldiers alone, carrying a sign of peace. He was shot, only the first of many Blackfeet killed that day.

Weakened by disease, beaten in battle, stalked by hunger and with their tribal society non-functional, tribe after tribe signed a treaty with the U.S. government.

The Indians not only were without options, but it is doubtful that they understood

Utes could live without intrusion by whites. But almost immediately, both gold and silver were discovered in the San Juan Mountains and the mountains were filled with miners.

Ouray was considered a great mediator by the U.S. government. The Utes considered him a traitor. Ouray felt the Indian had to change his way to survive and he joined the white effort to assimilate the Utes into the white society. In 1873, Ouray signed another agreement with the U.S. government that turned 6,000 sq miles (15,540 sq km) of Ute land to miners—almost one-fourth of the reservation agreement of 1868.

In an attempt to demonstrate to Indians they could succeed in an agrarian civilization, Ouray and his wife, Chippeta, lived on a farm near Montrose, Colorado, cultivating lands and raising sheep and cattle.

But after repeated contact with the Great White Father in Washington, Ouray died knowing his life's work had failed. Chippeta remarried and lived in a traditional teepee much of the time until her death in 1924.

Conforming to White Ways

By 1871, the U.S. had stopped treaty-making with the Indians. Through a series of government programs, attempts were made to force Indians to adopt white people's ways.

First they were all assigned to agencies where food and goods were to be distributed

destruction in the high suicide rates Indians experience.

Attempts to educate Indians were even less successful. Teachers spoke English in boarding schools where using any native tongue was discouraged to the point of punishment if children were found speaking anything but English. Not only did children not understand subject matter, but they were separated from their families and tribes and experienced severe trauma because of those separations.

Indian lawyer and writer Vine Deloria, Jr., of Denver, has written, "Tribal society is of such a nature that one must experience it from the inside. Being inside a tribal universe is so comfortable and reasonable that it acts like a narcotic. When you are forced

and Indians were forced to learn farming.

The Dawes Act of 1887 gave Indian heads of families 160-acre (64-hectare) allotments, opening the rest of the reservation lands to white settlers.

Indians were a highly spiritual people. Because the "superior" whites had no concept of any religion except their brand of Christianity, the move to "Christianize" the Indians diluted their native faith with a demoralizing result. Many Indian spiritual leaders see a direct result of that spiritual

Left, a native Indian concentrates on the rodeo; and right, a native dance at the Crow Indian Festival and Rodeo in Montana.

outside the tribal context, you become alienated, irritable and lonely. In desperation, you long to return to the tribe if only to preserve your sanity."

Throughout the government's attempt to assimilate the Indian, a paternalistic attitude existed that encouraged dependence.

In 1924, native Americans received citizenship from the U.S. government, but it was not until 1948 that they could vote in every state in the union.

The Indian Reorganization Act

In 1934, the Indian Reorganization Act reversed the Dawes Act, saying that no tribal lands should be parcelled out in individual allotments. Annual authorizations of $2 million for the purchase of tribal land were established. Credit funds for incorporated tribes were set up. Loans for vocational training and academic study were provided. The power of tribes as self-governing units was established. Although funds to enact many of these provisions were never fully appropriated by Congress, the policies of the Indian Reorganization Act were theoretically much better than the federal government's next idea.

In 1953, the United States adopted a policy of termination in its relations with Indians. Land and capital were distributed to individuals who were not prepared to handle either. The tribe was destroyed as a powerful economic unit.

laration of Indian purpose was drafted. "Indians ask for assistance, technical and financial, for the time needed, however long that may be, to regain in the America of the space age, some measure of the life they enjoyed as original possessors of the land."

Indians were ripe for the civil rights movement of the 1960s.

They staged a fish-in in Washington State where they had been denied the right to fish. They took over Alcatraz Prison off the West Coast of California. In 1968, the American Indian Movement (AIM) was founded. Leaders said they formed AIM because they were tired of having nothing to say about their own destiny. That organization took over the Bureau of Indian Affairs (BIA) office in November, 1972.

Concurrent with the termination policy was the Relocation Program. It was designed to take Indians off reservations and place them in the city. It proved to be just a new form of disaster for the Indians.

Indian Assistance

In 1946, a Claims Commission was established to settle all grievances with Indians by cash payments to them with the objective of cutting off all financial aid. By 1951, 852 land claims had been filed—a legal brouhaha that defied resolution since many claims overlapped each other.

In 1961, most tribes were represented at a government-called conference where a dec-

Recovering the 'Loot'

When they left the BIA, they took an estimated $750,000 worth of art objects which they said missionaries stole from the Indians many years ago. They left behind a statement which read: "Gentlemen: I do not apologize for the ruin nor the so-called destruction of this mausoleum. For in building anew, one must first destroy the old. This is the beginning of a new era for the North American native people. When history recalls our efforts here, our descendants will stand with pride, knowing their people were the only ones responsible for the stand taken against tyranny, injustice, and the gross inefficiencies of this branch of a corrupt and decadent government."

It is poetic justice that the arid lands many tribes were forced onto are now discovered to be rich with mineral resources.

Most tribes hired legal counsel long before the energy issue became critical in the States. Those lawyers negotiated contracts for lumbering, mining and farming on Indian lands. They lobbied state and local governments to address Indians' rights and make concessions without the expense of a trial.

From those lawyers, tribes have discovered that the way to fight the white man is in his own courts of law, and they are winning.

Rocky Mountain tribes are among the 25 tribes who in 1975 formed an organization to protect their energy resources. That orga-

nization calls itself The Council of Energy Resources Tribes (CERT).

From a CERT annual report come these words: "On a hot and dusty western summer day in 1875, two cowhands stopped their horses by a creek running deep through Indian territory. The animals refused to drink and the men looking closely, found the water to be covered with a thick, sticky black substance neither had ever seen before. They were the discoverers of oil on Indian land.

Left, native Indian and Congressman, Ben Nighthorse, in his shop "Campbell Creations"; and right, a beautiful Indian girl at the Fort Hall reservation.

Natural Resources

"A hundred years later, more than 13,000 oil and gas leases involving tribal lands were on record, accounting for over 23,000 separate producing wells. The largest open-pit uranium mine in the world and the largest surface coal mine in the country were both operating on Indian lands."

Indian lands contain one-third of low sulfur strippable coal lands in the West, half of the privately owned uranium in the United States and substantial deposits of oil-shale and geothermal energy.

While Indians own valuable resources, many continue to live in poverty. They were assured that the federal government, acting as their trustees, would negotiate the best possible agreements for the exploration and production of these newly needed resources.

CERT was formed on the premise that if they took control of this energy and managed it wisely, it could become the foundation for economic development on their reservations.

CERT's goals are: To ensure an equitable return for resources, to assist tribes in protecting those resources, to aid each tribe in the capability to manage its resources for itself.

Peter MacDonald, immediate past chairman of the Navajo Nation and former CERT Chairman, said, "Ongoing federal support for CERT and for other tribal energy programs is proving to be among the most cost-effective investments yet made in our country's energy future.

"Real progress, in the view of my people, must transcend profits. It must outlast generations. It must help us realize a vision articulated by Chief Joseph of the Nez Perce a century ago: "Let me be a free man—free to travel, free to stop, free to work, free to trade where I choose, free to choose my own teachers, free to follow the religion of my fathers, free to think and act and talk for myself . . . for this time, the Indian race is waiting and praying."

There is an effort by most tribes to recapture their spiritual values, native tongue, history and legends. Tribes are still affected by high unemployment rates, high suicide rates, alcoholism and infant mortality.

The freedom MacDonald speaks of will be found in leaders like himself—articulate, well-educated and sophisticated. Like oppressed people throughout the history of the world, American Indians are developing a leadership that will hold its own against further tribal and personal violations.

Rocky Mountain Area

0 ——— 120 miles
0 ——— 200 km

Calgary

CANADA

Saskatchewan R.

Medicine Hat

Regina

Gull Lake

Continental Divide

Glacier
Nat'l. Park

Kalispell

Havre

Fort Peck
Lake

Culbertson

Missouri R.

Great Falls

MONTANA

N. Dakota

Coeur
d'Alene

Lewiston

Missoula

Helena

Lewistown

Garrison Res.

Butte

Miles City

Livingston

Billings

Salmon

Dillon

Yellowstone R.

Lemmon

Madison R.

R O C K Y

IDAHO

Yellowstone
Nat'l. Park

Cody

Sheridan

Powder R.

S. Dakota

Boise

Dubois

Rapid City

Arco

Grand Teton
Nat'l. Park

Thermopolis

Snake R.

Jackson

Twin Falls

Pocatello

Lander

Casper

M O U N T A I N S

WYOMING

Kemmerer

Great
Salt
Lake

Ogden

Scottsbluff

Elko

Rock Springs

Nebraska

Salt Lake City

Vernal

Craig

Rocky Mtn.
Nat'l. Park

Cheyenne

Estes Park

Provo

Boulder

Ely

UTAH

Green River

Denver

Fillmore

Grand Junction

**Colorado
Springs**

Nevada

Capitol Reef
Nat'l. Park

Colorado River

Canyonlands
Nat'l. Park

Pueblo

Arkansas R.

Zion
Nat'l. Park

Bryce
Canyon
Nat'l. Park

Glen Canyon
Nat'l. Rec. Area

Durango

COLORADO

St. George

L. Powell

Arizona

Mesa Verde Nat'l. Park

Trinidad

New Mexico

Oklahoma

Continental Divide

Taos

Texas

Gallup

R. Grande

Flagstaff

Santa Fe

Kansas

A GUIDE TO THE GUIDE

The Rockies—a mountain land where Indians roamed—now boasts charming mountain towns, sophisticated cities and exciting activities. *APA's Insight Guide to The Rockies* helps you explore it all in the following recommended order.

First we present you with themes basic to the hearty Rockies lifestyle. "The Outdoor Rush" describes the variety of outdoor pastimes available in these spectacular mountains.

The Rocky Mountains is "Ski Country U.S.A." Many claim here is the greatest snow on earth. Dude ranches, ski lodges and resorts have sprung up everywhere so you can ski the peaks in style. "Ski Resorts" tells you how, when and where to get the best out of the champagne powder.

Still in the festive mood, it is apt to discover when and where the "Celebrations in the Mountains" are, so that you may plan your trip through the Rockies to coincide with some of these great events and happenings.

Visitors also flock to the many National Parks and Monuments scattered throughout the Rockies states. Some of the most dramatic landscape and wildlife in the world are here. The National Parks section gives you pointers on how to visit and what to look for in the Yellowstone, the Grand Tetons, the Rocky Mountain and in Utah's National Parks. Don't miss the helpful photographic tips following that section.

Next we lead you on a basic tour of the Middle Rockies states beginning in Denver, the gateway to the Rockies, and the surrounding cities and towns known as Colorado's Front Range.

The "Colorado Mountain Towns" nestled in the Rockies are a treat to visit and are full of mining history. "Aspen" in particular, a Colorado mountain retreat rivalling Denver in popularity, has an aura all its own.

Then your drive to Durango, south of Denver, takes you through narrow passes and wide open meadows to authentic Western streets almost frozen in time. And don't miss Canyon Country nearby. The Royal Gorge and the Black Canyon here reveal dramatic evidence of ancient geology at work.

Moving north to Wyoming, explore its wilderness and on the way visit Jackson Hole. Encounters with wildlife and the proximity of the Grand Tetons make this an awe-inspiring area. Then allow a few days at the Buffalo Bill Historical Center in Cody to view four superb museum collections. On the way out of town enjoy the Wapiti valley and some of the best dude ranches in the West on the outskirts of Yellowstone Park.

Also within reach is Bozeman in Montana "Big Sky" country. Farmers and modern cowboys here live with their rich lore of gold seekers and mountain men.

Travelling south through Idaho towards Utah you'll arrive at state capital Salt Lake City where 100 years of Mormon history come to life. This unique American subculture is a powerful social force today. From here the superlative ski areas in the Promontory Ranch north of the Great Salt Lake is close by.

The Rockies—a place well worth exploring. Come share in the adventure. . . . .

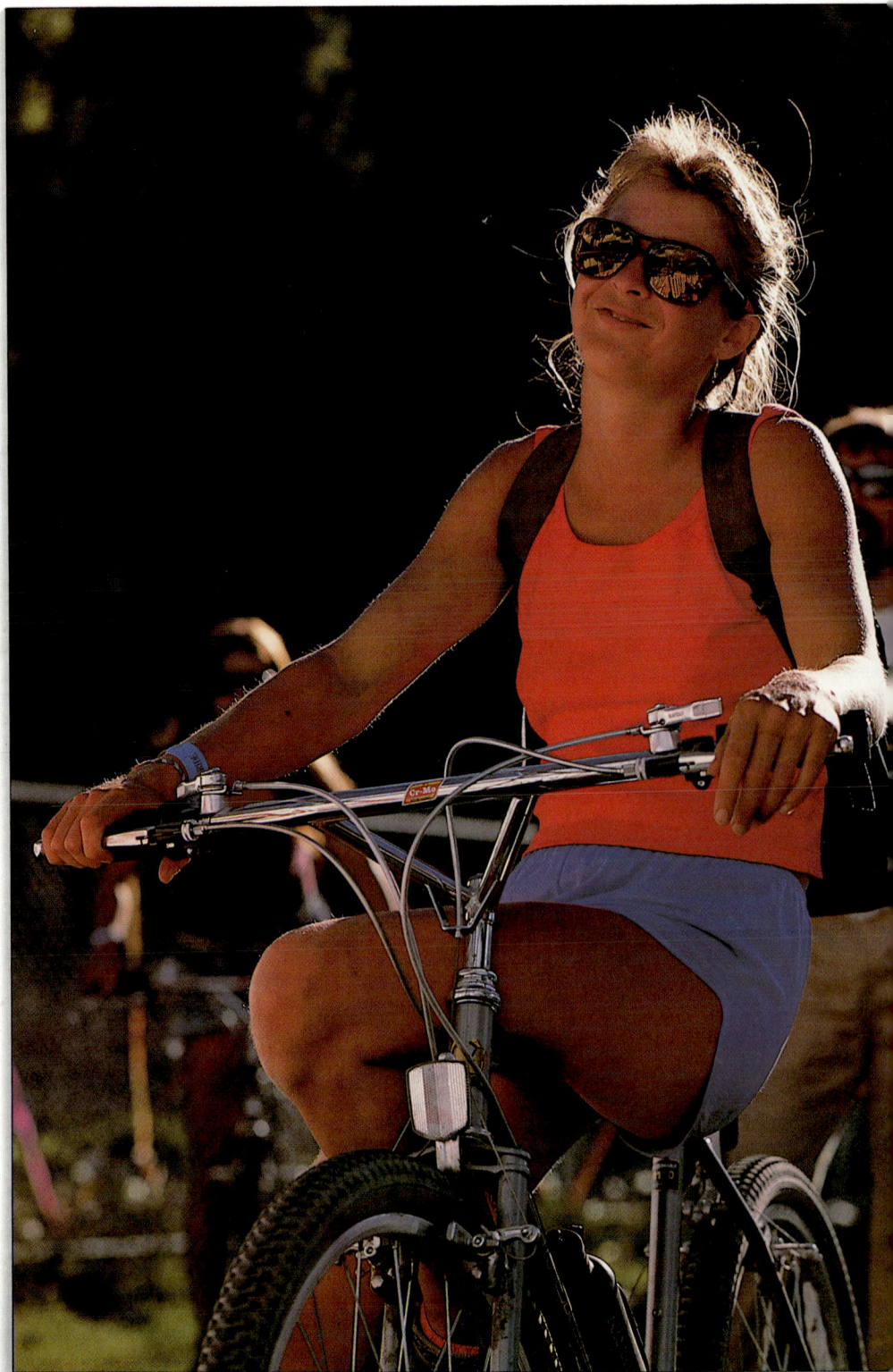

THE OUTDOOR RUSH

From the first recorded history of Rockies settlement, adventurous travellers have been coming to the area for various reasons. Not only to seek their fortunes in the rich gold and silver fields, but to settle the land and take advantage of the moderate climate and the vast resources of the varied terrain. The region's earliest history is not written but is recorded in paintings on the canyon walls in protected locations along the Colorado River near Lake Powell and in the ruins of the Cliff Dwellings at Mesa Verde.

Those early Rocky Mountain residents were drawn to the area for the same reasons as the white explorers and adventurers who came later; and, even more recently, as the vacationers who still make their way to the remote villages and mountain hideaways. The rich land and natural resources, spectacular scenery, and opportunity for adventure and personal fulfillment are what draw people, almost magically, to the Rockies, and have for more than 200 years.

The acquisition of the Rocky Mountain region with the Louisiana Purchase in 1803 made it accessible for settlers, trappers, hunters, and those seeking their fortunes in gold and silver. Brief forays or exploration parties made their way into the mountains. Included in their member was Zebulon Pike who, in 1806, discovered the mountain that bears his name, and Lord Gore whose reputation has been embellished as the years have gone by.

Lord Gore was an English nobleman who travelled in style during his hunting trips that included cooks and servants, and the luxury of frequent hot baths in his tent. His large brass bathtub was part of the equipment that normally accompanied Lord Gore. Today, an entire mountain range bears his name, and stirs curiosity and imagination in the campers and backpackers who take the time to trek the ancient trails.

More and more people ventured into the unknown territory from the 1830s to the 1850s. But not until the fall of 1858 was gold discovered in the hills west of Denver which sparked the rush that brought instant attention and tent cities to the relatively uncharted territory.

Just six years later, in 1864, the silver boom was on. Some of the rough-and-tumble mining towns turned quickly into rich and fabulous cities with opera houses, magnificent homes and personalities as broad and booming as the men and women who lived in them. Silver Baron H.A.W. Tabor is among the most notable, who established, lost and regained his fortune in Leadville, then made his mark on the society of Denver. He built the Tabor Opera House in Leadville and later the Tabor Grand Opera House in Denver.His first wife, Augusta, was a strong woman whose work ethic scorned Tabor's glamorous and flamboyant lifestyle. When Tabor moved to Denver, he married Baby Doe, a beautiful, young woman who enjoyed the exciting society that Tabor's riches provided. Baby Doe died penniless, trying to work the Matchless Mine near Leadville. Tabor admonished her before his death "never to sell the Matchless," because it would once again make her rich. Now, the Matchless Mine is open to visitors and takes history buffs into the rough world of the early miners. The Tabor Opera House has reopened as a visitors attraction, but the city of Leadville is far from the booming community that once boasted more than 12 theaters, many of which were "wine theaters" of questionable reputation.

On the Trail to Relaxation

Following the gold and silver boom, the region's cattle, agricultural and mineral reserves boosted the economy and allowed cities to flourish along the rivers, at highway junctions, natural springs and hot springs. The hot springs, vacation spots for the earliest settlers and once believed by both Indians and whites to have exceptional healing powers, still attract thousands of visitors. Among the most noted are the mineral hot springs at Eldorado Springs, Idaho Springs, Hot Sulphur Springs, Ouray, Mount Princeton, Pagosa Springs, Redstone and Glenwood Springs, the home of the largest spring-fed hot springs pool in the world. While some of the hot springs are well-known and accessible vacation spots, many can be reached only by jeep road or hiking trail in summer or by cross-country skies in winter.

Ironically, what draws people to Colorado most is also the state's biggest barrier: the Rocky Mountains. More than 50 peaks in the Colorado Rockies top 14,000 feet (4,250 meters), and more than half the state is covered by rugged mountain terrain or high plateaus laced with deep valleys and canyons. Etched by glaciers and erosion, layers of cliffs line canyon walls, creating the trails that early settlers faced and the adventure for today's hikers.

People still flock to the region to play or to seek their fortunes among the rocks and abundant resources. Most of the Rockies' industry relates to mineral resources or agriculture. The travel industry occupies an extremely important spot in the economy and it relies most heavily on the region's natural beauty and resources.

Recreation, relaxation, vitality, adventure, beauty, excitement—just a few of the varied reasons why people continue to visit the Rocky Mountains. An even greater variety of activities keeps them busy. From the sophisticated, modern, and elegant resorts that entertain skiers, conventioneers, and summer guests in a planned and ulti-mately civilized manner; to the back-country experiences where the hardy undertake almost the same risk and hardship of the early traveller, the Rockies have it all.

Because the Rocky Mountain states rely heavily on tourists, they have made it a point to develop a transportation and hospitality industry that encourages return visits. The interstate highway system allows easy access to major areas and links with well-maintained local roads which, in a few short miles, take visitors to regions that appear as untouched and pristine as they were 100 years ago. With a little extra effort, either by taking one of the numerous backcountry jeep trails or by going it alone, on foot, horseback or trail bicycle—you can reach restricted wilderness areas where no motorized vehicles break the silence. The only sounds are of the wind in the trees, the rushing stream at the valley floor, and the wildlife that goes about its daily business with an occasional scolding at intruders. Only minutes from the door of many Rocky Mountain communities, you can get away from it all and feel alone in the solace that Mother Nature

Balloons line up at the start of the Avon Balloon Race in Colorado.

maintains to replenish the mind and soul.

Victorian Elegance

As a Rocky Mountain vacation begins, in evidence are the quaint Victorian homes and buildings that sprang up at the peak of the gold and silver rush. Nothing was spared in many of the homes, with gingerbread wood-working surrounding the leaded glass windows that overlook mountain vistas. At the decline of the gold and silver boom, the rich communities suffered setbacks and homes fell into disarray. Beautiful and opulent landmarks, such as the Tabor Opera House in Leadville and Teller House in Central City, where the street in front was paved with 30 solid silver bricks and which was known for the large painting of a beautiful woman, commonly called "the face on the barroom floor," closed their doors to the richly attired gentlemen and ladies of the late 1800s.

The recent rush of tourists has given new life to the Victorian towns. Homes have been restored either as private residences, bed-and-breakfast locations

Sailing through water and clouds at Grand Lake.

or even boutiques and museums. While visiting one of the mining towns, it is appropriate to dive completely into the romance of the Old West and stay in one of the rooming houses. Today, summer visitors enjoy opera, symphonies and plays at a number of the restored opera houses. The opulent chandeliers, woodwork and decor have been authentically restored so guests can feel they are living in the 19th-Century affluent society.

Moving away from the atmosphere and relative formality of the villages and towns, the pioneering spirit of the West remains. The hustle and bustle of modern cities begin to fall away as you enter the mountain communities. The transformation continues as you move into the spaces and activities that are now so accessible throughout the Rockies.

The rush to the Rockies is not impeded by lack of transportation. Those arriving by car and reluctant to venture beyond that mode of transportation can see a large part of the states. Roads to mining towns are generally good, and many of the historic locations or ghost towns are found on jeep roads. While not for the faint of heart in many cases, taking time to visit some of the ghost towns is greatly rewarding. Jeep trails are ranked from nearly passable by a normal passenger car to a white-knuckled ride in a four-wheel drive vehicle. Narrow, winding roads that once provided access for residents travelling by wagon or on horseback are still the only ways to reach some of the ghost mining towns. But the vistas are spectacular, and, once at the destination, wandering among the fallen buildings and searching for artifacts left behind by departing citizens is rewarding. Tourists can let their minds wander and imagine what life was like in the encampments, from the bold and bawdy days when gold and silver finds were commonplace to the cold and desolate winters when the price of gold and silver dwindled and settlers suffered.

Jeeping to ghost towns is not the only choice, however. Taking restricted or jeep roads into the backcountry allows hikers to strike off on foot and push still deeper into the wilderness.

For those who wish to leave the driving and route selection to someone else, organized jeep tours are offered in almost every corner and valley of the Rockies. Local Chambers of Commerce or Information Centers can provide names of jeep outfitters and recommend routes that suit either the adventurous or the timid.

The Great Outdoors

The high moutain streams and lakes are a fisherman's dream, yielding brook trout, browns and firm-fleshed lake trout. Depending on the area, bait or fly fishing is recommended. For backpackers or hikers, finding a mountain stream is just as enjoyable as fishing itself. Most mountain communities boast a fishing guide operation that not only has checked out the finest and most productive fishing spots, but also constantly monitor the most effective bait choices for each season. Some guides all but guarantee that fishermen will leave with breakfast in their creels, but even if the fishing is unproductive, the Rocky Mountain scenery always makes the trip worthwhile. Guides can be hired to supply equipment as well as expertise in most areas, and, depending on season and location, will take their charges to the destination by boat or jeep.

For other sports enthusiasts, big game and bird hunting is abundant in the Rockies.Many guides and outfitters who handle jeep and fishing tours will also take care of details for hunters. A number of dude or working ranches accommodate hunters in fall, and offer an entire range of services. Some ranches or outfitters handle only lodging, while others provide horses, guides, cooks and every piece of equipment necessary for an extended stay in the woods. Materials supplied are almost certainly accompanied by many tall tales of years past and the big trophies that they didn't quite bring home.

Hiking and climbing into those unique and special wilderness spots is a pastime that can occupy a day, a weekend or entire summers in the Rockies. The area is networked with hiking trails maintained by the United States Forest Service. Maps are available through the Forest Service and at many information centers. Colorado has 11 National Forests that encourage everything from car-camping in the numerous campgrounds to a backcountry experience. Once again mountain guides and outfitters can help with equipment, guides and routes if visitors

Grinning and pushing over Independence Pass (CO).

Grinning and pushing over Independence Pass (CO).

are novices to backpacking. No one should strike off into the wilderness without first becoming properly equipped and learning how to use the equipment. Mountain weather changes frequently and rapidly, and what starts out as a sunny day can be punctuated by a snowstorm even at the height of summer. Many Rocky Mountain states boast—or caution—that somewhere in the high country, it snows during every month of the year.

Come Spelunking!

The unique outdoor activities that bring the hardy enthusiast to the Rockies include rock climbing and caving or spelunking. Neither of these demanding sports should be attempted by anyone who is unfamiliar with them. There are numerous rock-climbing schools throughout the area where, under the watchful eye of guides and well-trained instructors, students learn the art of rock climbing just as they learn to respect the technical knowledge needed to complete exercises and journeys successfully and smoothly.

Cavers and spelunkers should also be properly outfitted and guided to their destination. While caving can be exciting, it is surrounded by superstition and tales of wild adventure. The lure of the unknown is probably the basis for most of the spectacular stories about nature's underground, but those who venture into the deep should be well prepared, not only for where they are going, but also for what they are getting into. Climbers and cavers should check in with the regional Forest Service office both upon entering and leaving their destination.

For a more civilized approach to caving, Cave of the Winds, near the Broadmoor and Colorado Springs, is operated commercially for tourists. The stalactites, stalagmites, flowstones and other eleothems are typical of what cavers find.

Highways are not the only means of transportation throughout the Rockies. While the waterways are not noted for transport or big boats and sailing, river rafting has become a significant alternative for the adventure-seeking resident or guest. River rafting is generally done on inflated rafts carrying a dozen or more people but many prefer canoes,

Rough and tumble rafting on the Colorado River.

kayaks, or smaller inflated rafts. As a rule, because of the amount of whitewater throughout the region, only experienced canoe and kayak enthusiasts ply the wild rivers. Whitewater rafting companies, on the other hand, are as abundant as other guide services provided in the Rockies.

Classifications identify the rivers' ruggedness— from Class 1, an easy river with small waves and generally sandy, accessible beaches; to Class 3 with medium-sized or high irregular waves and passages dotted with boulders and rocks; to Classes 5 and 6 where only the most experienced boatmen dare to travel. A thirst for whitewater adventure can be quenched in the Rockies. Rafting trips can be booked for part of a day or a full day or a week-long adventure that takes boaters through deep canyons otherwise inaccessible. Camping and river rafting go hand in hand; once on shore, a hike into the desert or woods along the river takes boaters even farther from the bustle and smog and pressure of everyday city life.

Networks of rivers throughout the mountains provide plenty of opportun-ity for a relaxed daytime float or a whitewater thrill in thundering torrents.

Water Sports and Campouts

Other water sports are available in the Rocky Mountain states, but to a far different degree from coastal regions or states with vast waterways. Because of the rugged mountain terrain, lakes tend to be smaller and winds changeable and unpredictable. While the cold and often shallow water does not lend itself to swimming, sailboarding or water skiing in many locations, sailing can be exciting and a test of ability—the small size of the lakes and unpredictable winds require quick maneuvering.

Sailboarding with wetsuits is becoming increasingly popular at many lakes that allow body contact, largely because of the strong and active resident and visitor population and the relative ease and size of required equipment.

A number of mountain lakes allow motor boats and water skiing, but in some areas, skiers prefer wet suits. Some mountain lakes allowing water skiing are Bonny Reservoir, Grand Lake, Shadow Mountain and Green

A quiet resting place for man and beast.

Mountain. Dillon Reservoir in Summit County allows motor boating and sailing, but swimming, sailboarding and water skiing are not permitted. Lakes and reservoirs near metropolitan areas are abundant and full water-sport activities are usually permitted. Chatfield and Cherry Creek Recreation areas near Denver are particularly popular and accessible. Or a trip to Rifle Gap in the western part of Colorado, where artist Christo Jvaacheff hung the 400-foot-high (120 meter), 1,250-foot-long (380 meter) orange curtain, may be worth the time and effort, not only for the sailing but also for the scenery.

Back to the lure of the Old West, horseback trips into hidden canyons and valleys are among the finest and most relaxing ways to get acquainted with the wilderness. Guides and outfitters abound in nearly every mountain village and along major or secondary highways. For an hourly fee, guides take even the most inexperienced rider on a safe trail ride. Or, better yet, plan ahead for a breakfast ride at the crack of dawn in the crisp mountain air. The guide will have the horses ready and will take you to a camp where the cook has steaming coffee and a hearty breakfast ready to appease the appetites of dudes and wranglers alike. For a crowd less inclined to rise with the early birds, there is always the evening steak ride or wagon ride. Guests are led to a hidden spot where the fire crackles and the steaks sizzle. The evening almost always includes tales of the Old West or at least the wranglers' experiences when they "was just young-uns," pushing cattle or riding their horses to school in the blizzard of 1949.

Enthusiasts who want to go further into the mountains can take a packtrip lasting several days. Most outfitters will supply everything except personal articles. A packtrip by horse can be coupled with fishing or hunting for the real enthusiast; however, wandering off into the wilderness with a few good friends on horseback, and with no plans other than enjoying the scenery and each other, is fulfillment enough.

"Up, Up and Away"

Getting high in the Rockies is easy, with the rarified air, incredible scenery and changing vistas around each corner,

Freshwater fish are abundant in the Rockies lakes.

and the variety of things to do. But for those who want to get even higher, hot-air ballooning has become a new and exciting pastime. Whether you want to soar over the meadows and villages just to snap a few photographs and for the thrill of it all or to learn something about ballooning as a sport, an increasing number of balloon ranches throughout the western states are ready to fulfill your desire. Some of the ranches are connected with dude ranches and offer a variety of activities; others specialize in ballooning and balloon rides.

You'll find balloon ranches or balloon rides in the plains areas, along the foothills, and in high mountain valleys that afford enough space for take-off and landing the large, colorful crafts. Don't forget your camera, as the panoramas will excite you at every turn of the head.

The thoroughly active person will find bicycling in the Rockies a challenge. Steep climbs and exhilarating descents are the rule in all but a few mountain locations. In many communities and counties, a good system of bike trails links cities and towns 20 or more miles (32 km) apart. Some trails climb mountain passes or meander along mountain streams where the refreshing sights, sounds and smells of the outdoors take much of the effort out of the climb. Being in good physical shape before embarking on one of the mountain passes is imperative.

Renting a bicycle and pedaling around the villages and into the surrounding valleys is pleasure that can be enjoyed by almost anyone. Many winter-time ski rental stores switch to bicycles and fishing tackle in summer. They can recommend trails that are a joy to those who want fresh air and light exercise or can point out the more challenging rides.

Bicycling in the Rockies has long been a local favorite. The Coors International Bicycle Classic, the richest bicycle race in the United States, was born in the Rockies.

Tennis is one sport that requires equipment light enough to be taken along on almost any vacation or day trip, and tennis buffs will be delighted to find that nearly every resort town or mountain community has a number of courts available to guests. Many resort

Climbing Fremont's Peak (elevation 13,722') in the Wind River Mountains, Wyoming.

hotels have installed courts that are in use year-round. Equipment can be rented at most facilities, and lessons and full ternnis shops abound. There are even high-altitude tennis camps that will literally take your breath away.

Try a Hole-in-One or a Bucking Bronco

If you want more than a stroll in the woods, why not a stroll on the golf course? More and more 18-hole courses designed by luminaries such as Jack Nicklaus and Robert Trent Jones II are springing up in the Rockies. In Vail Valley alone, there are four public and one private course, and just an hour's drive away in Summit County is the beautiful Keystone course. The challenge to golfers extends beyond the usual as courses are frequently narrow and filled with many natural hazards. Designers have taken advantage of the natural lay of the land and complemented their courses with large stands of pine, mountain streams, rolls and hills, and turns that follow the valleys. Accurate ball placement is required on most mountain courses. In addition, because of the thin air, the

A lone climber finds himself between a rock and a hard place.

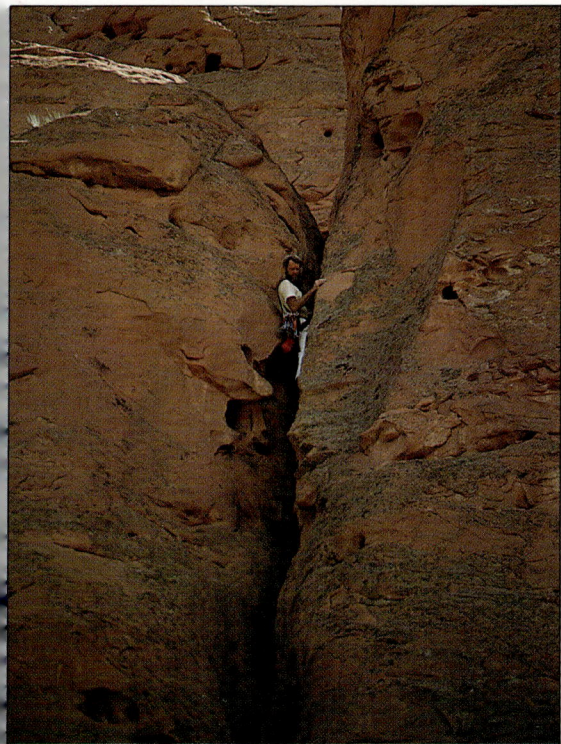

ball travels farther. Major adjustments in club use are required. The pro shop will be able to advise you, or a lesson with one of the local pros giving tips on how the course plays will work wonders in keeping scores low and spirits high.

But the Rockies aren't just for the active, the young and the brave. Spectator sports are numerous throughout the area. For one more taste of the old West, there is the rodeo—the sport that developed when cowboys turned skills required for their work into one of the nation's most popular events. Cheyenne Frontier Days is one the most noted rodeos in the world, drawing crowds from across the country for a week of fun and competition. In January, cowboys flock to Denver for the National Western Stock Show and Rodeo. In summer, you'll find rodeos up and down the Rockies: at state and county fairs, local rodeos and wild rides, and even – "little-britches" rodeos where the littlest cowboys are found each weekend riding broncos and spinning tales.

The essence and history of rodeo is captured at the Pro Rodeo Hall of Champions in Colorado Springs. Schedules of the more than 40 professional rodeos are available there. For more refined viewing, the Rockies abound with symphonies, art shows, and dance and theatrical performances, from travelling casts to community theaters. Schedules for summer music, art and drama festivals are available through local Chambers of Commerce or information centers.

While summer overflows with adventures and activities, fall becomes a wonderland as aspen trees turn to burnished gold contrasting strikingly with the deep green pine forests and bright blue skies. A weekend jaunt into the mountains is a regular fall activity for front-range residents and is a must for visitors in September and October. The aspen or "quakies" shimmer in the sunlight as they reach brilliant gold tones. Green and gold are primary fall colors here, and Indian summer days bring out the best in the aspen. Warm, sunny days beg you to take a hike in the woods to enjoy the fleeting days before snow falls, and coupled with the frosty nights encourage the leaves to turn gold. While it rains or more often snows a bit in October, Indian summer is generally the rule. Rocky Mountain locals will tell guests that fall is one of the best times in the mountains. Warm days that encourage outside play are precious, and the already spectacular scenery takes on new beauty.

Come Ski the Rockies

Leaving warm weather behind is a natural for the Rockies. While winters were the bane of travellers, settlers and miners, they are the sustenance of the travel and tourist industries. Colorado and the Rockies have earned the name of Ski Country, U.S.A., with hundreds of resorts and ski areas dotting the maps. From the luxury resorts such as Aspen, Vail, Deer Valley, Beaver Creek and Snowbird; to the smaller, intimate ski areas such as Loveland Basin, Telluride, Redlodge, or Jackson Hole, the Rockies offer an area for every taste and inclination. You can find accommodations fit for (and often used by) kings and heads of state or stay in bed-and-breakfasts, pensions or dormitories that are easier on the budget. But, once on the mountainside, the Rockies will make anyone feel like royalty. Downhill or alpine skiing is perhaps most popular throughout the mountain winter resorts, and it doesn't take an expert to enjoy the thrills. Complete programs are available for beginners who thought they would never venture into the cold mountain air; some become enthusiasts who readily join après-ski conversations with stories of excitement and accomplishment just as impressive as those of seasoned powder hounds.

In the steep and deep Rockies, expert skiers are constantly challenged, if not by taking lessons in the latest techniques, then by constantly changing conditions on expert slopes.

Cross-country skiing or touring is gaining in stature among Rocky Mountain skiers. It's easier on the pocketbook than downhill, both in equipment cost and because lift tickets aren't generally required. A skier no longer has to be a super-conditioned athlete to enjoy the sport. More sophisticated equipment, eliminating the need to be a waxing expert and adding instant ease and enjoyment to the sport, has made a tremendous impact over the past five to 10 years. A number of resorts are grooming cross-country trails or setting tracks for guests, some without charge and some asking a track use fee. In addition, the U.S. Forest Service marks and maintains (to a varying degree) trails throughout the National Park System which are usually free to the public. Maps can be obtained from the local Forest Service office or from information centers.

Winter Pleasures

Cross-country centers or ranches are springing up around the Rockies. Here one finds comfortable rustic accommodations set in valleys that afford miles and miles of skiing during the day, often followed by dips in hot springs or hot tubs. Spend a week or a day and take the trails at your own pace. Cross-country skiing can be a lively workout or, like a stroll in the park, a leisurely enjoyment of the wonders that wintry nature has to offer.

Cross-country centers frequently include lodge or hotel rooms with family-style meals, reminiscent of alpine skiing, when everyone gets together at the day's end to talk about their achievements and laugh over their falls. The romance has not disappeared, it remains much of the backbone of the cross-country center. There are moonlight cross-country tours in the high mountain valleys, drenched in the long nighttime shadows from the full winter moon. With the reflection from the snow, you can ski almost as in daylight, but with lunar rays.

The motorized set will be happy to learn that snowmobiles are pushing into the mountain scene more frequently. While they are restricted in some areas where the wilderness is protected, snowmobile trails are marked and easily accessible. Most communities catering to the tourist trade are near or adjacent to guides or outfitter companies that rent snowmobiles.

The lure of the Rockies and the rush to enjoy its riches has not diminished over the past 100 years. Adventure is still abundant and remains the watchword for most visitors. For others, the sheer beauty, immensity and solitude create not only relaxation but also excitement. The private spots that many residents or visitors find may truly have exceptional healing powers. It's no wonder that the rush to the Rockies continues.

Happy Rockies hikers reflect on the natural beauty around them.

ROCKIES SKI RESORTS

Colorado is known as Ski Country/ USA, a title obviously well deserved when one looks at a map of the state. Dotted with day ski areas and destination resorts, the map looks as if it has been sprinkled with snow, just like the abundant peaks. Colorado is home to more than 35 ski resorts and is known worldwide for its consistent "champagne powder," the light dry snow that makes skiing a pleasure and a thrill for avid experts who seek out the face of Bell Mountain in Aspen or Vail's Back Bowls.

For most visitors, Denver is the first stop and the gateway to the Rockies. It is the largest city in the region and Colorado's capital. Busy Stapleton International Airport is the seventh largest in the country, shuttling traffic from distant as well as nearby locations. While Colorado is still known for its western flavor, it also has assumed, because of the great influx of winter visitors, an international flair that is evident both in the cities and resorts from the variety of languages and dialects that can be overheard.

Upon arrival in Denver, skiers can expect generally mild weather, frequently in the sixties, even in winter, and graced by regular snowfalls that often disappear in days without a trace. But the ski enthusiast should not despair. The weather in Denver and the surrounding plains is often surprisingly unrelated to the mountain areas where, when city folk are relaxing in the parks with a good book, skiers may be enjoying that peak experience of a run down a slope covered with eight inches of newly fallen snow. Average snowfall throughout the region is nearly 350 inches (890 cm), with many resorts receiving double that number before the season ends.

From Denver, travellers can reach their destinations quickly and easily with the assistance of coach and limousine services, a regular bus service and even taxis. Because the Colorado economy depends upon tourists for its health, transportation in the state is efficient and well-organized.

While mountain travel is generally pleasurable, travellers are advised to check on current road conditions prior to leaving Denver for their destinations. Colorado Ski Country/USA maintains an information booth in the Denver Airport that carries current road conditions as well as skiing and weather conditions at 35 resorts. In addition, Colorado Ski Country/USA can assist with lodging, travel routes and a variety of other details.

Once on the road, take time to enjoy the mountain views and allow adequate time to reach your destination. Winter travel can be slow due to road and weather conditions or to drivers who are inexperienced on snow-packed roads. Exercise patience and the journey from the plains to the mountains will be pleasurable.

The Destination Resorts

Towering snow-covered peaks, secluded valleys, Victorian mansions turned into quaint shops and restaurants, Alpine villages hiding boutiques and pizza parlors, luxurious hotels, festivals, competition, celebrations— all are part of the experience in Rocky Mountain ski resorts. From the rustic and once rich mining-towns-turned-resorts such as Aspen and Breckenridge or Telluride, to the new developments at Copper Mountain, Beaver Creek, Snowbird or Vail, skiers can find a full array of activities, day and night. The personalities of the old towns shine through in many locations and are assisted by traditional celebrations of the snow such as Ullr Fest, with new excitement added by the influx of today's adventure seekers to the areas. The newly developed resorts springing up in sheep and cattle pastures have learned from the old, European styles that have been popular with skiers for so long. At times, visitors might feel that they are strolling down a street in St. Moritz, rather than close to home, because of the Bavarian architecture and the number of international visitors. At the same time, visitors can expect the latest conveniences and luxuries, including gourmet meals, fast food, shopping at its finest, and recreational activities to fill the days and nights of both skiers and non-skiers.

Ski The Summit, one of the first destinations for skiers travelling west from Denver, offers four ski areas and villages that suit many preferences. The

Keystone Complex includes Keystone Mountain, North Peak and Arapahoe Basin ski areas, and the modern Keystone Village. **Arapahoe Basin** is Colorado's highest skiing point. At an elevation of 12,450 feet (3,800 meters), the views are as breathtaking as the rarified air. Peaking well above the timberline, the jagged mountains are similar to the Swiss Alps. The season at Arapahoe Basin extends well into June. The Colorado sunshine combines with cool high-altitude temperatures to keep the snow light and moods high throughout spring skiing. Skiers of all levels find satisfaction on these slopes, and the most advanced challenge themselves on the Pallavicini or East Wall in narrow chutes that cascade from rocky heights. During the week, the locals' favorite time to ski, there are smaller crowds and relaxed ski experiences remembered from seasons past.

Keystone Mountain has become known as "the cruiser" on slopes like "Jackwhacker," "Last Hoot" or "Go Devil" for those who want just enough of a challenge but with the security of well-groomed intermediate and beginner trails that boost any ego and style. Keystone takes most of its trail and lodging names from the logging and mining operations that first brought settlers to the area. The remains of disused mines are dotted throughout the valleys and add to the ambience of the old west.

North Peak, opened in 1984, is a $15 million expansion that adds a six-passenger gondola, 14 new trails and exciting advanced terrains to neighboring Keystone Mountain. The new terrain is accessible from the Summit House at Keystone as well as from River Run Plaza, situated one-half mile east of Keystone Mountain Village on

Skiing in the olden days.

108

the Snake River. North Peak is for those who become bored with the consistent and reliable trails on Keystone Mountain; 58 percent of its terrain is for expert and advanced skiers. The gondola whisks skiers to the summit in 10 minutes. Then it challenges them with trails like the 1¾-mile (2.8-km) "Cat Dancer" or the popular bump run "Geronimo." A favorite steep but well-kept trail is "Starfire."

The calendar at Keystone is packed with activities that meet a variety of skier's interests and abilities. Recently, Olympic medalists Phil and Steve Mahre established their training center at Keystone. The week-long program is designed for everyone, from the never-ever to the expert racer. The gold and silver medalists are joined by their former coach as they present a training program utilizing exercises developed around natural skiing motions and using visualization as mental preparation. Included in the Mahre Training Center package is lodging, lift tickets, six days of ski instruction, meals and parties.

Cross-country fans of any level enter some of the most spectacular Rocky Mountain backcountry on the 20 miles (33 km) of prepared trails in the **Arapahoe National Forest.** Lessons on both cross-country and telemarking are offered through the Keystone Cross-Country/Touring Center. For an extra-special experience, a moonlight cross-country tour, including dinner, is recommended. It gives that extra dose of romance to a winter vacation.

There's no lack of activities off the slopes. The outdoor skating center is the largest of its kind in the country and the season lasts from early December through mid-March. At the day's end, a horse-drawn sleigh takes guests to dinner at the old **Soda Creek Homestead**; advance reservations are required. Or, for the adventuresome, snowmobile tours of the backcountry are available at **Tiger Run**, a few miles from Keystone.

Tired of the snow? The John Gardiner Tennis Center at Keystone offers two indoor courts year-round (12 more for outdoor play in the summer), lessons, clinics and matches. A special vacation touch is presented by the Condominium Grocery Service. For your convenience, Keystone will do your shopping for you and have your condominium completely stocked with groceries and fresh produce when you arrive. The resort makes

it literally impossible for you not to have a great and relaxing stay.

Information on a winter vacation in Keystone is available through the Keystone Resort Association or, if you want to check skiing conditions, telephone 303-468-4111 for a daily update.

A Skiing Tradition

Historic **Breckenridge** presents a direct contrast with Keystone's modern buildings and conference facility; old Victorian homes and bright paint combine with the enthusiasm of the local community. A few years ago, Breckenridge was a down-trodden old mining town that just happened to be the site of Summit County's largest ski area. With an injection of capital from investors, such as the ski company and local businesses, Main Street nowadays fairly sparkles with life and personality. On the side streets, visitors will find a variety of hidden pleasures, from restaurants to lodges. Quaint is one way to describe Breckenridge today, but that implies it's a place to visit where there is no action. Not true! Much of the excitement and enthusiasm of the old west remain in this rejuvenated community.

Skiing events such as the World Freestyle Championships and the Mogul Challenge dot the calendar. But the highlight of the winter season is Ullr Fest in January. Ullr, the Nordic god of snow, is honored in a week-long celebration which includes a parade that's second-to-none. It features inventive floats, and snow and ice sculptures line Main Street. All are created by the townspeople, who dedicate themselves to making the event fun for visitors. Fireworks, crowning of the Ullr King and Queen, and a moonlight cross-country tour complete the activities.

Complementing the Ullr Fest is the World Freestyle Invitational, an event that brings freestyle ski competitors together for the greatest contest in the country in ballet skiing, moguls and aerials. The event garners national attention and is aired on television specials. Part of the fun is the celebrity ski race, where Breckenridge skiers rub elbows with stars from *V*, *Hill Street Blues*, *Family Ties* and even with players from the Denver Broncos football team.

You never need put on your skis to be part of the fun in Breckenridge, although you would be missing a lot if you didn't. **Maggie Pond** is excellent for ice skating, snowmobile tours are just around the corner, and the cross-country center offers 28 miles (45 km) of trails along with complete lessons, ski rental and "warming hut" facilities.

Once the skis are on, skiers can undertake helicopter trips into the Colorado backcountry, in addition to more than 1,275 acres (516 hectares) of skiing on the mountain. Powder helicopter skiing is not for the faint of heart; it's for those who enjoy the challenge of wilderness skiing in remote terrain. The rewards are excitement and solitude.

On Breckenridge's two mountains, Peaks 8 and 9, are 95 trails. Fifty percent of the slopes are rated for expert skiers alone, but there's no lack of terrain for intermediates and beginners. **Mach I** is the super mogul run that is the site of the Bump event in the Freestyle Championships and the Annual Breckenridge Mogul Challenge. Mach I has been judged to be one of the most difficult mogul courses on the International World Cup circuit—it's definitely not for the casual cruiser. But nearby Peak 9 rates 87 percent of its trails as beginner and intermediate. The challenge is to ski them all during one winter vacation while still having time for the other activities in the resort. Favorites among the intermediate skiers are "American" for friendly bump skiing and "Gold King" for those who prefer groomed trails.

Several special programs punctuate the Breckenridge season. Book three or more consecutive nights, and the fourth night and next-day's skiing is free. Ski Free is available through the Breckenridge Resort Association—an extremely popular program, to say the least.

A full ski school program includes the regular complement of lessons, a women's three-day skiing seminar and the Peak 8 Nursery and Junior Ski School which handles infants aged two months or older.

Historic Charm in the Rockies

The Camel Sprint Series gives recreational skiers a chance to test their speeds on a safe and controlled track. It is the one time in the season when it's both safe and acceptable to go as fast as your legs and heart will allow.

True to the old west flavor of the resort, the "Telemark" returns each spring. Skiers dress in 1880s costumes and compete on a six-mile (10-km) course, moguls and in the classic telemark style.

Getting about as high as you can in the Rockies for the figure-eight competition in Horseshoe Bowl brings the ski season to a close. For the competition, two skiers start at the same point at an elevation of about 12,200 feet (3,720 meters) and cross each others tracks, making a series of "8's" as they ski down the fall line—almost a springtime tradition in the mountains.

Health Clubs and Olympic Workouts

Ski the Summit's final resort is **Copper Mountain**, nestled in Wheeler Flats at the upper end of Ten Mile Canyon. The image of Copper contrasts with that of Breckenridge. It looks more like a modern European resort with its tall, straight-walled buildings that maximize the minimal space. The village has recently developed into one in which guests can find all the customary goods and services, with the added advantage of being within a 30-minute drive of Vail and other Ski the Summit areas.

A new addition to Copper is the health club, which provides facilities in which to relax and soothe aching tired muscles, or to exercise for those who didn't get enough on the slopes. Jacuzzis, steam rooms, saunas, racket-ball courts, tennis courts, 25-yard lap pool, aerobics room, Nautilus, weight rooms and a staff masseuse complete the menu at the athletic club.

Copper now has five triple and nine double chair lifts, along with three surface lifts that serve 70 trails. The on-mountain programs available to skiers are abundant, beginning with the Belly Button Babies (two months to two years) and the Belly Button Bakery where the kids cook and bake, play indoor and outdoor games, and do crafts. Once the kids reach six years of age, they move on to Junior Ranch and Senior Ranch. The learn-to-ski programs expand to intermediate and hotshot, covering the entire mountain. Youngsters are supervised throughout the day.

For grown-ups, there are Women's Skiing Seminars, Early Season Ski Clinics to hone skills at the beginning of the year, and the usual lessons and value-conscious packages.

Copper Mountain is proud of its commitment and involvement with the U.S. Ski Team. In November, the team arrives at Copper for early on-the-snow training, and is joined by recreational racers at the Salomon/Copper Mountain Recreational Race Camp. Copper hosts the U.S. National Alpine Championships each year, bringing to town top competitors from around the world. Copper has hosted both the men's and women's team competition, and the commitment continues year-round to provide some of the finest racing and recreational skiing available in the state.

Copper is truly a family atmosphere; a self-contained resort that is large enough to provide challenge on the slopes and plenty of après-ski action, yet small enough to be intimate and comfortable; and a place where the entire family can be independent, yet very much together.

Vail, a Cosmopolitan Town

Vail is Colorado's largest single-mountain ski resort, which says a lot but not the whole story. There's a complete village with more than 70 restaurants and shops that literally take days to explore. About 22 years ago, Vail was nothing more than a green valley and sheep pastures intersected by Gore Creek and a highway. Vail Village streets now reflect an international flair dominated by Bavarian architecture. Where summer flowers fill the window boxes, winter finds them sparkling with lights and evergreen boughs. The cosmopolitan atmosphere is repeated throughout the diverse boutiques and punctuated with accents from around the world.

The broadest variety of housing can be found in **Vail** and **LionsHead villages**, from large hotels to pensions and intimate lodges to bed-and-breakfast. Depending on the level of service desired, guests can either check in for complete personal care at the **Marriott** or **Westin**, or rent a condominium or luxurious private home and be strictly on their own. Lodging information is available either directly through the hotels and lodges or through the Vail Resort Association toll free numbers.

The largest single winter event is the

Flying through the air on a cold winter's morn.

American Ski Classic. Lasting for almost a week, the Classic includes World Cup Racing, which brings the top racers from around the world to compete for points in World Cup standings. In 1984, gold and silver medalists, Phil and Steve Mahre, raced in and retired in Vail after the slalom races that followed the Olympics.

Former President, Gerald R. Ford, a skiing enthusiast himself, hosts the Jerry Ford Celebrity Cup, an event that draws notables from the worlds of sports, politics, media and screen to Vail. The third piece of the American Ski Classic is the Legends of Skiing, a unique race that features former Olympic and National Team greats from every Olympic skiing country. Olympians from the 1930s ski and share an easy camaraderie with those just off the circuit, then go on to captain the Celebrity Cup teams.

Come Race Every Which Way

American Ski Classic events are divided between Vail and Beaver Creek, just 10 miles (16 km) west. The entire community gets into the act with parades, fireworks, charity film showings and art displays that benefit the Jimmie Heuga Center for the Physically Challenged.

The final celebration takes shape in Mountain Madness, a wacky welcome of spring and joyous farewell to the snow. For two weeks, local residents and guest race in the Rental Cup or the Great Race—on cross-country and downhill skis, across swimming pools, on tricycles and other "vehicular conveyances," all done in ski boots. A treasure hunt, lasting the entire two weeks, offers prizes to those unraveling clues given by the local media and able to locate them on the mountain.

Special lodging rates are offered through the Vail Resort Association for Mountain Madness and two other value periods. Early December and the month of January are value periods during which snow conditions are generally good to exceptional, the crowds are small, and the essence of the resort abounds. Value seasons and Mountain Madness entice skiers away from the peak Christmas and President's Birthday weekend periods when the village and the mountain are

Cross-country skiers enjoying the view at Crosscut Ranch, Montana.

112

crowded with vacationers.

All this can be found in the villages; the mountains have yet to be explored. In addition to Colorado's champagne powder, Vail is probably best known for the expansive **Back Bowls**—780 acres (316 hectares) of uninterrupted vistas and ungroomed snow plunging from an elevation of 11,250 feet (3,430 meters). The steep consistent fall line entices powder hounds to line up at the top after a recent snowfall, awaiting the first signal from the ski patrol that signifies the bowls are open. They are quickly swallowed up in the enormity of the naturally open terrain.

But for those not yet ready to tackle expert-only terrain, Vail has **Game Creek Bowl**—10 sq miles (25 sq km) of skiing terrain. The longest run at Vail, **Riva Ridge,** begins at the mountain top on gentle slopes that build the ego. Then Riva pitches down toward **Tourist Trap** and becomes a pleasantly challenging advanced run that winds its way into the village. The western part of the mountain is served by a six-passenger gondola that towers above 200-foot (60-meter) trees, making an impact on the landscape. Over the entire mountain, 18 lifts serve slopes ranked 30 percent easiest, 40 percent more difficult and 30 percent most difficult.

The **Vail/Beaver Creek Ski School** is the largest in the world with more than 475 instructors, many of whom are multi-lingual. The school is noted as a leader in developing ski technique and methodology, and was the training and development ground for the American Teaching Method, now used by certified ski schools across the United States and recognized worldwide. The full array of ski school programs are presented with Super Classes for those who like lots of skiing, complemented with instruction and intensive workshops in powder, mogul skiing, racing and any discipline of particular interest.

"By the Light of the Silvery Moon..."

The cross-country center introduces novices to the serene sport of ski touring and polishes the skills of more accomplished "skinny skiers." Beginning on the golf course and when technique allows, branching out to the numerous trails in the White River National Forest with their guides, the cross-country program is one of the largest in the country. Special features include the Gourmet Cross-Country Tour and a Moonlight Tour offered on full moons. For the Gourmet four, skiers accompany their instructor into the backcountry and are treated to an exceptional meal prepared by the developer of the program.

Under a full moon, a lucky group takes a guided tour on **Shrine Pass** (or another location selected by the experienced guides). The crisp mountain air and moon-lit snow create an incomparable experience.

Beaver Creek, touted at its opening in 1980 as "the last resort," has become one of the most luxurious, yet affordable and approachable destinations in Colorado. The difficulty, time and investment involved in obtaining permits required to develop ski areas and the accompanying villages and facilities caused the "last resort" designation to be assigned to Colorado's seventh largest ski area. True to detailed master plans, there are eight lifts, five triple and three double chairs. The triple chair lifts are so efficient—getting skiers on the slopes and out of the lines—that a wait in a liftline is almost unheard of at Beaver Creek, even during peak season. The slope design takes advantage of Mother Nature's U-shaped valley. Few bottlenecks exist even where numbers of trails and several on-and-off-mountain routes converge. Skiers get to the lifts and up the hill from locations close to their hotels.

Many skiers have called this a cozy mountain, one with an unhurried atmosphere, few crowds and a complete variety of terrain. At the top of the mountain, a beginner's area is set aside for skiers who have just learned to turn and stop. The views, consistent snow and a long scenic run back to the bottom at the end of the day make this an enjoyable run.

Intermediate terrain invites cruisers to ski much of the middle of the mountain and newly opened **Larkspur Bowl,** where one can find anything from moguls to the large, sweeping expanse of snow and seemingly endless turns to the valley in the bowl.

Slopes for the Experts

For the experts, the "Birds of Prey" await. Some of the steepest, longest and most challenging slopes in the Rockies are **Peregrine, Goshawk** and **Golden Eagle.** While they are steep and long, the bumps have remained friendly and telemark skiers are frequently seen dancing through the moguls on Peregrine under chair nine—truly a delightful sight and one worth riding this chair.

Centennial, a 2¾-mile (4.4-km) top-to-bottom run was designated as the downhill course for the 1976 Olympics when Beaver Creek was suggested as the site for Alpine events. Colorado voters vetoed the Olympic bid, which allowed planners to proceed at a deliberate pace to create the present mountain and village. "Centennial" is a delightful trail with relaxing gentle sections punctuated with steeper plunges. It twists and turns with the natural terrain to keep essentially all of the skiing in the fall-line.

The on-mountain gathering place is **Spruce Saddle,** an award-winning log-and-cedar building with spectacular views and a sunny deck crowded with sun worshippers on nice days. While at Spruce Saddle, sample lunch at **Rafters,** an inviting table service restaurant with delightful specialties such as baked apples stuffed with cheese and a mouth-watering dessert cart.

The Vail/Beaver Creek Ski School just opened a cross-country center at the top of the mountain. Novice to expert cross-country skiers can strike off on set tracks across the top of the mountain. When ready to return to the village, they have their choice of riding the chair back down or skiing one of the intermediate or advanced trails under chair 12.

Once back in the village, a free horse-drawn sleigh takes skiers or shoppers back to their lodges.

The noted winter events in Beaver Creek are the Mountain Man Winter Triathlon that sets competitors off on cross-country skis, snowshoes and finally ice skates. The grueling course goes to the top of the mountain twice before its finale on Nottingham Lake in Avon.

Aspen, the International Challenge

Aspen presents the skier with four completely separate ski mountains linked by shuttle bus service and a lift ticket that is good any day at **Aspen Mountain, Snowmass** and **Buttermilk.** Add $1 per day to add a fourth mountain, **Aspen Highlands.** Four mountains at your disposal ensures plenty of skiing, from the face of "Bell" for powder hounds to numerous intermediate and beginner runs at Buttermilk, to the expansive "Big Burn" at Snowmass. One can stay for weeks and never become bored.

Highlighting Aspen's calendar are Winterskol and the Subaru Aspen Winternationals. Winterskol is a five-day festival featuring a bevy of winter events including zany skiing contests, ice hockey, balloon races, snowshoe races, a torchlight parade that dances down the mountain, and the Winterskol Parade—probably the oldest winter parade in the Rockies. Winterskol occurs in January, when lift tickets are discounted and most businesses offer tremendous savings on everything from meals and lodging to skiwear and furs.

Aspen has long been a major part of the international ski racing scene and the Winternational returns with World Cup Downhill and Giant Slalom events. Bill Johnson, the Olympic Gold Medalist, stopped in Aspen to thrill crowds on the Americas Downhill and is expected to return to capture the title again.

For those who are not yet afficionados of ski racing, Aspen developed a unique "trailblazer" sign system that makes it easy to trace the path the World Champion racers take while discovering the history of Aspen and World Cup Racing.

Although Aspen is one of the oldest resorts, it has not stopped growing; "Steep and Deep" has just been added to Snowmass. "Hanging Valley" and "Cirque" contrast 120 acres (48 hectares) of expert-only terrain. Those who don't feel the need for that kind of challenge should try the newly improved and expanded restaurants, such as **Ullrhof,** which includes more seating capacity, lockers and an accessory store with a woodburning stove to chase away the chill on cold days.

In Aspen, the mining town that experienced its first boom in 1880 when silver was discovered, and its second when the ski boom in the 1940s revived the dying community, one finds an upgrade and renovation boom going on. New hotels are being added and many lodge owners are pouring millions of dollars into improving their facilities. The historic **Jerome Hotel** is receiving a $12 million injection for renovation and reopens after 14 months with a nightclub, formal dining room and cafe, and

105 rooms that reflect the personality of modern Aspen as well as the charm of the old hotel.

Getting to Aspen is easier than ever now that Grand Junction is a viable airline gateway. From Denver, one drives for about four hours via Interstate 70, or flies Aspen or Rocky Mountain Airways. Weather conditions can sometimes delay flights into the mountain airport. From Grand Junction, skiers connect with ground transportation that takes about half as long as the drive from Denver, and no mountain passes to negotiate. Travel agents and tour operators have details on reaching Aspen via Grand Junction.

Steamboat Ski Area and **Steam Village** are where the skiers and cattle ranchers shake hands and say "howdy." A complementary relationship exists between the two very different enterprises and that gives Steamboat much of its personality. The ski area adjacent to the old ranching community, first opened in 1962, was called Storm Mountain. In 1964, the name was changed to Mount Werner in honor of Buddy Werner, an Olympic ski racer killed in an avalanche while filming a movie. Werner was raised in Steamboat, and the Werner family remains a vital part of the ski operation and the town.

The resort has responded to the growth of the ski industry with its own growth; 400 acres (160 hectares) of intermediate skiing has just opened in **Sunshine Bowls** graded slopes. This enticing terrain is adjacent to the already noted expert trails in Priest Creek that plunge from Sunshine Peak to the bottom of the Bowl. Steamboat sports a new restaurant, **Ragnar's**, that settles into the Rendezvous Saddle building. Ragnar's is named after Ragnar Omvedt, a Norwegian ski jumper who set a world record on Steamboat's historic Howelson Hill in 1915. Ski jumping played a large part in the development of the ski industry at Steamboat.

While the quiet atmosphere of the western winter is ever-present, constant energy is created by the numerous events at the ski mountain. Billy Kidd, another Olympic skier who makes his home in Steamboat, fills his race camps with eager recreational skiers for six and four-day sessions throughout the winter.

A time exposure of night skiers carrying torches creates a beautiful effect.

Joining the new west and rodeo with today's ski resort is the Cowboy Downhill, now more than 10 years old. The Cowboy Downhill was developed when Larry Mahan, six-time All Round World Champion cowboy on the pro rodeo tour, and Billy Kidd invited several cowboys competing in Denver's National Western Stock Show up for some post-rodeo skiing. Everyone had such a good time that the Cowboy Downhill developed into one of the greatest events of the Rocky Mountain winter.

The Winter Carnival in February is a traditional celebration of how skiing came to the valley. Ranchers, cowboys and visitors get together for a week of racing, ski jumping, sled races, cross-country/hot air ballooning, a parade and "ski jouring." The carnival began in 1913 when Carl Howelsen, "The Flying Norseman," arrived from Norway with skis strapped to his feet and got the local youngsters all excited about ski jumping. Carl convinced the locals that snow could be fun rather than just an annoyance for the ranchers. And they are still convinced.

The Steamboat Springs Stampede finishes off the year. The highlight event is the wacky Cardboard Classic in which competitors race in a "vehicle" made of cardboard, tape and glue. Lots of lodging, shopping and lift ticket bargains are available as are abundant spring snow and sunshine.

Ski Options at Jackson Hole

Jackson Hole, Wyoming, is one of those ski mountains that skiers looking for the big challenge just can't stop talking about. Three thousand acres (1,215 hectares) of terrain is 2½ miles (four km) wide and 4,139 feet (1,260 meters) from top to bottom. It regularly receives 38 feet (12 meters) of famous Rocky Mountain dry powder snow. The two mountains comprising Jackson Hole are served by five double chair lifts, one triple chair lift, and a 2.4-mile (four-km) aerial tram that carries skiers from **Teton Village** at the base to the top of **Rendezvous Mountain** where experts find steep chutes and ridges filled with champagne powder.

Jackson Hole is well-known for its ski school and a wide variety of programs for recreational skiers and racers. Pepi

Left, couple returning to the warmth of a hut after a snowshoe hike. Right, a St. Bernard carries a drink to skiers in trouble.

Stiegler, the Olympic skier, directs the programs, including Star Test International's PSIA proficiency test, Children's SKIWee sponsored by SKI magazine, and Stiegler's racing camps that feature daily ski instruction, video taping and après-ski options such as tennis and racquetball.

Cross-country skiing abounds in the Jackson Hole area. At Teton Village adjacent to the lifts is the **Jackson Hole Karhu Cross-Country Ski Center**, and nearby are **Togwotee Mountain Lodge Center** and **Spring Creek Ranch Ski Touring Center**. Surrounding Jackson Hole, the backcountry and Grand Teton National Park are webbed with marked trails. An easy guide to the cross-country areas is available from the Jackson Hole Chamber of Commerce, as is information on lodging and restaurants for the resort towns of Teton Village and Jackson Hole.

Big Sky Country

Montana is known as Big Sky Country because of its vast size and frontier environment. The western part of the state is dotted with ski areas and charming hideaways for guests who prefer a vacation at a secluded spot with local flair. Some of the longer trails stretch for three miles (4.8 meters), and the season in Montana lasts from mid-November through April at most ski areas. **Big Sky, Big Mountain** and **Red Lodge** are the largest and most noted of Montana's ski areas, but 11 other areas round out the list.

Big Sky sports two gondolas, a triple chair, and three double chairs serving 55 miles (88 km) of alpine trails. With a vertical drop of 2,800 feet (854 meters) and 400 inches (1,016 cm) of Rockies powder falling each year, Big Sky draws skiers who want to make the best of a ski vacation in a unique location.

Big Mountain has a vertical drop of 2,145 feet (654 meters) with 43 runs situated on 33 miles (53 km) of ski terrain. Nearer to Billings, Red Lodge offers 30 slopes from which to choose, covering 25 miles (40 km), and has a vertical drop of 2,016 feet (615 meters).

Much of the fun of skiing in Montana is staying at many of the ranches, lodges or country inns that open their doors to winter visitors. Many of the ranches provide family-style meals, horse or mule-drawn sleigh rides, snowmobile trips and vast cross-country trails upon which those taking a break from alpine skiing can really get away from it all for a day in the wilderness. Accommodations at the inns and ranches vary from single rooms without baths to fully-furnished condominiums. Advance reservations are recommended at most lodges.

Up-Market Skiing at Deer Valley

The front of Deer Valley's trail map calls the resort "Unspoiled, Uncrowded and Uncommonly civilized," and truly it is. Touted as Utah's answer to Colorado's Beaver Creek in gentility, it is already known for the fine food that is offered all over the mountain. Where else can one find salmon en croûte at the ski area cafeteria? The **Snuggery** at mid-mountain **Silver Lake Lodge** and the **Huggery** at the base area **Snow Park Lodge** set the stage for some of the finest ski-area cuisine anywhere.

It's the above-and-beyond frills for which Deer Valley is becoming famous: like the uniformed "ski valets" who unload the car and lead you to the slopes, or the free-of-charge Ski Corral where skis are watched during lunch or après-ski, and free coffee refills.

The mountain itself is known for its forgiving and relatively intermediate terrain. For those wanting to treat themselves to a relaxed and luxurious vacation, Deer Valley is just the place. And it's a short drive from Snowbird and Alta, the Utah resorts that draw the most demanding expert skiers and powder hounds. To combat the reputation of being too easy, additional advanced terrain has been opened up in "Mayflower Bowl" in Deer Valley.

The village at Deer Valley presents guests with more luxurious choices such as **Stein Eriksen's Lodge**. Eriksen, an Olympic medalist, is Director of Skiing at the new and noteworthy resort. In addition to greeting guests at the lodge and attending to details, he escorts VIPs around the mountain with that famous Norwegian smile and effortless skiing style that has become his trademark.

Ski Utah makes its winter ultimate escapes incredibly easy. The organization offers information and booking routines for 15 winter resorts including the big, well-known areas like **Snowbird, Alta, Park City** and the smaller but no less enticing **Sundance, Crystal**

Mountain or **Brighton**, and the better known cross-country ski areas.

One of the greatest advantages that so many of the Utah resorts have is the proximity to the International Airport at Salt Lake City. Located on the edge of the plains, Salt Lake City provides a hub for additional lodging, restaurants and a metropolitan entertainment and activity center nearly at the base of the ski mountains. Working half day and arriving at a Utah resort in time for a few runs before the end of that day is entirely possible and a feature that more and more people are taking advantage of all the time.

Utah's skiers who want more than skiing within the area boundaries can opt for the Interconnect Adventure Tour. The five-area tour is modestly priced and takes the adventurers from Park City to Snowbird, Alta, Brighton and Solitude ski areas with the aid of a guide licensed by the United States Forest Service. Tour participants will ski some of the slopes within the individual resorts and then go out of bounds on the way to the next destination. The tours require skiers to be in good physical condition because hiking and skiing some ungroomed slopes is a regular part of the day. Shorter Interconnect Tours visiting four or three areas are available. All are subject to weather or snow condition cancellations. Groups are limited to four to 14 skiers. Obtain information from Ski Utah, Inc.

Nestled just 31 miles (49 km) up Little Cottonwood Canyon from the Salt Lake International Airport are Snowbird and Alta resorts. Known worldwide for their breathtaking slopes and deep, deep powder, Snowbird boasts 500 inches (1,270 cm) of the white gold each season, stretching from mid-November right into mid-June when the weather permits. Serving the mountain are seven chair lifts and a 125-passenger tram that whisks skiers 2,900 feet (884 meters) up from the base over a distance of 8,395 feet (2,559 meters). The upper tram terminal perches at 11,000 feet (3,350 meters) in altitude and affords skiers a 3.3-mile (five-km) run through **Gad Valley** starting out from the summit in a spectacular bowl that challenges experts and then dropping into the intermediate trail, **Lower Bassackwards.**

Snowbird's Slopes, Steep and Deep

The ski runs in Utah have gained the reputation of being electrifying, and with good reason. With a vertical drop of 3,100 feet (945 meters) and 50 percent of the trails being rated advanced expert, the impression is realistic. Snowbird's slopes are steep, deep, sometimes wide and sometimes quite narrow but almost always exciting. But the resort doesn't cater only to the seasoned skier who is looking for more challenges. Thirty percent of the terrain is rated intermediate and 20 percent beginner, almost the perfect combination according to resort planners who insist that expert skiers command more acres of skiing because they cover ground more quickly than less experienced enthusiasts.

Snowbird is one of the only winter resorts that promotes a summer ski season. When most people are packing away their skis and digging out golf clubs and tennis racquets, those who haven't gotten enough spring skiing and racing flock to the week-long Summer Ski Race Camps that extend from mid to late May through mid-June. The

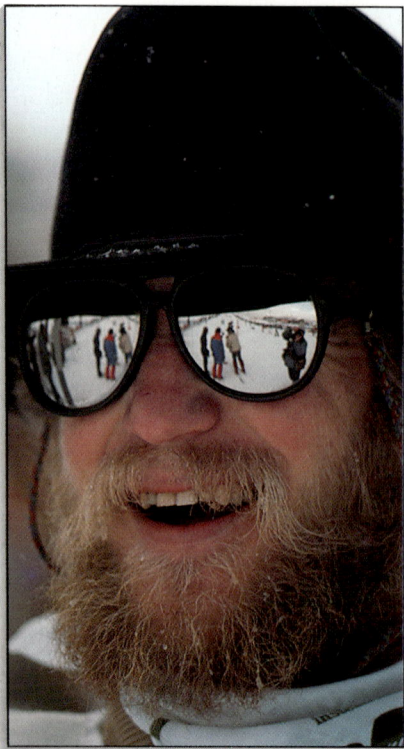

A hearty cowboy downhill skier enjoying the famous event.

camps draw coaches from the Professional Ski Instructors of America Ski Team to Susie and Ken Corrock, the Olympic medalists. The race camp package includes meals, lodging, coaching and lifts in the bargain price.

Snowbird's events calendar begins in December with Christmas festivities and extends through a variety of races, from the Coca Cola Cups and finals for recreational skiers through the Masters Series races and Telemark competition.

Variety doesn't stop with the terrain and activities at Snowbird. The village offers several options for lodging and dining, all within short walking distance of all the other services and activities. Many of the lodges have sports or spa facilities to complete the amenities offered here, one of North America's newest and most spectacular resorts.

Sun Valley and the Stars

A cowboy skier ropes himself a "wild filly."

Sun Valley, Idaho, holds the unique position of being the first American Ski Resort and for erecting the first chair lift in the United States in 1935. Sun Valley has attracted Hollywood stars since its beginning, and continues to do so.

The ski mountain now sports 16 chair lifts serving 64 trails. **Baldy, Warm Springs** and **Dollar Mountain** make up an incredible variety of skiing that keeps enthusiasts loyal. Sun Valley is surrounded by several other small mountains that are accessed by lifts but the three-mountain complex remains the star.

The village grew up around the **Sun Valley Lodge and Inn**, first started in the resort's infancy by Avere II Harriman, the noted diplomat, businessman and politician. Located about five miles (eight km) from the lifts, the classic lodge offers housing surrounded by complete resort services.

Slopeside lodging is available at **Warm Springs** and **River Run**, near the Sun Valley complex.

Idaho supports many other ski resorts. Of note are **Switzer** which overlooks **Lake Pend Oreille**, the largest lake in the state. **Bogus Basin** near Boise lets skiers partake of the slopes from 10 a.m. to 10 p.m., drawing the after-work crowd from nearby.

START
FRONTIER AIRLINES

CELEBRATIONS IN THE MOUNTAINS

"Something Hidden. Go find it.
Go look behind the Ranges –
Something lost behind the Ranges.
Lost and waiting for you. Go!"
   – From *The Explorer*
   by Rudyard Kipling

The Rocky Mountains are known for the diversity of experience they offer. For the lover of sports or art, nature or culture, summer in the Continental Divide is a parade of festivals and happenings. If you want to arrange some extraordinary encounters with Rocky Mountain people, plan your journey through the Rockies to coincide with some of these events. The Rockies have become the summer festival territory of the United States with celebrations taking place everywhere. Lists of happenings in most areas, from environmental and cultural to athletic activities, are available from chambers of commerce and travel agencies.

Denver, Colorado's capital city, is teeming with events and festivals. The Denver Center for the Performing Arts has a wonderful theater company that stages both local and hit Broadway plays all year round. The Boettcher Concert Hall, which the *New York Times* says can take anything a symphony orchestra can deliver, is the home of the renowned Denver Symphony Orchestra, and one of the best musical auditoriums in the world. Great performers are frequently known to stop here on national tour. Many exciting community outreach events occur during the year, such as the Festival Caravan which promotes greater understanding of other cultures. A new and different summertime event is The Breakaway dance festival, in which the local youngsters get together for a breakdance competition.

In Denver, there are also many museums and art galleries that offer exceptional special events. Spending a few days in Denver gallery-hopping will expose you to some of the best art in the world.

Heading down south towards Durango – on probably one of the most beautiful roads in the country – you'll be taken through the

Preceding pages, cowboy downhill ski contestants run the good race. Left, stop and pose for a portrait at the Renaissance Festival in Larkspur, Colorado; and right, dressing in period costume is part of the fun at the Renaissance Festival.

San Juan Mountains and to the popular ski resorts of Aspen and Vail.

One of Aspen's biggest summertime attractions is the Aspen Music Festival, which includes chamber music and modern jazz and attracts world-renowned musicians.

Vail also has a series exciting events. The Avon Hot Air Balloon Race in the middle of the Rocky Mountains is a visual delight. All through the summer, balloon races are held in different areas in the Rockies. Del Norte in Southern Colorado has a balloon farm for the serious balloonists.

The Telluride Festivals

State Highway 145 winds its way down through the San Miguel Mountains and ends at Telluride, which is nestled 8,745 feet (2,665 meters) in the midst of the towering San Juans. It has been rediscovered by a new generation that appreciates its magnificent snowcapped mountain slopes. Telluride is a year-round resort. Several Rocky Mountain Festivals are held here, including the Dance Festival, the Wine Festival, the Chamber Music Festival, the Lunar Cup 4th of July Ski Race, the Hang Gliding Invitational and the well-known Telluride Blue Grass Festival. Film buffs who also like the mountains will enjoy the popular Telluride Film Festival held in the summer, which brings together filmmakers, film stars, climbers, mountain men and outdoor enthusiasts.

The Telluride Blue Grass Festival is a spectacular event started in 1973 by a small, local blue grass band called "Fall Creek." Today, *Esquire Magazine* says, "Over its ten-year run, Telluride has established itself as the country's premiere progressive blue grass event." Thousands of country music lovers arrive for a weekend of the best blue grass music in the Rockies. The setting is a large field backdropped by the snow-peaked San Juans. It's a carnival with food stalls, craft booths and musicians playing on stage while people sit, stand, dance and play frisbee.

All types of people pitch their tents on a

Great Lakes of Colorado include Grand Lake, the largest natural body of water in Colorado, Shadow Mountain Lake and the man-made Lake Granby. People from all over the United States come to sail here, as Grand Lake has the world's highest registered yacht anchorage and hosts the traditional Lipton Cup Race in August. There are several marinas and boat facilities, and you can bring your own boat or rent one. Classical sailing regattas are held regularly every summer.

The Big Bicycle Event

Another historic event is the Coors Classic. This is not just a bicycle race, but a strenuous climb through mountain towns

field in town, and the city bustles with action. Little groups of musicians jam the street or the parking lots. The atmosphere is very casual and relaxed, and it allows country music fans to get together to appreciate the best professionals in the field. Throughout the years, this festival has hosted the finest blue grass musicians, including Leon Russell, Willie Nelson, John Hartford, Roseanne Cash, The Band, New Grass Revival, Hot Rize and many others.

At the top of the list of visual experiences is the Winter Park Cool Water Revival held at Lake Granby in August. This windsurfing regatta lasts for an entire weekend. Located on Lake Granby, the setting is perfect for a host of colorful windsurfing events. The

like Vail and Aspen and desert towns like Grand Junction and Cheyenne, Wyoming. Bicycling an accumulated climb of 50,000 feet (15,240 meters), the participants thrive on speed and danger.

The Classic began as a two-day event in Boulder in 1975, and was called the Red Zinger Bicycle Classic. Mo Siegel, president of Celestial Seasonings Herb Tea Company, wanted to show the entire world — or at least the people in Boulder — "that it was time for Americans to get out of their cars and get onto their bicycles." He saw the use of the bicycle as one way to deal with the shortage of world oil. Thus, the Red Zinger Bicycle Classic was born and named after Mo Siegel's brand of tea.

In 1980, the sponsorship of this Classic was transferred to the Adolph Coors Company based in Golden, Colorado. Spectators love the Coors Classic. During July and August, you can catch the race at Vail, Boulder, Aspen, Estes Park, Denver, or even at the Colorado National Monument where a new tour, "Tour of the Moon," was recently added. Write to Coors Bicycle Classic, 1540 Lehigh, Boulder, Colorado 80303, for schedule information.

Package tours are available to see the entire 11-day Classic or just a part of it. In 1984, more than 30 international Olympic teams participated. Today, this 750-mile (1,200-km) event is the premiere men's cycling event in the United States and the world's most important exhibition race for

The Crown Theatre in Notting Hill is the location for the Royal Entertainment. Belly dancers, caravans and wandering players take the stage from time to time. The Celestial Seasonings Pavilion in Tumble Downs features music, madrigals, magic and merry-making. Great Shakespearian actors roam the fairgrounds while witty young lasses force kisses on you. Try the apple fritters and other Renaissance delicacies. It's all fun, action-packed and continuous entertainment on 20 acres (eight hectares) of Renaissance Country.

Fort Hall was built by a Bostonian in 1784 for the purpose of trading with the Indians and the trappers. The building became the common boundary between British and American trappers west of the Rockies.

women.

The Colorado Renaissance Festival, held on six consecutive weekends in June and July, offers a trip back in time. Located at the base of the Rocky Mountains, in the shire of Larkspur, between Colorado Springs and Denver off Interstate 25, this is an event in which the whole family can really experience the 16th-Century European marketplace, with nearly 200 craftspeople demonstrating and selling their wares to an eager public.

Left, the Bluegrass Festival is a major annual event at Telluride, Colorado; and right, cyclists round a bend in fast motion in the renowned Coors Bicycle Classic.

During this time, the Shoshone and Bannock tribes were living in quiet harmony. Though some tribes roamed the Fort Hall area, no connection between Fort Hall and the two tribes existed when the Fort was established. Today, this reservation is the home of the Shoshone and the Bannocks, and the center of many Indian events. The trading post and shopping complex have beautiful and intricate buckskin and beadwork; it is some of the best craftmanship you'll ever see.

The Shoshone Bannock Festival features a variety of arts and crafts stalls selling exquisite Indian jewelry, leather goods, beadwork and other unusual Indian items. Hot dog and hamburger stands are plentiful, but it's hard to top the authentic Navajo Tacos. When you attend this event, you can either stay at Pocatello and commute daily or camp out on the reservation in areas well-prepared for campers.

Operas and Rodeos

Central City Opera Festival is one of Colorado's oldest summer festivals. This nationally famous festival takes place in the 1878 Opera House at the old gold mining town of Central City, 35 miles (56 km) west of Denver. For opera lovers, Colorado College at Colorado Springs hosts the Colorado Opera Festival in July. Another nationally important music festival is the Colorado Music Festival held at the 1896 Chautauque Auditorium in Boulder. For five summertime weeks, a series of chamber music concerts is held. Also of interest are lectures, symposia, concerts, films and exhibits.

Wyoming is another Rocky Mountain state bursting with festivals and events. One of the most important is the rodeo, held throughout the state during the summer. A list of dates and locations can be obtained from the Chambers of Commerce. As far as rodeos go, the Big Daddy of 'em all is Cheyenne Frontier Days, which began in 1897 when 15,000 people cheered cowpony races, pitching and bucking broncos, a pony express and a battle between Sioux Indians and United States Cavalry. It was so successful, it lasted two days. Today, Frontier Days lasts 10 days. The world's best rodeo is combined with a fabulous mile-long parade, superstar entertainers, free breakfast, square dancing, Indian Dancing and an excellent Old West Museum. More than 1,300 top professional cowboys compete for nearly $500,000 in prize money.

In Montana, too, you can join the locals in foot stompin' rodeos that go on almost every weekend during the summer. From the College National Finals Rodeo in Bozeman to the Wild Horse Stampede in Wolf Point, Montana has much to offer rodeo fans. Another special happening is the State Fiddling Championship held every July in Polson, on the south shore of Flathead Lake. Immerse yourself in the music of some 500 members of the Montana Old Time Fiddlers Organization.

Two of the biggest Indian pow-wows in the nation are Crow Fair in Montana and, in August, the Shoshone Bannock Festival at Fort Hall, Idaho. Most Indian reservations have a variety of events and festivals, and lists can be obtained by writing directly to reservations.

Some of the special events at this festival are the inter-tribal pow-wows, Miss Sho-Ban Contest, "Little Princess" presentation, Indian Relay Races, Horse Shoe Tournament, dance contests, Indian stick games, softball and, of course, the All-Indian Rodeo. The parades are colorful and artistic, where you can see the traditional Indian attire in all its glory. Beautiful leather clothing, beaded dresses, feathered headdresses, decked-out horses — it's a wonderful sight. At the pow-wows, tribespeople dance into the night to the rhythm of drums. The native Indian events have a flavor all their own. Instead of the glamour and finesse that some of the other Rocky Mountain festivals demonstrate, a sincerity and simple, earthy feeling unites all the participants here.

Fish or windsurf Colorado's largest lake, watch the Jerry Ford Invitational Golf Tournament at Vail, visit the Ballet Aspen Summer Dance Festival, see the Pikes Peak Climb, run in the Estes Alpine Classic — how does one choose the best festivals? The choices are unlimited, so plan your time carefully. The Rockies are a great place to begin your escape or to start an adventure. Every festival and event in the tall mountains will let you experience an unforgettable "Rocky Mountain High."

Left, Cheyenne father and daughter celebrate the old ways and right, a Cheyenne Indian dance contestant in full feather.

NATIONAL PARKS IN THE ROCKIES

A trip to the well-preserved natural wonderlands known today as national parks readily conjures up images of the past. One can only imagine what took place before the white man arrived, before ski lodges, before paved highways carrying Winnebagos and windjammers, before tackleboxes and snowmobiles – it was a time when huge herds of buffalo roamed free amid towering mountains teemed with deer, elk, moose and grizzly bears.

The first people to live in this area were American Indians who coexisted in harmony with the environment for centuries. But others eventually arrived to disrupt the peace. The Louisiana Purchase opened the way for American trappers to penetrate the Rocky Mountain region, and they took immediate advantage of the opportunity.

John Colter, a fur trapper, is believed to have been the first white man to enter the area which is now Yellowstone National Park. Working as a hunter for Lewis and Clark, Colter left the expedition as it returned to the United States. Joined by two trappers, Forest Hancock and Joseph Dixon, he turned once again into the wilderness for yet another winter.

In the spring of 1807, Colter met the keelboats of the trader Manuel Lisa, who was ascending the Missouri River to establish a trading post in Yellowstone, at the mouth of the Big Horn River. Colter was persuaded to return to the mountains to "Manuel's Fort," from where, in the winter of 1807-08, his epic journey began.

Colter's Secret

Lisa, for whom Colter was then working, sent him out to drum up trade with the Indian tribes. He passed through Pryor's Gap, past a thermal region (near present-day Cody, Wyoming), crossed the mountains into Jackson Hole, and most likely journeyed across Teton Pass into the Teton Valley. Heading north up the Snake River, Colter entered the present boundaries of the park. He crossed the Continental Divide eastward and, high up on this

Preceding pages; river snakes through the Grand Teton Mountain Valley; and rock formations of Bryce Canyon National Park. Below, tourists should keep their distance from the wandering wildlife in Yellowstone Park.

plateau, laid eyes on a vast expanse of water — the Yellowstone Lake. Following the Yellowstone River north, Colter discovered the Grand Canyon of Yellowstone and its two magnificent waterfalls. But for a time, the wonders of the Yellowstone region were Colter's secret, shared only with the Indians.

Three years later, Colter returned to St. Louis and reported his discoveries. His accounts of the strange phenomena of the wild west was regarded with disbelief. Scoffers labelled him a "plain and fancy liar," and laughed at his descriptions of boiling hot springs, bubbling mud pools, and gushing geysers. They coined it "Colter's Hell," the name by which Yellowstone was known for many years. Although his stories were discounted by the public, Captain William Clark outlined Colter's course on the expedition's map, marking it "Colter's route in 1807."

Bridger's Tall Tales

Of the trappers who eventually entered the region, Jim Bridger became the most well-known. At the end of a three-year trapping stint in Yellowstone

A Yellowstone park ranger offers advice to visitors.

country, Bridger also returned to St. Louis. His incredible reports met with the same disbelief; newspaper editors called his stories too "preposterous" to print. Bridger, esteemed as a truthful man until his Yellowstone tales, figured since he was gaining a reputation as a liar, he might as well earn it. So in Paul Bunyan style, he spiced up his tales a bit.

"And a fellow can catch fish in an icy river," drawled Bridger, "pull it into a boiling pool, and cook his fish without ever taking it off the hook." He also told of an old Indian Medicine Man who cursed the region with instant death, transforming a flourishing forest into hard, cold stone. Today, Yellowstone visitors still admire those petrified trees along Specimen Ridge.

No serious exploration of Yellowstone occurred until several years after the days of Bridger and other early trappers. The 1849 gold rush brought a few fortune seekers to the area, but, finding no gold, they pressed on to California. The decline of the fur trade led to the trappers' subsequent departure. Danger from Indians and a general lack of interest in exploration — especially during the predominating cold and snowy months — were good enough reasons for most to continue avoiding the area. The Civil War kept the government busy in the east, so official expeditions or geological surveys weren't conducted either. It became, once again, a nearly forgotten wilderness.

After Colter's initial penetration, the second important expedition to the Yellowstone region was the Cook-Folsom-Peterson Party in 1869; it was the first exploration based on curiosity rather than profit. The three explorers scouted the area, where they observed the geysers, hot pools, and other principal points of interest. But, as with Colter and Bridger, their reports of Yellowstone's wonders were never believed.

Lost and Found

In 1870, however, the stories circulating were sufficient to warrant formation of the first official exploration party — the Washburn-Langford-Doane Expedition. The party was official insofar as the prominent men were given a five-man military escort. One of the members of the expedition, Nathaniel P.

Langford, later served as the first superintendent of Yellowstone National Park.

In less than four weeks, the expedition discovered and reported on most of the sights about which John Colter and Jim Bridger had told tales 60 years earlier. The journey was marred by one unfortunate mishap. One member of the party, Truman C. Everts, was separated from the others and spent "37 days of peril" in the wilderness. Unassisted by today's park rangers, walkie-talkies, or the National Guard, the expedition turned into a search party. During the search, the team stumbled upon the area now designated the Upper Geyser Basin. With awe, they tagged the world-famous geyser with its present name, Old Faithful.

After some time, the loss of Everts to the wilderness turned the adventure sour, and the despondent crew headed home. To their surprise and relief, the wayward Everts returned safely from the area, accidentally rescued by another party of explorers. Possibly out of sympathy for his hardships, a moun-tain was named after him — Mount Everts.

The Nation's First National Park

A year later, in 1871, a scientific and military expedition led by Dr. Ferdinand V. Hayden substantiated the reports of the previous expeditions. An official photographer, William H. Jackson, was taken along to record the wonders.

The Hayden Survey reports, along with the accounts of the Cook-Folsom-Peterson and Washburn-Langford-Doane expeditions, resulted in the wondrous Yellowstone country being brought to national attention and, subsequently, led to the Congressional bill that created the nation's first national park. Overwhelmingly passed by Congress in early 1872 and affixed with President Ulysses S. Grant's signature on March 1, 1872, the Yellowstone Park Act set aside more than 2 million acres (810,000 hectares) for the enjoyment of the public.

"Be it enacted by the Senate and House of Representatives of the United States of America in Congress assem-

Two young elk lock horns in a territorial contest.

134

bled, that the tract of land in the Territories of Montana and Wyoming, lying near the headwaters of the Yellowstone River ... is hereby reserved and withdrawn from settlement, occupancy, or sale under the laws of the United States, and dedicated and set apart as a public park or pleasuring-ground for the benefit and enjoyment of the people."

For 14 years, Park supervision was in the hands of a series of five superintendents. Properly developing and preserving the Park was a monumental task. So, from 1886 to 1918, managing the Park became the U.S. Army's responsibility. Abuses occurring under the attempted civilian management were finally brought under control. After 32 years of military law and order, a more mature attempt at civilian supervision was made.

The National Park Service

Bull moose are seen in watery areas at dawn and dusk.

In 1916, Congress established the National Park Service "to promote and regulate the use of the ... national parks, monuments, and reservations" to "conserve the scenery and the natural and historic objects and wildlife therein ... by such means as will leave them unimpaired for the enjoyment of future generations." Today, the National Park Service actively assists more than 90 nations who have adopted the national park concept in establishing and expanding their own national park programs.

Currently, more than 340 units in the United States National Park System are attended yearly by 300 million visitors. Sometimes, a summertime map navigator may become a bit confused for his road atlas reveals not only national parks, but also national forests, national monuments, national recreations areas, national historic sites and national landmarks. Each area has been established according to its geological, historical, cultural, archeological or scenic value. While national monuments generally consist of one outstanding feature and national forest resources are managed to produce a sustained yield, national parks stand alone as unrivaled vacationlands, unique areas — nature's grandest expressions — preserved for the purpose of enriching the lives and lifting the spirits of their visitors.

YELLOWSTONE NATIONAL PARK

"There is something in the wild romantic scenery of Yellowstone which I cannot describe; but the impressions made upon my mind while gazing from a high eminence on the surrounding landscape one evening as the sun was gently gliding behind the western mountain and casting its gigantic shadows across a vale were such as time can never efface from my memory ... for my own part, I almost wished I could spend the remainder of my days in a place like this where happiness and contentment seemed to reign in wild romantic splendor." Such was the sentiment of Osborne Russell, who was a trapper in the region until late in the 1830s.

In the northwest corner of Wyoming sprawls the **Yellowstone National Park,** the nation's first and still the largest of the 33 national parks. It remains one of the most thrilling holiday attractions available, drawing millions of cosmopolitan visitors yearly.

The effects of continual geological processes — building up and tearing down the landscape by radically different agents of fire and ice — are probably more visible today in Yellowstone than any other place in the world. Immense mountains uplifted from the sea, the aftermath of a succession of volcanic eruptions, against a backdrop of ice-etched and water-carved rocks and canyons: the vastness and variety of these attractions, each unique and outstanding, bewilders visitors and presents newcomers with a difficult decision — where to go, what to see, and what activities to plan. Be well-prepared before beginning your Yellowstone adventure to benefit as much as possible from your trip. Write to the National Park Service in Washington, D.C. for specific and very useful information.

Contained within Yellowstone's 3,472 sq miles (8,992 sq m), more than 2 million acres (810,000 hectares), are hundreds of impressive sights. Take advantage of the many friendly visitor and interpretive centers in the Park; inquire about special attractions in each area and make sure you keep a step ahead in your planning.

The Yellowstone boundary creates a common bond between Montana, Idaho, and Wyoming, and the five separate entrances access attractions at all points of the compass.

In 1805, based on information received from the Indians, Lewis and Clark sent to President Thomas Jefferson a progress report which included a map on which "Yellow-Stone" appeared in English, thereby permanently naming the river as the Missouri River's principle tributary. Seven years before, full rendering of the river's name into English was made by explorer-geographer David Thompson, who had visited the Mandan towns near present-day Bismarck, North Dakota. The yellowish sandstone bluffs, conspicuous along the lower course of the river, most likely inspired the name that eventually lent itself to the entire Park. Yellowstone's glorious **Grand Canyon,** with its towering 100-foot (30-meter) cliffs, is a rainbow of colors. Highlighted by the **Upper and Lower Falls,** the canyon is considered the most photogenic region of the Park.

From Mudpots to Hot Springs

Almost every visit to Yellowstone includes a stop in the **Upper Geyser** to witness world famous **Old Faithful** spouting hourly. Although Old Faithful enjoys the limelight, Yellowstone's entire thermal theater is the world's most extensive area of geyser activity, harboring more than 10,000 thermal features. Only in Iceland, New Zealand and Siberia are there comparable thermal wonders.

Heat from the enormous reservoir of molten rock remains relatively close beneath the earth's surface, sustaining the spectacular hot water and steam phenomena. Though geysers, hot springs, mudpots, and fumaroles are all hot springs technically, the only difference is the end result of their activity. A geyser erupts, a hot spring flows, a mudpot emits both water and steam, and a fumarole issues just steam.

The most spectacular features are the geysers, for which Yellowstone is justly famous. Yet it has earned its name as the most popular national park, not simply because of its displays, but because of its wildlife. As a wildlife sanctuary, Yellowstone is unparalleled, with untamed creatures roaming free in unspoiled surroundings. Yellowstone, provides a perfect habitat for a variety

Preceding pages, eerie thermal activity at Mammoth Hot Springs, Yellowstone. Left, Clepsydra Geyser blows its top in beautiful patterns.

of creatures, all essential to one another. The area remains largely in the same natural state as it was when designated a protected park in 1872.

A Wildlife Extravaganza

Yellowstone's larger animals include the infamous bears, buffalo, elk, mule deer, pronghorn antelope, bighorn sheep, coyote and lynx. On rare occasions, wolf and mountain lion have been spotted. Birds such as the bald eagle, Canadian goose, osprey, rare trumpeter swan, California and ring bill gull, white pelican, a variety of ducks, and a host of other species share the wilderness with mountain whitefish, grayling and cutthroat trout — the only three gamefish native to Yellowstone — and German brown, brook, lake and rainbow trout.

Due to early liberal feeding restrictions, the black bear (in colors varying from cinnamon to brown to black) and the occasional grizzly could be spotted easily along the roadside. In an effort to restore natural balances within Yellowstone, however, the major dumps, where bears were fed garbage from the hotels and inns, were closed in 1969. Bears could no longer depend on the dumps for food, and visitors no longer see them nearly as often.

Endless varieties of trees and profuse gardens of flowers (in season) provide a rich habitat for the Park's wildlife. Ninety percent of Yellowstone is forested, and a staggering variety of flowers populate this botanist's paradise. In spring and summer, it is difficult to find a spot in the Park where flowers are not growing in abundance.

As if the terrific spectacle of the present were not enough, a frozen glimpse of the past has been dramatically preserved. A fascinating consequence of the volcanic era in Yellowstone is the fossil forests, an area covering more than 40 sq miles (100 sq km) along the northeastern border of the Park. Trees stand amazingly erect in the same place and position in which they originally thrived.

Whether your mode of travel within the Park is bicycle or mobile home, and whether your accommodations include room service at one of the comfortable lodges or a canopy of stars in the backwoods, Yellowstone National Park supplies a rich setting for a wide variety of activities. The regular Park season generally runs from the first week in May through Labor Day (first Monday in September). Limited services are available earlier and later in the year. Camping throughout the season is on a first-come first-serve basis, with most campgrounds open between mid-June and mid-September. Check at the entrance gates for information on open campgrounds and available campsites upon your arrival at Yellowstone.

Within Park boundaries, you will be impressed with the professional and courteous services rendered by local rangers. The National Park Service conducts extensive programs daily in which the Park and its features are explained. In addition to displays and audio-visual programs at visitor's centers and conducted walks and hikes, talks and films are presented each evening during the summer season at amphitheaters.

More than 100 miles (160 km) of trails lead to remote sections of the Park. Some are easy walks of a few hours, including self-guided nature trails, while others are strenuous hikes and climbs that require hiking skill and stamina.

Yellowstone angling means plenty of

The colorful morning glory pool at Yellowstone is a wonderful sight.

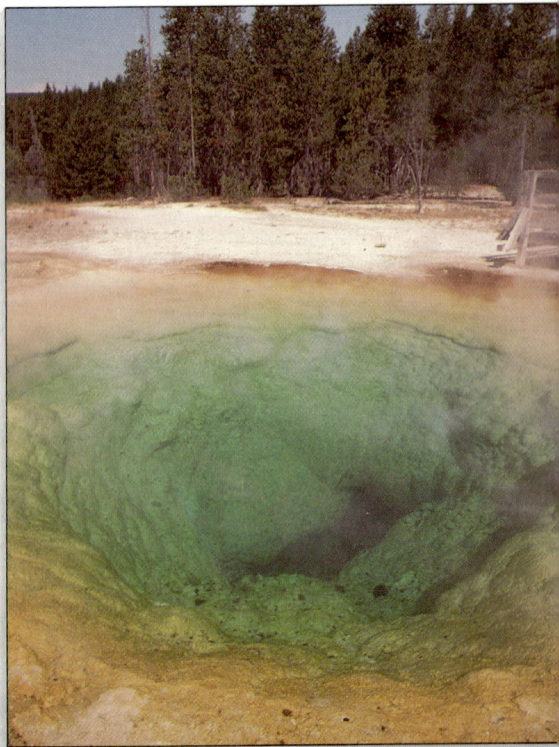

action. Fishing licenses are required and can be obtained free of charge upon request. Be sure to check with any ranger station, entrance gate or visitor's center regarding seasons and other relevant regulations.

With the exception of Lake Tihicacea in Peru, **Yellowstone Lake** is the largest lake in the world at this altitude of 7,731 feet (2,350 meters). The most significant body of water in the Park, the lake is renowned for its black-spotted, or cutthroat trout that have made it a world famous fishing area.

Permits are also required for all types of vessels. For launching larger vessels, marinas and ramps are available on Yellowstone and Lewis lakes. Other designated areas are reserved for canoes and row boats. **Shoshone Lake** is a favorite with canoeists.

For those visitors who want to get out on the water but can't bring their own crafts, the Park offers boat rides.

Yellowstone's breathtaking scenery naturally makes it a photographer's paradise. Tumbling waterfalls, steaming hot pools, rare wildlife, bounding fields of flowers — the splendor of summer in Yellowstone must be personally experienced to be truly appreciated. Yet some maintain that the quiet beauty of Yellowstone in winter is best. Hushed by a thick blanket of snow covering the landscape from early October until June, winter is truly another world — a silent world of unearthly shapes and contours where waterfalls freeze in mid-plunge and trees are wreathed with frost. Even as Yellowstone appears to be sleeping, the lively wilderness saga continues, and it can only be witnessed by the adventurous. Only snowshoes, cross-country skis, snowmobiles, or snow coaches allow first-hand access to the winterscape where elk patrol the white meadows, bison plow through deep snow, and Old Faithful remains true to its name. Tours of the Park can be arranged from Jackson, Pahaska, TeePee, or West Yellowstone from mid-December to mid-March. Or you can obtain comfortable lodging deep in the heart of the winterland in either the Old Faithful or Mammoth Hot Springs areas. Whatever season lures you to Yellowstone, the nation's first national park remains foremost with its unparalleled beauty, opportunity and natural enjoyment.

Spray and sky meet as Yellowstone's most famous geyser, "Old Faithful," bursts like clockwork.

'BEAR WITH US'

The magnificent grizzly bear is rapidly becoming a creature of the past — a vanishing symbol of our national heritage. The grizzly bear has acquired two popular reputations, as either a vicious killer or a cuddly "Gentle Ben." Fatal maulings receive so much media attention that an exaggerated impression has been created; the Gentle Ben image, on the other hand, is also unrealistic. The real grizzly rarely has been introduced to the American people. The truth about him lies somewhere between the two extremes.

The largest and most formidable of carnivorous North American animals, the grizzly is potentially dangerous. Fortunately, he minds his own business most of the time and doesn't allow himself to become addicted to panhandling like the more common black bear.

Their invulnerability and ferociousness in direct confrontation has long earned grizzlies the respect they deserve. Lewis and Clark provided early scientific reports on grizzly bears. Captain Lewis recorded, "... these bears being so hard to die rather intimidated us all; I must confess that I do not like the gentlemen and had rather fight two Indians than one bear."

The romantics look at him from a different point of view. "If bravery comes from the heart, his heart is very big for he is very brave," admired western artist Charles Russell.

In all fairness to the vanishing grizzly bear, we must admit that his brave self-defense of his own territory is responsible for his criminal reputation.

Of the thousands of grizzlies who once roamed freely throughout most of western North America, fewer than 1,000 have survived. They are limited to the wilderness areas of Montana, Wyoming and Idaho.

Complete extinction has taken place throughout most of the grizzly's historic range. It seems the grizzly and the Indian have shared a similar fate. Affectionately referred to by mountain men as Old Ephraim, the grizzly was firmly planted in North America long before the first European ventured to these shores. Like Indians, grizzlies were marked for destruction by the

same natural enemy, the white man, who exemplified the sweeping wave of "civilization," an undeniable force that swept across the new frontier from coast to coast. To our national shame, the war cry of our western frontier armies became "the only good Indian is a dead Indian." Cattlemen and stockmen employed a similar cry against every grizzly.

The factor most responsible for the grizzly bear's destruction in the United States was introduction of the domestic cattle industry into the grassy mountain valleys and open ranges west of the Great Plains. As the nation grew, the demand for beef also grew. Cattle were brought by the thousands into grizzly country, and most of them roamed free and wild. Grizzlies quite naturally cultivated a taste for beef. The slow-moving cattle were easy prey for the carnivorous bears, and the grizzly quickly became the cattleman's foremost predatory enemy. For most cattlemen, the new, improved high-powered repeating rifles and packs of trained hunting dogs made slaughtering every possible grizzly bear relatively safe and easy.

A large population of grizzlies still exists in Canada and Alaska, but this fails to pacify many in the United States. Aldo Leopold, for one, says, "Relegating grizzlies to Alaska is about like relegating happiness to heaven."

The advent of ultra-light backpacking equipment allows hardy campers to venture into the most remote recesses of the grizzly's dwindling domain. As the number of confrontations between grizzlies and recreationalists increases, Old Ephraim once again becomes a menace to human safety. These confrontations are actually more hazardous to the grizzly, as any bear involved in a mauling is usually shot by authorities. The grizzly's low reproductive rate cannot compensate for its increased mortality.

Overall knowledge of grizzlies is the best safety precaution when visiting bear country. Get tips from the local rangers on how to pack and store your food for camping so as not to attract unwanted visitors. Never go near a cub or you'll arouse the mother's wrath, and menstruating women should be prewarned not to go near a grizzly area. When you venture into these areas, remember that you're a foreigner in a king's domain, so your best manners are in order.

A fearsome grizzly, known for its slightly humped back, wanders through a mountain field.

TETON NATIONAL PARK

Standing in northwest Wyoming, just south of Yellowstone National Park, are the majestic **Grand Teton Mountains,** the outstanding feature of the **Teton National Park.** The mighty Teton mountain range is tiny as mountain ranges go, but because they "come from nowhere" and explode abruptly from the valley floor to a summit of almost 14,000 feet (4,265 meters), they are incredibly picturesque. The blue-gray pyramid-like Tetons are among the most noble creations of the American West. Soaring more than a mile (1.6 km) above the Sagebrush Flats and morainal lakes of Jackson Hole, the imposing Tetons are a striking example of the fault-block type of mountain formation (in contrast to the results of volcanic action in Yellowstone).

By geological standards, the Teton range is a young mountain range, the youngest in the Rocky Mountain system, and it's still growing. A series of upthrusts over a period of time progressively exposed this great block of the earth's crust. As the earth cracked along a north-south line, the outer crust faulted under tremendous pressure deep within. The western block tilted upward and the eastern block sank, accounting for the tremendously steep eastern face of the mountains and the gentle western slope.

For hundreds of years prior to the early 1800s, the Indians held undisputed dominion over Teton country. They frequently crossed the passes into the basins on warring expeditions or to hunt and fish, but they didn't stay long. The winters were too severe in Jackson Hole for permanent settlement and the land was left virtually untouched.

On his trek to Yellowstone country in 1807, the intrepid John Colter crossed the Teton range, probably making him the first white man to enter the area.

For the next few decades, known as the Fur Era, the Tetons became the center of activity for fur trappers and traders representing both American and British interests. By 1845, the trappers had left the Rockies, and — for the next four decades — the valleys near the Tetons were deserted except for a few

Horsepacking adventures enjoy the grandeur of the Teton Mountains.

wandering bands of Indians.

As the frontier closed in, several government expeditions passed through Teton country, naming many of the natural features. In the late 1880s, the first permanent settlers homesteaded the valley, augmenting their meager earnings by arranging summer lodgings for visitors and guiding dude and hunting parties. Setting apart Jackson Hole as a national park was discussed as early as 1890, but many of those interested in preservation owned ranches in the area they felt should be protected. This distinguished the Teton situation from the Yellowstone, where no one had ever lived.

As Jackson Hole developed economically, socially and recreationally, certain individuals, societies and government groups kept alive their interest in the national park idea. The greatest single benefactor was John D. Rockefeller, Jr., who in 1925 purchased privately owned lands within the area to accomplish the shared purposes of those dedicated to preserving it.

Unaware of the operation at hand, Congress voted to create Grand Teton National Park on Feb. 26, 1929. The Park was about one-third the size of today's Park, protecting only the immediate mountain range and very little of the valley floor. In 1949, the lands purchased by Rockefeller were conveyed by Jackson Hole Preserve, Inc. to the Secretary of the Interior as a gift to the people of the United States. The deeds covered 33,455 acres (13,540 hectares) in Jackson Hole, and represented $2,000,000 and nearly 25 years of tenacity and endless patience. The present-day Grand Teton National Park, created by a Congressional Act on Sept. 14, 1950, combined the former Park with newly acquired land, expanding the Park to almost 500 sq miles (1,300 sq km).

One's first impression of Teton is naturally inspired by the looming Teton range, but it isn't the whole picture. There are also dozens of lakes shimmering like a row of jewels at the foot of the peaks. Hidden behind fringes of trees or up a short stretch of trail, most of them are reached only by leaving the highway behind. **Jackson Lake** is the largest body of water in the area. Marinas are available and sail boating is allowed only on Jackson Lake. Power boats are permitted on Jackson, Jenny and Phelps lakes; the others are reserved for noiseless hand-powered crafts.

The Grand Teton National Park and Jackson Hole have no monopoly on the **Snake River,** one of the cleanest left in the United States, although it extends 17 miles (27 km) south through Jackson Lake. Of its 1,000-mile (1,600-km) traverse from the Continental Divide near Yellowstone National Park to its confluence with the Columbia River near Pasco, Washington, just 40 miles (65 km) of the Snake River are spent in Teton country. Compared to the lakes, the Snake River harbors a wealth of aquatic life, due to the enriching quality of the abundant shoreline. It supports a plant complex which, combined with countless insects, supplies food for the profuse fish population. The fish, in turn, become a tasty meal for more than skilful anglers. Herons, mergansers, eagles, ospreys, otters and other terrestrial predators also rely on the Park's aquatic food pyramid. Of the several varieties of game fish luring thousands of fishermen to the waters of the Tetons, the Snake River cutthroat trout — found only in the Snake's watershed — is unique. Fishing regulations within

A windstorm at the top of a Grand Teton peak in Wyoming.

the Park conform to Wyoming's laws.

A highlight of Jackson Hole is a float trip on the Snake River, one of the best ways to experience the Park's wildlife and outstanding scenery. Local commercial operators conduct raft trips — either all-day or half-day scenic or exciting whitewater adventures. The Snake River regains its free-flowing character at the **Jackson Lake Dam.** This is the 27-mile (43-km) section of the river within the Park that is most appealing to floaters. On a float trip, you don't have to tote your backpack, watch the trail or mind your horse. You just watch the wildlife and the scenery as the guide recounts the local lore and nature identifications. As the Teton range glides by, you may see bald eagles, ospreys, moose, great blue herons, Canada geese, beaver, otters and a variety of ducks in the same primitive setting appreciated by the territory's earliest inhabitants. You can float the river in your own craft, but a permit is required — kayaks, inflatables and canoes are the best. For a truly exciting experience, whitewater excursions are available for the adventurous. A word of caution: do not underestimate the power of the Snake. Write the Park for information about hazards, regulations, equipment and best travel times for floating the Snake River.

To make best use of your time in Teton National Park, stop first at the **Moose Visitor Center** (south end) or the **Colter Bay Visitor Center** and ask the rangers about Park activities and services. The National Park Service presents the Park's many features in movies, slide shows and talks at amphitheaters near the major campgrounds.

On the Trail

Besides the museums and historical displays, great family activities like self-guided nature trails at **Jenny Lake** and **Colter Bay** are available. These are the shortest trails, from one-half to two miles (.8 to 3.2 km), just a fraction of the more than 200 miles (322 km) of hiking trails in the Park. The valley trails, running along the base of the Teton range to the lakes in front of the mountains, are shorter and less demanding than the mountain trails. But these valley trails will pique your interest and help you decide if you want to hike

Snow can be seen on mountain tops all year long in the Rockies region.

further into the mountains. Half-day and all-day hikes into the canyons between the Teton peaks are more difficult, requiring uphill and downhill efforts, but the rewards in mountain views, wildflowers and wildlife are worth it. For overnights in the backcountry, a free backcountry use permit is required.

Grand Teton National Park is considered one of the country's finest areas for general mountaineering, offering an exceptional range of climbing difficulty. The mountains are unusually accessible, rising sharply as they do on the eastern side. No expedition is required to reach the peak, but many climbers find it convenient to pack in and set up base camps in high-country locations. The old rock is very hard and mostly free of slides, with cracks and ledges for hand and footholds.

Ask a Ranger

The **Jenny Lake Ranger Station** is the center for climbing information and registration in the Park. The National Park Service requires all climbers to register in person before climbing and to sign out afterwards. Climbing conditions are best from mid-July through late September.

Seasonal changes dominate the Park, bringing warmth and life, winter and stillness in their turn. Winter weather in the Teton range is severe, bringing heavy snowfall, high winds and extreme temperatures. But winter activities gear up just the same in mid-December. One good snowstorm can turn Jackson Hole into a winter wonderland, covered with up to seven feet (two meters) of snow. Cross-country ski, ice fish, snowshoe, mountaineer, ice skate, snowmobile and observe the wildlife and scenery in or near the Park. In addition to specially designated winter camping areas, lodging within the Park is available at **Flagg Ranch, Triangle X Ranch** and **Signal Mountain Lodge.** Nearby Jackson offers full tourist services year-round.

So, whether you are cruising down **John D. Rockefeller Jr. Memorial Parkway** and appreciating the Teton range from a distance, or scanning the John D. from the summit of one of the majestic Teton peaks, the Grand Teton National Park is awesome from any angle.

A split rail fence and wildflowers frame the distant mountains.

ROCKY MOUNTAIN NATIONAL PARK

In north central Colorado, the snow-mantled peaks of **Rocky Mountain National Park** rise high above fresh green alpine valleys and glistening lakes. With 71 peaks reaching over 12,000 feet (3650 m) and nearly 40 miles (64 km) of the Continental Divide running through it, the Park is often referred to as the "top of the continent." Any visitor to Rocky Mountain National Park is immediately humbled by the magnitude and grandeur of the surrounding mountainscape.

Gigantic Earth Movements

The history of Rocky Mountain National Park is one of gigantic earth movements. Geologists confirm that a great sea once covered the area. Yet today's magnificent mountains, the smooth and gentle slopes on Trail Ridge, the U-shaped valleys, and the uptilted rock strata are fascinating evidence of the powerful forces of change in nature.

A unique feature of the Park is the marked differences found with the changing elevations. In an exhilarating trip over the 38-mile (62-km) Trail Ridge Road, you traverse a quantity of life zones equivalent in number to a round-trip of the Arctic Circle. The best evidence of these differences, besides visitors' difficulty in breathing comfortably at greater altitudes, is the diverse plant life.

At lower levels, open stands of ponderosa pine and juniper grow on the slopes facing the sun; on cooler northern slopes, the Douglas fir reaches skyward. Embellishing streamsides are blue spruces intermixed with dense stands of lodgepole pines. Groves of aspen appear here and there, and meadows and glades are speckled with wildflowers. Above 2,970 yards (2,715 meters), forests of sub-alpine fir take over. Gaps in these cool, dark forests produce wildflower gardens of rare luxurious beauty where the Colorado columbine reigns. Grotesque, twisted trees hug the ground at the upper edges of this zone. One-third of the Park is actually above the treeline, where trees

Delicate alpine tundra in Rocky Mountain National Park.

disappear and the harsh, fragile world of alpine tundra predominates. More than one-quarter of the plants here can also be found in the Arctic.

The modern Ute and Arapahoe were the most recent Indian inhabitants of the Rocky Mountain National Park region. Several thousand years earlier, other Indians – of whom little is known – also used the region for hunting. Meadows and hills teemed with elk, antelope, bighorn sheep, bear, deer, beaver and other game. Winters were apparently too cold for these semi-nomadic peoples, and no tribe claimed the land as home.

Settlers Arrived

In the early 1800s, after the United States acquired the region through the Louisiana Purchase, white men began tentatively exploring this country. Explorers, adventurers and famous mountain men trappers passed through the Park. In 1806, Lt. Zebulon Pike's expedition was the first to see and record Long's Peak, the highest mountain in the Park, named for Col. S.H. Long who led a party along the foot of the mountain 14 years later. However, he never actually climbed it himself.

The first white man to live in Rocky Mountain was Joel Estes. In 1860, Estes settled his entire family in the grassy meadows of the forest-rimmed valley which now bears his name; they lived there for six years.

Estes Park and parts of Rocky Mountain National Park are the only areas in the United States that were once the private hunting preserve of a European nobleman. The Irish Earl of Dunraven was so impressed by the scenery and abundance of game on his 1872-73 hunting trips that he ordered his agent to buy the place. At one time, he owned or controlled about 15,000 acres (6,070 hectares). Other settlers disagreed with the earl's notion that the Park was his own private domain. Court settlements stemming from charges of fraudulent land-grabbing methods reduced the earl's holdings to 8,000 acres (3,240 hectares). In 1906, he sold his remaining land to two men, one of whom was F.O. Stanley – of Stanley Steamer fame – who also built the sparkling white Stanley Hotel, which has overlooked Estes Park since 1910 from its grassy knoll

Endless fields of poppies on the mountain slopes.

north of town.

The gold rush of the 1850s that established Denver and such roaring mining towns as Central City and Blackhawk did not affect Rocky Mountain. Estes was never a boom town. A mining boom did occur in the 1880s in what is now the west side of the Park, and a small but exciting community grew up on the shore of Grand Lake at the Park's western entrance to serve the needs of the new mining camps. But only low grade ore was found, the mines were soon abandoned, and the disappointed miners hitched up their mules and drifted away.

Establishment of Rocky Mountain as a National Park is historically linked with the name of one man — Enos A. Mills, the "father" of the Park and a famous naturalist. At his own expense, he spent seven years promoting the idea of a national park, making many trips from Colorado to Washington, New York, and other centers of influence. His enthusiasm, reports and lectures laid the groundwork that eventually led to legislation setting aside the area as a national park in 1915.

By the mid-1920s it was apparent that the Fall River Road, which first opened to traffic in September 1920, was quickly becoming inadequate. The views from the road on the east side were restricted by large rocks and trees and the west side traversed a series of such hair-raising switchbacks that the pleasure of the view was substantially diminished. Furthermore, the snow-removal problem kept the Park superintendent up many spring nights worrying about whether the road would be cleared by mid-June for the tourist season.

The National Park Service began a determined search for an alternate route in 1926, one which would provide moderate grades, gentle curves, few places of heavy snow accumulation, and, most importantly, unparalleled views of spectacular scenery.

Almost immediately, the search narrowed to Trail Ridge, which derived its name from the Ute Trail traversing its entire length. The trail, travelled by both Ute and Arapahoe Indians, was used to cross from Middle Park through Estes Park, where game was particularly abundant, to the high plains lying to the east of Front Range. The trail was also used by miners travelling across the

The renowned Stanley Hotel in Estes, Colorado, with its old world style.

150

divide to Lulu City and other mines in the Colorado Valley as early as the 1880s. And, with the coming of the 20th Century, the trail was used increasingly by vacationers travelling between Estes Park and Grand Lake on foot or horseback.

Visiting Requirements

Stop at one of the four Rocky Mountain visitor's centers and become acquainted with the Park. The **Headquarters Visitor Center** on the east side and the **Grand Lake Visitor Center** on the west side are open year-round. Guided walks, campfire talks, and other services begin in early June and extend into September.

Rocky Mountain is a park for hikers. More than 300 miles (480 km) of trails provide access to the Park's remote sections so you can get away from the crowds and savor the streams, meadows, mountains and wildlife. For detailed information on elevations, lakes, and hiking trails, purchase a U.S. Geological Survey topographical map or other guide at any visitor counter. To remain overnight in the backcountry, you will need a backcountry permit, available free at Headquarters or the West Unit Office. Some areas are closed to overnight camping and danger from avalanches exists, so plan your trip carefully; check with park rangers for the latest information on areas in which you plan to travel. Rangers can also suggest the most lightly used trails and what to watch for along the way.

You won't see any wolves or grizzly bears; they are already extinct in Colorado. Common larger animals remaining are elk, deer, bighorn sheep, coyote, beaver and a few black bears. And, of course, many varieties of birds abound.

Park Mountain Leason

About 3 million people come to Rocky Mountain National Park each year, and many of them can testify to how difficult it is to acquire a campsite during the peak summer season. A beautiful time of year to consider a trip to Rocky Mountain National Park is in September or October when the weather is pleasant, the aspens are golden, and the crowds are gone.

Weather is a concern to everyone here, for weather determines what you can do, where you can go, and how long you can stay. Primarily due to differences in altitude, slope and exposure, the high country of Rocky Mountain National Park produces a variable weather pattern. Another consideration is the drastic difference between daytime and nighttime temperatures. Summer days reach well into the 80s (26°C) and drop into the 40s (4°C) at night.

The Continental Divide runs along the crest of a range of high peaks in a northwest to southeast direction through the center of the Park. Because of this, there are two distinct weather patterns. One is typical of the east side (Estes Park) and the other of the west side (Grand Lake).

The cold waters of the high Rocky Mountains may not produce large fish, but you just can't beat the mountain scenery as a soothing fishing environment. Remember, though, you must have a valid Colorado fishing license, and the use of live bait is prohibited. Some streams and lakes are closed to protect the greenback cutthroat trout, which is being reintroduced into its natural habitat. So check with the nearest ranger station before going fishing.

For the climber, Rocky Mountain National Park offers a variety of challenging ascents throughout the year. A park concessionaire operates a climbing school and guide service providing mountaineering instruction. For more information and details, contact park headquarters.

Horses and guides can be hired at two locations inside the Park on the east side or from a number of liveries outside the east and west Park boundaries during the summer season.

Winter means snow in the Rockies and snow means skiing — cross-country skiing in the lower valleys, winter mountaineering in the high country, and downhill skiing at **Hidden Valley.** Access roads from the east are kept open, providing winter travellers with a panorama of the high mountains.

Most travellers to Rocky Mountain National Park stay pretty close to the Trail Ridge Road, but do take time to get to know the lesser-known parts of the Park. There is much to see, to do, to ponder and to appreciate here at the "top of the continent."

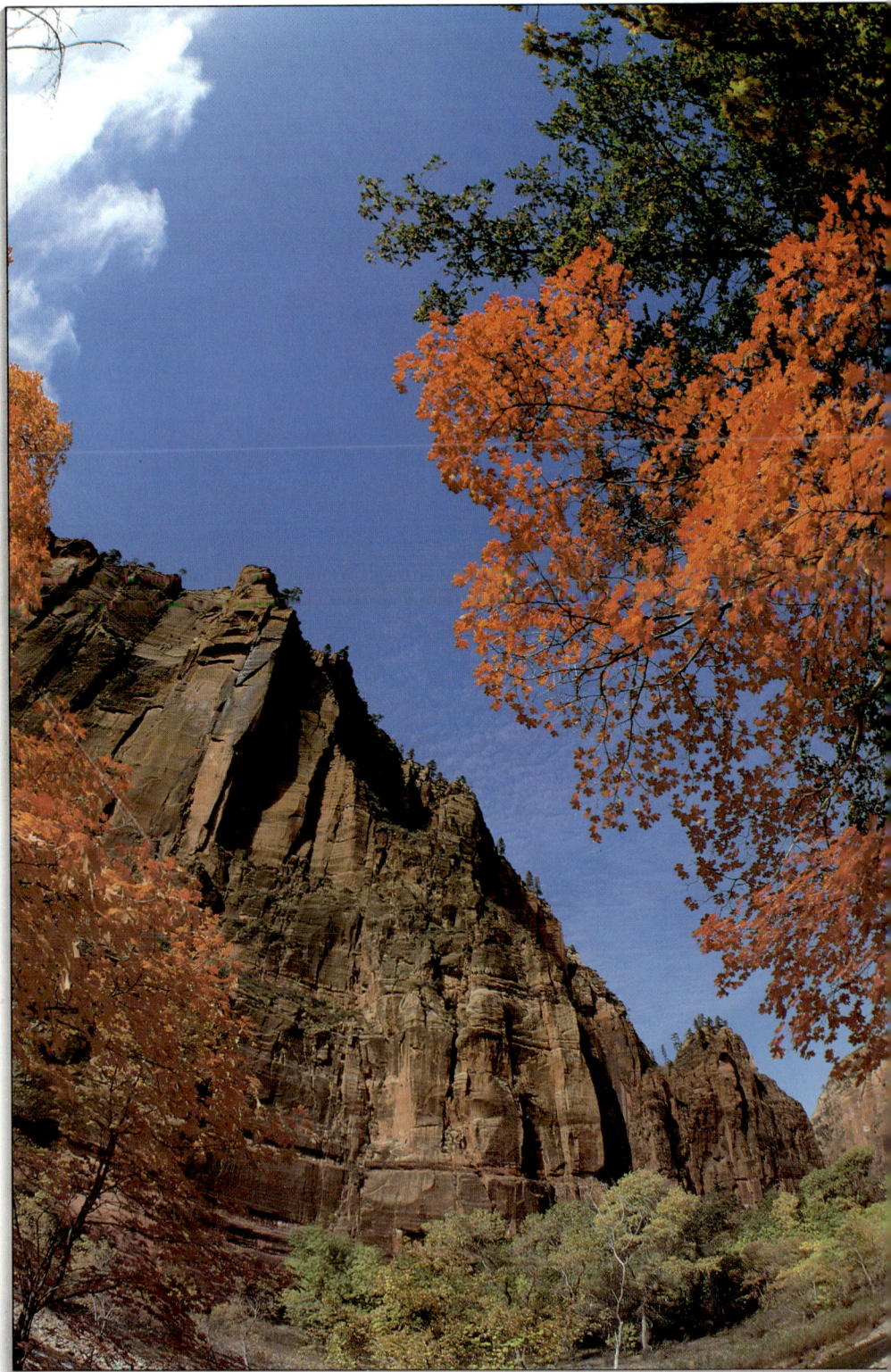

UTAH'S NATIONAL PARKS

Located within a 200-mile (320-km) circle, each of Utah's five national parks exhibits a flavor and personality of its own. Though the geological forces working in each park are identical, the effects are not.

Zion National Park

Powerful upheavals combined with the erosive forces of wind, rain, frost, and the **Virgin River** have cut through Navajo sandstone creating what is now **Zion National Park.** Zion is the grandfather of Utah's national parks and one of the nation's oldest. It contains some of the most colorful, deep, narrow canyons, sheer rock walls and unique formations in the plateau country of southern Utah. Vividly colored cliffs tower above the scenic route along the floor of Zion Canyon. This narrow, deep canyon is the centerpiece of the Park.

On most days, the Virgin River winds peacefully through the canyon. Frémont cottonwoods, willows and velvet ashes along its banks provide shady spots for picnics or short walks. Mule deer and a wide variety of birds seek refuge from summer's extreme midday heat beneath this canopy. Other wildlife, including ringtail cats, bobcats, foxes, rock squirrels and cottontails, rest under rocky ledges.

Most of the rock formations can be seen from roads which pass through the Park; however, the best way to view Zion is on foot or horseback. Self-guided trails lead to the major formations. Among the most popular is the one-mile (1.6-km) trail, **Gateway to the Narrows,** beginning at the **Temple of Sinawava.** Arrangements for guided horsepack trips are made at **Zion Lodge.**

Three campgrounds are located within Zion. The Visitor's Center, at the south entrance of the Park, is open year-round. In addition, the **Zion Canyon Scenic Drive,** the **Zion-Mount Carmel Highway** and the **Kolob Canyons Road** are open all year. Zion's roads introduce you to the Park's spectacular cliff-and-canyon landscape. Once within Zion, you can drive, bike, hike or take the guided tram tour, depending on your time and interests.

The Visitor's Center at the north end of the Park is open year-round. Here, useful information is available free, as well as interesting exhibits and a slide program. The Park also offers a variety of interpretive programs in summer and fall, including human and natural history talks, campfire programs, view talks, guided nature walks, and special interest walks. Camping spots are available year-round in the Park; however, drinking water is available only during the summer months. Accommodations and services can be obtained within the Park and the surrounding towns.

Capitol Reef National Park

Capitol Reef National Park lies in the slickrock country of south central Utah, an area where water has cut monoliths, arches and mazes of canyons out of a sandstone-and-shale desert. Massive gorges, scarps and artifacts of the Columbian Indians of the Frémont Culture are contained here.

The term "reef" as applied to land formations means a ridge of rock that is a barrier. Capitol Reef was named for

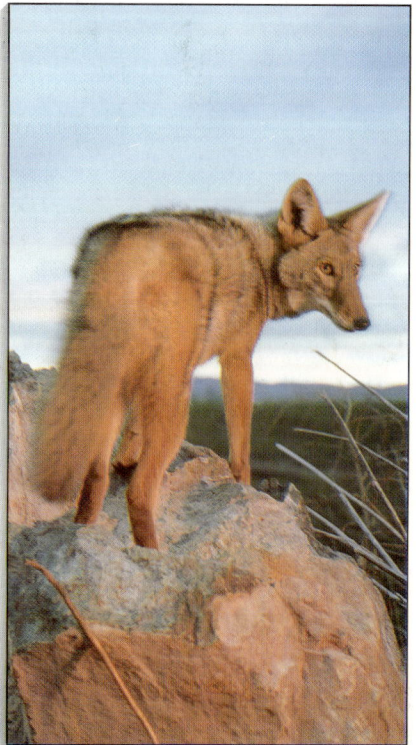

Preceding pages, the dramatic "delicate arch" is the focal point of Arches National Park (Utah). Left, fall foliage at its colorful peak in Zion Park (Utah); and right, a coyote watches an approaching storm.

one of its high points: **Capitol Dome,** which resembles the dome of the U.S. Capitol. The Park has been penetrated and explored only in the past 100 years and much of it still remains a rugged wilderness.

The domes of Capitol Reef are part of **Waterpocket Fold,** a 100-mile-long (160-km) bulge in the earth's crust which contains pockets eroded into the rock that catch thousands of gallons of water each rainfall. The layer upon layer of rock was, once, a tidal flat whose ripple marks are now hardened into stone. At another time, dunes drifted across the land, eventually consolidated into crisscrossing beds of sandstone.

The most spectacular experiences are off the main highway on graded or dirt roads. Marked roads lead to ancient petroglyphs, waterpockets and magnificent overlooks. The Park's remote sections are accessible only over rough backcountry roads. Spring and fall are ideal for backcountry hiking and camping because of the mild temperatures.

Driving to Canyonlands is an adventure in itself. Since the park is located a vast distance from anywhere, gas is hard to come by. The closest service station is 60 miles (96 km) away and water is hard to acquire. Piped water is available only near the campground in the Needles district; anywhere else in the Park, you'd better provide your own or be prepared to get mighty thirsty. Visitors should also contact rangers at north and south entrance information centers for road conditions.

Hiking, jeeping or scenic flights are great ways to explore the rugged wilderness of Canyonlands; but, for many, the ultimate recreational experience is a never-to-be-forgotten river ride down either the Green or Colorado River and through **Cataract Canyon.** Commercially operated float trips, led by licensed guides, are the most popular. Guides are also available in nearby communities for overland trips into the more remote areas. Primitive campsites are located in four-wheel drive areas of the Park.

Arches National Park

The largest concentration and greatest collection of natural stone

"Triple arch" at Arches National Park dwarfs visitors below.

arches in the world lies on the **Colorado Plateau** in southeastern Utah's red rock country. All stages of arch formation and decay are found in **Arches National Park.** The forces of wind, water and time have carved the incredible arches within the 115-square-mile (300-sq-km) Park.

Bryce Canyon National Park

Unlike Zion, the mood in **Bryce Canyon,** located 50 miles (80 km) northeast of Zion, is light and lacy. Delicate rocky pinnacles and spires are colored in pink, white and rust shades.

Though called a canyon, Bryce Canyon is actually a series of "breaks" in 12 large amphitheaters. These breaks plunge down 1,000 feet (305 meters) in multicolored layers of limestone. The many shapes and forms in stone conjure all sorts of images: walls, windows, minarets, gables, pagodas, pedestals and temples. Photographs usually emphasize the otherworldly magnificence of Bryce Canyon. As light shifts with cloud movements or as the sun rises or sets, the changing scenery passes before you in vivid color.

The main geological features of Bryce are easily seen from overlooks along 35 miles (56 km) of paved roads. The best exposure to the Park, however, is on foot or horseback. Trails range from one-half to 23 miles (0.8 to 37 km) and most of them are self-guided.

The forests and meadows of Bryce Canyon support a remarkable diversity of plant, animal and bird life. Three distinctive plant communities thrive here — the pinyon junipers in the canyon, the ponderosa pine forests on the plateau in the main park area, and the fir spruce forest at Rainbow Point, the highest elevation in the Park.

Mule deer are the largest mammals at Bryce Canyon. They can be seen on summer mornings and evenings in meadows and along park roads. Cougars, also called pumas and mountain lions, are the most secretive animals in the area. A huge rodent population, together with jackrabbits and cottontails, are preyed upon by small populations of night hunters including badger, skunk, bobcat, weasel, ringtailed cat, gray fox and coyote.

More than 164 species of birds, ranging from tiny swifts to golden eagles,

A panoramic view of the incredible Bryce Canyon National Park.

visit Bryce Canyon annually. Meadow-larks, bluebirds and robins are active in meadow areas.

To the daytime visitor, it may seem that — except for lizards, chipmunks, and squirrels — only a few animals live in the park. But most, like the ringtail cat, fox, mountain lion and deer, are simply nocturnal. The best time to view wildlife is at dusk, dawn and after dark.

From May through September, you can join a park naturalist on a walk or attend informative evening campfire programs. The main Visitor's Center, as well as the Capitol Reef's two camp-grounds, are open year-round.

Canyonlands National Park

In southeastern Utah, the **Colorado** and **Green Rivers** merge midway in **Canyonlands National Park** to form the wildest river on the continent. Entrenched in twisting ravines, they cut deep into the earth, almost 1,500 feet (455 meters), creating the spectacular canyons responsible for the Park's name. The outstanding quality of Canyonlands is its variety of form and color — the combined effects of substance, time, and

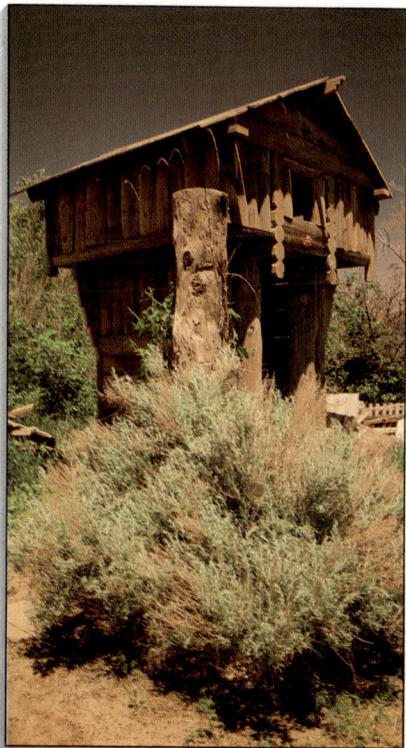

erosion.

Isolated high mesas and deep can-yons, obstructive broad rivers and sheer cliffs affect the distribution of plants and animals just as they also res-trict man's movements in the area. The desertlike lands look desolate and emp-ty, but are occupied by plentiful plant and animal life. Bighorn sheep, mule deer, cougars, bobcats, coyotes, foxes and pronghorn are at home here, as well as rodents in great variety and numbers. Along the rivers are beaver, shorebirds, ducks and other wetland animals.

Bird life in Canyonlands is especially diverse because of the wide range of habitats. Totally different conditions may occur within very short distances, and birdwatchers find a rich variety of species throughout the year.

Paved and graded state roads allow access for passenger cars to the Park's overlook areas and some interior areas, but Canyonlands is basically a paradise for four-wheelers and backpackers. Much of the Park's 337,570 acres (136,600 hectares) is still unexplored and provides great opportunities for adventure.

Arches National Park's trademark is **Delicate Arch,** an isolated rocky rem-nant standing on the brink of a canyon, with the white-capped LaSal Mountains as a backdrop. Spires, pinnacles, and balanced rocks perched atop seemingly inadequate bases vie with the arches as scenic spectacles. Early explorers thought the huge arches — **Landscape Arch** is the world-record-holder with a span of 291 feet (88 meters) — and monoliths were remnants of a lost cul-ture, like Stonehenge in England.

Many of the more than 90 sandstone arches are seen from the paved roads running through the Park, but, to prop-erly appreciate their magnificence, leave your car and take a short walk along the well-marked footpaths.

At the Visitor's Center, you can see a color slide orientation program, the geology museum, history exhibits and other maps and publications. Ask also about the popular naturalist-led Firey Furnace Walk and obtain a self-guiding tour booklet which includes information coordinated with numbered stops along the Park road.

Take your time exploring and be pre-pared for the astonishing scale that is so special in Utah's National Parks.

Left, unique lifestyles abound in Capitol Reef National Park; and right, erosion patterns can be seen clearly in the rocks of Zion.

The very word "tundra" conjures an image of coldness, flatness, desert land or even waste land. The word really describes a kind of vegetation, an area with a specifically different ecosystem; it defines the land beyond the tree limit, whether in the North Pole or in the mountains. "Alpine Tundra" is delicate mountain land above the timberline in the Arctic regions of the North and South Pole. In both these areas, the vegetation and climate is similar. This flower-rich meadowland which grows beyond the limit of trees, is similar to a miniature "forest."

The mammoth sky and towering mountains contrast significantly with the delicate microscopic tundra flowers.

In alpine tundra country, the high contrast of the snow-capped mountains and the sky at this high altitude is intense. It's a deserted area with no trees, very few animals and nothing man-made — just you, the boulders and the mountains. Since there's twice as much ultra-violet radiation and 25 percent more light, the dazzling brightness confuses your perspective of scale, making distant mountains look much closer and more defined. The light gives the alpine tundra a mood of elation. The thin air holds less heat, making it about 30 degrees cooler than the

valley. Sunglasses, sunburn cream and plenty of warm clothing and good hiking boots are essentials if you plan to explore the tundra grasslands.

In 'Lilliput' Land

Tiny wildflowers struggle to survive under the severe weather conditions of cold, wind, snow and strong sun. Daisies in your garden may grow to be three feet (one meter) tall, but here the same plant toils almost vainly to reach a height of about one-third inch (one

cm) at full term. It's magical to come across one of these tundra grasslands — like being in Lilliput, where everything is so perfectly miniaturized. You will have to bend down low or even crawl on your belly to see up-close the tiny forest that exists at the tips of your toes.

Tundra is composed of various dwarfed shrubs, sedges, mosses, grasses and flowering plants. Even though these stunted living things can withstand rigorous and bitter winters accompanied by stormy summers, they are extremely fragile and delicate and should not be trampled. Sometimes, hundreds of years are required to achieve the growth you see. Flower buds begin growing a few years ahead to get to full bloom. They are usually well-formed by the end of the summer to protect themselves when winter sets in.

The plants are small and stay low to the ground. They can dodge the mountain wind, though they are still exposed to severe winters. As a group, alpine tundra have fewer and smaller leaves and less flowers. The grasslands themselves are spotty, the growth is thick in some areas and desert-like in others. Sedge turfs, however, are like thick lush rugs and spaced sporadically over an area. The alpine flower sometimes looks

oversized compared to its leaves, because growth is only stunted at that portion of the plant below its flower.

The meadows abound in the Rocky Mountain region. Trailridge Road in the Rocky Mountain National Park has a tremendous view of tundra slopes, and just a few meters from the main road in the Rocky Mountain National Park are fields of tundra flowers. The early Indians used this ridge as an east-west traverse across Colorado mountains in the summer. The trail is still clear,

Left, wildflowers are everywhere in the Rockies, including on the wagon wheel (above).

even though used years ago; tundra vegetation takes a long time to recover from that type of travelling. More than a million people visit Trailridge Road each summer, and the visitor-pressure is hard on alpine tundra plants. Keep in mind that the plants are extremely delicate; if you step on them, they will be permanently damaged.

Summer in the Tundra

As the growing season is short, the summer is a good time to enjoy the alpine tundra. When the sky is blue during July and August, the tundra is fresh, bright and beautiful, truly a visual delight. Some of the other easily accessible areas in the Rockies where you will see Alpine Tundra in summer are Independence Pass, the road from Red Lodge to Cook City in Montana, the northern entrance to Yellowstone, and most of the forests whose mountains rise above the timberline.

In these high elevations, few animals choose this environment for their home. Most of the larger animals leave the mountains during the winter, as grazing is poor. Smaller animals who have adapted to the harsh climate and stay through the year are the pocket gopher, meadow mole, mouse, shrew, marmot, pika and weasel.

A common small animal is the yellow-bellied marmot, a large rodent that looks like a woodchuck. On scenic turnoffs, you will spot these two-foot-long (½ meter), 10-pound (five kg) creatures being trained by tourists to beg for handouts. But feeding them interrupts their natural feeding cycle and can be harmful to them. Their long front teeth can be detrimental to you. Other friendly creatures, such as rock rabbit, chipmunk and pine squirrel also roam the tundra.

Most of the alpine areas do not have paved roads, trails or easy accessibility — one way in which the alpine tundra has been preserved. With the development of mountain tourism in modern times, trailbikes, snow-mobiles, jeeps and four-wheeled vehicles have disrupted the peaceful tundra world. During winter and fall, the most delicate stages of the alpine plants, vehicle tracking can do permanent damage. Conservationists today fear the alpine tundra may become endangered.

NATIONAL MONUMENTS

The nationally preserved areas we know as National Parks and Monuments offer visitors a new perspective. These places, where nature still thrives, ensure that forthcoming generations will be able to enjoy these "islands of hope." National Monuments in the United States are unique places set aside for the preservation of one particular outstanding feature. Fifteen National Monuments located in the Rockies highlight both geologically and historically spectacular sights. All are worth a visit and a few are highlighted here.

North America's tallest sand dunes are preserved at the **Great Sand Dunes National Monument**. The Dunes are piled at the foot of the Sangre de Cristo Mountains, located in the San Luis Valley in South Central Colorado. A geological and recreational wonder, the Sand Dunes are formed as winds heap up billions of sand grains, building low sand hills against the mountains.

The essence of this place is to be found in the contrast of light and shadow, desert and forest, sky and dune, valley and mountain. Whether jumping off a dune peak, relaxing in the sand, or watching the sun go down behind the San Juans, visitors find the Sand Dunes truly magnificent.

In west-central Colorado, nature has sculpted 18,000 acres (7285 hectares) of towering monoliths and strangely beautiful rock formations. Here in the **Uncompahgre Highlands**, the earth's crust has been worn down by constant erosion. Dinosaur bones, petrified logs, colorful stones and prehistoric Indian artifacts have been discovered in the canyon floors. The 22-mile (35-km) **Rim Rock Drive** goes around the walls of **Red, Ute, No Thoroughfare** and **Monument Canyons** and a scenic tour of the landscape.

At **Florissant Fossil Beds National Monument**, 40 miles (64 km) west of Colorado Springs, remains of fossil bones can be seen embedded in the rock.

Dinosaur National Monument, is located in the northeast corner of Colorado and stretches into the edge of Utah. Fossilized dinosaur remains are found here. The Quarry Visitor's Center, 20 miles (32 km) east of Vernal, features a world-famous display of dinosaur fossils and is open daily, year-round.

Located 23 miles (37 km) east of Cedar City, Utah, is **Cedar Breaks National Monument**, a natural ampitheater with limestone formations, mountain meadows, alpine flowers and picturesque scenery. A six-mile (10-km) paved rim road encircles the fields and forests, affording numerous vistas of the Breaks. A Visitor Center, picnic area and campground are open during the summer.

One of the seven natural wonders of the world, **Rainbow Bridge National Monument** in Utah is the largest natural rock bridge on earth. The bridge reaches 290 feet (90 meters) in height and 270 feet (85 meters) across. Rainbow Bridge can be reached by foot or horseback, but the best approach to the monument is by boat on Lake Powell. Take the 50-mile (80-km) water route from Wahweep Marina to the landing in Bridge Canyon and walk half a mile (one km) up to the bridge.

The three sandstone bridges (Kachina, Sipapu and Owachomo) forming **Natural Bridges National Monument**, can be seen along a eight-mile (13-km) paved road 42 miles (67 km) west of Blanding, Utah. Museum exhibits and educational information are available at the Visitor's Center. A large photovoltaic solar system was installed to provide electricity to the Monument's facilities. The system's 96 solar panels produce 130 HP (100 kilowatts) of electricity at peak power.

In south central Idaho, immense lava fields studded with cinder cones and huge central depressions form **Craters of the Moon National Monument**. The first U.S. astronauts practiced their "moon walk" on this amazing landscape that resembles lunar craters. The 86-sq-mile (220-sq-km) volcanic National Monument is open for exploration. Naturalists at the Visitor's Center are also available to help you get acquainted with the area.

Big Hole National Monument, 12 miles (20 km) west of Wisdom, Montana, marks the site of a surprise attack on Chief Joseph and 800 other Nez Perce Indians. The tribe had been avoiding the U.S. Army for two months when they were attacked by Col. John Gibbon and 182 of his men. The Nez Perce successfully evaded the army by setting fires and forcing the soldiers to retreat while they fled. The Monument is open from Labor Day to Memorial Day, where you can tour the battlefield and visit the Museum and Visitor's Center.

Another site history buffs will appreciate is the famed **Custer Battlefield National Monument**, 15 miles (24 km) from Hardin, Montana. Known as "Custer's Last Stand," the 1876 battle between Sioux and Cheyenne warriors and Lt. Col. George Armstrong Custer's troop of 225 men is the most famous Indian Battle in U.S. history. Walking along the bluffs that concealed Indian warriors from Custer's troops you will see the memorial graveyard of the unfortunate Seventh Cavalry.

In southwest Wyoming, the **Fossil Butte National Monument** proves that this part of the country was under water at one time. Rising 7,500 feet (2,285 meters) from Twin Creek Valley is a concentration of fossilized fresh water fish preserved in sandstone; this unique find became a National Monument in 1972.

Northeast Wyoming's **Devil's Tower National Monument** is a unique formation rising 1,280 feet (390 meters) above Belle Fourche River. The tower itself is 600 feet (182 meters) tall and is composed of phonolite, a volcanic rock, that rings when struck. It can be seen for nearly 100 miles (160 km) before reaching it. The Sioux Indians called the tower "Mapo Tipi" meaning "Bear Lodge." It is said that three young maidens were attacked by grizzly bears while picking flowers. The girls climbed on top of a large boulder for protection. (A sympathetic god had allowed the rock to grow.) The persistant bears never reached the top, but their claw prints can be seen as vertical grooves along the tower. After the bears left, the Indian damsels lowered themselves from the rock with ropes of flowers. The famous Indian chief, Sitting Bull, is said to have prayed atop "Mapo Tipi" many times for victory over the Whites.

In more recent times, Devil's Tower made an exciting location for Stephen Spielberg's science fiction film, *Close Encounters of the Third Kind*. Located at the foot of the tower is a large prairie dog "town," protected since 1933; when the animal was put on the endangered species list.

Hikers cross the next hill in the Great Sand Dunes National Monument (CO).

TAKING GOOD PHOTOGRAPHS

If you are like most travellers, you enjoy the reminders and evocative images photos of your trip can bring to mind. The Rockies cover a spectacularly varied region; there are endless possibilities for capturing on film scenery, wildlife and natural phenomenon. Be prepared for this land of challenges, use your imagination, and keep the following photo tips in mind when shooting in the Rockies:

Landscapes: Decide whether your photo will be wide angle or telephoto, or both. Choose a center of interest and compose

the shot to accent that subject. (Avoid always centering horizon and subjects.) **Best Light:** Sunrise, late afternoon and sunset. Side lighting is an excellent way to maximize drama. Be careful to avoid looking at the sun through the camera lens—it can cause eye damage.

Snow: Automatic light meters tend to underexpose snow and ice. Open the aperture a stop or two to compensate. If optical lens flare is an undesired effect, make sure the sun is not in the lens.

Wildlife: Keep your camera ready. stay at a safe, unobtrusive distance; a fixed telephoto or zoom lens is ideal. In your car, a small bean-bag over the door frame (win-

dow open) makes a good lens support. **Best Light:** At dawn and dusk, when most animals feed. **Exposure:** Set ahead of time (use a higher shutter speed (1/250th) and a wider aperture (f-8) to free yourself to concentrate on your subject.

Wildflowers: Focus is critical when photographing delicate alpine wildflowers—and depth of field gets shallower the closer you get. Use a macro lens for extreme close-ups. A tripod isn't necessary if wind is calm and light adequate. **Best light:** early morning, late afternoon and shade. Remember, you can make your own shade!

People and Events: For candid and action shots, pre-set exposure and approximate focus on your telephoto lens. Then browse, ready to catch an interesting face unaware. For a studied pose, windowlight and shade provide good portrait lighting. Indoors or out, use a portable flash when possible to ensure adequate lighting of your subject.

Architecture: Tilting up will cause distortion; when photographing monuments or buildings try to keep your camera parallel to the ground. When possible, find a spot higher than the base of the building, and shoot from there. **Best light:** Afternoon or morning. Accent the facade by throwing one side of the building in shade.

larly take on a new dimension in fog.

Taking Advantage of Existing Weather

Overcast: This is a great solution to portraits when you don't have a flash. Many subjects that don't photograph well in sunlight make excellent subjects under overcast skies.

Rain: You can capture raindrops during the daylight when the background is dark, or illustrate the reflecting neon signs in wet city streets at night. In rainy weather,

Technical Tips

Night Shots: To photograph night fairs, festivals or floodlit buildings, bracket from 1/2 second to 1/125 second exposure at a wide aperture (F-L 1.5). Cities are best photographed just after the sun has set. When shooting landscapes lit by the full moon, use a tripod and try 30-second, one-minute, two-minute, and four-minute exposures.

always carry an umbrella to protect your equipment, or put the camera in a loose plastic bag, with an open hole around the filter, with lens poking through.

Storms: The breaking or clearing of a storm brings forth the elusive rainbow. If you are patient, the resulting photograph will be highly dramatic.

Fog: Take advantage of this condition. For some cities and landscapes, fog is an essential part of the local flavor; forests particularly take on a new dimension in fog.

Aerial: A small plane or helicopter, with the door removed or window opened, is a successful way to photograph. If you plan to shoot through windows, be sure to clean them before leaving the ground, and shoot out of the shady side of the plane. Use a high shutter speed (1/250 or 1/500) and focus on infinity. Slower films (ASA 64 or 100) give best results. Use your body to absorb any vibrations, and remember to keep your horizon straight!

Rivers and Waterfalls: Long exposures (1/8 second or longer) produce a fluid motion image when shooting fast moving water. Use a tripod at slow shutter speeds.

Left, focus close-up with a powerful lens to capture the alpine tundra; and right, this inspiring point provides the ideal view of Yellowstone Canyon.

THE FRONT RANGE OF COLORADO

The great Continental Divide, which runs the length of two vast continents, is an effective population and weather barrier. Nowhere is this better demonstrated than in the Rockies of Colorado. The Front Range, as the eastern slope of the Rockies in Colorado is called, is where the mountains end and the plains begin. The Front Range is a booming megalopolis that extends from Pueblo in the south, through the cities of Colorado Springs, Denver, Boulder, Longmont, Greeley and Fort Collins, near the Wyoming border. As soon as the foothills begin to rise to the west this densely settled area gives way to huge expanses of wilderness and small mountain towns.

Though Denver is a mile (1.6 km) high, the weather is considerably balmier there than it is just a few miles away, up in the mountains. Most of the storms that regularly drop a foot or two of glistening powder snow on the ski slopes have used up all their moisture in the mountains by the time they reach the Front Range. Denver receives only eight to 15 inches of precipitation a year, about the same as Los Angeles, and has as many sunny days a year (over 300) as Miami. Summers can be hot, but the low humidity keeps it relatively comfortable.

The Early Explorers and Settlers

The white man's history of settlement on the Front Range is little more than a century old. Lieutenant Zebulon Pike got part way up the peak named after him in 1806, but he and his men followed the eastern slope of the Rockies south, never really broaching the mountains. In 1849, when hundreds of thousands of people were migrating West in the Gold Rush to California, Denver was still a quiet valley belonging to the Ute Indians and a handful of itinerant mountain men. A few of the mountain men, such as Jedediah Smith and Bill Williams, had explored the Colorado Rockies while they were trapping beaver, but the majority of the trapping and exploration was concentrated to the north, in the Wind River Range of Wyoming.

The first gold strike at Cherry Creek in 1859 attracted enough miners to create a small tent town where Denver now stands, but it was the rich lode found at Clear Creek a year later that brought 15,000 people to the area in a matter of months, and over 50,000 within a year, in the famous "Pike's Peak or Bust" gold rush. These immigrants eventually settled along the length of the Front Range in Colorado, and from there made forays into the mountain wildernesses to look for the ore that would make them rich.

Growing Pains

It took only a few years for ambitious Denverites to create a reasonably well-governed, though somewhat wild city, complete with a mayor, aldermen, police and street commissioner. A commercial section of the city was established around what is Larimer Square today, and a residential section was built, complete with ornate Victorian homes. After a fire in 1863, wooden buildings were forbidden, and impressive brick structures replaced them. But in spite of the enthusiasm of the town fathers, the Denver area went through a major slump for nearly a decade after the first gold strike. Colorado was too isolated, the ore was too difficult to get out of the mountains for refining, the necessary milling machinery too expensive to import, and marauding Indians were scaring away many potential settlers. The Indians were taken care of by a series of massacres that all but exterminated the Rocky Mountain tribes.

The problem of isolation was finally solved when the Denver Pacific and Union Pacific railway lines were completed in 1870. These branches from Kansas City and Cheyenne created another, though smaller, boom in Denver when towns sprang up along the line. These first railway lines fueled further entrepreneurship, and by the early 1880s, the Denver, Rio Grande and Sante Fe railroads had laid nearly 2,000 miles of regional track along the Front Range and into the mountains.

It was the discovery of silver in Leadville that put Colorado back on the map for another decade. Those mines, which earned $11.5 million in 1880, and others

that opened up on the Western Slope attracted another wave of immigrants to the area. Denver, the gateway to the Rockies, reaped many benefits from the silver rush. Other industries grew as well. Huge stands of timber were cut for building mine shafts, and coal was mined in great quantities to fuel locomotives and warm homes. Once the Easterners learned how to use irrigation ditches, agriculture thrived in Greeley, Longmont, and Fort Collins. Cattle ranching became established in eastern Colorado. The University of Colorado was organized in 1877, to be followed by Colorado Agricultural College, the University of Denver, and the Colorado School of Mines. Pueblo became a center for smelting. These were the industries that continued to carry Colorado economically through the 50s.

The Early Sightseers

Thanks to the railroad, the Rockies attracted tourists early on. An estimated 200,000 people travelled to Colorado in 1878 to see its scenic wonders. Among the more popular spots were Idaho Springs, which had a first-class

To Cheyenne
Speer Blvd.
Valley St.
Water St.
Union Sta.
20th St.
Blake St.
16th St.
15th St.
13th St.
Larimer St.
Lawrence St.
Arapahoe St.
Curtis St.
Champa St.
Stout St.
California St.
Arapahoe St.
Curtis St.
Champa St.
Stout St.
California St.
Welton St.
N. Broadway
Washington St.
Welton St.
Lawson Park
Denver Art Museum
South Platte River
Bus Terminal
U.S. Custom House
Downing St.
E. 2
Mile High Stadium
Denver Center for the Performing Arts
E. 20th Ave.
E. 19th Ave.
E. 18th Ave.
Sports Arena
Larimer St.
Lawrence St.
Municipal Auditorium
13th St.
Tremont
E. 17th Ave.
E. 16th Ave.
Park Ave.
Champa St.
Speer Blvd.
U.S. Mint
Civic Center
State Office Bldg.
E. Co
W. 14th Ave.
State Capitol
E. 14th Ave.
W.13th Ave.
Cherokee St.
Library
Colorado Heritage Center
Molly Brown House Museum
Valley Hwy.
Cherry Creek
Speer Blvd
Bannock St.
E.12th Ave.
Mariposa St.
Kalamath St.
Santa Fe St.
Inca St.
Acoma St.
S. Broadway
Lincoln St.
Sherman St.
Grant St.
Logan St.
Pennsylvania St.
Corona St.
Downing St.
E. 11th Ave.
E.10th Ave.
E.9th Ave.
W. 8th Ave.
Grant- Humphreys Mansion
W. 7th Ave.
To Colorado Springs

hotel and hot springs for the health-oriented; the Hotel de Paris and a scenic narrow-gauge railway trip in Georgetown; the Stanley Hotel in Estes Park; and the famous health spa of Colorado Springs, with its sumptuous Broadmoor Hotel, wealthy clientele, and invigorating mineral hot springs. In fact, the dry, crisp mountain air and numerous hot springs made Colorado a major destination for tuberculosis victims and others with respiratory illnesses. Dude ranches also thrived, and to lure evermore visitors, Colorado's business community dreamt up many number of celebrations and festivals.

With the Silver Panic of 1893, the Front Range went through yet another slump but was once again bailed out by the discovery of gold at Cripple Creek — the richest strike ever made in the United States. By this time the town fathers of Denver had learned the value of boosterism, and they poured their new wealth into parks, trees, fountains, statues, curbed streets, a capitol building, and a civic center — the wild, muddy, disreputable boom town was becoming respectable.

Children enjoy the fabulous Arts Center Mall in Denver.

The Mile High City

Through the early part of the 20th Century, until after World War II, Denver was little more than a sprawling cow town — quiet and stable, with little of the growth, glitter, and glamour of a big city. When the energy boom hit, Denver turned out to be in the perfect location to take advantage of it. In addition to being the geographical headquarters for the west's massive coal reserves and oil shale deposits, the climate was good, and there was plenty of room for housing and industry. It wasn't long before the Front Range became a leading area for solar research, thermal power and wind power. Many oil exploration companies moved their headquarters to the growing city, along with major corporations such as IBM, Kodak, John Mansville, and Frito Lay. The latest boom has been in the hi-tech industries, turning the Front Range into the Silicon Valley of the Rockies. The federal government has a huge complex in west Denver, giving the city the second highest number of federal employees in the nation.

All this has meant tremendous

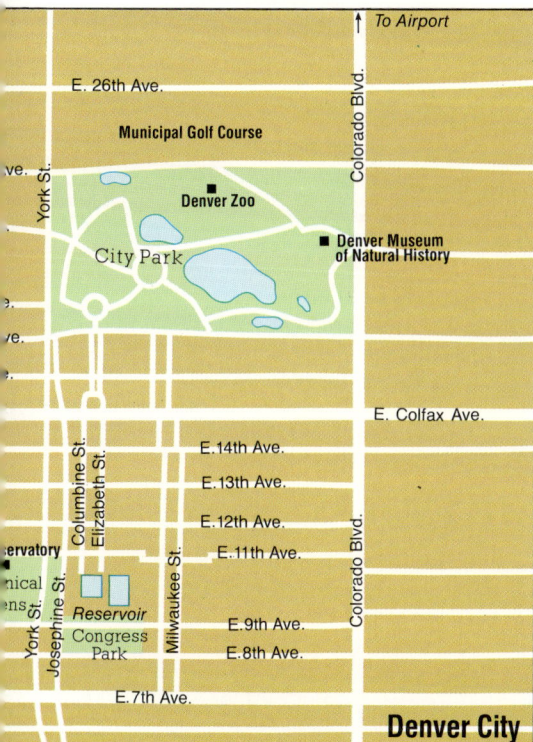

Map: Denver City

- To Airport
- E. 26th Ave.
- Colorado Blvd.
- Municipal Golf Course
- York St.
- Denver Zoo
- City Park
- Denver Museum of Natural History
- E. Colfax Ave.
- Columbine St.
- Elizabeth St.
- E.14th Ave.
- E.13th Ave.
- E.12th Ave.
- Milwaukee St.
- E.11th Ave.
- ervatory
- nical ens.
- York St.
- Josephine St.
- Reservoir
- Congress Park
- E.9th Ave.
- E.8th Ave.
- Colorado Blvd.
- E. 7th Ave.

growth for Denver in the past decade — a 30 percent increase in population, 16 new skyscrapers, and a sense of cultural and economic well-being. The majority of the three thousand or so people who move to the Denver metro area every month are young and well educated — Colorado's capital city has one of the youngest median ages and highest percentage of college graduates in the United States. A few of the city's other superlatives also reflect the high population of active young people — it has more sporting goods stores per capita than any other city in the world, and it leads the nation in movie attendance per capita.

Garden Greens

For the most part, Denver is an easy and pleasant city to live in. Parks were built in abundance from the very beginning and, as a result, there are 205 of them in Denver alone, and 20,000 acres (8,000 hectares) of mountain parks are operated by the city. Cherry Creek and the South Platte River, which run through the heart of Denver, are lined with bicycling and jogging trails. Pedes-trian skywalks and bridges make it possible to get around the downtown area without fighting traffic.

Most people en route to the Rockies at least drive through Denver, but it's well-worth it to stop and spend a couple of days exploring the city itself. There's no better place to begin to get a sense of the history and development of the Rocky Mountains than Denver. The downtown area is spanking new, clean, and full of exciting shops and museums. Because of downtown Denver's pollution problems and traffic congestion, it's cheaper and easier to park outside the downtown area and take advantage of the well run bus system. The mountains that keep Denver's climate mild also create weather patterns that allow air to settle into the valley, creating one of the worst pollution problems in the country. The city government has gone to great lengths to encourage residents and visitors to take public transportation, walk, ride bicycles — anything but drive a car. Free shuttle buses leave both ends of the 16th Street Mall (at a mile, one of the longest pedestrian malls in the country) about every 90 seconds,

Denver city skyline.

172

putting the entire downtown area within easy walking distance.

Downtown Denver: A Walking Tour

The best place to begin a tour of a capitol city is, of course, the **State Capitol** building. On the 13th step is a marker informing you that you are exactly one mile high. Denver calls itself the Mile High City for obvious geographical reasons, but after a few days there it will become clear that the young city is as high on itself and as full of itself as a college freshman. Ninety-three steps up into the Capitol rotunda is an open-air deck with fabulous views of the city and the Front Range. On a clear day it's possible to see the Rockies from the Wyoming border south to Pikes Peak, about 150 miles (240 km).

This view will also give a good feel for the layout of the city, which can be confusing at first. Outside of the downtown area, the streets run north-south and east-west like most cities, but suddenly in the downtown area they seem to go every which way. It's thought that when General Larimer laid out the city streets

Picturesque homes in Georgetown, Colorado.

in 1858, he pointed them at Long's Peak, which rises 14,000 feet (4000 meters) to the northwest, giving them a northwest, southeast orientation. The impressive building with the white pillars directly in front of the Capitol is Denver's **City and County Building.** In a tradition that goes back to the turn of the century, the Christmas lighting display on and around the City and County Building rivals anything in the world. Between the Capitol and the City and County Building lies **Civic Center Park,** with large expanses of green lawns, gardens and shade trees — a nice place to rest the feet and stroll.

A short detour to the east of the State Capitol building is the **Molly Brown House and Museum**, an outstanding example of the way the upper middle classes lived at the turn of the century. Molly Tobin followed her brother to Leadville in 1884, where she met and married J.J. Brown. It was after the Browns moved to Denver that Molly sailed on the ill-fated voyage of the Titanic. According to legend she herded a group of immigrant women and children into a lifeboat. Dressed in a chinchilla cape and waving a small pistol she always carried, she kept the men at the oars rowing until rescue ships arrived, earning herself the nickname of "The Unsinkable Molly Brown." Between 13th and 8th avenues on or just off Pennsylvania Street are more than 40 historical houses and mansions dating from the turn of the century.

Museums and Dioramas

Going back to the State Capitol area, a block south of the Civic Center Park is the **Colorado Heritage Center,** a new museum which details Colorado's colorful past from the ancient Anasazi Indians, who lived at Mesa Verde, to the space-age skyscrapers that tower above the city. The highlight of the museum is the dioramas depicting old forts, Indians on a buffalo hunt, gold mining, and a particularly large and superbly crafted one of Denver as it appeared in 1860 before it was destroyed by fire and flood. This is also the place to see some of the finest old glass plate photographs ever taken of the West, in the collection of William Henry Jackson's work.

Heading west, around the Denver Public Library, is the **Denver Art Museum** designed by Gio Ponti of Italy. The 28-sided structure with a Corning gray glass tile "skin" and fortress-like roof is a work of art itself. It houses what may be the finest collection of Indian art in the world, as well as a complete range of other art exhibits. For those with a penchant for money and museums, this walking tour can be continued to the west and north, back towards the 16th Street Mall, to the **United States Mint** (free tours but no free samples), the **Denver Firefighters Museum** and the **Trianon Art Museum and Gallery,** which has a fine collection of 18th- and 19th- Century furniture and art from all over the world.

At 17th and Tremont streets is the triangular **Brown Palace Hotel,** a grande dame hotel built in 1892. Even if you don't stay there, it's worth a look at the nine-story atrium, topped by a Tiffany stained glass window, and the sumptuous lobby. You can still see the entrance to a tunnel that once led across the street to Denver's fanciest bordello and gambling hall, the Navarre. The tunnel was constructed so that Denver's finest couldn't be spotted entering that notorious den of iniquity. The Navarre now houses the new **Museum of Western Art,** a treasure trove of paintings and sculptures by such renowned Western artists as O'keeffe, Remington, Russell, Moran and Bierstadt.

Street Mall Shopping

The 16th Street Mall is the place for shopping, even if just window shopping, and perhaps some espresso at an outdoor cafe. Denver is justifiably proud of the new glass-enclosed **Tabor Center,** an architectural triumph filled with fancy shops and restaurants. Street musicians, jugglers, fountains, banners, hanging plants and brick walkways give the whole area a festive air. At the north end of the mall is the historical **Larimer Square,** where it all began in Denver. There are 18 renovated Victorian buildings, gas lamps, and an atmosphere reminiscent of Denver's early days. Larimer Square's Oktoberfest is a rollicking festival patterned after the one in Munich.

Yet another centerpiece of a glittering and sophisticated new Denver is the **Center for the Performing Arts,** the most complete performing arts center in the country, located a few blocks southwest of Larimer Square. The space age architecture is dazzling, and the **Boettcher Concert Hall** in-the-round is the first of its kind in the United States. The complex is larger than Lincoln Center in New York City. It houses four theaters, the nation's largest resident acting company, a film center, and one of the most advanced recording and voice research centers in the world.

Other Roadside Attractions

Three miles (4½ km) east of downtown Denver is the outstanding **Museum of Natural History.** As expected in a natural history museum, there are dozens of dioramas of animals from all over the world, including many Colorado species. But for kids − both old and young − the **Gates Planetarium** and the new **IMAX Theatre** are a special treat. You don't just look at solar systems and galaxies in the planetarium, you travel to them. If that doesn't take you far enough into space, stick around for one of the laser light shows. In the

ravellers
scape
om the city
the
ountains.

Greater Denver

Stapleton International Airport

Peoria St.
Chambers Rd.
Park Lane Park
Aurora
Ave.
E Colfax Ave.
70
wy.
E 6th Ave.
FB
Buckley Air National Guard Base
Havana St.
ameda Ave.
225
Mississippi Ave.
Chambers Rd.
le Drive
Hampden Ave.
Dam
Cherry Creek Lake State Rec. Area
Cherry Creek Lake
Airline Road

0   2,5   5 miles
0   50 m   1 km

IMAX Theatre are 30 specially designed speakers, the biggest movie projector made, and a large story screen, all of which combine to make you see, hear and feel the movies as if you were actually there – heaven on earth for movie buffs and hi-technophiles. Across City Park from the museum is **Denver's Zoo.**

For plant lovers the **Denver Botanic Gardens** have a nice selection of orchids and tropical plants as well as many special outdoor gardens. The Rock Alpine Garden is a great place to get a head start on identifying some of the plants you'll be seeing in the mountains.

Denver also has its share of amusement parks. **Elitch Gardens,** east of downtown, is the oldest and the biggest, with a roller coaster rated among the nation's top 10, a beautiful old carousel, and a summer stock theater named the **Elitch Theatre Company.** It's a pretty place, with plenty of flower gardens, fountains and pools. Others include **Lakeside Amusement Park,** north of Elitch, and **Heritage Square** in Golden, 12 miles (19 km) west of Denver, which has a reconstructed Colorado city from the 1870s, a narrow guage railroad and

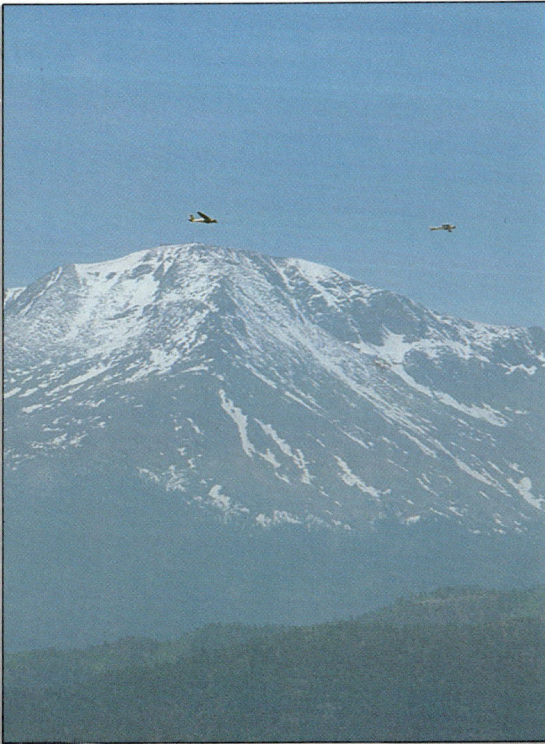

an alpine slide.

Coloradans, and Denverites in particular, are loyal and often fanatical fans of the Denver Bronco football team, which plays its home games in **Mile High Stadium,** located just west of the downtown area off Colfax Avenue. In fact, thanks to sellout attendance, lusty Colorado vocal cords, and inadvertently good acoustics, the stadium has the highest recorded crowd noise level in the country. For sports fans, there is **MacNichols Arena** where the Nuggets play basketball and the Flames play hockey, two dog racing tracks, and a horse racing track.

The fact that Denver is a major trade center for ranching is never more evident than in January when the National Western Stock Show brings thousands of cowboys into town for 10 days of rodeo, exhibits, shows and auctions.

Denver After Dark

There are more than 2,000 restaurants in Denver, and, like any big city, there's a little bit of everything and a few regional specialities. Steak is the most obvious specialty, but buffalo and venison are also frequently found on menus. Rocky Mountain rainbow trout is especially good if it's fresh – be sure to ask. Mexican food is Denver's international specialty, but the best authentic Mexican food is often found in unlikely looking neighborhood dives rather than the slick, downtown spots.

It's easy to dance the night away in Denver, thanks to an unusual zoning situation in **Glendale,** southeast of downtown Denver, that has a concentrated cluster of discos, saloons and restaurants in an area served by one vast parking lot. Disco live bands playing rock, country and swing; they're all there, from the glitter to the funk, with some uniquely Denver touches like two outdoor volleyball courts and in one bar, saddles instead of bar stools. Some other spots in the Denver metro area with a concentration of nightlife can be found along East Hampden Boulevard, South Parker Road, South Monaco Boulevard, and on East and West Colfax.

Outdoor concerts are something special at **Red Rocks Amphitheatre,** 12 miles (19 km) west of Denver. The 8,000 seats are built into a natural amphitheater of red rock walls that rise

400 feet (122 meters) on two sides, with a great view of Denver on a third side. Most of the top-name artists featured play pop, rock and country and Western, but the surrounding sandstone has also reverberated with the sounds of classical music and jazz.

South of Denver

The southernmost city in the Front Range is **Pueblo,** about 100 miles (160 m) south of Denver. This diminutive little city began its life as a trading post, conveniently located at the confluence of a number of trails coming out of the mountains and at the confluence of the Arkansas and Fountain rivers. Before New Mexico became a part of the United States, it was also the first watering hole north of the border, not far from Taos. When the Rio Grande railroad was routed through Pueblo, it became one of the largest ore smelting towns in the country, and to this day it remains a largely industrial city with the Colorado Fuel and Iron Mills (CF&I) the largest employer in the county. Pueblo is also a trading center for the agricultural and ranching areas which surround it, but it

remains something of a political, social and economic backwash. It's here that the adobe buildings of the southwest begin to appear, evidence of a large Hispanic population that increases as one goes south.

The high point of the year in Pueblo is the Colorado State Fair, held for 10 days in the last week of August through Labor Day. Thousands of people from all over the West come for the rodeo, horse racing and all the other attractions that go along with a state fair.

The Sangre De Cristos

There are some beautiful drives through the San Juan mountains to the east and south of Pueblo. At Walsenburg, south of Pueblo, State Highway 160 follows the Cucharas River, then forks. State 12 to the south continues along the river, through a series of mountain valleys, the small Spanish village of La Veta, over Cucharas Pass, and back down into arid lowlands. State 160 heads for **Great Sand Dunes National Monument,** an anomaly in the verdant San Luis Valley. The 10-mile (16-km) stretch of multi-hued, shifting sand can be explored by foot or by jeep. **Medano Creek,** which flows along the east side of the dunes, is a pleasant spot to hike or just cool the feet.

From Walsenburg it's possible to head for Pueblo, Colorado Springs, or Denver by back roads. One of the most scenic roads is via State 69, which goes northwest through the Huerfano River Valley and the San Isabel National Forest. (Ask at Walsenburg first about the road, since a section of it is gravel.) Just outside of Gardner is Gardner Cone, a large standing rock surrounded on two sides by piñon trees. The sweet, rich piñon nuts which ripen in the fall are a delicacy. From Gardner the road climbs to **Promontory Divide** with magnificent views of Crestone Peak and the Crestone Needles, part of the Sangre de Cristo (blood of Christ) mountain range. To the north is the green **Wet Mountain Valley.** The valleys on either side of this divide provide a study in cultural contrasts: the Huerfano river valley is largely Hispanic, with adobe buildings. In the Wet Mountain Valley, which was settled by Europeans, mostly Germans, are white wooden farmhouses, red barns and silos.

At **Westcliffe,** a classic Western ran-

Families pose at the Air Force Academy chapel.

ching town, turn east onto State 96. Silver Cliff was once Colorado's third largest town, but faded as quickly as it grew in the boom and bust mining days. This route goes back to Pueblo, or take State 67 north to Florence and Canon City (covered in "Canyon Country" chapter of this guide).

From Tourist Town to Air Force Base

Until World War II, Colorado Springs was a pretty and opulent little town. Then business leaders decided the bloom might eventually fade from the tourist rose and invited the military to settle there, luring them with 35,000 free acres (14,000 hectares). The military came in full force, first with **Fort Carson,** then with **Ent Air Force Base,** headquarters of the North American Air Defense Command, which dug itself into a massive and expensive cave in the side of Cheyenne Mountain. The last military branch to move in was the **Air Force Academy,** which, for the military, is unusually imaginative architecturally. One of the highlights of the Air Force Base is the falcon training. Beautiful falcons are raised (some from eggs) and trained by cadets. They perform often at the football games. Visitors can tour some of the buildings of the academy and watch the Cadet Wing march to lunch every weekday at noon.

Today Colorado Springs is an odd combination of unchecked urban sprawl, tourist traps, old castles and mansions, and lovely, exclusive neighborhoods. There are literally dozens of attractions from the **Hall of the Presidents Wax Museum** and the **Cheyenne Mountain Zoo** to the **American Numismatic Museum** (of old coins, medals, etc.) and Flying W Chuckwagon Supper and Western Show. The **Van Briggle Pottery Studio** conducts pottery demonstrations and tours of the studio throughout the day. **Seven Falls** and the **Western Museum of Mining and Industry** are two attractions that should also be included in your itinerary. The high points of the natural attractions include the **Garden of the Gods,** 700 acres (280 hectares) of huge standing rocks the Utes believed were invading giants turned to stone by the Great Manitou, and of course, **Pike's Peak.**

Two Air Force cadets show how to train falcons.

Pike's Peak Country

Cripple Creek and Colorado Springs can be approached from Canon City by a dirt road that's a continuation of State 67 – ask first in Canon City about road conditions, though. On the backside of **Pike's Peak,** nestled in a valley created by a long-extinct volcano, is one of Colorado's most famous towns. **Cripple Creek** was the site of one of the largest gold strikes in the world and once supported a population of about 50,000. It now hovers between the status of a ghost town and a tourist attraction, uncertain of its identity but possessing a quiet charm. Some of the residents still remember the old mining days, others have moved there for the small town atmosphere and the beauty of the surrounding mountains.

A narrow gauge train passes through the deserted mining camps that surround Cripple Creek, on its way to Anaconda, one of the largest of the old mines. At the Mollie Kathleen gold mine it's possible to descend 1,000 feet (300 meters) in a miner's cage, to see the conditions the early miners worked in and the equipment they used. There's still plenty of gold around too. A couple of places in Cripple Creek give gold panning lessons – you never know, you might strike it rich!

The **Imperial Hotel** is a good reason to spend the night in Cripple Creek. The only original Cripple Creek hotel still standing, the Imperial has many of its original furnishings. But the high point of a stay there is the **Victorian Melodrama Theatre** (when the villain appears the audience hisses), one of the best in the country.

Like so many Rocky Mountain towns, **Colorado Springs** began as a mining town, but it soon became Colorado's first and finest destination resort, a haven for the wealthy seeking health and beauty or a cure for respiratory illnesses in the dry mountain air and hot mineral springs at the "Saratoga of the West." Railroad magnate William Jackson Palmer literally created the town in the 1870s, envisioning it as a utopia inhabited by teetotaling, well-to-do, educated citizens. Thanks to some judicious advertising there was a healthy English population in the town, giving it snob appeal. By the early 1900s the town had begun to open its door to

Waterplay in the hot springs of Colorado.

tourists of all classes, a change initiated through the efforts of Spencer Penrose, a wealthy developer and one-man chamber of commerce. In the span of a decade he had an auto road and a cog railway built to the top of Pike's Peak; constructed the Cheyenne Mountain Highway; bought and renovated the Broadmoor Hotel and Casino; built a zoo, a polo field, an indoor arena; donated libraries and civic buildings; and advertised with a flamboyant zeal that promised success.

Manitou Springs is an old spa town perched in a valley above Colorado Springs, near the mineral springs whose name it bears. Many of its houses and streets hug the steep hillsides, and much of the original Victorian architecture remains. In terms of attractions, Manitou Springs is essentially an extension of Colorado Springs, with its **Buffalo Bill Wax Museum, Miramont Castle, Cave of the Winds** and the cable car ride to the top of **Mount Manitou.** The cog railway to the top of Pike's Peak begins at Manitou Springs.

There are two back roads through the mountains from Colorado Springs to Denver, both very scenic. Either continue on State 67 on a narrow, winding State 24 then north on State 285, which is a major road.

North and West of Denver

The metropolis of the Front Range in Colorado extends north from Denver to Fort Collins, only about 50 miles (80 km) from the Wyoming border and Cheyenne. **Golden**, just west of Denver, is best known for the **Coors Brewery.** Free tours – and samples – are available. Above Golden on Lookout Mountain is **Buffalo Bill Cody's Grave and Museum,** with lots of interesting memorabilia and history, and excellent views of Denver. Railroad buffs will enjoy the **Colorado Railroad Museum,** also located in Golden. Nearby **Evergreen** is a quiet, attractive little town, mainly catering to people who have second homes there, including a few celebrities. **Evergreen Lake** is a pleasant place for swimming and boating in the summer and ice skating in the winter.

One of the most scenic loop drives in Colorado begins in Golden on State 6, which winds up Clear Creek Canyon

Mountain traffic twists through a rocky pass.

along an old railroad bed and through many short, dark tunnels. State 119, which branches off to the right leads to Central City and a back road to Boulder through Rollinsville and Nederland.

Central City is one of the best preserved of the old Rocky Mountain mining towns. The huge strike there was nearly Denver's undoing when most of the population dropped whatever they were doing to head for the "richest square mile on earth." Many of those who struck it rich built the impressive and picturesque stone and brick buildings that still perch on the sides of the narrow valley. The narrow streets, plank sidewalks and beautifully renovated buildings are very effective in taking the traveller back in time. The **Teller House,** where President Grant, Oscar Wilde, Baron de Rothschild and a host of other rich and famous names once stayed, is a Historic Landmark hotel and a great place to spend the night or just have a good meal at reasonable prices. Don't miss the famous **Face Bar,** featuring Madeleine's face on the barroom floor. The Opera House next door has a dinner theater during the winter months, and in July an opera with some outstanding productions plays there.

True to the rollicking Rocky Mountain spirit, Central City holds a no-holds-barred celebration in June called Madam Lou Bunch Day in honor of the "sporting house girls" of a bygone era. The Original Bed Race is held on Main Street, and in the evening locals and visitors alike don their finest attire for the Madam and Miners Ball.

Backtracking to Interstate 70, **Idaho Springs** was first a mining town, then a health spa, centered around the hot springs which once brought Ute Indians from near and far. The **Indian Springs Resort** is the place to enjoy the healing hot water of the springs, which are funneled through two tunnels underneath the hotel, one for men and one for women. It's also possible to rent a private bath. The hotel is not fancy, the rates are low, and there are often good country bands playing there on weekends.

About 20 miles (32 km) west of Idaho Springs off I-70 is **Georgetown,** yet another well-preserved old mining town with quiet, narrow streets, well-preserved Victorian buildings and a

A ranger makes his rounds in the Garden of the Gods, Manitou Springs (CO).

host of gift shops. The narrow gauge railway, the Georgetown loop, runs a precipitous route between Georgetown and Silver Plume, and it is among the best of the narrow gauge rides in the state. A narrow, switchbacking road just north of town (not for the faint of heart) leads up to **Guanella Pass** through a number of Rocky Mountain life zones from lush green meadows and aspen groves, through conifer forests, to the sparse vegetation of the alpine tundra at the top. This is a good drive for plant lovers and for day hikes to the surrounding peaks.

Boulder may also have the largest concentration of brains in the Rockies. From 1876 until just a few decades ago, Boulder was a quiet little university town with few paved roads and lots of scenic views. Then the natural beauty of the setting and the convenience of a large university attracted NCAR (the National Center for Atmospheric Research), IBM, the Ball Corporation, Rockwell International and a dozen other large, clean-industry corporations. Neodata Services takes care of subscriptions for dozens of national magazines. Many medium-sized hi-tech electronics firms have located in Boulder, and the city is overflowing with small publishing houses. Celestial Seasonings went from a home style operation to a major corporation in less than five years and radically changed the tea drinking habits of Americans.

Boulder is also a cross section of the West in that it's perceived as a place of opportunity and a young, energetic, optimistic town. The prevailing open-minded attitudes of the populace have encouraged the growth of holistic health clinics, health foodstores and other hallmarks of alternative lifestyles which proliferate and thrive in Boulder alongside a passion for the latest in hi-tech, from electronics to bicycle parts.

Back at Idaho Springs is State 40, one end of the famous **Peak to Peak Highway,** a long and spectacular road over Berthoud Pass, past Berthoud Ski Area, Winter Park Ski Area, through Granby and past the Great Lakes of Colorado — **Grand Lake, Shadow Mountain,** and **Granby Reservoir** (see "Mountain Towns" for more details). From Granby the road becomes State 34 and follows the North Fork of the

Window shopping in Central City, Colorado.

Colorado River through the green and lovely Kawuneeche Valley, up to Rocky Mountain National Park and Trail Ridge Road, the highest paved road in America. From there the road descends to Estes Park, back to the Front Range.

Estes Park is the gateway to Rocky Mountain National Park, a busy little Western town in the summer. The beauty of the valley, which is surrounded by the snowcapped peaks of the Continental Divide, is unmatched. In the late 1800s the Earl of Dunraven purchased the Estes Park valley with hopes of making it a big game hunting park and preserving its natural beauty. His dream didn't come true, but a few years later, thanks largely to the efforts of naturalist Enos Mills, **Rocky Mountain National Park** (for details, see "Rocky Mountain National Park" chapter) was officially established. On winter weekends hundreds of Coloradans head for Estes Park and the mountains above for cross-country skiing.

A pleasant stop en route to Wyoming is **Fort Collins,** a busy, pretty, unspoiled little city that did indeed begin as a fort. But for most of its life, Fort Collins has been a prosperous agricultural and university city. The sugar beet industry put Fort Collins on the map and **Colorado State University** adds a touch of sophistication. To the south, **Loveland** is probably most remembered on Valentine's Day when hundreds of thousands of people send heartfelt greetings through the post office there. A few miles farther south, **Longmont** is a typically Western town, with a long, wide Main Street and lots of pickup trucks and cowboy hats in evidence.

Boulder

Boulder is a microcosm of trends in Denver, or some say, it's the other way around. Though it has the feeling of a town, it has to be called a city these days, with all the amenities of one and then some. As a stroll down the Boulder Mall will attest, the city has a large population of the young and the fit — jogging, bicycling, skiing and aerobics classes are the norm. The city caters to this passion for exercise with over 30 miles (48 km) of jogging and bicycling paths, and with bike lanes on major streets. Many more miles of hiking trails criss-cross the greenbelt, an undeveloped oasis at the edge of town ex-

tending into the foothills. Beginning rock climbers come from all over to challenge the Flatirons, the uplifted red rock that towers over the city to the west.

The arts thrive in Boulder. The Colorado Music Festival sponsors classical concerts in the outdoor amphitheater at **Chautaqua** every summer, but there is also a year-round philharmonic orchestra, half a dozen theaters including the university-sponsored Shakespeare Festival in the summer, a mime school, bands, chamber choirs, a center for the visual arts, and dozens of galleries — the **White Horse Gallery** is nationally known for its collection of Indian and Western art. For the best in jazz, the **Blue Note** has a longstanding tradition of attracting top-name musicians. The **Hi-Lo Inn** is a funky Western bar with live music ranging from swing to Country Western and a lively dance floor. There are a dozen or so singles bars hopping with live music and disco seven nights a week.

From old time music halls and mining towns, to bustling cities, you'll find it all in Colorado's Front Range — the most exciting part of the state!

Below, Garden of the Gods in Colorado Springs; right, canoeing on Grand Lake.

184

COLORADO MOUNTAIN TOWNS

The Continental Divide and its mountain ranges occupy two-thirds of the state of Colorado, making most communities on the western slope mountain towns. The following tour will encompass the highlights — the most picturesque, historically interesting, and scenic mountain towns of Colorado, as well as some particularly panoramic back roads.

Back roads are for the adventurous — dirt or gravel roads in the Rockies should be approached with caution. Ruts, washboards and washouts can be rough on any vehicle. Sturdiness, reliability and reasonably high axles are a must for all of the back roads mentioned in this section. High water at creek crossings and mud slides can also be a problem. Ask locally before travelling on them and start off with a full tank of gas.

There's a certain amount of etiquette involved in travelling on back roads: uphill vehicles have the right of way on narrow roads; closed gates should always be securely refastened; slow down for horseback riders and hikers — some horses aren't used to traffic, and nobody likes to eat the dust raised by cars.

Never drive off the road; alpine tundra and meadows are delicate and may take decades to recover from tire scars. It's illegal to pick columbine flowers; they're on the endangered species list and, besides, they wilt almost immediately after picking and so will you when you could be fined $300 for doing so.

The Great Lakes of Colorado

One of the best ways to begin a tour of the Colorado Rockies is with Rocky Mountain National Park (dealt with in detail in the National Parks Supplement section).

Granby and its surrounding lakes are the southwestern gateway to the park. The log buildings around the lakes are mostly summer homes. At one time, Granby was a year-round supply depot for miners prospecting in the surrounding mountains. Grand Lake, Shadow Mountain Reservoir, Lake Granby and

Colorado

the Willow Creek Reservoir are a series of interconnected lakes known as the "Great Lakes of Colorado."

Grand Lake, the highest yacht anchorage in the United States, is dotted with boats all summer and, frequently, a regatta of some sort is going on, sponsored by the local yacht club. Windsurfer, sailboat and motorboat rentals are all available.

A number of legends haunt Grand Lake, which is called Spirit Lake by the Utes. According to one legend, when the Utes were attacked by the Cheyennes and Arapahoes, they sent their women and children out to the middle of the lake on a large raft for safekeeping. During one great battle, the Utes won, but a violent thunderstorm created a maelstrom of wind and waves on the lake, drowning all the women and children. The mists that rise on the lake are, legend says, the restless spirits of those women and children.

South of Granby, U.S. Highway 40 goes either southeast to the ski area of Winter Park, or northwest through Hot Sulphur Springs to Steamboat Springs. This is a spectacular drive, first along the uppermost reaches of the great Col-

orado River, past the mining and ranching town of Kremmling, then a steady climb up and over Rabbit Ears Pass (look for the rock formation that gave the pass its name) to descend into the Yampa Valley and Steamboat.

Cowboy Country

Steamboat Springs is a divided town in more ways than one. At one end is the ski mountain and the dense clusters of condominiums and shops that surround the base. A few miles down the road, one arrives in Steamboat Springs proper, a genuine one-street western town with the attendant cowboys, farmers and saloons.

A series of ads sponsored by a condominium development company which included the promise that they would "take the cowboy hat off Steamboat" was met with little enthusiasm by locals and visitors — Steamboat's cowboy image is an integral part of its charm.

Seasonal celebrations, such as the Winter Carnival during the second week of February, have the usual resort-style parades and races, but are particularly fun because of enthusiastic

Preceding pages, the snow covered slopes of Steamboat (CO). Below, skiers take the lift to the top of the run.

local participation in such events as a cross-country skiing and muzzle loading biathalon, and ski-joring contests down Main Street in which the contestant on skis is towed by a galloping horse.

Winter and summer, something's always happening at the city recreation complex on the edge of town, which has a ski jumping complex, ice-skating rink, rodeo grounds, tennis courts, softball, rugby and soccer fields and a racetrack. A ride up the gondola at the ski area provides panoramic views of the mountains to the north and east, and the Flat Tops Wilderness to the southwest.

Steamboat Springs is in many ways the perfect Rocky Mountain playground in the summer. With Routt National Forest to the north and east, a hiker or horseback rider could theoretically go all the way to the Wyoming border and beyond without hitting a town or a road.

Good jumping-off points for hikers are to the north at Slavonia or at the South Fork of the Elk campgrounds at the edge of the Zirkel Wilderness. **Hahns Peak Village,** 24 miles (40 km) north State Highway on 129, is an old gold mining camp that was once the Routt County seat. Nearby are a host of campgrounds and **Steamboat Lake,** which is apt to be dotted with colorful sails in the summer. The Yampa and Elk rivers provide good fishing, kayaking and tubing. **Fish Creek Falls** is a 283-foot-high (85 meter) series of waterfalls. To get there, take Third Street to Fish Creek Falls Road, then drive four miles (six km) east. As the name indicates there are a number of hot springs around Steamboat. Ask at the Chamber of Commerce for those that are open to the public.

South of Steamboat, State 131 winds along the Yampa River through a beautiful ranching valley. **Oak Creek** used to be inhabited by a large hippie population that mingled somewhat uneasily with retired miners and ranchers. **Phippsburg** is an old railroad town with a good cafe. Stop in at the Antlers Cafe & Bar in **Yampa** for a dyed-in-the-wool taste of the Old West. This used to be a major stage stop between Wolcott and Steamboat, and is now a local hangout, complete with a stuffed golden eagle, old oil paintings, and a bar that's seen a lot of history go by. Farther down the road at **Toponas** is another relic, a

Experienced windsurfers head their sails into the wind.

general store called the People's Store.

At Toponas the road forks, and State 134 heads back east over Gore Pass. The pass and the Gore Range were named after Sir George Gore, an Irish nobleman who hired mountain man and scout Jim Bridger to lead one of the earliest hunting parties in Colorado in 1855. The party consisted of more than 40 men, and a long parade of carts, wagons, horses, dogs and oxen. Unfortunately, Gore's name was fitting, for he and his party reputedly killed uncounted thousands of buffalo, bear, deer, elk and antelope. The Ute Indians were almost driven to kill Gore, so worried were they that their winter meat supply would be depleted by his careless and bloody killing spree.

Summit County and Beyond

The Gore Range continues south to the Summit County area, which can be reached either by continuing south on State 131 or by heading south at Kremmling on State 9. **Summit County** is a series of valleys off Interstate 70 between the Eisenhower tunnel and Vail pass, encompassing the resorts of **Dillon, Keystone, Breckenridge** and **Copper Mountain.**

The town of Dillon grew up around **Dillon Reservoir,** one of the largest bodies of water in Colorado and another haven for boating fans in the Rockies. Keystone and Copper Mountain grew up around the ski areas that rise above them.

Breckenridge bills itself as the "oldest authentic Victorian mining town in Colorado." The town does indeed have many colorfully restored Victorian homes, shops and western saloons, surrounded by modern hotels and condominiums that fill up during the winter. Breckenridge also has hiking, horseback riding and festivals that bring so many people to the Rockies in the summer.

When Colorado was made a state in 1876, Breckenridge was somehow left out of the process. The miffed town elders finally decided to become an official part of the state and the country in 1936, on the condition that the town be a "free and independent kingdom three days each year." And so, for three days every August, visitors and residents of Breckenridge are in "no-man's land" —

Late season snow clings to the hollows of the Red Mountain Pass from Ouray to Silverton (CO).

naturally there's a parade, barbecue and dance to celebrate the event.

Two roads head south out of Breckenridge, both scenic and historic drives. One is gravel, crossing the Continental Divide at Boreas Pass, where it drops into South Park. Many remnants of the mining days are visible on this road, which used to be a major stage route and narrow gauge railroad track. State 9 is the other road, crossing the Continental Divide at Hoosier Pass, then dropping down into Alma and Fairplay. Mount Silverheels is named after a dance-hall girl who bravely nursed the miners of Alma through a smallpox epidemic, when nobody else would come to help, before she mysteriously disappeared.

State 9 follows the South Platte River into **Fairplay,** a small town of log cabins whose local hero is a burro named Prunes. Burros were indispensable workers and companions to early miners. Prunes lived in Fairplay for all of his 63 years, and when he died, a monument was built in his honor. When his owner died a few years later, he was buried next to his burro.

During the last weekend of July, the town of Fairplay sponsors the World Championship Pack Burro Race over Mosquito Pass. This hilarious event is publicized by a bumper sticker that says, "Get Your Ass Over the Pass." The **South Park City Museum** in Fairplay is a street of old buildings preserved from the days when Fairplay was a boom town, complete with a general store stocked with patent medicines.

The Roads to Leadville

From the Fairplay area, there are two ways to Leadville. The back way is over Weston Pass, a beautiful drive, but the road can be virtually impassable at times, so check locally before trying it. The other road is U.S. 285, which goes through the South Park Valley to Buena Vista, then north on U.S. 24 along the Arkansas River and past the Collegiate Range to the west. Every year, alumni groups gather to climb their respective peaks – Yale, Harvard, Princeton, Columbia – but one doesn't have to be an Ivy Leaguer to enjoy this magnificent section of the Sawatch Range.

South of Buena Vista is Salida, and on the other side of Poncha Pass is the San Luis Valley, flanked on one side by the Sangre de Cristo (Blood of Christ) mountains and on the other the San Juans. The **San Luis Valley** is a long, flat, rich ranching area with the protective mountains rising steeply on either side. **Salida** is a pretty little town, but the drive between Monarch Pass, west on Highway 50 and Salida is one of the most scenic anywhere.

The halcyon days of **Leadville** are in the past. It was once, thanks to its abundant gold mines, one of Colorado's biggest, richest, busiest cities. Mining magnate H.A.W. Tabor spent fortunes erecting the still-standing stone buildings; presidents, royalty and celebrities walked the streets; railroad and stage lines were busy and profitable.

Active or even semi-active mining towns are not really pretty places, and Leadville is no exception. Huge slag piles, crude shacks and surrounding mountains denuded of timber do not contribute to the charm of a town. But the panoramas from the town are breathtaking. Leadville is trying hard to recapture its past, and has a number of museums worth stopping to see, among them **Healy House** and the **Dexter Cabin.** The **Matchless Cabin** is a sad

Left, seasons greetings from Keystone, Colorado, in ski country; right, a snow bunny checks out the skiing action.

reminder of the woman who inspired the opera *The Ballad of Baby Doe*, Leadville is still a mining town, but, these days, most of the digging activity takes place 12 miles (19 km) north at the huge Climax molybdenum mines.

Vail Village

Vail is reached by heading north on U.S. 24 from Leadville over Tennessee Pass. **Vail** and the nearby brand-new towns of Avon and Beaver Creek were built purely for their fabulous skiing — there is still nothing in the United States that compares to Vail's back ski bowls. The modern little village of Vail has grown from a wide spot in the road to a chic resort that attracts celebrities and money like a magnet.

Though the usual Rocky Mountain outdoor attractions are better found elsewhere in the summer, Vail has made up for it with two months packed with glamorous events. The Summer Vail Kick-Off Celebration during the first week in June does just that, with gondola rides to the top of the mountain, lawn parties, barbecues, music, golf and tennis matches. The fun and glitter continues throughout the summer with "It's a Small World," a convocation of puppeteers from around the world; the Coors International Bicycle Classic; a Pro-Celebrity Tennis Classic at Beaver Creek; a Big Band Swing Festival; and much, much more.

Into the Heart of the Rockies

To reach Aspen from Leadville, head south on State 82, which passes Twin Lakes, then heads up and over the Continental Divide via Independence Pass. For those with a fascination for wolves, the **Inn at Twin Lakes** serves hearty, basic meals and is home to a few wolves, which are sometimes chained to the bar inside.

The name **Aspen** is universally recognized enough to have deserved a special chapter of its own (see "Aspen Mystique" in Features section). A half-dozen campgrounds and trail heads veer off State 82 as it winds its tortuous way down into the Roaring Fork Valley from Independence Pass. The Grottoes and the Devil's Punch Bowl, strange formations and caves carved out of the rock by the Roaring Fork River, are great places at which to picnic and swim

(the Devil's Punch Bowl can be dangerous at high water).

Once in Aspen, hikers can head out in almost any direction to find unpopulated trails, streams jumping with rainbow trout, hanging lakes and challenging rock faces. The **Maroon Bells,** twin peaks towering above a small lake, is one of the most photographed scenes in the Rockies. Reservations must be made well in advance for a space at the Maroon Bells campgrounds.

Behind the Bells is a vast wilderness area that would take months to thoroughly explore on foot. On the other side of the Elk Range, to the west, is Castle Creek. At the end of this road is **Ashcroft,** an old ghost town that has groomed cross-country trails in the winter. The **Pine Creek Cookhouse** at Ashcroft serves simple but superb lunches for very reasonable prices. For a day hike in Aspen, nothing beats **Hunter Creek,** a hanging valley and ghost town just east of Red Mountain.

Heading west out of Aspen on State 82, turn left at Carbondale, where Mount Sopris rises majestically out of the valley. Here State 133 winds south and west along the Crystal River.

Wheeler Opera House, Colorado.

Across the river is an old railroad bed with occasional chunks of marble scattered along it. These are droppings from the mine at Marble.

But first there's **Redstone.** This little town began as a somewhat eccentric utopian community, envisioned by a mining magnate who built the nearby **Redstone Castle.** His dream was a company town where everyone would share and nobody would ever go hungry — while he, as feudal lord, ruled from his castle. The castle is open for tours and is reportedly haunted. The **Redstone Inn** has been renovated and serves excellent food.

Still on State Highway 133

Farther up the road, **Marble** once had a population of 2,000, and supplied the marble for the Lincoln Memorial and the Tomb of the Unknown Soldier in Washington D.C. The handful of log cabins there now are summer refuges, and nearby is the base for an Outward Bound school. The marble mine, a few miles away, is a surrealistic, cavernous, echoing hole in the mountain, worth taking the trouble to hike up to.

Continuing on State 133, the road winds up and over McClure Pass, and eventually into a valley that, blessed with warm weather and rich soil, produces some of the tastiest peaches in the world. Paonia, Delta and Hotchkiss are filled with fields and fruit orchards — this is the place to stock up on cherries, apples, peaches, and vegetables.

The dirt road over Schofield Pass, from Marble to Crested Butte, is strictly for four-wheel-drive vehicles and even then, is frequently impassable. From Paonia, there's a reasonably well-maintained dirt road that goes over Kebler Pass and then east into Crested Butte, or continues south to Gunnison over Ohio Pass.

Crested Butte is one of the few ski resorts that has retained much of its small town atmosphere, thanks to its isolated location. As the crow flies, it's just over the Continental Divide from Aspen, but by car, Crested Butte is a long way from anywhere. Best known for the copious amounts of powder that fall on its ski slopes during the winter, the town also offers all the requisite Rocky Mountain attractions during the summer.

A shadowy view of Maroon Bells Peak, Colorado.

Crested Butte drew national attention a few years back, when a large mining company decided to move in and extract valuable molybdenum from Mount Evans which towers above the town and gives it a name. Knowing that Crested Butte would never be the same with a gigantic bite taken out of the mountain and massive slag piles heaped up below, a grassroots movement was organized to stop the mining company. Money and expertise poured in from all over the state and the nation, and after a long tedious battle, the mountain stayed intact.

At the Top of the World

Heading south now, and skipping past Gunnison which is covered elsewhere (see Canyon Country), are the idyllic mountain towns of Ouray, Telluride and Silverton. **Ouray,** named after a Chief of the Utes, is a high mountain valley with steep mountainsides rising all around it. The town is small, friendly and quaint, with a couple of hot springs to soak in. The **Beaumont Hotel, Wright's Opera Hall,** the **Elk Lodge** and the **Western Hotel** are all buildings of historical value.

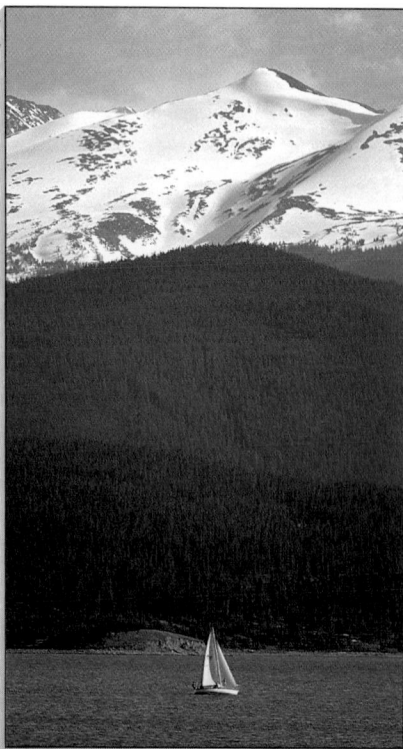

The surrounding mountains hold some of the most spectacular hiking and jeeping country in the Rockies, with more 14,000-plus-foot (4,200-meter) peaks than anywhere else in the continental United States. East of town is a wonderful campground nestled into a huge natural amphitheater.

A good day hike is up the trails of **Box Canyon,** along Canyon Creek, which plunges dramatically down to the valley in a series of waterfalls.

South of Ouray, along the "Million Dollar Highway" (named for the low-grade ores that it was found to be paved with after the fact) and over Red Mountain Pass, is **Silverton,** supposedly named when a miner claimed that "we might not have much else, but we got a ton of silver!" It is famous for the narrow gauge railroad that transports people between Silverton and Durango. The coal-fired locomotives chug and puff along the Animas River on the same line that was once used to haul $300 million in silver and gold out of the mountains.

Backtracking north on U.S. 550, turn onto State 62 at Ridgway, where the old buildings are reminders of busy mining days. A few miles past Ridgway is a very special spot called the Dallas Creek East Fork campground, usually uncrowded, with Mount Sneffels in the distance. State 62 continues over Dallas Divide to Placerville (where the road to Telluride forks off).

Telluride is another ski resort that has remained small and charming because of its remote location. The steep narrow valley, with snowcapped peaks at one end, is reminiscent of Switzerland. There are beautifully restored old buildings and friendly local bars. The bank in Telluride once had the dubious distinction of being robbed by Butch Cassidy.

At the end of the valley, a steep, switch-backing road that eventually becomes very rough leads up to **Bridal Veil Falls,** which plummets dramatically off a cliff. Another spectacular waterfall cascades in **Bear Creek Canyon.** Telluride's ski slopes haven't earned it as much renown as its summer events have-the Telluride Jazz Festival, Bluegrass Festival and Film Festival are internationally known and well-attended events. Reservations are needed and tickets bought months in advance.

Left, scenic sailing on Lake Dillon, Colorado; right, a typical January day at the Snowmass ski resort, Colorado.

THE ASPEN MYSTIQUE

Aspen has a glamour and mystique all its own. This special quality is more than the jetsetters and celebrities who make it their second home, more than the strict zoning regulations which have kept out the "shake-and-bake Bavarian village" look of other resorts. There's something special about the valley itself that has been inspiring philosophical visionaries and bartenders alike to settle in Aspen for more than a hundred years.

How long the Ute Indians lived in the Roaring Fork Valley before the white man

state. Leadville was already a well-established town when the first strike in the Roaring Fork Valley was made near Independence Pass (where the ghost town of Independence still stands). Even today, the road over Independence Pass from Leadville is tortuous and high enough to be closed most of the year. In Frank L. Wentworth's book, *Aspen on the Roaring Fork,* is a description of one resourceful settler's trip over the pass. Henry Gillespie asked Henry Staats to assess some of his claims in Aspen, but was afraid the trip from Leadville might

made his appearance is not known, but they fought to keep it, killing 11 of the valley's first settlers (who named it Ute City) and an army troop investigating the attack. But the lure of rich silver veins overcame the fear of Indian attacks, and the miners quickly edged them out by sheer force of numbers and a series of massacres.

The Sherman Silver Purchase Act in 1878 inspired settlers to risk the wrath of Indians and explore the Rockies of western Colorado. Under the act, the federal Treasury Department bought silver ever month and had it coined into silver dollars. The rush for gold, that originally populated the Front Range of Colorado, now became a silver rush that began to populate the rest of the

be impossible because the snow was so deep. He reported that many people were on the trail to Aspen, and some of the them had been trying to get there for three weeks. Staats assured Gillespie he could reach the town in three days.

He had five wooden boats made which he and his men pulled up and over the pass. "Then, we began to get into the crowd of people trying to get to Aspen. There was not a man among them realized that night was the time to travel over soft snow. There were over a hundred men along that trail in 10 or 12 miles rigs of all kinds, sleds, snow-shoes, pieces of tin and baggage of all descriptions. About one-half of the outfits were going back to Twin Lakes to get more grub. The trail looked like a herd of cattle had passed over it. We made camp, borrowed two or three frying pans and made up enough bread to last us through.

"Word was passed around that we traveled at night, so quite a number waited until we got ready about 10 or 11 o'clock. We struck bare ground about 10 miles down the trail and had hard sledding from there on."

As so often happened in the early mining towns, most prospectors staked claims, then

per as well), Wheeler virtually took over the fledgling town. He surveyed the mining camp, laid out a townsite, renamed it Aspen after the trees on the surrounding mountainsides, staked out many claims, then went on a lecture tour to promote the many virtues of Aspen.

Men like Jerome B. Wheeler (no relation to Clark Wheeler), President of Macy's in New York, saw long-term potential in the town and put as much into it as he got out of it. Wheeler was lucky enough to be a partner in one of Aspen's richest mines, the Mollie

sold out to wealthy Easterners, who had the capital to open a mine. Many of the street and building names in Aspen are reminders of these early developers and promoters.

Gillespie went to Washington to drum support for mail service, a telegraph line and a road into town. B. Clark Wheeler made a 17-day trek over the pass on snowshoes after hearing rumors of the rich veins of silver in the valley. Being a natural leader and promoter (many said a swindler and claim jum-

Preceding pages, nightlife in Aspen, Colorado. Left, a solitary skier slides through a clearing; and right, a sleepy Aspen neighborhood awakes to a blanket of snow.

Gibson. With that bonanza, he built a smelter, a bank, an opera house and a hotel. He was also involved in a marble quarry, coal and iron mines and a ranch. By 1889, Aspen boasted a population of 8,000, the most advanced mining equipment available, 10 churches, two schools, two railroads, three daily newspapers, and a county courthouse. Handsome brick buildings housed shops, and splendid Victorian homes lined the streets of the residential areas. Even then, Aspen had a certain panache, a sense of sophistication. The wives of the silver barons formed a literary and a temperance society. Their husbands built polo grounds and a race track. D.R.C. Brown, father of one of the founders of the Aspen Skiing Corporation, started an electric company, making Aspen the first town in Colorado with electric street lights.

Waking up from the Silver Dream....

For all of its respectability, however, Aspen was still a mining town. The miners worked shifts around-the-clock; in fact, it was torch-bearing miners coming off a late shift on Aspen Mountain who started Aspen's tradition of skiing down the mountain in torchlight parades. Plenty of saloons catered to the miners, and a red-light district flourished on Durant Avenue.

When the U.S. government repealed the Sherman Act and de-monetized silver in 1893, Aspen was the largest silver camp in

developing skiing as a recreational sport in Aspen in 1936. They built a lodge below Mount Hayden, part of the ridge between Castle and Maroon creeks, and planned to build another at Ashcroft. Even while Flynn was touring the country to raise money for a ski lift, tourists were coming to ski, climbing the mountains under their own power. Famous European skier Andre Roch moved to town, formed the Aspen Ski Club, and gave lessons. By 1938, a crude WPA-built tow was taking the first of Aspen's recreational skiers up the now-famous Aspen Mountain.

World War II put a stop to the early dreams of Aspenites. Billy Fiske became a pilot and was shot down and killed. His death ended the development of Mount

the world and the busiest town between Denver and Salt Lake City. Because the town was completely dependant on silver for its economic well-being, most of the mines shut down, banks and businesses closed, and the population decreased by 1,000 almost overnight. People continued to leave steadily over the next few decades, and by 1930, less than 600 people lived in the sleepy little town. It was a shadow of its former self, with rows of empty houses available almost for the taking.

...And New Dreams of Skiing and Culture

Three young dreamers named Ted Ryan, Tom Flynn and Billy Fiske the potential for

Hayden as a ski resort. But as fate would have it, the U.S Army's 10th Mountain Infantry Division ski troops trained at Camp Hale near Leadville. Word quickly got around that Aspen was a lively little town with good skiing, and many went there on leave. Among those to return to Aspen after the war with big plans were Freidl Pfeifer and Steve Knowlton, who ran the Golden Horn restaurant for many years. Pfeifer joined forces with Chicago businessman

Left, Windstar's founder and singer John Denver; and right, a magician/bartender in Snowmass (CO) entertains his patrons.

202

Walter Paepcke to lease D.R.C. Brown's mining claims on Aspen Mountain, and the Aspen Skiing Corporation was born.

Meanwhile, Walter Paepcke and his wife, Elizabeth, had even more grandiose plans, which, ultimately, were to make Aspen the cultural mecca it is today. Paepcke was not only an astute and highly successful businessman, but an intellectual and a visionary as well. He formed the Aspen Company and bought real estate, including the Hotel Jerome and the Wheeler Opera House. The Jerome was modernized and the Opera House was opulently refurbished under the direction of Bauhaus designer Herbert Bayer. Paepcke wrote to potential investors, "Definite plans are underway to provide opportunities for man's complete life – to earn a livelihood, to enjoy nature and physical recreation, with facilities at hand for his enjoyment of art, music and education." Aspen's mandate hasn't changed since Walter Paepcke wrote that in the late 1940s.

Oil-rich Texans and New York City socialites followed the celebrities, and the drug dealers followed the money. And yet, the fast lane is a very small part of what Aspen is all about. One may catch a glimpse of a Kennedy on the chair lift, or bump into Robert Wagner grocery shopping at City Market, but the jetset is actually there infrequently and plays a very small part in the day-to-day life of the community.

Though drug dealers are arrested with some frequency, the actual crime rate is extremely low. Most Aspen residents with families feel there's no better place to bring up a child, with the excellent school system, the emphasis on outdoor recreation and fitness, and the cultural events available. The very wealth of activities, events, celebrations and outdoor recreation should make it obvious to even a transient visitor that most Aspenites are just too busy, and work too hard, to be part of the non-stop party circuit envisioned by many to be the Aspen way of life.

Nevertheless, like all resort communities, there are places to see and be seen, and certain rules of etiquette. Little Nells and The Tippler are après ski favorites for both tourists and locals. Abetones, Andres and the Ute City Banque have never gotten rave reviews for their very expensive food, but the ambience is all glamour and glitter for the après ski crowd. Locals tend to favor the Hotel Jerome Bar, Little Annies (the barbecue is excellent), and the Red Onion. Andre's disco and The Paragon are hot spots after dinner. The Crystal Palace has long

been famous for its hilarious dinner show routines and excellent food. Of course, with more than 100 bars and restaurants, it's difficult to make generalizations, and almost any place is bound to be hopping in the winter and summer.

As for etiquette, an Aspen local never approaches a celebrity for an autograph; never wears fur boots, designer jeans or gold chains; and always refers to Aspen Mountain as Ajax, its original name.

The International Design Conference, held in the music tent in mid-June, is the first event in Aspen to signal the coming of summer. Designers of everything imaginable – shoes and race cars, buildings and computers, movies and graphics, come from all over the world to attend a week's worth of lectures, seminars and special events. A few weeks later, the Music Festival begins.

Aspen is a seasonal town. Though it can accommodate up to 30,000 visitors, the permanent population hovers around 13,000. In winter and summer, the streets are filled with cars and pedestrians; there are waiting lines at restaurants; and hotels and lodges are fully booked. In spring, the town is almost deserted, and for good reason – spring is mud season in the Rockies. Fall used to be off-season too, a gloriously peaceful season of warm Indian summer days, crisp nights, and golden mountainsides of aspen trees. Now the rest of the world is catching on. The Aspen Film Festival in September is gaining a national reputation for picking the best of the independently made films of the year. An Art Cart Derby, sponsored by the Aspen Center for the Visual Arts, features zany designs on wheels and a death-defying race down a street below Aspen Mountain. There's a County Fair in Snowmass and a rodeo, and a group of people who dons red jackets and black hats and jump over fences on horseback, chasing hounds who are chasing coyotes – Aspen's version of the English fox hunt.

Snowmass

Snowmass Village, located in the Brush Creek Valley about 10 miles (16 km) southwest of Aspen, was incorporated as a town in 1967. It has done nothing but grow eversince, sprouting condominiums, fancy homes on the ski slopes, hotels, lodges, shops and restaurants at an astounding rate. Its success is due to its plethora of excellent intermediate ski runs, its determination to cater to families, and the marketing and business acumen of the Snowmass Company, its major development company. The success of Snowmass is also due, in part, to its proximity to Aspen, something the little village may be forever trying to get over.

Soon after its beginnings in 1950, the Aspen Music Festival expanded to include a summer music school and quickly attracted the most famous names in the world of classical music. From June through August, strains of music can be heard everywhere in Aspen — on the mall, where student groups play and pass the hat; and in the famous tent of the west end of town, where concerts are held most afternoons and evenings. While connoisseurs will want to buy a ticket and listen to concerts inside the tent, dozens of people always bring blankets and picnic baskets to enjoy the music and sunshine for free on the grass outside the tent.

tournaments. It seems everyone is outdoors, riding horses, hiking, rock climbing, hang gliding, kayaking, fishing, jeeping — or just sitting in the mall soaking up the sun and watching the world go by. Local nightclubs feature everything from folk, jazz and country to disco, rock and punk.

Aspen also has its special holidays. The 4th of July is always wild and crazy, with an Independence Day parade down Main Street and any number of peripheral goings-on, including fireworks against the backdrop of Aspen Mountain. On Halloween, the mall and every bar in Aspen overflows with costumed revelers out to see and be seen — in disguise. Winterskol is a mid-winter celebration in January, complete with ski races, parades, costumes balls, contests and

Summer also brings Ballet Aspen, whose winter home is Salt Lake City, to leap and plié gracefully through the all-too-short warm months. As the ballet company has grown, toured and attracted international renown over the years, it has also spawned a school in nearby Snowmass. For theater lovers, the Aspen Playwright's Conference, hosted by the Pilgrim Theater Company, gives new playwrights the opportunity to stage their works, under the critical eye of well-known directors.

Aspen bursts at the seams with events during the summer, with crafts fairs; rodeos and rock concerts; balloon, sailboat, bicycle and running races; horse shows and polo matches; tennis, golf, softball and volleyball

whatever else the Chamber of Commerce can dream up to give one and all a good time.

One of the treasures of Snowmass is the **Anderson Ranch,** which offers summer classes, seminars and workshops in a range of arts, from pottery and photography to woodworking and print making, taught by internationally known artists. Visitors can shop at the Ranch's gallery, and attend a variety of exhibits held throughout the summer. Snowmass has also put itself on the map with the Snowmass Balloon Races, held in the early summer. The sight of dozens of balloons rising in the dawn light against the backdrop of the Rockies is a photographer's dream.

Farther west, in Old Snowmass, is Windstar, a place, an organization, a vision that only Aspen and the 70s could have produced. With John Denver as a figurehead and financial supporter, Buckminster Fuller as a mentor, and Amory Lovins as a nearby resident, Windstar thinks of itself as the new Aspen Institute, dedicated to solving problems relating to alternative forms of energy, building, heating and growing food. They also have classes, seminars and workshops.

Because of the scarcity of inexpensive housing in Aspen, thousands of people who consider themselves Aspenites have migrated to the bedroom communities of Basalt, El Jebel and Carbondale. But Aspen remains the pot of gold at the end of the rainbow, a magical valley filled with people determined to keep it that way. The jetset and those who follow in their wake are fickle, and will probably move on, but Aspen will always have its great skiing, its charm, sophistication, roaring river, and the mountainsides of whispering aspen trees that inspired its name.

The Goethe Bicentennial in 1949 was the event that brought Aspen national attention. Patterned after the Salzburg Music Festival in Germany, and dreamt up by Paepcke and a group at the University of Chicago, it attracted scholars, philosophers and social and cultural leaders from all over the world, including Albert Schweitzer, Thornton Wilder, Jose Ortega y Gasset, Arthur Rubinstein, Gregor Piatigorsky, Dimitri Mitropoulous and Bruno Walter. Some of Aspen's most enduring and successful institutions were born out of the Goethe Bicentennial: the Aspen Institute for Humanistic Studies, a "think tank" for intellectual, political and cultural leaders; the International Design Conference; and the Aspen Music Festival.

Aspen Gets into the Fast Lane

Through the 50s and 60s, Aspen continued to grow. Ski bums flocked into the valley, living six to a shack and working three jobs so they could take advantage of Aspen's fabulous skiing. Aspen Highlands, Buttermilk and Snowmass gave the small valley three choices of ski mountains. Shops, restaurants, condominiums, and expensive homes proliferated. Those who loved the small town atmosphere of Aspen saw the writing on the wall and elected "slow-growth" candidates to run the city and coun-

Left, Aspen music lovers under the tent; and right, a wagon full of funlovers celebrating Aspen's Winterskol Festival.

ty. Building heights were restricted, neon and billboards were banned and strict zoning controls were adopted. The Holiday Inn was relegated to a spot outside the city limits (it's been turned into condos), and McDonalds was only recently allowed to operate. The stringent growth controls successfully limited the number of people who moved into the valley, but it also made property values shoot up to the out-of-control level, until buying a home became out of the question for most residents.

Somewhere along the way, the jetset — the fur coat, cocaine and "the second home" crowd — decided that Aspen was the place in which to be, and gave the town a reputation for drugs, sex and life in the fast lane. It's hard to deny that such an element does exist

— in fact, it would be naive to do so. One only has to drive by the rows of Lear jets parked at the airport, or look up at the multi-million dollar homes in Starwood, an exclusive residential area on a mesa west of town that is home to celebrities such as John Denver and Jill St. John. Other part-time residents include Jack Nicholson, Don Henley and Glen Fry of Eagles fame, Jimmy Buffet, and journalist Hunter Thompson, one of the few genuine long-time celebrity residents. Hack journalists and marketing executives have thrived on this image; it would also be naive to say that Aspen, which has had a car, a pulp novel and a soft drink named after it, hasn't also thrived on all this economically.

DURANGO, COLORADO

She sits astride **El Rio de las Animas Perdidas** (River of Lost Souls), serving as gateway to the San Juan Mountains. Her foundation is cultural diversity, her wealth is historical abundance, and the estimated 1.5 million tourists who seek her out annually are her life's blood.

Durango, Colorado, did not just happen as most western towns did. More than 105 years ago, she was intentionally given birth to by the builders of the Denver and Rio Grande Western Railroad – William Bell and Alexander Hunt – who paid $500 for the 160-acre (65-hectare) site on a bend in the river. In September 1881, Charles Perrin surveyed and plotted the town, and within a month it was booming.

Rails were already pushing over the Continental Divide (the watershed that separates the easterly flow of rivers in the United States from the westerly flow), and Durango was ready for their arrival. When the first train arrived later that first year, 3,000 people already called Durango home.

Among other things, Durango served as a rail hub for 70 years. In the early 1950s with rail lines leading out of the town closing down, many thought they were witnessing the demise of the "Queen City of the West." But that was about the time the tourists found Durango. One of the rail's major attractions is the narrow gauge line between Durango and Silverton, which annually carries 150,000 travellers through breathtaking mountain wilderness.

The narrow gauge railroads that linked the mining towns of the west to each other and the outside world were the brainchild of Gen. W. J. Palmer of Denver. A Durango hotel – **the Palmer House** – still bears his name. In 1890, Palmer envisioned the expediency and utilization that could be gained if rails were set 36 inches (90 cm) rather than 56½ inches (140 cm) apart, as standard rail lines were. The closer-together rails made cutting rail beds into the sides of mountains much easier, as well as bringing ore out of those nearly inaccessible mining camps. Now, the narrow gauge lines that networked the mountain towns are almost a thing of the past. Rail buffs seek out the remaining two

Preceding pages, on the road again in the breathtaking San Juan Mountains (CO). Left, Thunderbow—Durango's mountain man.

for a ride before the narrow gauge railroads slide completely into oblivion.

The planned community was really a latecomer to the area. Four years earlier, Animas City, just to the north, had been founded. It is now part of Durango. Ignacio, to the southeast and headquarters for the Southern Ute Tribe, already had a rail line. Silverton, to the north near the headwaters of the Animas River, was a booming mining town with mule trains carrying out ore. And to the south, Farmington, New Mexico, at the mouth of the Animas River and a trade center for the Navajo Tribe, was well-established. Hispanic farmers had been cultivating the lands along the Animas for years. And hundreds of years before that, the Anasazi had lived in the great settlements of Mesa Verde, Colorado, 45 miles (72 km) west of Durango; Aztec, New Mexico, 36 miles (58 km) south of Durango; and Chaco, New Mexico, 96 miles (154 km) south of Durango. Indications are that the population of those ancient settlements was greater than the number of people who live in the area today.

Irrigation, road and trade systems stretched from the area all the way to the center of the Toltec Empire in the Valley of Old Mexico, 62 miles (100 km) north of the present Mexico City. Sometime during the 1300s, the Anasazi disappeared, but the telltale signs of their civilization draw part of the great number of tourists to southwest Colorado. Less than one hour from Durango, the Mesa Verde ruins have been declared a world cultural heritage site. About six years ago, when an international committee set out to identify historical sites which deserve preservation because of what they tell about man's cultural heritage, Mesa Verde was among the eight chosen.

Durango is now highly multi-ethnic, being born into a community of Indians, Hispanics, Anglos, Scandinavians, Italians, Germans and Irish. (The last four races came later.)

From Silver Smelter to Uranium Mill

The narrow gauge railroad that now serves only travellers once carried supplies to the miners around Silverton. And after the town's founding fathers moved a smelting operation from Silverton to Durango, the trains brought back the ore to be smelted on their return trips.

The smelter changed its occupation in 1942 when the United States Vadium Corporation built a uranium mill at the site. Uranium milled there was sold to the Manhattan Project, the federal government's venture into the manufacture of the first atomic bomb. In 1963, the "military secret" across the river south of town was closed, but the residual uranium tailings pile that was created during the mill's 20 years of existence keeps Durango in the national news regularly as the U.S. Environmental Protection Agency scratches its collective head about how to make the low-level radioactive mound easier to live with.

History records a couple of memorable shootouts in Durango's early days, both related to the never-ending turf-rights western feud between cattlemen and sheep men.

One was between the "badmen" from Farmington and from Durango on the mesa east of town in April 1881. Within a month, Durango became incorporated, elected a city council, and passed 11 ordinances. Durango wanted a more sophisticated image than that of a gunfighter town.

Gunshots also awakened the town the same year when some cowboys rode down Main Avenue shooting holes through the tent that served as the newspaper office. The woman editor, who had hauled her printing presses from Leadville, had drawn the fire by an editorial she had written.

A Walk through History

The town is rich with historical architecture. Many homes are restored originals. The mortuary has a round turret room on one corner where pallbearers now sit during funeral services. At one time, that turret room held a poker table, and legend has it that large sums of money and property changed hands there nightly.

The three-story sandstone **Newman Building** at Eighth Street and Main Avenue once housed the Smelter National Bank, and parts of the bank's vaults, which extended through the upper two floors, are still visible.

The **Strater Hotel** at Seventh Street and Main Avenue has been housing notables since 1887. Its Victorian architecture is enhanced with fur-

Don't miss riding the thrilling Silverton-Durango narrow gauge railroad.

210

nishings collected from 100 years ago. The scantily clad ladies with their net stockings and plumed hats who serve in the hotel's bar, the **Diamond Bell,** could be stepping right out of the last century. The hotel, just a block from the railroad depot, also includes the **Diamond Circle Theater.** The Diamond Circle and the **Abbey Theater,** also within a block of the train station, have nightly presentations during the summer months which include everything from serious drama to monologues to international dancing demonstrations and the tourist's favorite, vaudeville.

There are three amateur theater groups in Durango. The locally written and cast *David's Star* has been on the stage at the Abbey for several Christmas seasons, and those who have seen it generally agree that one viewing is not enough.

The **Fine Arts Auditorium** at Fort Lewis College also stages many productions from near at hand and far away. The Four Corners Opera Association performs during the summer months.

Scattered among those history-rich buildings are the Irish pubs: **Clancy's** and **Father Murphys;** the Mexican can-tinas: **Dos Juans** and **Franciscos.** Durango has a reputation for its fine restaurants and interesting lounges. Places like the **The Palace** and **Sweeneys** enjoy an international reputation.

Art Selection

Like restaurants, art galleries abound. **Gallerie Marguerite** houses outstanding Western oils. **Kathleen Warner Fine Arts** specializes in both paintings and sculpture and **Noble Galleries** shows work of both national and local artists, of which there is a plethora, from potters to glass workers, painters, carvers and jewelers.

If one could manage a visit to every art gallery in the Rocky Mountain region, among the most memorable would be Durango's **Toh-Atin Gallery.** At 145 W. 9th St., the gallery has a reputation for handling the finest in handmade Indian art and crafts. Handwoven Navajo tapestries adorn the walls. Cases of handmade silver and gold jewelry with turquoise, shell, coral and jet display the talents of artists such as Andy Kirk, Jimmie King, Jr., Preston Monogye, Mary Marie, Jimmie

Cattle graze beneath the San Juans in Ridgeway, Colorado.

Harrison and Ben Nighthorse Campbell.

Gallery owner H. Jackson Clark has been collecting Navajo weaving since 1957. Not only is he recognized as one of the most knowledgeable men in the field, but his collection, much of which hangs in the **United Bank of Durango** on Main Avenue, is one of the most extensive in the world. The display represents three centuries of Navajo weaving, all accurately dated and documented.

The Navajo weaving collecting is a reminder that you cannot separate the Durango of today from the Durango of the past.

Trimble Springs, begun in 1882 a few miles north of town in the Animas Valley, was an internationally known health resort with visitors claiming "miraculous" cures from bathing in the naturally hot mineral waters. It burned to rubble in the late 1950s.

The first liquor reportedly was brought into the area by wagons from Santa Fe, New Mexico. Like most places where men do hard physical labor, saloons sprang up overnight, some of which were fronts for brothels and gambling houses. Right after the saloons came the churches. The first minister in Durango, the Rev. Mr. C. M. Hogue, an ex-gambler and a Texan, was converted, and reportedly jumped on a gambling table in a local drinking establishment one night. He asked for a cut of the take just before he called the gamblers to prayer. He wanted a cut of the take for the new church he was trying to build in the burgeoning little town.

That church, **St. Mark's Episcopal,** opened its doors February 1, 1881, and is still going strong. A year later, the Catholic Sisters of Mercy arrived and opened a school and a hospital, both of which survive today as **St. Columba School** and **Mercy Medical Center.**

Like many western towns quickly built of lumber and heated with wood fires, Durango experienced a disastrous fire in 1889. The prominence of brick and sandstone buildings seen today stems from knowledge gained from that fire.

A Natural Movie Set

Small Town Vamp was the first of a about 45 major movie and television

A western belle greets you in a Durango portrait studio.

shows filmed in the Durango area. That first film was shot by the late Jim Jarvis, a local man. The film *Around the World in 80 Days* saw the narrow gauge railroad in action. Perhaps the best known movie filmed in the area was *Butch Cassidy and the Sundance Kid,* starring Robert Redford and Paul Newman. The shot of the two of them jumping into the river was filmed at the Trimble Lane bridge over the Animas River.

Adding cultural and academic interest to the community is **Fort Lewis College.** It had its beginning as a military fort southwest of Durango during the last century. The site became a normal and industrial training school for Indians. The school taught agriculture and industrial arts from 1911 to 1927, when the state legislature authorized two years of college courses to be taught. In 1933, high school classes were dropped and the school became a junior college. In 1956, moving the campus from its rural setting to the mesa east of town spawned more controversy than the original 1881 shootout. In 1962, Fort Lewis became a four-year baccalaureate degree-granting college. It has a current enrollment of 3,500 students. The campus joins the city's 18-hole golf course and the in-town Chapman Hill ski slope. It has a swimming pool, playing fields, tennis courts, stadium and track, and like most campuses, hosts well-known speakers, musical presentations and dramas.

Durango's two major celebrations each year draw participants and onlookers from nearby and far away. The Navajo Trail Fiesta is in late July or early August, and Snowdown takes place the last weekend in January. The first began in 1935, the latter in 1979. The fiesta includes parades, rodeos and usually horse racing. It draws bullriders, barrel racers and horse fanciers of all kinds. Snowdown activities include everything from a bartender's contest to serious winter sport competition, including both cross-country and downhill skiing.

Visitors who arrive in Durango on Halloween may feel as if they have arrived in the Land of Oz. Six blocks of Main Avenue are blocked off for the evening's festivities, which finds as many as 5,000 people — that's nearly half the town's population — parading in the most outlandish and creative costumes seen anywhere. It is not uncommon for participants to work on their costumes all year.

The summer arts fair takes over the **Old High School Park** on Main Avenue the second weekend in July, with artists and craftspersons from all over the southwest, working at, displaying and selling their creations.

One of the favorite souvenirs that many tourists take away with them is an old-time photograph of themselves in the costume of a trapper, sheriff, brothel madame or saloon girl with all the proper props like guns, parasols, furs and garters. Two such studios operate on Main Avenue.

At an elevation of 6,500 feet (2,000 meters), Durango's surrounding geography provides the natural setting for river rafting, hiking, mountain climbing, hunting, fishing and skiing.

One-and-a-half million tourists annually make Durango seem like something more than a small town. But it really isn't. In more than 100 years, only 9,000 people have increased the population. It would be a challenge to find such a small place that is such a bubbling melting pot of historical, current and anticipated events.

A Silverton boy rides past the colorful shops.

the Snake River near Moran Junction. Mule deer are mostly seen by the traveller who hikes the mountain trails. In the summer the deer prefer the lower slopes; in spring and fall, they move between the mountain slopes and their wintering grounds south of Jackson.

In spring, moose often feed in open ponds. Many browse in the Willow Flats close to Jackson Lake Lodge. In summer, they move into the spruce and cottonwood forests along the river bottoms. In fall and winter, the moose move into open country where they can be easily observed. Moose are animals of unpredictable temperament, and observers should exercise caution, especially with moose cows and their calves.

Elk are more shy than moose, and more difficult to see. They usually rest in deep forest during midday, so the early morning and late afternoon are the best times to observe this member of the deer family in the open.

The **National Elk Refuge**, one of six major wildlife refuge areas in Wyoming where visitors can watch animals and birds in their natural surroundings, was established in 1912 when nearly 20,000 elk in the Jackson Hole region were starving during a severe winter. Residents of the valley raised $1,000 to buy hay for them, and the Wyoming State Legislature appropriated $5,000 for additional feed. Congress then set aside 1,000 acres (405 hectares) as a winter refuge for elk. The area has been enlarged since that time, partly by over 1700 acres (680 hectares) bought and donated by the Izaak Walton League and partly through later land acquisitions of the Federal Government. Elk migrate onto the refuge in late October and November, and they leave the refuge for the summer in early May. Visitors may take sleigh rides among the elk from December 26 to April 1, 10 a.m. until 4 p.m.

The **Bridger Teton National Forest** encompasses three sides of Jackson Hole. Its three-and-a-half million acres (1.4 million hectares) and seven ranger districts are supervised from the Jackson headquarters.

A visit to **Yellowstone National Park** is an opportunity to see a variety of wildlife. Year-round accommodations are available south of Yellowstone in the Jackson Hole area.

A study in contrasts—red rock,

Happy travellers pose for a family portrait in front of arch made of deer antlers.

green forests and snowcapped summits mirrored in clear lakes vie for attention in Jackson Hole. No matter the season, the silent splendor of Jackson Hole will make any traveller's vacation a memorable one.

The **Moose Visitor Center** is open from 8 a.m. to 7 p.m. daily. An information and Interpretive Center Museum is operated by the National Park Service, and its exhibits illustrate the mountainman fur-trade era in Jackson Hole.

The **Colter Bay Visitor Center**, open from 8 a.m. to 7 p.m., houses the **Indian Arts Museum**, where the David T. Vernon Indian art collection is featured in exhibit rooms.

The Outdoor Life

As the early mountain men discovered, camping is a good way to experience Jackson Hole. Campsites abound throughout the region in Teton County, Grand Teton National Park, and Bridger-Teton National Forest. Be sure to take along your insect repellent, though. There are times when Wyoming seems to contain every biting insect

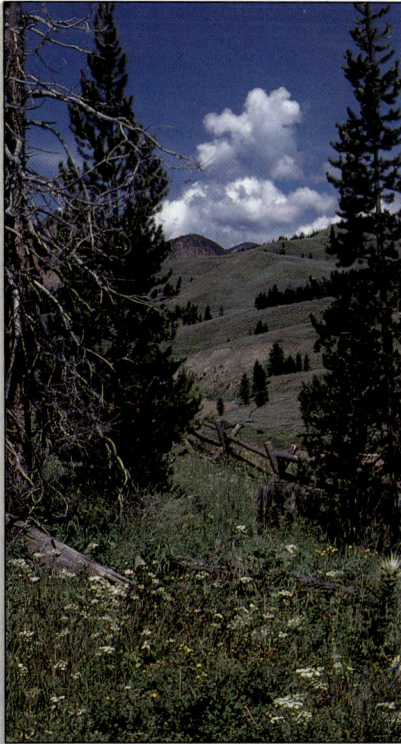

known to entomological science from green-eyed horseflies to humming swarms of mosquitoes.

Whether boating, rafting, wading, swimming, canoeing, fishing—Jackson Hole is a watersports paradise. Paddle on a crystal clear mountain lake, or thrill to a whitewater trip through one of the canyons of the Snake River. Jackson Hole's lakes (**Jenny, Leigh** or **Jackson**) yield Mackinaw trout up to 50 pounds (22.5 kg), or snag a native cutthroat trout in one of the fine streams (**Hoback, Buffalo** or **Snake Rivers**).

Modes of transportation are as varied as the tourists themselves—take a sleigh ride through the National Elk Refuge and see the sleigh races in January and February or view the scenery from a helicopter, glider or hot air balloon. Ski (downhill or cross-country) or snowmobile any of the three major ski areas (**Grand Targhee Ski Resort, Jackson Hole Ski Corp.** and **Snow King, Inc.**). Ride the Jackson Hole Aerial Tram, the Snow King Mountain chairlift, or the Alpine Slide—they'll whisk you away for a breathtaking view.

Autumn in Jackson Hole beckons the big game hunter. Sports enthusiasts from around the world flock to the area when the hunting season opens to stalk the country's largest herds of elk and moose, Hunters will also find mule deer, mountain sheep and black bear.

Seeing the wildlife is as exciting as hunting it. A pair of binoculars, a little knowledge of animal habits, and "taking your time" can reap thrilling rewards. Ducks and geese are common along the Snake River or on ponds that are free of ice. White pelicans migrate through the area, and trumpeter swans can be seen on Christian Pond, east of Jackson Lake Lodge, during all but the coldest of winter months. Black Bear are occasionally spotted along the lower mountain trails and have been known to wander into campgrounds and picnic areas. It's important to keep in mind that they are wild animals and if approached can do severe injury to people. Antelope can be found in the summer months but they don't winter in the area. Bighorn mountain sheep can be seen in Grand Teton National Park—most likely from the trail over the Mount Hunt Divide, between Open and Granite Canyons, or in the vicinity of Gros Ventre Slide just east of the park.

Left, a picturesque mountain meadow; and right, winter visitors get quite close at the National El Refuge, Jackson.

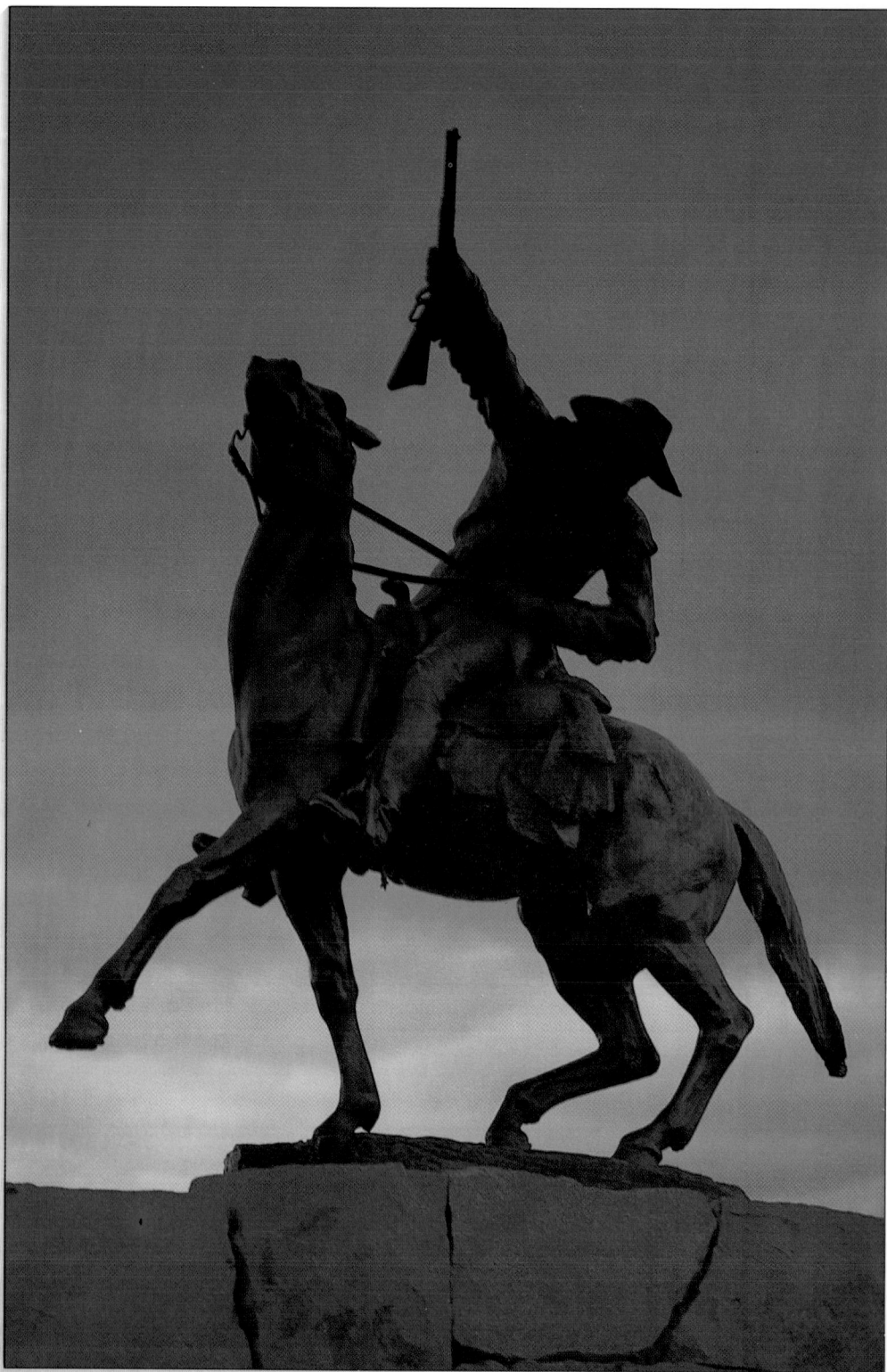

CODY COUNTRY WYOMING

Yellowstone, America's first national park, attracts millions of visitors each year. It is one of the few pristine and pure environments left; wild animals roam freely in the vast forests, and the waterfalls spill into rivers filled with trout that make some of the best fishing in the country.

One of the best kept secrets of this spectacular area is the **East Yellowstone/Wapiti Valley** connecting the East Gate of Yellowstone National Park and **Cody**, Wyoming. A vast magnificent view includes the **Shoshone National Forest**, America's first wilderness area to be designated a national forest. The traveller is hard pressed to watch the road ahead with his attention being caught by the forest surrounding him on all sides and eagles soaring above the majestic mountains and meadows. Tall stands of pine trees protect herds of deer, elk, moose and the occasional bears. Buffalo herds wander outside the Park boundaries to graze in the Valley.

Several campgrounds tucked into the forest area invite the traveller to stop long enough to gather memories from a world that has existed for eons and has somehow survived here in this Wyoming land. A stop along this primitive area is an opportunity to regain one's senses; campers are free to hike, backpack, take advantage of photographic skills, lean back against a shady pine tree, and watch the river flow by or observe the wildlife in its natural habitat.

The Shoshone River follows the road into Cody, Wyoming, changing from raging, white water into flowing contentment. There are many places along the river banks where you can watch the trout jump and beavers building their dams. Several times a day, river floaters in rubber rafts can be seen riding the currents, and the traveller is torn between breathing in his surroundings or hurrying into Cody to arrange his own river trip.

As the road leads out of the dense forest land, the valley widens and color is rampant as red rock formations stir the imagination. Formations named Holy City, Laughing Pig, Elephant Rock and Ptarmigan look down from great heights and are met by stands of pines and breathtaking valleys. Sprinkled along this roadway between Yellowstone Park and Cody are guest ranches and lodges where rustic comfort is available. Many of the guest lodges are hidden from view so travellers must watch for signs indicating where they may be found. Accommodations are modern but manage to combine convenience with true western flavor.

Saddle Up and Ride the Range

A stay in a guest ranch or lodge in the Wapiti Valley or any other scenic area surrounding Cody is an opportunity to get away from a crowded and fast-paced world that is oftentimes saturated with pollution. Here in this Wyoming country is vast uncluttered space, clear clean skies, and water so pure you can drink from the running rivers and waterfalls. The ranches and lodges offer horseback rides into the wilderness, camping, cookouts, hikes and backpacking and huge homecooked meals three times a day. Not the least of the pleasures of world is at day's end when one can gaze into star-filled skies and see galaxies

Preceding pages, the 19th Century "Old Trail Town" near Cody. Left, wild Buffalo Bill Cody is immortalized in sculpture; and right, Buffalo Bill's Wild West Show posters were an art for themselves.

and sparkling constellations with complete clarity.

The ranches are run by cowboys and cowgirls who are not much different from their predecessors at the turn of the century. These people have the same skills and heartiness of the frontier days, and they work from sunup to sundown caring for the horses and cattle, fencing the rangeland, and keeping the buildings in top condition. On their days off, the ranch hands head into Cody where they can kick up their heels in a western nightspot called **Cassie's** or compare stories and dreams with their contemporaries at the **Silver Saddle Lounge** or the **Proud Cut Saloon** across the street.

William F. ("Buffalo Bill") Cody was the founding father of the town of Cody and his influence is still strongly felt. Buffalo Bill first entered the area in the 1870s and saw its tremendous development possibilities. He returned with friends and named the site Cody in 1895. By 1902, the town was incorporated and Colonel Cody opened **Irma Hotel**, named after his daughter. The Irma Hotel, now a historic landmark, is still a gathering place for the community and an attraction for visitors.

Buffalo Bill Historical Center

After the Colonel's death, an association was formed to preserve his memory and to immortalize his contributions to the setting of this portion of the frontier, Gertrude Vanderbilt Whitney was commissioned to do a historic sized sculpture. The sculpture is named *The Scout* and was dedicated in 1924. It sits on the west edge of Cody and was the beginning of a tribute to the American frontier heritage that has today become the world-famous **Buffalo Bill Historic Center**.

The Historical Center, a four-part museum, is usually a complete surprise to visitors who have not made the trip to Cody especially to see it. It sits with the Rocky Mountains as a background and has no resemblance to the original log cabin that sufficed at the beginning of this memorial effort. It is a huge modern structure built, for the most part, of rock and is composed of four separate museums—truly the Center of the West. The four sections are **The Plains**

Artist Charles Russell captured the Wild West in *The Jerkline.*

Indian Museum, The Whitney Gallery of Western Art, The Winchester Arms Museum and **The Buffalo Bill Museum**. Together, there are over 100,000 sq feet of exhibit space.

Throughout the summer season, you can see tour groups from all over the world in the Historical Center, as well as an occasional celebrity. Writers and television personalities have found it a facinating institution on which to focus because of its rare and diverse collections of western memorabilia. Visitors should allow a minimum of three hours to tour the Buffalo Bill Historical Center—a week would be even better! Also during the summer months, there is a special exhibition of artworks, usually featuring the most famous Western artists in history.

The Plains Indian Museum, guardian of cultures, traditions, customs and the creativity of the plains area tribes of the United States is a wondrous world that one cannot see without a deepening understanding, appreciation and awe. The Whitney Gallery of Western Art is one of the major Western art museums in America and displays artworks by great artists including Bierstadt, Miller, Moran, Catlin, Sharp, Remington and Russell to name but a few. Remington and Russell are well known as Western artists and their work is often compared. The Winchester Arms Museum, one of the most prestigious of its kind in the world today, has over 5,500 firearms and projectile weapons and is perhaps the most complete documentation of weaponry in the world. The collection was started by Oliver Winchester in 1860 and moved to Cody in 1975. The Buffalo Bill Museum displays hundreds of items that belonged to its namesake as well as memorabilia, artifacts, artworks and photographs illustrating the development of the American West. The visitor is treated to the memorabilia from Annie Oakley's days to Buffalo Bill's Wild West show. The sum offers an educational opportunity that is unsurpassed. It is doubtful that such rare and complete collections of Western American history can be found anywhere else in the world.

Carnivals and Celebrations at Cody

Those looking for *replicas* of early western frontier towns will be dis-

Old Sioux Indians dress patterns, c. 1860.

appointed, as Cody has remained untouched by a plastic facade. Cody is a small community and its residents have chosen to call it home for personal reasons: year round outdoor recreation, spectacular scenery and fresh open spaces—luxuries in today's fast-paced world. They drive two miles (three km) out of the city limits and can be completely alone, or they can go downtown and be surrounded by friends. With the abundance of wildlife nearby, game hunting is excellent in the Cody area. Fishing is also rewarding.

In the summertime, this otherwise quiet community has an entirely different atmosphere. Visitors from all over the world come to Cody to take part in the unique attractions and enjoy the natural environment. Cody boasts that it is the Rodeo Capital of the World! Other towns may claim the same distinction but Cody does offer a rodeo every night of the summer which is PRCA sanctioned. And the cowboys and cowgirls who ride in the Cody rodeo are serious competitors; many of those riders go on to become the best in the business.

June is a great month to visit Cody.

The weather is usually ideal and there are special events sponsored by the Buffalo Bill Historical Center. One such is The Frontier Festival held on the north lawn of the Historical Center. People bring their special skills and wares to the Festival and spend two days demonstrating and selling arts, crafts and foods authentic to the turn of the century. Demonstrations on spinning, weaving, saddle making, hide tanning, log hewing, Indian beadwork, and the preparation of frontier foods, can be watched from booths all arranged within the Festival area. Throughout the Festival, entertainment is provided by groups who specialize in traditional Western music and contests are held between outfitters as they race, pack saddles, and shoe horses.

An Indian Powwow is another exciting June event. Participants invited from Plains tribes all over the United States and Canada, compete throughout the day in a variety of singing and dancing competitions. All entrants wear traditional tribal clothing and make a day that is entertaining and educational.

On July Fourth, Cody holds a celebration that attracts thousands of

Crow Indians headdress, c. 1830.

visitors. The Stampede Days begin in the mornings with a parade down the main street. After lunch, contestants compete for championship titles at the Stampede Rodeos. Families enjoy picnics and parties, and the city park fills with crowds who come to take part in the entertainment. The day finishes with a bang, as the fireworks display lights up star-filled skies.

Throughout the summers in Cody, the days may begin with a river float down the Shoshone River in the Wapiti/ East Yellowstone Valley. Then it's on to **Old Trail Town**, which has been widely publicized by media such as *Good Morning America* and *National Geographic*, and is also a must-see on your vacation. Every building in Trail Town remains as it was originally. They have only been moved to Trail Town to be preserved for future generations; they make up a complete town, being furnished authentically from the livery stable and saloon, to the cabins that were lived in by famous frontiersmen.

Cody Country—the spectacular scenery of the Wapiti/East Yellowstone Valley, the abundant wildlife, the community of Cody, and the Buffalo Bill Histor-

ical Center—brings back the reality of the West. A couple of weeks spent in the area will provide an appreciation of why those pioneers struggled so valiantly to settle this part of the world, and why they overcame such hardships to reach their destination.

Throughout the world, people value the legend of America's west. For the most part, that lifestyle, with its attitudes, recreational opportunities and open spaces, are a thing of the past. Replicas and imitations can frequently be found as recreations of a past era, but Wyoming and the Cody Country are alive and well. Cowboys are really cowboys who earn their living riding the Wyoming ranges. Shopkeepers are often third generation residents who understand the quality Cody offers them and their families, and who would not consider giving it up for city benefits. Whether a family is growing up in Cody or visiting, they enjoy the experience together. Cody has a lot to offer everyone. So load your camera **and bring lots of extra film, gather your** casual clothing for action or relaxing, and show your zest for "cowboy country" as it is today!

Buffalo Bill conferring with his Indian friends, Red Cloud and American Horse.

CHEYENNE, WYOMING

On the sun swept prairie where the plains meet the mountains, Cheyenne, the capital of Wyoming, had its humble but hardly modest beginnings in 1867 when the Union Pacific Railroad tracks were laid through this site on its way to the West Coast. The city was named after the Indian tribe "Shey-ah-nah" who roamed these territories and occupied the present-day southeastern part of Wyoming. The railroad brought all types of characters to Cheyenne and most of them never left. It was a wild frontier town possessing over 60 saloons and by 1868, 300 businesses were supported by hunters, trappers, railroad men, laborers, artists, engineers, Sioux, Pawnee and Cheyenne Indians, gamblers, musicians, promoters and gunmen. The only law enforcement for this unruly community known as "Hell on Wheels" was a gunny sack hooded "vigilance committee." Their nightly activities (including some lynchings) subdued some of the law breaking and motivated the more trustworthy citizens to elect a real sheriff. Some of the realities of early Cheyenne were cheap liquor, good pay and high stakes for gamblers, confident men, promoters and robbers.

Grenville Dodge, Railroad Surveyor General after surveying the town site, organized his first camp on Crow Creek in west Cheyenne. This camp ideally situated at the junction of many major routes had direct access to military activities throughout the region. Soldiers and workers alike were recovering from a four-year war, and had become familiar with quick decisions and instant action. White ruffians, angry Indians and straying bullets made death a common affair. The cemetery was as important as the saloon, and the bad folks and workers were "dying to get in." In 1868, a reorganized vigilance committee assumed a strong standby taking law and order into their own hands. They passed severe judgment on most matters; 12 men received death penalties the first year. As the railroad moved West, it took some of the transient population with it. Cheyenne continued to evolve into a flourishing town and had a thriving depot for army supplies.

An important contribution to the progress and development of Cheyenne economy was the booming livestock industry. In the early 1800s, due to cattle raising, Cheyenne was the most wealthy per capita city in the world. It was during the height of her economic development that the world famous "Cheyenne Club" was built. In this exclusive club the cuisine of the imported chef was known from coast to coast. The club was luxuriously furnished in English style and had many wealthy members who spent their summers in Cheyenne and their winters in Europe. One of the most notorious paintings in the state, Paul Potter's *Bull* finished by Nesker in 1885, which hangs in the reception room of the Chamber of Commerce, is said to have been the cause of the dismissal of one Cheyenne Club prominent member. The member, a wealthy cattle owner, shot a hole through the painted bull's front leg because he considered the painting a travesty on Wyoming livestock.

Most of the members were well-to-do cattlemen who spent time in the "Cheyenne Club" sipping rich wine and determining policies that affected the

Preceding pages, rodeo cowboy ropes a steer for excited fans. Left, a bronco rider gets the ride of his life; and right, a flag bearer rides high in a Cheyenne parade.

cattle empire throughout the West. The rich nutritious grasslands that surrounded Cheyenne were the main reason that some ranchers started sheep ranching in 1890. In the northwest corner of Cheyenne is the site of the Old Court House where Tom Horn was hung in 1903. As sheep ranching became a threat to the cattlemen, a major feud developed. Horn, a range detective, was hired by wealthy cattlemen to do away with rustlers and other trouble makers, namely the sheep ranchers. It is said that he was suspected of killing many offenders before he was convicted for killing 13-year-old Willie Nickell. Horn was promised $500 to kill the rancher Nickell, but accidently killed his son, Willie. Horn was held in jail for many weeks prior to the execution. As the hanging day drew nearer, the "Cattleman-sheepman range feud" was building up and Horn escaped jail. Rumors spread that the cattlemen were "fixing things" so Horn could escape before the hanging. After the hanging, Nickell had insisted that he should see the body but he was refused permission by the county attorney saying that it could cause a riot. This led many to

believe that the law had been bought and like some American "bad guy" celebrities, Tom Horn had been seen in various parts of Wyoming since he was hanged. While cattlemen held their own for a while, sheep interests eventually took over bringing much prosperity to the state. Today sheep farming is vital to Wyoming's economy making her sheep industry the second largest in the country.

'The Magic City of the Plains'

During the late 1800s, Cheyenne was known as 'The Magic City of the Plains.' In the history of Cheyenne, transportation played an important role. In 1870, beef was shipped to Europe for the armies fighting in the Franco-Prussian War. There was a time in Cheyenne when over 200 wagons had engaged more than 400 men to operate the daily Cheyenne-Dreadwood Stage Line. The Stage Line carried mail, gold bullion that was discovered in the Black Hills and, of course, passengers. In 1875, the gold outfitting prospectors and miners came to Cheyenne with long string teams hauling mining machinery, provi-

The Anoka High School band in front of the Cheyenne Capitol Building.

248

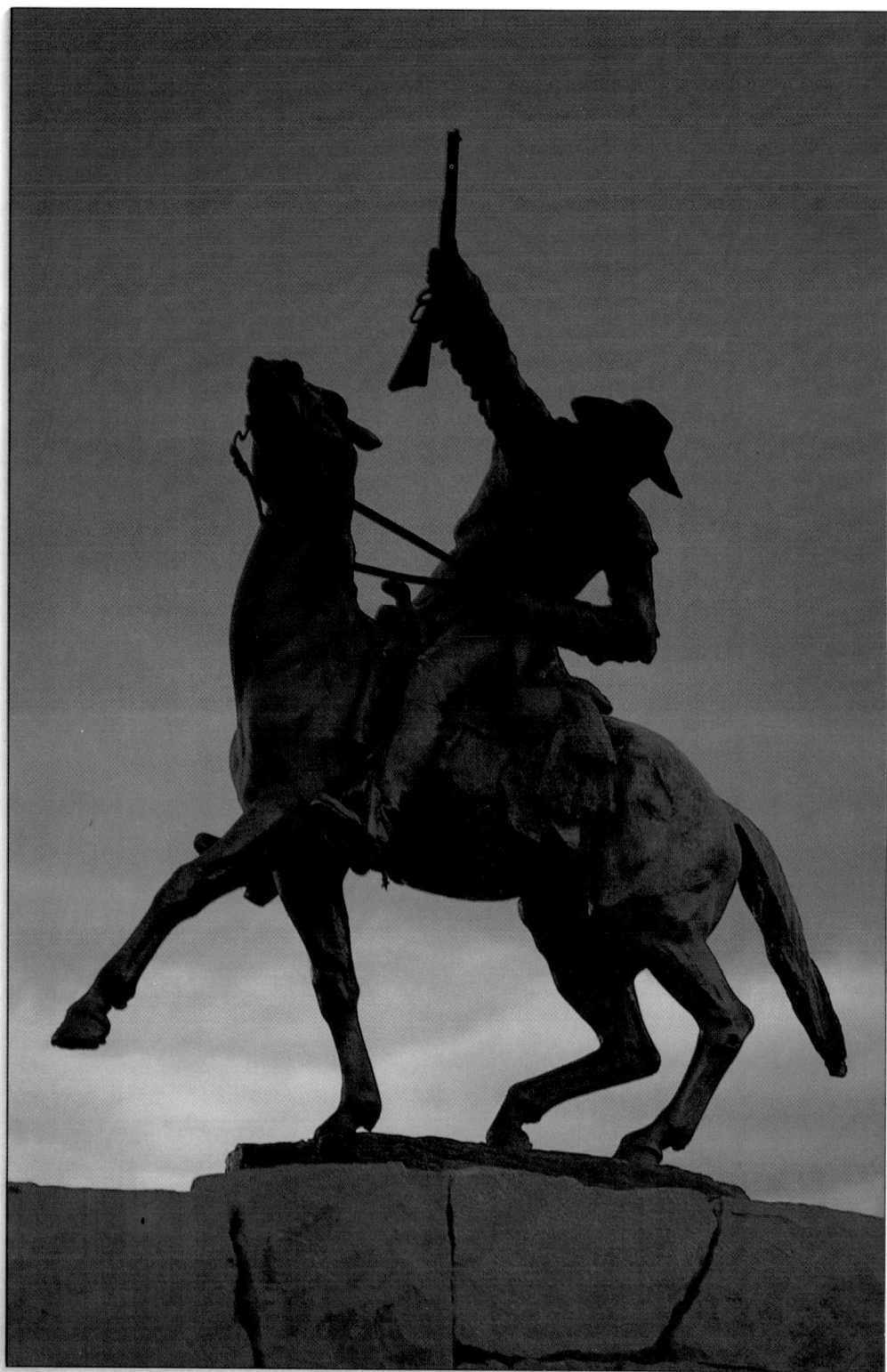

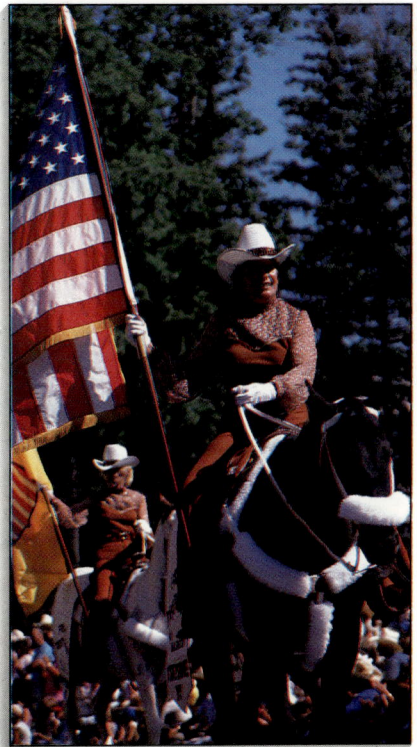

sions and thousands of passengers.

Diverse activity and a versatile population created a busy social life in Cheyenne. The Opera House featured many Broadway Productions on their way to San Francisco. Lavish balls, parties, dramas, literary and musical functions, and art exhibits added to the cultural life of the community, which far surpassed many of other cities of this size in the East.

This highly developed cultural life still exists in Cheyenne. There is an active symphony theater, concerts, museums, art shows and many musical and cultural organizations. Cheyenne caters to the University population of Laramie which is only 50 miles (80 km) from here. The Cheyenne gunslingers bring the old West to life with reenactments of gunfights and other activities all through the summer (daily except Sundays) in the **Old Town Plaza** in downtown Cheyenne. Melodramas complete with olio acts are performed twice every night from mid-June through mid-August at the Atlas theater.

The last week of July brings the Cheyenne Frontier Days, the year's most spectacular event and "The Big Daddy of 'em all." This event has been called "where the pavement ends and the West begins," "honest to goodness, bronc stompin' jumping up and down Western family fun,"... The city comes alive in the true Western fashion. Boots, cowboy hats, blue jeans, Western shirts ... the spectrum of attire here varies from the conventional to high fashion designer outfits. You can capture the magnetism and flavor of this place in its heyday! The early Frontier Days which started in 1897 were held on the prairies north of town. The spectators usually came with their umbrellas to avoid the rain and to shoo away bucking broncos or steers.

Nowadays before the celebration, Cheyenne natives dress up in big hats, high heeled boots, and Western shirts. Native Indians congregate from different parts of the country to participate in the Indian Village and Plains Indian Dancing which is the most colorful part of the event.

Cheyenne Frontier Days Rodeo is claimed to be the largest outdoor rodeo in the world attracting the best rodeo performers with its high prize money of

Square dancers whoop it up during Cheyenne Frontier Days.

nearly half a million dollars. Every rodeo cowboy covets the Frontier Days trophy buckle which is awarded to the cowboy with the best performance. Each afternoon during this event the world's best cowboys compete for the grand payday against some of the nation's wildest stock. Thousands of fans and spectators thrill as cowboys and cowgirls, professional and amateur, compete with wild-eyed brahma bulls, the roughest, meanest and largest animals in the show. Press from all over the world come to cover the event. Special press areas (press box at the roof top) and a portion of the arena are reserved for international writers and photographers. Every once in a while press photographers have to run for the fence to avoid the attack of an angry charging brahma bull. The atmosphere is exciting, the action wild and fun-packed. Some of the other special events at the rodeo are bull riding, saddle Bronc, calf roping, steer roping, steer wrestling, chuckwagon racing, bull fighting, pony races, wild horse races, and the naming of the all-round cowboy to the one who wins the most points in the individual events.

Every one of the Cheyenne Frontier Days Rodeos (except the first one) began with a big parade. An elaborate spectacle was held in 1898 when Buffalo Bill himself led the grand parade with his Wild West Show. For a number of years after that, the parade emphasis died down with the exception of Theodore Roosevelt's visit in 1910, and when the event celebrated its Silver Anniversary in 1921. In 1925, the Frontier Committee started improving the parade and introduced the theme, "Evolution of Transportation," which is still maintained.

Today the Frontier Days Parade is an incredible experience and possibly one of the best parades in the country. The same parade is watched by thousands as it goes through Cheyenne on four different days. The parade boasts of having the largest collection of horse-drawn vehicles in the world. The pageant features the progress of transportation in United States since 1860. On display are Prairie Schooners, stagecoaches, lumber wagons, freight wagons, express wagons, carryalls, surreys, single buggies, antique cars, high wheel bicycles, dogcarts, miniature passenger trains,

The old Union Pacific railway station still stands in Cheyenne.

racing gigs and many other modes tracing the "evolution of transportation." The parade is further enhanced with historic floats, marching bands, equestrians, baton twirlers, Rodeo Queens, Plains Indian Dancers, and many other colorful groups.

The Frontier Days carnival has a wide variety of rides in the midway area of the fairgrounds. This goes on all nine days of the Rodeo. Concessions, games, and all types of merchandise from turquoise jewelry to Western Hats and belts are available. Every night some of the best country entertainment in the States performs on the fairgrounds. Other family fun includes events like chili cook-offs, free pancake breakfasts and square dancing. The Old West Museum, The Governor's invitational art show and sale and the Indian Village make this nine-day nonstop adventure one that is fun, educational, and cultural.

A Railroad Depot and the State Capitol

The **Union Pacific Railroad Depot** in downtown Cheyenne is worth a visit. This Romanesque building is uniquely designed and still serves as the Union Pacific Station. At the far end of the street is the **State Capitol** with its sparkling gold leaf dome; it can be seen from anywhere in the city. Though the first territorial government met in Cheyenne, it did not have a permanent building for the legislature until 1888. In April of 1890, three months before Wyoming was admitted into the Union as a State, this French Renaissance Capitol building was completed. The capitol occupies two full city blocks and is a part of a 14-acre (six-hectare) complex of State buildings and offices.

Within the confines of the Capitol, the history of Wyoming comes to life. It was here that the first woman governor in the United States (Mrs.) Nellis Taylor Ross was elected. (She later became the first woman director of the United States Mint.) The first woman justice-of-the-peace in America, Esther Hobart Morris, a Wyoming native, has her statue in front of the capitol.

In the summertime on weekdays, guided tours of the capitol begin every 30 minutes. The beautiful marble floors, woodwork, stained glass, wildlife display and a historical photo-

Two bisons fight it out on the open range.

graphic display are some of the features of the tour.

Parks for Relaxation

Cheyenne's numerous parks are great for family picnics and relaxation. "Old Number 4004 Big Boy" is the world's largest locomotive and can be seen on display at the **Holiday Park.** Until 1956, this massive engine did the work of two conventional steam engines, carrying 28 tons of fuel and 25,000 gallons of water.

The **National First Day Cover Museum** in Cheyenne is the only museum of its kind in the world. This well-preserved collection is of first day covers of the rarest and most valuable stamps in the world. Its worth is nearly a million dollars. The museum stays open Monday through Friday 9 a.m. till 5 p.m. and may be visited free of charge.

The **F.E. Warren Air Force Base** pioneered the operation of cattle herds, towns and the railroads in Wyoming. Today this site is used by the United States Airforce for the storing of Intercontinental ballistic missiles and the training of Air Force recruits. A tour of the Air Force Base can be easily arranged. Prior arrangements are necessary for touring the Wyoming **Hereford Ranch.** This Ranch has been in operation since 1883 and is one of the oldest and most prestigious western cattle businesses. Known for its top quality cattle, this ranch has had over 100 years of success.

There is a wide variety of motels, hotels, and restaurants for you to "hang your hat" in. If you expect to visit Cheyenne during Frontier Days, accommodations should be booked ahead of time. If you plan to explore the wilderness in Wyoming, stop at the Wyoming Travel Commission in Cheyenne on Interstate 25, and collect all the necessary information, maps and brochures you will need for your trip.

Not too far from Cheyenne, about 30 miles (50 km) are the **Vedauwoo Rocks,** a popular stop for rock climbers, photographers and picnickers. The name means "Earthborn" in the Cheyenne language. This jumbled mass of unusual rock formations are located on Pole Mountain between Laramie and Cheyenne.

A hardworking ranch hand drives the cattle out to pasture.

Laramie, the Gem City of the Plains

On your way out of Cheyenne West, about 50 miles (80 km) is the town of **Laramie** which is also one of Wyoming's oldest cities. The town was named after the legendary French-Canadian trapper, Jacques La Ramie, whose name was also given to a military post, a mountain range, a peak, a river, a county and a section of the Wyoming plains all in the Rockies area. La Ramie, a free trapper working the southeastern part of Wyoming, was said to have been killed by unfriendly Indians along the banks of the river that bears his name.

Laramie has a history and foundation very similar to that of Cheyenne. This city called "The Gem City of the Plains," made history by having the first woman in the world to serve on a court jury in 1870. Another "first" occurred when "grandma" Louiza Swain went to the polls and became the first woman in the world to vote in a general election. Wyoming was the first state in the country to give women the right to vote. This happened in 1869 when the Wyoming Territorial Legislature passed resolutions that offered "married women in their separate property, and the enjoyments of fruits of their labor," and a school law providing equal pay for female school teachers. Wyoming women were trailblazers in pursuing women's rights. The leader of suffragettes, in Laramie, Susan Anthony, rejoiced that Wyoming was '... the first place on God's green earth which could consistently claim to be the land of the free!"

The first chance for the vote came in 1870 when most of the one thousand women in Wyoming went to the polls. After the initial excitement, this event was soon forgotten. In 1889, when the State Constitution was being drawn, there was a threat to repeal suffrage. Mrs. Theresa Jenkins, a women's rights activist, organized a demonstration for every woman in Cheyenne to come to the Capitol and insist that they keep their voting rights. The demonstration was successful and that night Mrs. Jenkins went home and delivered a baby girl!

Laramie started as a temporary tent city in 1868, and today it is the third largest city in Wyoming and the home of the University of Wyoming. Besides the University, some of the other points of interest include the **Geological Museum,** the **Fine Arts Center** and the **Rocky Mountain Herbarium.** The Herbarium located on the third floor of the Aven Nelson Building, contains more than 320,000 specimens of Rocky Mountain plants and is one of the best known herbaria in the country. **Fort Sanders,** three miles (five km) from Laramie; **Laramie Plains Museum;** and the **Overland Trail Art Gallery** are also worth visiting. Laramie hosts a rodeo early July, a local square dance festival in August, and a 4-H county fair in mid-August.

As you travel through southeastern Wyoming, you will follow a similar course to that laid out by the early explorers and others who ventured in wagon trains along the Overland Trail. Wyoming was, and continues to be, "the land of the cowboy." In this ranching country, the quiet of the evening is broken by the bleating of the sheep. The sunsets, mountain peaks, and old trails never change. Most folk here take pride in maintaining the traditions of the Old West, while keeping in step with the world's technological developments in agriculture and farming.

A Wyoming cowboy prepares for the ride ahead.

BOZEMAN, MONTANA

Americans are fond of remembering the West's many mining camps as rambunctious and ramshackle towns thrown up overnight when gold or silver was discovered. Towns and cities of today's Rockies that had such beginnings proudly and nostalgically remind themselves and their visitors of their romantic heritage.

In doing so, they blithely overlook the certainly less romantic aspects of daily life. The myth would convince us that all the men in town spent every waking minute working their claims, and that the only women present were the gaudily dressed "soiled doves" of the saloons. When darkness fell over the diggings, the men repaired to saloons to consume rye whiskey – and nothing else – while playing poker until dawn.

Bozeman, Montana, did not start out that way. It came into existence because of the miners' needs. Men who devoted themselves to seeking elusive mineral riches during a short summer season had no time to plant crops.

Bozeman sits in a wide and fertile valley with mountains ringing the horizon. Even though we think of the concept as a 20th-Century one, Bozeman was a planned community. On August 9, 1864, a group of settlers sat down and decided to establish a farming community. They would make their money by supplying food to the mining camps located in the mountains north and west of here. The group voted to name their town for the man who had conceived the idea and who had brought some of them here, John M. Bozeman.

Bozeman Leads the Way

It was the beginning of a stable community. Some of the great Rockies family fortunes were begun by those who were wise enough to venture west to serve as merchants, freighters, cattle ranchers and farmers. Untold thousands who came only for the precious metals went home penniless, while those who brought in and sold them the necessities of life profited and stayed.

John Bozeman seems to have learned that lesson the hard way. In 1862, he, too, came west to make his fortune as a miner, and failed. Wintering at Bannack, Montana Territory, he joined with John M. Jacobs in designing a shorter route north from Fort Laramie to Montana's new gold camps. Becoming known as the Bozeman Road, it was popular with gold-seekers for three years, although it was far more difficult and dangerous than the competing route laid out by former mountain man Jim Bridger.

Red Cloud's War

Hardship was not to stand in the way of those afflicted with gold fever. Bozeman's route offered less water, less forage for the horses, and passed through the prime hunting land of the Sioux Indians. Having been pushed westward long enough by white settlement, the Sioux were by now unwilling to give up this game-rich area. Led by Red Cloud, they fought. The new wagon route became known as the "bloody Bozeman," and the Sioux efforts are still remembered as Red Cloud's War. Red Cloud and his people won, and the U.S. Army

Preceding pages, cheerleaders strut their stuff down Main Street in the Bozeman Sweet Pea Festival, Montana. Left, morning light over Lone Mountain, Montana; and right, a special sight—the great horned owl.

officially closed the three-year-old route.

John Bozeman, having initiated the problem, retired from guiding wagon trains over his route after the first year. Upon the founding of Bozeman, he settled there to farm and to serve as a probate judge. But in 1867, as John was travelling into eastern Montana to solicit a flour contract with the army, he was killed by Blackfeet Indians. They were not the Sioux, but perhaps it was poetic justice.

In death as in life, John Bozeman assisted his namesake town. Bozeman residents appealed to the federal government for military protection from Indian raids such as the one that killed their founder. They received Fort Ellis, a cavalry post which, naturally, became another market for the produce of Gallatin Valley farms surrounding the town. By 1880, when it was 16 years old, Bozeman had 3,800 residents, but its subsequent growth has been much slower: 50 years later, the population had not quite doubled. Today Bozeman has 22,000 people, half of them students at **Montana State University.**

Studying at "Moo U"

This public institution opened as the Agricultural College of the State of Montana in 1893, with eight enrolled students and no campus. Although it is now a university, and the largest in the state's system, it is known as "Moo U" by those who remember its beginnings. Important research into improved crop and livestock production continues at the university; there is also an excellent film and television department, along with art, architecture, engineering, social services and nursing programs.

On the university campus is the **Museum of the Rockies,** a well-designed modern museum dedicated to telling the story of this region from prehistoric times to the 20th Century. The museum sponsors summer season paleontological and archeological digs, which have uncovered significant dinosaur remains as well as evidences of Native-American cultures. Finds from these digs as well as farming relics are on exhibit.

Special changing exhibits feature art or historical objects from the museum's collections, as well as works by contemporary western artists and artisans. An

The story of John Bozeman is depicted in this town mural, Bozeman.

annual western art show and sale occurs from late June to mid-July. The museum is open seven days a week during summer, closed Mondays during winter and on all national holidays. Admission is free; group tours can be arranged on request.

Bright Lights to Red Lights

Cultural events centered on the university are not the only ones Bozeman offers. Like many other small and isolated Rockies towns, Bozeman has a tradition of self-sufficiency in entertainment. In 1890, the ornate **Bozeman Opera House** opened, hosting various musical and theatrical performers — from Sarah Bernhardt to Al Jolson — and lecturers over the years. For a different clientele, a red-light district of at least six "sporting houses" (of prostitution) operated in a most businesslike way. From 1900 to 1912, each house paid a monthly fine to city hall for breaking the law. The opera house and the "sporting houses" are long since gone.

The 1970s saw a rebirth of interest in preserving historic Bozeman buildings. All along Main Street, the central downtown business district, brick "business blocks" dating from the late 19th Century were restored to their original exterior appearances. Even though their interiors are modern stores and offices, a stroll down Main Street is a pleasant view of the west's past.

Bozeman supports 15 small art galleries and dealers, offering exhibits and sale of works in all media from weaving to photography, painting to jewelry, from artists around the western United States.

The Sweet Pea Arts & Crafts Festival

The annual Sweet Pea Arts & Crafts Festival (the second week in August) combines display and sales with a carnival-like offering of foods, outdoor musical performances and open-air theater by Shakespeare, performed by a Montana repertory company that tours the state each summer.

The Sweet Pea Festival began in 1906, celebrating a major industry in town: production and packing of seed peas for sale to farmers throughout the nation, and canning of peas for food consumption. During World War I, the festival was discontinued, and wasn't revived until 1978. By then, the seed pea and canning industries were gone from the town, but many backyard gardens still blossomed annually with sweet pea flowers, so the sweet pea festival was resurrected.

Cattle ranching is also a part of Bozeman's heritage, and so, too, is the cowboy. "Cowboy art" is available in the galleries — realistic paintings of western landscapes and ranching scenes past and present. Cowboy cafes offer the hearty food that fuels ranch hands for long days, and western clothing stores supply their Stetson hats, Levi jeans, bandanna handkerchiefs and boots with heels designed for various kinds of work. Cowboy bars offer country-western music for listening or dancing.

Educated Cowboys

In mid-June, Bozeman welcomes the National Intercollegiate Rodeo Association Finals, a rodeo for the best student competitors from more than 200 colleges in the United States, including 10 in Montana. These are young people attending college on rodeo scholarships, who have qualified for this event by their performances in rodeos between competing schools during the preceding academic year. They are competing both as individuals and as team members representing their schools.

A specially-groomed arena at Montana State University houses the Finals events, each night for a week. Related events include a "Miss College Rodeo" pageant, a cowboy golf tournament and an art show.

Because of its small size, Bozeman does not offer mass transportation. But visitors who rent cars to tour the surrounding area will find it worthwhile, summer or winter.

Bridger Bowl, north of town, offers downhill ski slopes noted for their dry powder snow. Next to it in the Bridger Range is **Crosscut Ranch,** a year-round facility with 12½ miles (20 km) of groomed cross-country ski trails in the winter and a guest ranch in the summer.

West of Bozeman on I-90, the **Madison Buffalo Jump** vividly explains how Plains Indians hunted the buffalo in the ages before they had horses. Working toward a cliff such as the one at this site, they herded the animals into a stampede over the side. At the kill site below, the buffalo were slaughtered and butchered in a process putting to use every part of the animal — hide, meat, bones, sinews, even bladders (which became inflated "footballs" for children's play). Interpretive signs at the Madison Buffalo Jump explain the use of the site as a camp during the buffalo preparation, and tell of archeological finds from the area.

Neighboring Scenic Parks

The nearby **Headwaters State Park,** also along I-90 and well-marked, is where the Jefferson, Madison and Gallatin rivers converge to form the **Missouri River.** Within the park, visitors experience the land as Captain Meriwether Lewis did on July 27, 1805, when the Lewis and Clark expedition reached this point. He noted in his journal (in his own spelling style): "we arrived at 9 a.m. at the junction of ... the Missouri and the country opens suddonly to extensive and beautifull plains and meadows which appear to be surrounded in every direction with distant and lofty mountains ..."

Interpretive signs tell the story of this area's use before whites came, and of the Lewis and Clark expedition. One of their purposes in exploring the vast "Louisiana Purchase" of lands obtained from France was to discover the fabled "Northwest Passage," a hoped-for water route to the Pacific Ocean. At the headwaters of the Missouri, they knew that no such water route existed, for here the Missouri stopped.

South of Bozeman, through the beautiful **Gallatin Canyon,** is one of the gateways to **Yellowstone National Park.** Throughout this area of clear streams and lushly green-forested mountains peaks are guest ranches with year-round recreation facilities, including skiing, fishing, pack trips, horseback riding, golfing, swimming and primitive or deluxe lodgings.

About one day's drive north from Bozeman is **Glacier National Park,** which crosses from Montana into Canada as Waterton Park. It is aptly named for the glaciers that remain upon its craggy, glacier-sculpted peaks, providing some of the most breathtaking scenery in the Middle Rockies.

An opening in the Shoshone National Forest from Red Lodge Road.

Glaciers and Eagles

Glacier Park is not nearly so developed with road networks and tourist facilities as is Yellowstone National Park. Only one road crosses from the east to the west entrance — **Going-to-the-Sun Highway,** which crosses the Continental Divide on Logan Pass. This narrow road, built for yesteryear's smaller cars, is cut shelf-like high up on the solid rock of the Garden Wall escarpment. It does truly seem to head for the sun.

These mountains show well the effect of glaciation on the hard rock faces when a mammoth ice sheet once covered the region. Cirques, or high mountain basins scoured out by glaciers, are in evidence, but the remaining glaciers are tiny by comparison to the ancient ones.

Alpine meadows of wildflowers bloom in late spring and early summer, and perpetual snowfields allow visitors to go cross-country skiing in the warm summer sun. While the park is open in some areas for winter cross-country skiing, Going-to-the-Sun Highway cannot be cleared of snowdrifts until June — and snows begin again in September or October. This is definitely a place to visit in summer.

At a lower elevation, however, is one of the grand sights of the Rockies. In October, bald eagles, an endangered species protected here, swarm to feed on spawning salmon. Visitors are allowed within sight of hundreds of the birds, but binoculars are worthwhile.

Camping and Bears

Hiking is the way to see Glacier Park, and trails exist thoughout. Backcountry camping is allowed, and campgrounds and lodges by lower elevation roadsides are provided. This is a prime home for dangerous grizzly and black bears, so park rangers close campgrounds or trails where bears have been sighted. Visitors are alerted to such situations upon arrival.

Bozeman and its environs offer a way of life centered upon outdoors activities. From active sports to scenery viewing, here is the essence of the Middle Rockies.

Rock croppings decorate this lake in the Custer National Forest.

SALT LAKE CITY, UTAH

Years ago, Salt Lake city enjoyed the reputation of being a strait-laced provincial western town. In the eyes of the "well-travelled" visitor, only two distinctions redeemed the city from mediocrity. One, as the capital of the Great Basin kingdom of the Church of Latter-Day Saints (Mormons), Salt Lake City seemed like a foreign land to most Gentiles (non-Mormons)—an exotic encounter in his own homeland for the American visitor and a unique experience to those travelling from abroad. The distinct Latter-Day Saints' heritage left an indelible imprint on the city's history, architecture and lifestyle, which visitors readily discern. Two, the city's physical setting also placed Salt Lake City in the guidebooks as a memorable place to visit in the western Rocky mountains. The city's matchless setting between the towering, jagged, snowclad Wasatch Mountains to the east, and the copper-pitted Oquirrh Mountains to the west, with the blue Great Salt Lake shimmering off to the northwest, brought tourists to this city of Zion in moderate droves.

But after scanning the peaks and vistas, "bobbing" in the unsinkable salty waters, gawking at the Mormon citizenry and suspecting everyone of polygamy, boredom set in and soon the visitor asked, "Is there life in Salt Lake City after the local Woolworth's closes?" The answer was no.

But not today! For Salt Lake City is a premiere urban oasis in a rising new American West. The city now has not only vistas and virtue, but also vitality. Due to a wave of outside influences during the last decade—the influx of energy-related and electronics industries, banking and corporate interests—coupled with the phenomenal growth of Wasatch ski resorts (only minutes away from downtown), Salt Lake City has leaped into modernity boasting a contemporary, cultured, uncrowded, vibrant lifestyle envied by all its Rocky Mountain urban rivals. Salt Lake City is still a "clean" city, but at no time is it ever dull.

This prosperity has created a benign tension between those "of the kingdom" and those outside the kingdom, placing the city squarely at a crossroads between the new "Gentile" growth and the saintly heritage of the region. So far, a beneficial balance has been struck between the two, making the area a Rocky Mountain Zion for all!

Temple Square

By day, the heart and hub of Salt Lake City is the sandstone and adobe walled 10-acre (four-hectare) grounds of **Temple Square**, naturally the place to begin a visit. Shortly after their arrival at Salt Lake Valley in 1847, Brigham Young, with cane in hand, consecrated this site between two forks of City Creek for the construction of the church's temple. For over 40 years thereafter, oxen teams dragged and hauled granite blocks from nearby quarries in the Wasatch Mountains until the majestic, six spired neo-Gothic Latter-Day Saints (LDS) Temple stood completed. Gold-leafed and conspicuously statued atop the Temple is the angel figure of Moroni, blowing his horn to announce the Second Coming of Christ. The Temple itself is used for the holy ordinances of the LDS church, such as baptisms, weddings and family "sealing" ceremonies, and is open only to Mormons with "recommends" from their ward bishops. But the general public can amble about within the manicured grounds of Temple Square (a delight at Christmas time, when it is aglitter with thousands of lights) where two **Visitors** Centers provide exhibits of Mormon history and beliefs. While on the Temple grounds, of note is the **Sea Gull Monument** commemorating the "miracle of the gulls," who saved the Mormon pioneers' first crop from swarms of crickets, and **Assembly Hall**, a place of worship. And one should not miss a visit to the acoustically sensitive home of the Mormon Tabernacle Choir, the **Tabernacle**, and its magnificent organ with 11,000 pipes, considered to be one of the world's finest pipe organs.

From Temple Square it is only a short walk in several directions to other noteworthy LDS church sites in this district of Salt Lake. Going out the west gate of Temple Square you cannot miss the mausoleum-housed **Museum of Church History and Art** where religious exhibits on church leaders, western art, the Mormon westward migration, and other subjects provide additional knowledge to the traveller. Directly east of Temple Square is a full block clustered with Church related buildings. Passing out the south gate of Temple Square and heading east, the route is marked by the **Brigham Young Monument** (depicting Brigham Young, the frontiersman Jim Bridger and the Shoshone Indian Chief Washakie) and the elegant **Hotel Utah**, one the West's finest historic hotels. Directly north and east, the hotel is flanked by magnificent fountains, flowered gardens and leisurely lawns that comprise the grounds to a complex of other noteworthy LDS buildings.

A Genealogical Library

Dominating this complex is the towering twenty-eight story **Church Office Building**, where the LDS genealogical library (largest in the world) is located. Almost one million rolls of microfilmed records of births, baptisms and deaths from around the world are housed in its archive collection, and a staff of librarians, speaking forty languages, will guide you to the

roots of your family lineage. When your eyes tire of searching parish records, take the express elevator to the twenty-sixth floor, where an observation area provides the best panoramic view other than from a Wasatch mountain top. Views of the Great Salt Lake, the Wasatch and Oquirrh Mountains, Capitol Hill, downtown Salt Lake City and a postcard view of Temple Square will refresh your vision.

Brigham's Beehive House

Directly south from the Church Office Building, across the plaza, are the former residences of Brigham Young and many of his 27 wives. The **Beehive House** (1853-1854), on the southeast corner of the block, was the official residence of Brigham Young, where as an LDS church president and Utah territorial governor he received many prominent visitors. The charming three-storied Federal and Greek revival styled residence, which is now a National Historic Landmark, is named for the unique hand-hewed beehive sculpture resting on the roof's cupola; and its

Salt Lake City

restored interior pine paneled walls and period decorations quickly draw you to the Mormon past. Next door stands the **Lion House** (1855), a "supplementary" domestic residence for Brigham Young and his wives where many of his fifty-six children grew to age. An impressive sculptured stone lion guards this communal residence's entrance. The main floor lodged Young's many wives in individual quarters, and the twenty gabled dormers on the second story marked the rooms of the older children. Though the Lion House is closed to the public (the LDS church now uses it for social purposes), more of the Mormon pioneer past can be discovered by walking westward back to the Brigham Young Monument and heading three blocks northward on Main Street, passing the elegant **McCune Mansion** (home of Alfred McCune, a mining pioneer and millionaire) on the right, to the **Daughters of Utah Pioneers'** or **Pioneer Memorial Museum**. The volunteer D.U.P. Museum is crammed, nook and cranny, with pioneer memorabilia, from doll to military collections— enough Mormon paraphenalia and belongings to overwhelm any visitor.

A stained-glass frontier woman in the Pioneer Museum, Salt Lake City.

The State Capitol

Across the street from this monument to the Mormons', the secular world of the Gentile past and present begins with a tour of the **Capitol Hill** area. The Renaissance Revival copper domed **State Capitol**, the temporal seat of power in Utah, overlooks Temple Square and the rest of the valley. On a clear day or night, from the steps beneath its Corinthian marble columns, the perfect photographic view of the Wasatch Mountains and the platted streets below is seen. Inside rises a 165-foot (50-meter) rotunda, arching over the building's attractions: the 23-karat gold-leaf state reception room, an exhibition hall displaying Utah's attractions and history, and marble staircases leading to the galleried chambers of state government. Outside there is a 40-acre (16-hectare) park with lawns and strolling gardens and other sites to visit such as the restored **Council Hall** (first meeting place for the territorial legislature), **White Memorial Chapel** (a Gothic steepled former LDS chapel), and **Memory Grove**, a secluded park in **City Creek Canyon** east of the Capitol where many downtown workers spread out picnic lunches on the banks of City Creek.

Surrounding Capitol Hill are two historic residential districts. West of the State Capitol is the **Marmalade Historic District**—its streets named after fruits—where many early English and Scandinavian immigrants resided. East of City Creek Canyon and accessible from Temple Square is the **Avenues Historic District**, where one can find a wide variety of residential architectures, including many restored Victorian houses. A number of mansions and buildings here are noteworthy and within short walking distance from Temple Square. They include the **Cathedral of the Madeleine** (a gray sandstone Catholic Romanesque style church with stained glass sanctuary windows) and the mansions of two prominent Utah silver magnates who owned the Silver King Mine in Park City, the **Keith-Brown Mansion** and the **Thomas Kearns Mansion**, which is now used as Utah's governor's mansion.

Tracing the way back to Temple Square, you can shrug off spiritual values in favor of the commercial and cultural ones found in the downtown district of Salt Lake.

Shopping Districts

The secular life begins with downtown's many shopping areas which are easily reached from all of Salt Lake's major hotels. Commercial Salt Lake City is compactly and conveniently arranged to meet all one's shopping dreams. South of Temple Square is **Crossroads Plaza** (America's largest downtown shopping mall) where close to 100 shops and stores, three movie theaters, 22 restaurants or cafes, and a sports mall are all available. Across Main Street from the plaza, an additional 60 beautiful stores and restaurants are located in the **ZCMI Center**, operated by the LDS church. In addition, three blocks west of Temple Square (reached by a turn-of-the-century trolley car) is a 30-acre (12 hectare) multipurpose residential and commercial complex, the **Devereaux Plaza** at **Triad Center**. It features fine shops, restaurants, private social clubs, an ice skating rink, and the restored **Devereaux Mansion** at the center of the complex.

The vitality of Salt Lake's shopping district is only a small reflection of the growing prosperity and energy of the city. Almost daily, a new construction crane lifts its head toward the desert blue skies as the moribund pre-1970s lifestyle fades into the distant past. An energetic cultural and recreational life is evident everywhere in Salt Lake City. Ice cream parlors and movie houses, popular local weekend diversions, still abound, but now there is a Gentile night life as well!

Capping Salt Lake City's new cultural life are a number of nationally acclaimed restaurants and dozens of hot nightspots and clubs. No "liquorbythedrink" (one word in Utah) except in private bottle clubs (where visitor memberships can be purchased) is still the norm, but the nightlife in Salt Lake is no longer just a night of bingo, as new "to-be-seen-at" social clubs proliferate and compete to meet the demands of Gentile immigrants and local "jack" (inactive) Mormons.

Cultural Activities

Summertime is Salt Lake's best downtown season. The city now features a variety of activities for both

The inspiring Mormon Tabernacle Choir.

Mormon and non-Mormons alike, such as arts and ethnic festivals where one can buy local crafts and art works with one hand while eating Greek souvlaki and Navajo tacos with the other. Or one can buy tickets to shows and entertainment at the nearby **Salt Palace Convention Center**, where activities range from concerts, circuses and rodeos to cheering Salt Lake's own professional basketball team, the Utah "Jazz."

If one has "higher" culture in mind, Salt Lake City has everything in the performing arts any cosmopolitan visitor could desire, for this western urban center is an oasis of culture in the Rocky Mountains, where many nationally acclaimed music, theater and dance companies now reside. **Symphony Hall**, an architectural and acoustical gem, houses the world-renowned **Utah Symphony Orchestra**, while next door the **Salt Lake Art Center** offers the best work of Utah artistry along with visiting national exhibits. Several blocks away at the **Capitol Theatre**, performing arts have no equal in the Rocky Mountain West when the **Utah Opera Company** and **Ballet West** take to fulfilling their busy calendar of engaging works.

Medical Schools and Museums

Downtown Salt Lake is not the only attraction for those seeking entertainment and fun. Within easy access from downtown Salt Lake are other areas that offer varied experiences. To the east is Salt Lake's **Emigration Visitors District**, a scenic triangle of entertaining, historic, educational and cultural attractions situated near the mouth of **Emigration Canyon**. At the **University of Utah**, whose medical school implanted the world's first artificial heart in Barney Clarke, one can stroll around the vast, gardened campus overlooking the panoramic valley below, visit the collections and exhibits at the **Museum of Fine Arts** and the **Museum of Natural History** or tour **Fort Douglas**, a National Historic Landmark, which was established to protect the overland mail route and whose federal guns were trained on the Mormon settlers below to keep Utah Territory within the Union during the Civil War. From here, it is only a short hop to **Hogle Zoo** on Sunnyside Avenue, where 1,000 exotic animals await your visit. Directly across from Hogle Zoo, Utah's pioneer past comes

The Mormon Assembly Hall, Salt Lake City.

alive in a recreated typical Mormon settlement, **Pioneer Trail State Park**. The park's attractions include **"This is the Place" Monument**, commemorating the Mormon's entry into the valley, **Brigham Young's Forest Farm House**, an authentic social hall, a pioneer store, and pioneer craft demonstrations. It is an excellent picnic spot from which to observe what the pioneers may have felt as they entered the Salt Lake Valley from the Wasatch Mountains and saw the Great Salt Lake in the west.

Nostalgic Fun

The **Trolley Square District** is six blocks southeast of downtown along Seventh East. It centers around a series of renovated 1908 trolley car barns turned into a bustling, brick-paved shopping, dining and theater area known as **Trolley Square**, an area reminiscent of Boston's Faneuil Hall and San Francisco's Ghirardelli Square. A few blocks south on Seventh East is **Liberty Park** where on landscaped lawns under shady pines, one can enjoy watching people swim, play tennis, and paddle on the ponds. After visiting the park's ivory, two-storied adobe **Isaac Chase Home and Mill** with its period furnishings, take a leisurely walk and listen to the trumpeter swans, the rare Andean condor and hundreds of other bird species at the **Tracy Aviary.**

The **Other Side of the Tracks District** literally designates an area with a rich ethnic heritage on the west side of the railroad tracks that pass through the city only a few blocks away from downtown. Railroad buffs may want to visit the nostalgic **Union Pacific Depot**, where western scenes are depicted on murals and stained glass, or the renovated **Rio Grande Depot**, two blocks to the south and now the **Utah State History Museum**, which offers many exhibits on Utah's rich and varied past. Continuing west from these sites, one can visit the unique **International Peace Gardens** representing 18 countries, take a boat ride on the Jordan River, or travel out to the **Utah State Fair Grounds** for such seasonal events as the western style state fair during the second week of September.

Beyond the city's immediate environs, several of Salt Lake's scenic satellite areas, such as **Great Salt Lake Desert/Oquirrh Mountain Tour** await discovery in a day's drive. The **Great Salt Lake Park** is a must for any visitor. But because of rising waters in the early 1980s, swimming and picnicking will be limited for a few years. The lake, in one of its flooding cycles, has inundated the causeway to **Antelope Island**, and beautiful beaches, bird rookeries, and a small herd of buffalo (American bison) are temporarily inaccessible. Plans are underway to carry the public to the island by barges. Near the sailing marina on the lake's southeastern shores are breathtaking views of the Great Salt Lake, Antelope Island, mountainous **Stansbury Island** to the west, and spectacular sunsets.

Along the Western Shores

Travelling west along the lake's shores, one has many choices of what to do next. Far west of the **Oquirrh Mountains** are the **Bonneville Salt Flats**, famous site of numerous world land speed records. Nearer to the western side of the Oquirrh Mountains unfolds the fascination of the American West,

A skiing couple atop a Snowbird (Utah) mountain.

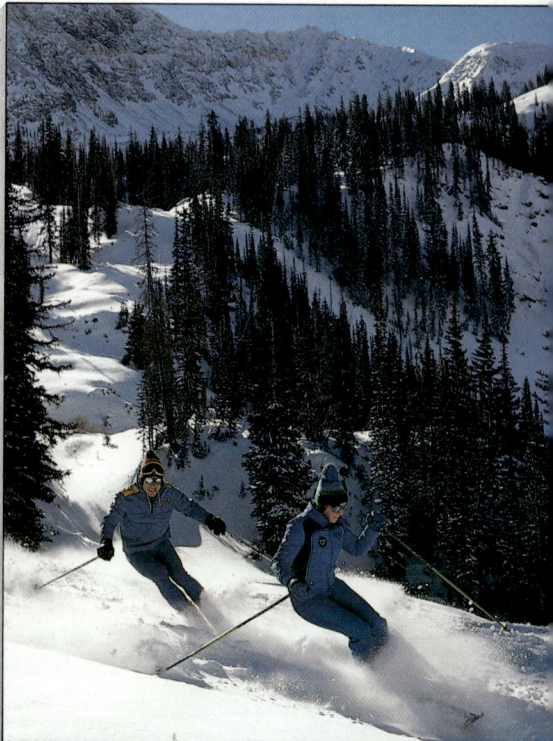

where Pony Express riders once carried the mail and where mining ghost towns named **Gold Hill, Ophir** and **Mercur** still capture the imagination. The culminating experience is a visit to the **Bingham Copper Mine** on the east side of the mountains, boasted as the "largest man-made excavation in the world, twice as deep as the Empire State Building is tall!"

Alpine Loop and Osmond Studios Tours

After touring the Great Salt Lake and sites west of Salt Lake City, the **Alpine Loop Tour**, 45 minutes south of the city offers a variety of activities including some of Utah's most popular scenic excitement. Start the day with a tour of the **Osmond Studios** in North Orem, visit **Brigham Young University**, the nation's largest private university, or even do some spelunking in famous **Timpanogos Cave National Monument**. Any one of these activities is only minutes away from the scenic beauty of Mount Timpanogos. Here one can wind pass thawing springtime mountain streams

on the nineteenth century **Heber Creeper Steam Train** trip to **Bridal Veil Falls**, or in summer windsurf on **Deer Creek Reservoir** below the mountain's majesty, or cast eyes on an incredible alpine autumn by driving along the scenic loop from **Provo Canyon** to **American Fork Canyon**. Or finally, one can snow ski all winter at **Sundance**, movie star Robert Redford's ski resort on the flank of the high peak.

"Powder Perfect" Canyon Country

Any season of the year, anywhere along the Wasatch Front there are exuberant experiences, but the best Utah has to offer is surprisingly only minutes east from downtown Salt Lake in **Wasatch Canyon Country**. This is a relatively small area containing seven major ski resorts, four in **Big and Little Cottonwood Canyons** on the western side of the range and three near Park City on the eastern side of the mountains. All offer the "Greatest Snow on Earth" in the winter, and, for all other seasons, the "Greatest Hiking on Earth."

The dramatic skyline of Salt Lake City.

"Powder perfect" is the only way to describe the skiing at **Alta** and **Snowbird**, both located in Little Cottonwood Canyon. With an annual snowfall of 500 inches of light, dry powder, and with lifts and trails unspoiled by crowds, you know immediately that from Thanksgiving to early summer you can anticipate the consummate skiing experience. Each resort presents a unique skiing vacation.

Skiing Sensations

The "Alta Experience" is considered "the" intimate mountain experience. Once you have experienced Alta, you will go home and brag about it. Lifts named Sunnyside, Sugarloaf and Supreme take you to fluffy virgin powder almost every morning, and the resort's leisurely lodge life of superb dining, cozy fires, saunas, jacuzzis and a 100 degree F (38°C) outdoor swimming pool all contribute to a memorable experience. On the other hand, Snowbird has the reputation as the "Giantkiller" and is Utah's fast-paced, ultrafashionable skiing resort. With 50 percent of its runs rated advanced/expert, this resort is a must for those seeking the ultimate breathtaking descent. The Garaventa tram ride to the top of 11,000-foot (3550-meter) Hidden Peak is just spectacular in itself. In addition to alpine grandeur, Snowbird has excellent lodges, dining and bars to entertain you through the night.

If you are searching for skiing that is less commercial, slower-paced and more family oriented, **Solitude** and **Brighton** ski resorts in Big Cottonwood Canyon are the best destinations. It is here that "locals" learn to ski. If you're friendly, one may even adopt you and show you his favorite secret slopes and runs.

"Greatest Snow on Earth"

From Big Cottonwood Canyon, it's over to **Park City** on the east side of the Wasatch Range, where one finds resorts ranging from ruggedly wild Parkwest to world class Park City to Utah's newest ski area, the "unspoiled, uncrowded, uncommonly civilized" Deer Valley. All three are located only minutes from the

Left, a monument to Mormon leader, Brigham Young; and right, one of Young's 57 wives—a typical Mormon frontier woman.

heart of frontier flavored Park City. This historic mining town, nestled in the heart of Wasatch ski and hiking country, has a lifestyle and lively nightlife to match. Uncommon vacation condos, boutiques, gourmet restaurants, private bottle clubs and such annual events as the winter **United States Film Festival** and the summer **Park City Arts Festival** have transformed this once booming Utah mining town into a wealthy skiing mecca and summer vacation spot.

On the outskirts of Park City is another one of Utah's favorite local skiing areas, **Parkwest**. Its rugged powdered terrain, reflected in runs named Bad Hombre, Slaughterhouse, and Massacre, gives clues to the challenge ahead. After testing your skiing skills there, a little more ambiance might seem enticing and the Park City ski resort is the answer.

Park City is the largest ski area in Utah presenting well balanced runs from wide open beginner slopes to famous powdered bowls like Jupiter, Blue Slip, and Puma that challenge the advanced skiers. But if pampered poshness is your dream, then your skiing destination is luxurious **Deer Valley**.

Valets will unload your skis, attendants will watch over them in special ski corrals, and Stein Ericksen, Olympic gold medal winner and resort director, will see that you have a relaxing and sumptuous skiing vacation.

Wildlife, Wildflowers and Waterfalls

The Wasatch canyons hold not only the "Greatest Snow on Earth" but also the "Greatest Hiking on Earth." In the spring, summer or fall, in any of the main canyons, like Big and Little Cottonwood Canyons, and lovely **Millcreek Canyon**, or in any of the smaller canyons, such as **Neff's Ferguson** and **Lamb's Canyons,** the traveller will find a hiker's and rock climber's paradise. Numerous well marked trails crisscross the canyons leading the hiker or picnicker to meadows of wildflowers full of wildlife, splendid pine and aspen forests or to hidden, but easily accessible, mountain streams, foaming waterfalls and pristine lakes. Hiking, scenery, photography, fishing, picnicking, and camping are all only minutes away from Salt Lake City.

A strip mining operation near Salt Lake City.

Joseph Smith

(1805-1844)
"I teach the people
correct principles and
they govern themselves."

MORMONS: "A CHOSEN PEOPLE"

Mormonism, the most American of major religions, always had an ambivalent relationship with the rest of the nation. Mormon (officially, the Church of Jesus Christ of Latter-Day saints is the name of the largest branch of followers of Mormon founder Joseph Smith) experience in many ways repeats American experience, but for more than the first half century of their history Mormons confronted fellow citizens across a gulf of seemingly endless hostility. They were considered a peculiar people with odd, unAmerican attitudes, and for awhile they toyed with the idea of building a separate nation. On the other hand, it is hard to imagine how Mormonism could have spread anywhere but the intellectually and socially turbulent North American frontier.

That frontier was the prime source of America's symbolic identity and national character. Mormon culture, born and nurtured on the frontier, selected from the available components of that identity, choosing from the Puritan sense of mission and divine selection, freemasonry's cult of secrecy and brotherhood, pseudo-intellectual attempts to explain American Indian origins, and the swirl of social, religious, and economic experimentation that gripped a young nation in the romantic era. of the early 19th Century. Mormons saw danger and excess in the wilderness, and they, like other Americans, tried to subdue it, pursuing an orderly, civilized ideal of neat farms and great cities—an ideal made possible by a steady, strengthening flow of immigrant converts to new orthodoxies like American ideology and Mormon theology. The parallels between the religion's and the nation's experiences became more apparent in the 20th Century after the Latter-Day Saints, under duress, abandoned their most idiosyncratic ways—polygamy, theocracy, and communalism—and reembraced middle class America. Further parallels occurred in the 1980s as a Mormon vanguard led the national shift to the political right.

Through much of their history, the Mormons sought to organize their society along different lines. Today, their culture's uniqueness is composed of the residue of that

Left, Mormon founder, Joseph Smith, had a vision; and right, a portrait of the imposing-looking Brigham Young.

distinct social order: their insulating sense that they are a different and special people, their rigid adherence to a set of values that they feel the modern world threatens, and an institutional framework that permeates their lives. Of course, they are no longer just an American people; they have achieved the international presence for which they worked hard. They are emerging as a major religon, not major on the scale of the world's largest religions, certainly—their million members don't compare with 50 million American Catholics, for example—but their

BRIGHAM YOUNG.—*For sketch of life see Annex No. 91.*

influence exceeds their numbers, and they are one of the world's fastest growing churches. Their 30,000 or so missionaries effectively spread a message first spoken by the son of an itinerant family in the primitive backcountry villages of upstate New York.

The "Burned-Over" District

Frontier New York, in the first three decades of the 19th Century, underwent cycles of religious revivalism that historians call the Second Great Awakening. In hectic camp meetings, wandering evangelists competed for the souls of traditionally irreligious frontiersmen. The "burned-over district," as upstate New York was known because of the fervor that swept across it, had been peopled largely by descendents of New England's fervent Calvinist settlers, people like Joseph Smith's Vermont parents. In 1820, Joseph, a 14-year-old confused over religious choices, sought answers in prayer and had the first of a series of visions in which God and others told how true Christianity had been lost from the earth. Between 1823 and 1827 the Angel Moroni, the last survivor of a chosen people who had inhabited pre-Columbian America, revealed the location of a buried set of gold plates that told the story of Moroni's people, the Nephites, and the ancestors of American Indians, known as the Lamanites. Using a special instrument buried with the plates, Joseph translated them, completing the Book of Mormon and

driven from the State."

After retreating to other parts of Missouri, they arrived in Illinois. Here Mormon culture truly blossomed, as the harassed people seemed to have found their "City on a Hill" on the swampy banks of the Mississippi, where they built the city of Nauvoo. Nauvoo was the largest city in Illinois of its time, and it benefitted from a liberal state charter which gave its government—Smith and fellow church leaders—almost independent powers, including its own army, the Nauvoo Legion. But the problems that had repeatedly alienated neighbors arose again: the Saints asserted that as a divinely chosen people they would inherit the earth, and with their industrious accumulation of property, occasional boasting and military

founding his church, with six members, in 1830.

From the moment his story leaked out, Joseph Smith and his followers were criticized, ostracized, and attacked by neighbors who considered him a charlatan. As membership slowly grew, the church moved, first to Kirtland, Ohio, where failure of a banking scheme in 1837 led to widespread apostasy and the leadership's retreat to Far West, Missouri. Devout Mormons expected to await the imminent second coming of Christ here, but instead they were violently attacked by Missouri mobs: 18 were massacred at the Mormon settlement at Haun's Mill, and Governor L. W. Boggs issued an order that the Mormons "must be exterminated or

potential, they seemed poised to do it by force. They also tended to vote as a bloc, giving them the potential to control close elections. Always there were their unorthodox beliefs, which by the 1840s were rumored to include polygamy. A breaking point came when Smith ordered a Nauvoo newspaper run by critical ex-Mormons closed down and its presses smashed. Joseph and his brother Hyrum were arrested and taken to the Carthage jail, where, in June 1844, a mob murdered them.

Enter Brigham Young

Rather than disbanding, the bulk of the Mormons then rallied around Brigham

Young, the head of their preeminent governing body, the Council of Twelve Apostles. In an unparalleled organizational feat (migrants were divided into companies of one hundred; support farms were established along the way; crews constructed trails and river ferries), Young led his people west in search of a new haven. Twelve thousand moved across Iowa in 1846, to Winter Quarters near present Council Bluffs. This was the jumping-off point for the journey to the isolated and barren valley of the Great Salt Lake, the place Young, as the head of the first 148 person migration, chose as their refuge. Between 1847 and 1869, the year of the railroad's arrival, Mormon parties annually crossed the Plains from Winter Quarters, from other Mormon settle-

Meanwhile, Brigham Young sought to build Joseph Smith's dream of the kingdom of God on earth. His visions of the new Mormon homeland were imperial: he proposed a new state of Deseret (the Book of Mormon name for beehive) emcompassing all of present-day Utah, Nevada and Arizona and parts of Idaho, Wyoming, Colorado and southern California. Young sent out parties, carefully composed of men with various useful occupations, to begin occupying this vast expanse. By 1855, a corridor of settlements stretched from Idaho down the west slope of the mountains to San Bernardino. California.

Mormons now had the chance for uninhabited, open practice of their experimental social philosophy. After years of persecu-

VIEW OF SALT LAKE CITY, LOOKING WESTWARD ACROSS THE JORDAN VALLEY.

ments and from overseas, where missionaries were at work. The Saints in Salt Lake City supported the poor's migration through donations to the Perpetual Emigrating Fund, which the migrants were expected to reimburse after establishing themselves. Some walked to Zion, pulling handcarts behind them, but in 1856 the Martin and Willie handcart companies started late and were trapped by snow in central Wyoming. In the worst tragedy of America's overland migration, between 200 and 225 died before relief arrived.

Left, a sketched interior of the Institute of Mormon Presidents; and right, a 19th Century view of Salt Lake City.

tion, the Saints had found an isolated home away from the rest of the United States.

A Theoracy in Utah

The organizational framework for Mormonism was the lay priesthood held by all adult males in the church. It was a patriarchal order that reached from priesthood holding fathers in the family through bishops of neighborhood wards (similar to parishes) through other ascending levels to Brigham Young, the prophet, at the top. The overland migration had strengthened organizational ties; in the mountain West these were refined and institutionalized. Young's own charisma built up members' loyalty and willingness to obey, but so did their sense of shared hardship and group destiny. Jedediah Grant, Mormon leader and first mayor of Salt Lake City, once said that Mormons' faith and testimony were different, much stronger, than that of other religions' adherents because the Saints were asked to believe so much more—especially God's appearance to men in modern times—in the face of great challenges. During the first years in the West, there was no clear line between ecclesiastical and secular government in Utah. Young was territorial governor, and church leaders held most government offices. Utah was, in effect, a theocracy where absolute obedience to a hierarchy was the norm.

That hierarchy pursued its goals of economic cooperation and self-sufficiency through careful planning. Living on the edge of the desert, the Saints first needed a different way of watering their crops than that used in the well-watered East. They hit upon the idea of extensive irrigation systems, the first widespread non-Indian use of irrigation in the United States. These systems were built by cooperative labor, and local church leaders allocated the water. They also distributed land for homes and farm fields according to members' perceived needs. The fields typically surrounded a small village, the focus of Mormon life, where the houses, farm buildings and stock corrals were situated in the middle of carefully laid out blocks. Each village strived toward its own self-sufficiency within the overall general economic and political independence of the kingdom of Zion.

Communal Living in the Mormondom

Manufacturing or raising specific products, especially those which otherwise would be imported, was encouraged and supported by the hierarchy. In the 1860s, the first of many local cooperative merchandising stores was opened (the modern ZCMI department store chain is a free enterprise descendent of these coops). Many of these operations included communally owned factories producing items such as clothing, furniture, textiles and dairy products. In the 1870s, Young encouraged the creation of United Orders in Mormon villages. In this most extreme Mormon communal experiment, members gave up private ownership of all property other than clothing and personal goods. Everything else was communally owned and managed. Most of these experiments, especially the United Orders, failed to achieve their ends, mainly because

of Mormondom's growing connections to the outside world and economy. That process began with the 1849 gold rush, which brought the desperate Saints a windfall in abandoned or traded goods as passing forty-niners lightened their loads to obtain badly needed Mormon farm products and livestock. Then it accelerated after the arrival of the transcontinental railroad in 1869.

The most infamous Mormon institution was polygamy. Joseph Smith first announced it to a small group of church leaders at Nauvoo. The extent of his own plural marriages is still debated. In the Rocky Mountains promised land, polygamy came out into the open, although only a small Mormon minority, those with enough wealth and influence, practiced it. But before long, it

was the rallying point for national anti-Mormon forces. The early Republican party, for example, campaigned against what is known as the "twin relics of barbarism," slavery and polygamy.

There were other reasons why Mormons by the mid-1850s found themselves in a state of renewed conflict with other Americans. Foremost were the complaints of several federally appointed territorial officials who felt thwarted by Utah's theocracy. Probably seeking to divert national attention away from sectional conflicts over slavery, President Buchanan in 1857 sent Colonel Albert Sidney Johnston, 2,500 soldiers, and a new territorial governor to enforce federal authority over the rebellious Mormons. In response, Brigham Young sent out guerrillas to harass the army, ordered his people to abandon Salt Lake City and retreat south, and prepared armed resistance. The bogged down army, after spending a winter in camp at Fort Bridger, accepted a settlement negotiated by an intermediary and marched through Salt Lake City without incident to establish Camp Floyd far south of the city. The Mormons, in return, accepted their new Gentile governor, although Brigham Young continued to be the real authority in Utah.

Mormons and Indians Unite

In a tragic sidelight to these tense events, Mormons and local Indians massacred 120 emigrants at Mount Meadows on the south

commander, Colonel Patrick Connor, was eventually known as the father of mining in Utah because he encouraged his soldiers to prospect in their spare time and helped develop some of Utah's earliest strikes. He was virulently anti-Mormon and hoped mining would encourage immigration of Gentiles to Utah. He was correct, and mining in places like Alta, Park City, and the Oquirrh Mountains eventually created a second, non-Mormon economy in the state.

After the Civil War, Congress stepped up its crusade against polygamy. In a series of acts culminating in the Edmunds-Tucker Act of 1887, stiff penalties were imposed for practicing polygamy. Polygamists were disenfranchised and prohibited from public office and jury duty, test oaths were intro-

California trail. Southern Utah Mormons, in the midst of a religious revival, were expecting the army's invasion. They knew that some haughty members of the emigrant train were from hated Missouri and had insulted other Mormon communities along the way. Many years later, John D. Lee, the only Mormon ever brought to justice for the crime, was executed at the massacre site.

During the Civil War, volunteer troops from California occupied Salt Lake City to insure Mormon loyalty to the Union. Their

Left, a Mormon temple in Utah; and right, Brigham Young University is famous for its football team.

duced, the church was disincorporated and its property confiscated, the Perpetual Emigrating Fund was dissolved, and women's suffrage was abolished. Federal marshals hounded polygamists throughout the state while church leaders went underground. In 1890 Mormon president Wilford Woodruff (Brigham Young had died in 1877) publicly advised members "to refrain from conducting any marriage forbidden by the law of the land," thereby surrendering to overwhelming federal power. With the Woodruff Manifesto, as it was known, and the admission of Utah to statehood in 1896 after 50 years of waiting, church members took their first steps toward reconciliation with the rest of the nation.

Mormons in the 20th Century moved further and further from their early attempts to build a perfect millennial community and embraced the more traditional social ideals of middle class America. Members at first entered the Democratic and Republican parties in roughly equal numbers, ceasing to be a solid voting bloc, but in more recent years, more of them have adopted the predominant Republican business ideology. The church's own economic strength rebounded gradually until after World War II, when the Latter Day Saints grew into one of the country's wealthiest religions, with major investments in real estate, communications, insurance, and elsewhere.

The Latter-Day Saints did not abandon their insularity, their sense of

SIGN OF MORMON STORES.—SALT LAKE CITY.

separateness—that, after all, derived primarily from their continued belief that they were a chosen people. In fact, while abandoning many distinctive practices and institutions that crossed the boundary between the religious and the secular, Mormon leaders sought to integrate religion all the more completely into members' lives. If the church no longer directed its members' political and economic lives (and it continued to have considerable influence on both), it sought to fulfill as many of their other needs as possible. It did so by finding church positions and responsibilities for all, by taking care of its needy through its own large welfare program, by providing a wide range of social activities—including athletics and entertainment—through wards and auxiliary groups, and by keeping in touch with members through an organized network so intricate that it could make most federal bureaucracies jealous. Members pay, not only a tithe of 10 percent of their income, but also contribute to a building fund, a missionary fund, and a welfare fund.

Cultural Differences

There are other distinctive cultural attributes of the Mormons—abstinence from alcohol and tobacco; the wearing of specially designed, sanctified undergarments; dedication to genealogical research; and the high value placed on education and the arts. But it was the increasingly conservative politics of many members, an attribute shared with many other Americans, which brought them much attention in the 1980s. Patriotism and the family were suddenly popular. President Ronald Reagan received his largest vote margins in Utah. He considered the Mormon West one of his prime constituencies, and brought a number of prominent Mormons (such as Education Secretary Ted Bell and pollster Richard Wirthlin) into government. When the 1984 Miss America pageant sought to recover from the scandal caused by publication of nude, sexually explicit photos of the incumbent, they turned to a squeaky clean Mormon, Sharlene Wells, as a more apt symbol of the American image they wished to convey.

Mormons, if anything, are fiercely partisan, and they take great pride in celebrities like Miss Wells. They loyally follow the careers of well-known members like entertainers Donny and Marie Osmond and ex-football star and television personality Merlin Olson. While there are many kinds of Mormons with widely different attitudes (political columnist Jack Anderson, for example, does not fit the Mormon stereotype and his religious persuasion is hence less well-known), there is still a striking uniformity among Mormons that lends credence to stereotypes. The Mormons, after all, remain a tightly unified people who largely conform to the wishes of church leaders. As such, they are a people apart, one subculture in the hodgepodge of American society.

Left, a typical Mormon's merchant's sign in the 19th Century; and right, representative Mormon leaders surround Brigham Young in the center position.

REPRESENTATIVE MORMONS.

1.—W. Woodruff.   2.—John Taylor.   3.—Mayor Daniel H. Wells.   4.—W. H. Hooper.   5.—President Brigham Young.
6.—Orson Pratt.   7.—John Sharp.   8.—George Q. Cannon.   9.—Orson Hyde.

Utah

Idaho
Wyoming
Idaho
Utah
Nevada
Great Salt Lake
Great Salt
Lake Desert
Wyoming
Utah
Colorado

0   30   60 miles
0   50   100 km

Golden Spike Nat'l. Historic Site
Smithfield
Bear Lake
Logan
Brigham City
Ogden
Farmington
Salt Lake City
Flaming Gorge Nat'l. Rec. Area
Brighton
Park City
Alta
Heber City
Bingham Canyon
Lehi
Orem
Timpanogos Cave Nat'l. Mon.
American Fork
Midway
Dinosaur Nat'l. Mon.
Vernal
Roosevelt
Fort Duchesne
Fairfield
Provo
Springville
Utah Lake
Ouray
Payson
Green R.
Fairview
Helper
Price
Manti
Castle Dale
Green River
Fillmore
Richfield
Fish Lake
Arches Nat'l. Park
Moab
Capitol Reef Nat'l. Park
Canyonlands Nat'l. Park
Colorado R.
Panguitch
Monticello
Cedar City
Cedar Breaks Nat'l. Mon.
Escalante
Bryce Canyon Nat'l. Park
Natural Bridges Nat'l. Mon.
Blanding
Zion Nat'l. Park
Cannonville
Lake Powell
Springdale
Glen Canyon Nat'l. Rec. Area
San Juan R.
St. George
Hurricane
Kanab
Utah
Arizona
Lake
Rainbow Bridge Nat'l. Mon.
Gouldings
Mexican Hat

UTAH, NORTH OF GREAT SALT LAKE

Its geography, its history, and its culture make northern Utah a land of transitions and contrast. Perhaps its most notable contrast is between the seclusion its people sought and the changes an intruding outside world kept bringing, but the contrast in its landscape, located astride a geological transition zone, is more readily seen. Two massive plates of the earth's crust clash together along the Utah, Idaho and Wyoming borders to form the energy-rich Overthrust Belt, one of America's most recent and productive oil fields. To the south and west is the Great Basin and its jewel, the Great Salt Lake, remnant of Lake Bonneville, whose prehistoric shore lines can be seen high on the mountain benches throughout northern and western Utah. To the north and east are towering mountains that arise abruptly from deep, expansive valleys formed by Bonneville and her children, the lakes and rivers of today. These valleys—Cache,

Weber, Ogden's, Bear River, Bear Lake, and other smaller ones along the lake—were retreats: first for Shoshones, Bannocks, and Utes who ranged east to contest Plains Indians for buffalo; later for mountain men who cached their furs, held their rendezvous, and spent their winters; finally for Mormon farmers seeking a refuge where they could build their communities in peace. Always there was an outside world beyond the valleys of different and potentially hostile competitors.

Then the railroad came and finally effectively tied America's regional cultures together. Fittingly, the transcontinental railroad was linked, the symbolic transition and tie between East and West pinpointed in the **Promontory Range**, north of Great Salt Lake. Today, the sense of passage from one world to another can still be felt in northern Utah. There are few areas in America where one can get a better feeling of climbing from lowland to highland than along the front rising to the east of Great Salt Lake. Approaching the Utah border from Wyoming or Idaho, a traveller can detect the subtle but apparent differences in the farming villages that announce the Mormon core region. But also within and around those villages there is a strong sense of change as an older, rural way of life gives way to national security, energy and recreation industries—to name but a few of the modern equivalents of the mid-19th Century railroad.

Utah Farmlands

Cache Valley, the heart of the remaining farm economy, is a good place to begin a visit to the region bounding Great Salt Lake's northern shores. Here where the winters are frigid, but the summers pleasant, are some of the most productive farms in Utah. Well-watered by Bear River and its tributaries, the beautiful green valley is almost completely surrounded by steep mountain ridges. Its name derived from the early trappers' practice of hiding their furs here. They called it Willow Valley, and many spent their winter layoffs here, taking advantage of the valley's abundant game.

Near the middle of the valley, on its eastern side where Logan River emerges from the mountains, is **Logan**. Upon approaching the city, a visitor may first see a castle high on one of Lake Bonneville's terraces. This is the **Logan Temple** of the Mormon church, an unornamented, gray limestone Gothic building with twin cupola-topped towers. Volunteer laborers constructed it with native materials between 1877 and 1884. The temple is not open to the public (although its grounds are), but a similar gray, cupola crowned building is only two blocks west on Main Street, and visitors are welcome. This is the **Mormon Tabernacle**, begun in 1865, and completed in 1890. Another two blocks west and north brings one to the **Cache Country Relic Hall** on the lower level of the Chamber of Commerce building. Run by the Daughters of Utah Pioneers, the hall contains a fine collection of pioneer artifacts, including clothing, furniture, tools, and art.

There are numerous historic buildings in Logan. The old **Lyric Theatre**, home of a modern repertory company, and the stately **David Eccles Home** are among the reasons **Center Street** is listed as a historic district on the National Register of Historic Places.

Utah State University, founded in 1888, sprawls across the benchland east of the city. Originally a land grant agricultural college, Utah State, like Logan, still has some of the flavor of its early years, both in its old buildings like **Old Main**, with its distinctive tower, and in its curriculum, which continues to emphasize programs in agriculture and natural resources. But it is now a complete university with distinctively modern facilities and a full range of course offerings. Each July and August, the campus hosts the Festival of the American West, including diverse activities ranging from a spectacular historical pageant to a fair, exhibits, reconstructed old West streets, and conferences, all celebrating and highlighting the frontier experience.

The Wellsville Area

South of Logan is Cache Valley's oldest settlement, **Wellsville**. Brigham Young first sent an exploratory party into this valley in 1847. Their report was favorable, but settlers didn't return until 1856 when Peter Maughan and a party of friends and relatives drove several thousand cattle and horses to

A view of Logan (Utah) with the dominant Mormon Temple.

the site of Wellsville, called "Maughan's Fort," for many decades. Several houses and other buildings have survived from the village's early years. The town sits at the foot of the **Wellsville Mountains**, which climb 5,000 feet (1,500 meters) from the valley floor, a rise made more impressive by their narrow base. They have one of the steepest mountain faces in the United States. A few miles east of Wellsville is another colorful early Mormon settlement, **Hyrum**, and outside it is the **Hyrum Lake State Recreation Area** with complete boating and camping facilities.

Making Cheese in a Valley

Heading back north on the highway between Wellsville and Logan, stop off at the **Ronald V. Jensen Historical Farm** and **Man and His Bread Museum**, a 120-acre (50-hectare) living museum where a large collection of steam powered tractors, harvesters, threshers, wagons and other antique farm equipment is kept operating. The Jensen farm is only one sign of Cache Valley's agricultural tradition. One only has to cross the valley from south to north,

passing through little villages such as **Mendon, Newton, Clarkston** and **Richmond** to see the hundreds of neat, modest farms among their dairy pastures and alfalfa fields. Although the area's farms produce varied crops, Cache Valley is best known for its cheese. A tour of the **Cache Valley Cheese Factory** in Amalga, north of Logan, and a taste of its product will demonstrate why. It's advertised as the world's largest maker of Swiss cheese; other equally tasty varieties are also made. The factory is the other side of the coin to the modest sized family farms, for agriculture in Cache Valley, like elsewhere, is big business. Five large cheesemaking firms, for example, employ some 1,500 people.

Cache Valley extends several miles across the state border into Idaho, where there are two sites important to the region's history. Five miles (eight km) north of Preston, Idaho, by the Bear River, is the **Bear River Massacre Site**, the place where a large band of Shoshone-Bannocks, accused of harassing overland migrants and settlers, camped in January 1863. Federal troops from Fort Douglas in Salt Lake City attacked them there. Led by Colonel Patrick E. Connor, the soldiers trapped the Indians in a ravine and, showing no mercy, killed at least 224. Their own casualties came to a total of 14 killed and 49 wounded. A few miles north of Preston, Cache Valley ends at **Red Rock Pass**, site of one of the world's great floods. After rising for thousands of years, ancient Lake Bonneville finally reached its maximum depth and broke through its rim here, draining into the Snake River.

Picturesque Sites

For peaceful mountain beauty there are few areas that can beat the **Bear River Range** east of Cache Valley. Start with **Blacksmith Fork Canyon**, reached from Hyrum. A high walled canyon with good fishing and plenty of picnic sites, its main attraction is the winter feeding of hundreds of elk at **Hardware Ranch Elk Preserve**. With a primary mission to maintain herds through the winter and keep them away from local farms, the ranch now attracts visitors who view the feeding elk from sleighs drawn by Clydesdale horses.

Logan Canyon is a pleasant 30-mile (48-km) drive, from the narrow rocky banks of the **Logan River** at its lower end outside Logan city to the high parklands and sinks at its top. Along the way are superb fishing areas for German Brown, Rainbow and Cutthroat trout; a steep one-and-a-half mile (two-km) hike to the giant 3,500-year-old **Jardine Juniper**; a number of caves for the adventuresome to explore; a roadside drink of clean mountain water at **Rick's Spring**; and many scenic campgrounds like the one at pretty **Tony Grove Lake**. In winter, try some quiet, out-of-the-way skiing at **Beaver Mountain Ski Area**.

Summer Activities at Bear Lake

From the summit above the Logan Canyon, look down on the breathtaking vista of the 21-mile (34-km) long, deep blue **Bear Lake** below. Summer boaters and water skiers flock to Utah's **Bear Lake State Park Marina** or other docks. Swimmers collect at **Idaho State Beach** on the northern shore or **Rendezvous Beach State Park** on the southern edge, and others find diverse pleasures at one

The sparkling Jupiter steam engine at Promontory Point, Utah.

of several resorts, like the largest at **Sweetwater**. The 200-foot (61-meter) deep lake also harbors the rare Bonneville cisco fish, which begins its run in January, attracting wading fishermen with dip nets to the ice-covered lake.

While small traditional Bear Lake towns like **Laketown** and **St. Charles** still retain much of their character, Bear Lake is showing signs of overdevelopment. Its beaches and nearby hillsides are crowded with resorts and summer homes, and the quality of its once crystal clean water is deteriorating. It once drained one way, into Bear River; now Bear River water is pumped back into the lake during the high runoff, a process gradually altering the temperature and ecology of the lake.

"Must-Sees"

To see truly rural Utah scenes, travel south from Bear Lake on State highways 30 and 16 to rustic, isolated **Randolph** and **Woodruff**. From the latter, head west, taking a seemingly endless climb past some of the most well-maintained and extensive snowmobile trails around to reach **Monte Cristo**, a spectacular picnic area among the clouds at 9,000 feet (2,740 meters). Then descend into **Ogden's Valley**, a rugged mountain valley with jagged edged **Pineview Reservoir** occupying much of its floor. Near the reservoir is **Huntsville** and the home of the late David O. McKay, one of the Mormon church's most revered prophets. Not far from Huntsville is the **Abbey of Our Lady of the Holy Trinity**, a Trappist monastery that welcomes visitors and sells its own bread and honey. There is plenty of skiing in the mountains surrounding Ogden's Valley—at **Snow Basin** to the south and at **Nordic Valley** and **Powder Mountain** to the north.

Ogden River drains west out of Pineview Reservoir down **Ogden Canyon** to the city of **Ogden**, all named after Peter Skene Ogden, the British fur brigade leader who passed this way in the 1820s. Ogden, Utah's second largest city, is where Miles Goodyear, commonly considered Utah's first non-Indian settler, built his home in 1846. He raised a garden and traded horses he bought in California to overland migrants. He eventually sold everything to early Mormon settlers, and now the **Miles**

A copper smelting plant near Magnavox (Utah) is hard at work.

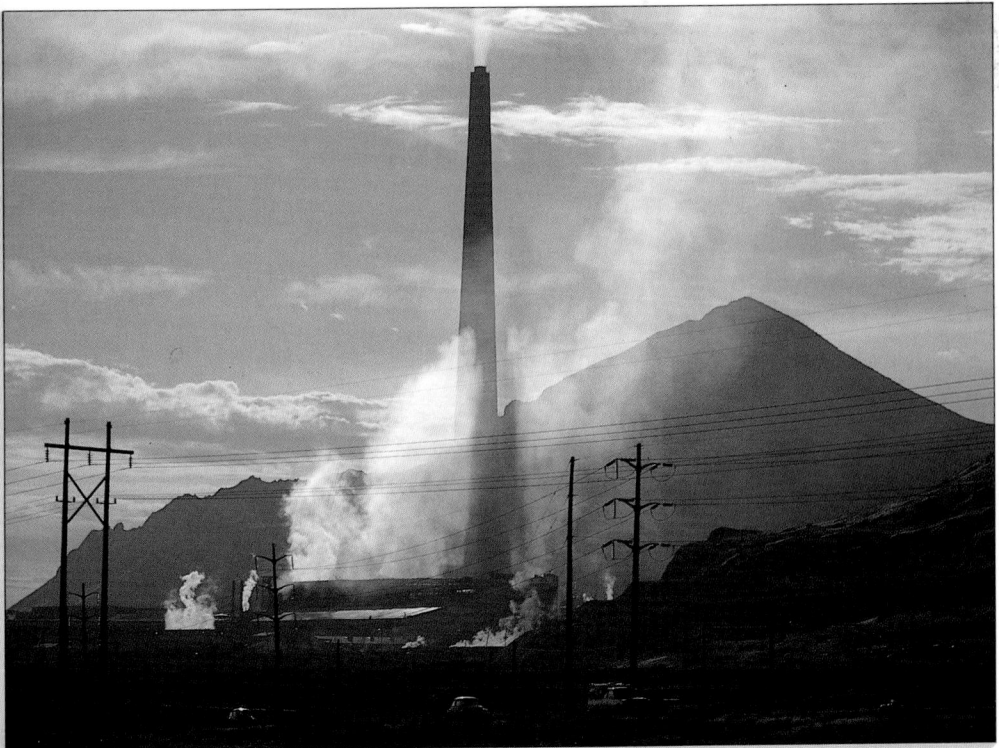

Goodyear Fort Buenaventura State Historical Monument, a reconstruction of his log stockade, commemorates him at a park off 24th Street in West Ogden. The actual **Goodyear Cabin** is located next to the **Daughters of Utah Pioneers Museum** on the same block as the Mormon Temple dedicated in 1972 and the older **Ogden Tabernacle**. A Visitors Center is located at the latter.

Ogden grew with the railroad, becoming Utah's non-Mormon city after the tracks arrived in 1869. It was then Utah's commercial connection to the outside. The **Union Depot** at 25th Street and Wall Avenue wasn't built until 1924, but it is a classic reminder of the railroad's importance to the city. Designed in the Spanish Revival style, it houses the **Railroad Hall of Fame Museum** and the **John M. Browning Firearms Museum**. It is also a part of the **Lower 25th Street Historic District**, a deteriorating area under restoration which once was the hub of Ogden business and society.

A good way to sense the **Great Salt Lake's** beauty and size, as well as the varied topography and changing society around it, is to follow the old railroad's route north around the lake's northeastern shore. First take the highway through **Willard**, the **Golden Spike Fruitway** where countless fruit stands offer the many products of local orchards. Next is **Brigham City**, most successful home of Brigham Young's nineteenth century experiments in cooperative living, where all belongings were consecrated to the community and numerous industries were communally owned and operated. West of Brigham City are the extensive marsh lands of the **Bear River Migratory Bird Refuge**, best visited in the fall or spring when hundreds of species of migrating birds pass the Great Salt Lake's shores. Turning west around the north end of the lake, one comes to **Corinne**, once the sin capital of Utah. Corinne, one of many western sin capitals spawned by the railroad is now a quiet Mormon village on the Bear River. Just before turning south to the railroad's most historic site, look north where the huge **Thiokol Wasatch Division Plant**, the world's largest manufactuer of solid propellant rocket motors, can be seen. It is only one piece of evidence demonstrating Utah's dependence on the national security industry and the federal government, known to be the state's largest employers.

In the Promontory Mountains, the **Golden Spike Historic Site** commemorates the joining of the Union Pacific and Southern Pacific in 1869. Drive south along the range to **Promontory Point** jutting out into America's inland sea. From here one can look south to **Fremont, Antelope** and **Gunnison Islands**. Far to the west is **Pilot Peak**, a point which served as a guide to the first emigrants trying to cross the desert to California. To the east is the **Wasatch Front** and urban Utah. To the northwest is lowland at the head of the lake's northwestern arm, where the **Locomotive Springs Waterfowl Management Area** (worth visiting just to see its surrealistically blue pools resting in the salt marshes) lies. Farther north are the **Raft River Mountains** and some of Utah's most remote little towns at their base. Looking at that vast scene and the lake itself, one can feel some degree of the threat, challenge and opportunity the first Mormon settlers faced when they chose to adopt this odd, diverse landscape as their home.

Below, weather-worn ranch woman shows the strains of time and toil. Right, an exuberant youth symbolizes the excitement of springtime in the Rockies.

288

guide
in
brief

GUIDE IN BRIEF

TRAVELLING TO THE ROCKIES

By Air

Most major and international carriers service the Western Rockies states of Colorado, Idaho, Montana, Utah and Wyoming. The major entry points to the Rockies are Denver in the east and Salt Lake City in the west. There are small airports covering the entire Rockies region. Some of the smaller airports are Colorado Springs, Pueblo and Grand Junction in Colorado; Boise, Twin Falls, Idaho Falls and Pocatello in Idaho; Bozeman, Helena and Great Falls in Montana; St. George and Moab in Utah; Jackson, Casper, Cheyenne and Laramie in Wyoming. Some of the local and regional airlines travel to these airports. The National Parks in the Rockies are easily accessible by air. The Jackson Airport is located in the Teton National Park. The other National Parks have airports within short distances of the Parks.

Stapleton International Airport

This airport is located 340 miles (550 km) west of the center of the Continental United States, just outside the city of Denver. Stapleton International Airport is the seventh busiest airport in the world and the sixth busiest airport in the United States, making Denver one of the major centers of air travel in the country. Trans-World Airlines is the major airline to Denver. Over 25 million people land at this airport every year.

(For listing of airlines, *see* appendix.)

Airport Transportation

Most of the major airports will have airport limousine services to take you to your hotel. Some hotels provide transportation back and forth from the hotel. Cabs are available outside the major airports. Yellow Cab has radio controlled cabs and can be reached at 1-800-525-3177.

Public bus service is available at some of the major airports.

Denver Airport Transportation

Airport Limousine Service Inc., 3455 Ringsby Ct., Denver, CO 80216. 1-800-525-3177. Leaves Door 10 every 25 minutes.
Yellow Cabs, In Colorado, 1-800-367-8294. In Denver, 292-1212. Elsewhere, 1-800-525-3177. $8.50 from downtown to airport. (approx)
Zone Cabs, 2358 Washington, Denver, CO 80205. 861-2323. Radio controlled cabs.

By Land

Bus

Greyhound and **Trailways** bus companies provide services to the main cities and towns in the five Rocky Mountain states covered in this book. There are many other bus companies that serve specific areas. Denver serves as a hub for intercity bus services with Trailways offering 40 daily arrivals and departures, and Greyhound offering 24. Check the Yellow Pages for a listing of local bus companies.

Denver, Colorado.

Greyhound, 1055 19th St., Denver, CO 80203. (303) 292-6111.
Trailways, 1055 19th St.. Denver, CO 80203. (303) 292-2291.

Salt Lake City, Utah.

Greyhound, 160 West South Temple, Salt Lake City, UT. (801) 355-4684.
Trailways, 77 South West Temple, Salt Lake City, UT. (801) 328-8122.

Cheyenne, Wyoming.

Greyhound, 1503 Capitol Ave., Cheyenne, WY 82001. (307) 634-7744.
Trailways, 820 W. 16th St., Cheyenne, WY 82001. (307) 634-2128.

Boise, Idaho.

Greyhound, 1212 Bannock St., Boise, ID 83706. (208) 343-3681.
Trailways, 1212 Bannock St., Boise, ID 83706. (208) 343-7531.

Bozeman, Montana.

Greyhound, 625 N. 7th St., Bozeman, MT 59715. (406) 587-3110.

Train

Amtrack is a leisurely passenger line that provides an excellent service from coast to coast. In Denver there are six daily arrivals and departures serving Los Angeles, Seattle, San Francisco and Chicago. Westbound trains pass through Glenwood Canyon, a spectacular route. Amtrack has rail passes for unlimited travel in the United States which can only be purchased from a travel agent overseas. (Amtrack — nationwide — 1-800-872-7245.) In Denver, Amtrack operates from the Union Station (893-3911). Amtrack office in Salt Lake City is located at 400 West South Temple (364-8562).

Taxis

Taxis are available throughout the Rockies area, and are seen more often in the big cities. Rates vary depending on the company. Long distance rides tend to be expensive.

Car Rentals

Visitors wishing to rent or lease an automobile after arriving in the Rockies area will find car rental offices in most tourist centers, airports and major hotels. Shop around for the best rates and terms. Most rental companies will rent their vehicles only to individuals at least 21 years old, (sometimes 25), having a valid driver's license (an international driver's license is acceptable) and a major credit card. Some companies will require a high deposit (sometimes as high as $500) in case you don't have a credit card. Check with your travel agent for special package rates for car rentals.

American International Rent-A-Car 1-800-527-0202
Avis Rent-A-Car 1-800-331-1212
Budget Rent-A-Car 1-800-527-0700
Hertz Rent-A-Car 1-800-654-3131

Highway Travel

Denver is served by interstate highways 25, 70, 76 and 225.

AAA Auto Club, 4100 E. Arkansas, Denver, CO 80222. 753-8800.
Colorado Ground Transportation Center, 12599 E. Bates Circle, Aurora, CO 80014. 388-5669. Ground transportation serves all major ski areas in Colorado. Hotel/condo reservation statewide.

Motoring Advisories

Winter Driving Tips

If you are stranded in a blizzard stay put in your car. Your car will be easier to locate than you. Run the heater in your car sparingly and be careful of carbon monoxide poisoning. Make sure your exhaust pipe is not blocked by snow. Open a "crack" in you window for ventilation. Running the car for 20 minutes per hour should keep you fairly warm and conserve gas.

Emergency supplies for winter travelling by car are a warm sleeping bag for each person travelling, extra winter clothes, high calorie non-perishable food, matches, candles, first aid kit, flashlight, transistor radio with batteries, pocket knife, shovel with a long handle, tow chain, small sack of sand, water jug, basic tools for repairs, signal flares, axe, spare quart of gas and a distress flag.

In the Rocky Mountain area you can expect a blizzard even in the early fall. Driving on icy roads demands more skill than driving on dry roads. Check the weather forecast before venturing out into the mountains. Don't drive on icy roads if you can avoid it. Postpone your adventure, its better than being stuck in the middle of nowhere in a snow storm.

TRAVEL ADVISORIES

Visa Regulations

Most visitors entering the United States, must have a valid passport, a visitor's visa and an international vaccination certificate depending on the country of origin. Canadian citizens entering the Western Hemisphere need not have a visa or a passport. Neither do Mexican citizens who possess a border pass.

At the port of entry the State Department of Food and Agriculture may inspect all produce, plant materials and animals to see if they are admissable under the current quarantine regulations.

Citizens of any country admitted to the United States on a single entry visa may visit Canada or Mexico for not more than 30 days and reenter the United States without a new visa, but only if the reentry falls within the original admission specifications.

Currency

The United States has no limit on the amount of money foreign visitors bring into the country. For your convenience, come with a supply of small bills, credit cards and travellers checks (preferably in U.S. Dollars).

The basic U.S. monetary unit is the dollar($) which is equivalent to 100 cents. Coins are minted in 1¢ (penny), 5¢ (nickel), 10¢ (dime), 25¢ (quarter), 50¢ (half dollar) and $1. Silver dollar coins are very rare. Nickels, dimes and quarters are accepted by coin operated vending machines, telephones and laundromats. Paper currency is printed in denominations of $1, $2, $5, $10, $20, $50, $100 and $1000 and are of the same color (greenbacks) with the value of each note clearly indicated on the bill.

Visitors who arrive by air can usually exchange their money at the gateway airport. Most shops and hotels in the Rockies area accept U.S. travellers checks. Foreign currency will have to be changed at the bank. Most banks are opened from 8am till 5pm on weekdays. Some banks are open till 1pm on Saturdays. In most states in the country there is a sales tax added to retail goods. This amount is different in each of the Rockies states.

Travel Information for International Visitors

Private and public agencies offer the foreign traveller to the United States special fares and discounts for transportation and accommodation. Some of these are outlined below.

Airlines

Visit U.S.A. is a discounted airline ticket offered by many domestic airlines with discounts up to 40 per cent off regular fares within the country. The requirements to qualify for this ticket is that you must live at least 100 miles (160 km) outside the border of the United States and you must stop in at least two cities (not including the arrival and departure cities). Visit U.S.A. tickets are valid for one year and tickets must be confirmed 7 days prior to your arrival in the country and reservations must be made outside the United States.

Bus Services

Greyhound and **Trailways** offer bargain rate passes for unlimited travel in the United States. The **Visit U.S.A.** bus tickets have to be purchased from your travel agent before you come to the United States. Discounted international rates are also available on point-to point travel that could be purchased either overseas or in the United States.

Accommodations

Many motels and hotels have reductions up to 35 percent for Visit U.S.A. participants. Hospitality packages offering prepurchased meals and accommodations are also available. Your travel agent can inform you about these benefits.

Tour Packages

A prepackaged tour is often a lot cheaper than if you tried to assemble it yourself. There are also a variety of special interest tours that are offered in the areas of art, sports, skiing, horse riding, theater, etc., that your travel agent can help you with. The local chambers of commerce can give you list of outfitters and guides that you can write to and make your own arrangements with. One of the most inexpensive ways for a family to travel in the Rockies is to travel by car and stay in campgrounds. This is only possible in the summer.

Hospitality Program

Many cities and communities in the United States have a "Meet Americans at Home" program where responsible citizens will help to make your visit a pleasant one. Some of these volunteers speak your native language. Write to the **U.S. Travel Service**, U.S. Department of Commerce, Washington D.C. 20230, and request the "Americans at Home" folder.

GETTING ACQUAINTED

Geography

The Rockies is the name given to a group of jagged, snow-capped peaks which run across the western part of North America. This chain of mountains stretches over 3,000 miles (4,800 km) and in some areas it is 350 miles (563 km) in width. The Rockies start in northern New Mexico and extend to the northern part of Alaska. They run from New Mexico through Colorado, Utah, Wyoming, Idaho, Montana and Washington. At the U.S. border the Rockies stretches into the Canadian Rockies.

This *Insight Guide* to the Rockies covers the states of Colorado, Wyoming, Utah, southeast Montana and the eastern half of Idaho.

The Rockies are known for their scenic beauty and natural wonders. Many of the nation's national parks are in the Rockies including the oldest and the largest, Yellowstone National Park and the Rocky Mountain National Park. The Rockies are the starting place of mighty rivers like the Arkansas, the Colorado and the Rio Grande.

Climate

The climate in the Rockies varies greatly depending on the season and location. Denver is almost a desert, receiving 15 inches (38 cm) of precipitation and 300 days of sunshine in a year. Denver's climate is ideal due to its low humidity and sunshine. Gold courses are active here even in January, as good weather prevails most of the year.

If you are a skier, the weather is perfect in the Rockies. Most ski areas have a dry climate, brisk temperatures, high elevations and unbeatable powder snow. In the summer most of the mountain areas are warm during the day and cool in the evenings. In most parts of the Rockies the spring and autumn are cool and crisp.

The hallmark of the weather systems in the Rockies is the changeabilty. There can be a 50°F (10°C) difference from one day to another. Along with its wonderful weather are the brilliant golden aspens in the fall, the picturesque snow covered ranges in the winter and the meadows of wildflowers in the spring and summer.

Clothing

As Rocky Mountian weather is so changeable, you should bring a variety of clothing to be comfortable. Most of the residents dress in layers so thay can peel clothes off till they are comfortable. Most clothing worn in the Rockies area is very casual and often very sporty. Denver, the capital of the Rockies, is the city with the most number of sports shops in the world.

In the summer you will need shorts, T-shirts, light-weight dresses and slacks for the mornings and sometimes a light sweater or jacket in the evenings. A hooded sweatshirt, sweatpants, and tennis shoes or hiking boots is good summertime mountain attire. In the winter you will need a warm winter jacket, scarf, mittens, sweaters, hat, woollen pants, jeans, and warm footwear. For the slopes you will need one warm ski outfit, ski gloves, ski hat and sunglasses or goggles. You can find these things in the many ski shops at the resorts. Skis can be easily rented. A sunscreen is essential in the mountains so you can avoid being a victim of sunburns and windburns.

Remember to bring along your swimsuit so you can enjoy the different hot springs located in different parts of the Rockies. Most of the larger hotels have swimming pools and health spas.

Time Zone

The Rockies is within the Rocky Mountain Time Zone. The time zone in all five Western Rockies states (Colorado, Idaho, Montana, Utah and Wyoming) is the same: one hour behind Chicago, two hours behind New York, and one hour ahead of Los Agneles. On the last Sunday in April, the clock is moved ahead one hour for Daylight Savings Time, and on the last Sunday in October the clock is moved back one hour returning to Standard Time.

Without taking Daylight Savings Time into consideration, when it is 12 noon in the Rockies, it is:
9 a.m. in Hawaii;
2 p.m. in New York and Montreal;
7 p.m. in London;
8 p.m. in Bonn, Madrid, Paris and Rome;
10 p.m. in Athens and Cairo;
11 p.m. in Moscow;
12.30 a.m. in Bombay, the next day;
2 a.m. in Bangkok, the next day;
3 a.m. in Singapore, Taiwan, and Hong Kong the

next day;
4 a.m. in Tokyo the next day;
5 a.m. in Sydney, the next day.

Etiquette

As in most parts of the United States, service personnel rely on tips for a large part of their income. Your gratitude in the form of a tip is most appreciated.

The accepted rate for porters at the airports is 50 cents per bag. Hotel bell boys, and porters expect at least 50 cents depending on the location of your hotel or resort. A doorman should be tipped if he loads and unloads your car. It is not essential to tip chamber maids unless you have an extended stay in a small hotel or resort.

In most instances 15 to 20 percent is the going rate for other services like taxi drivers, barbers, hair dresses, waiters, waitresses and bartenders. Some restaurants include a service charge if the group is large. Tipping is not necessary in cafeterias and self-service fast food restaurants.

Weights and Measures

Given below are the U.S. equivalents of metric units.
1 inch (in) = 2.54 centimeters (cm)
1 foot (ft) = 0.305 meters (m)
1 mile = 1.609 kilometers (km)
1 square mile = 2.69 square kilometers
1 U.S. gallon = 3.785 liters
1 ounce (oz) = 28.35 grams (g)
1 pound (lb) = 0.454 kilograms (kg)

Electricity

Most wall outlets have 110-volt, 60 cycle, alternating current. A transformer is necessary if you are using European or 220-volt equipment.

Liquor Laws

The legal age for consuming and purchasing liquor differs in each state in the Rockies area. In Colorado, alcoholic beverages can be served till 2am seven days a week. Legal drinking age is 21 and the purchasing age is 18. Colorado and the other Rockies states have very stiff drunk driving laws and visitors are advised not to drive while impaired. Utah is not a dry state. Once you understand the liquor laws it will be possible to get a drink. Legal drinking age is 21 and beer is served in all public bars. Certain licensed restaurants serve 2 ounce (62ml) "mini-bottles" of liquor. Retail liquor is only sold in state stores and a list of these stores are in the telephone directory. The minimum drinking age in Wyoming, Montana and Idaho is 19. The Federal Government has been urging all states in the United States to adopt a minimum drinking age of 21 due to rising drunk-driving accidents statistics.

Public Holidays

State, local and federal agencies may be closed during the following holidays. Local businesses, banks and schools may also be closed.
New Years Day — January 1

Martin Luther King's Birthday — February 12
Washington's Birthday — February 20th
Easter Sunday — First Sunday after spring equinox.
Memorial Day — Last Monday in May
Independence Day — July 4
Labor Day — First Monday in September
Columbus Day — Second Monday in October
Election Day — First Tuesday after the first Monday in November, of even numbered years.
Veteran's Day — November 11
Thanksgiving Day — Fourth Thursday in November
Christmas Day — December 25

There may be additional holidays in the different Rocky Mountain States for local events.

Embassies and Consular Services

There are some consulates and other foreign government representative located in Salt Lake City and Denver.

(For listing of embassies and consular services, *see* appendix.)

TOURIST INFORMATION

Tourist information and useful literature can be obtained from the tourist promotional agencies in each of the Rocky Mountain States. The following agencies will be very helpful.

Colorado
Denver and Colorado Convention and Visitors Bureau, 225 West Colfax Ave, Denver, CO 80202. (303) 892-1112.

Idaho
Idaho Travel Committee, Statehouse Boise, ID 83720. 1-800-635-2470.

Montana
Montana Travel Promotion, Dept. of Commerce, 1424 9th Ave. Helena, MT 59620. 1-800-548-3390.

Utah
Utah Travel Council, Council Hall, Capitol Hill, Salt Lake City, UT 84114. (801) 533-5681.

Wyoming
Wyoming Travel Commission, Cheyenne, WY 82002. 1-800-443-2784.

Chambers of Commerce

Cities and resorts throughout the Rockies have **Chambers and Commerce** to provide free information about the area. Accommodations, dining, shopping, medical, events, festivals, businesses, and other general information are areas in which they can be of assistance.

(For listing, *see* Appendix pages 319-323.)

Travel Information Sources

Colorado:

U.S. Forest Service, Rocky Mountain Region Office, 11177 W. 8th Ave. Lakewood CO 80225. 234-4185. (4-color map of any national forest, excellent guides showing trails campgrounds... etc., send $1 for postage)

Colorado Campground Association, 5101 Pennsylvania, Boulder, CO 80303. (Colorado maps, private campgrounds, fun things to do, send $1 for postage)

Colorado Climbing Guides Association, 1335 Broadway, Boulder, CO 80302.

Colorado Division of Highways, 4201 E. Arkansas Ave. Denver, CO 80222. 757-9481. (for information on Highway)

Colorado Division of Parks and Recreation, 1313 Sherman St. #618, Denver, CO 80203. 1-800-328-6338. (state parks, boating, RV and snowmobiling regulations, camping reservations 1-800-328-6338)

Colorado Division of Wildlife, 6060 Broadway, Denver, CO 80216. 297-1192. (for information on hunting and fishing)

Colorado Guides and Outfitters Association, P.O. Box 29022, Denver, CO 80229. 287-9080.

National Park Service, P.O. Box 25287, Lakewood, CO 80225. 234-3095.

U.S. Bureau of Land Management, 1037 20th St, Denver, CO 80202. 837-4481. (quad maps — $1.50, statewide public lands — $2)

U.S. Geological Survey, P.O. Box 25286, Denver Federal Center, Denver, CO 80225. 234-2832.

Idaho:

Lewis and Clark Country, Box 8936, Moscow, ID 83843. 882-3581.

Treasureland, P.O. Box 2106, Boise, ID 83701. 1-800-635-5240.

Magicland, Box 1844, Twin Falls, ID 83001.

Big Water Mountain Land Inc, P.O. Box 928, Sandpoint, ID 83864. 263-2161.

Pioneer Country, c/o Lava Hot Springs Foundation, Box 668, Lava Hot Springs, ID 83246. 776-5221.

Mountain River Country, Box 498, Idaho Falls, ID 83402. 523-1010.

Idaho Department of Parks and Recreation, 2177 Warm Springs Ave., Boise, ID 83712. 334-2154.

Idaho Department of Game and Fish, 600 S. Walnut, Boise, ID 83712. 334-3700.

Idaho Department of Transportation, 3311 W. State, Boise, ID 83707. 334-3664. (for highway information)

Idaho State Historical Society, 610 N. Julia Davis Dr., Boise ID 83707. 334-2120. (for information on historic sites and museums)

Idaho Bureau of Mines and Geology, Morril Hall, Rm 332, University of Idaho, Moscow, ID 83843. 885-7991. (for information on rockhounding and mining)

Aeronautics and Public Transportation Division, 3843 Rickenbacker, Boise, ID 83705. 334-3183. (for information on fly-in recreation areas)

Utah:

Utah State Division of Parks and Recreation, 1636 W. North Temple, Salt Lake City, UT 84116. 533-6011.

National Park Service, 125 South State, Salt Lake City, UT 84111. 524-4165.

Utah Travel Council, Council Hall Capitol Hill, Salt Lake City, UT 84114, 533-5681. (for information on travel, ski planning, campgrounds....)

Utah Division of Wildlife Resources, 1596 W. North Temple, Salt Lake City, UT 84116. 533-9333.

Ski Utah, Dept UTG, 307 W. 200 S. Salt Lake City UT 84101. 521-8102. (for information on and snow conditions)

Western River Guides Association Inc, 994 Denver St., Salt Lake City UT 84111. 355-3388. (for information on river running)

Antiquities Division, Utah Div. of State History, 300 Rio Grande, Salt Lake City, UT 84111. 533-5755. (for information on rockhounding and geology)

Utah Arts Council, 617 E. South Temple, Salt Lake City, UT 84102. 533-5895.

Utah Department of Transportation, 4501 S. 2700 W., Salt Lake City, UT 84119. 965-4000.

Utah Guides and Outfitters, P.O. Box 21242, Salt Lake City, UT 84121. 943-6707.

Montana:

Visitor Services, National Park Service, P.O. Box 168, Yellowstone National Park, WY 82190. (307) 344-7381, ext 2283.

Montana Campground Owners Association, KOA of Havre, Havre, MT 59501. 265-5012.

Montana Department of Fish, Wildlife and Parks, 1420 E. 6th Ave., Helena, MT 59620. 444-2535.

Bureau of Land Management, P.O. Box 36800, Billings, MT 59107. 657-6561.

National Park Service, Grant Kohrs Ranch National Historic Site, P.O. Box 790, Deer Lodge, MT 59722. 846-2070.

United States Forest Service, Northern Region, P.O. Box 7669, Missoula, MT 59807. 329-3711.

Montana Promotion Division, Department of Commerce, 1424 9th Ave., Helena, MT 59620. 1-800-548-3390.

Wyoming:

Wyoming Archives and Historical Department, State Office Bldg. East, Cheyenne, WY 82002. (for information on Wyoming museums)

Wyoming Recreation Commission, Cheyenne, WY 82001. (for information on state parks and historic sites)

Wyoming Geology Survey, P.O. Box 3008, University Station, University of Wyoming, Laramie, WY 82071. (for information on rockhunting and geology)

Wyoming Highway Department, Cheyenne, WY 82002. (for information on highway)

Wyoming Game and Fish Department, Cheyenne, WY 82002. (for information on hunting and fishing)

Wyoming State Office, Bureau of Land Management, P.O. Box 1828, Cheyenne, WY 82001.

Indian Reservations

Travelling through the Rockies allows you to discover vestiges of the colorful past of the Indian cultures... in sites, festivals, names, art, pagentry and descendants. The Indians have left a significant contribution in the Rockies area for at least thousands of years.

If you plan to visit any of the reservations, you could write to the tribal headquarters ahead of time and get the schedule of events. During the summer months pow-wows and festivals go on in most of the reservations which are culturally enriching events.

Colorado

Southern Ute Reservation, Tribal Headquarters, Ignation, CO 81137. (Mouche and Capote Ute Tribes)
Ute Mountain Reservation, Tribal Headquarters, Towaoc, CO 81334. (Wiminuche Ute Tribe)

Idaho

Coeur D'Alene Reservation, Tribal Headquarters, Plummer, ID 83851. (Coeur D'Alene Tribe)
Fort Hall Reservation, Tribal Headquarters, Fort Hall, ID 83203. (Shoshone and Bannock Tribes)
Kootenai Reservation, Tribal Headquarters, Bonners Ferry, ID 83805. (Kootenai Tribe)
Nez Perce Reservation, Tribal Headquarters, Lapwai, ID 83540. (Nez Perce Tribe)

Montana

Blackfeet Reservation, Tribal Headquarters, Browning, MT 59417. (Blackfeet Tribe)
Crow Reservation, Tribal Headquarters, Crow Agency, MT 59002. (Crow Tribe)
Flathead Reservation, Tribal Headquarters, Dixon, MT 59831. (Salish and Kootenai Tribes)
Fort Belknap Reservation, Tribal Headquarters, Harlem, MT 59526. (Gros Ventre and Assiniboine Tribes)
Fork Peck Reservation, Tribal Headquarters, Poplar, MT 59225. (Assiniboine and Sioux Tribes)
Northern Cheyenne Reservation, Tribal Headquarters, Lame Deer, MT 59043. (Northern Cheyenne Tribe)
Rocky Boy's Reservation, Tribal Headquarters, Box Elder, MT 59521. (Chippewa-Cree Tribe)

Utah

Goshute Reservation, Tribal Headquarters, Ibapah, UT 84034. (Goshute Tribe)
Skull Valley Reservation, Tribal Headquarters, Grantsville, UT 84209. (Goshute Tribe)
Southern Painte Reservation, Tribal Headquarters, Cedar City, UT 84270. (Southern Paiute Tribe)
Uintah and Ouray Reservation, Tribal Headquarters, Fort Duchesne, UT 84026. (Ute Tribe)

Wyoming

Wind River Reservation, Tribal Headquarters, Riverton, WY 82501. (Shoshone and Arapahoe Tribes)

ACCOMMODATION

The Rockies area and its surroundings, harbor thousands of rooms in hundreds of diverse types of lodgings. The variety ranges from cozy family managed motels to large, luxury hotels, from alpine ski lodges to campgrounds and, bed and breakfast accommodations. The Visitors Bureaus and Chambers of Commerce in the Rockies States have made the selection easier by compiling information on accommodation, rates, amenities, services, schedule of events....etc. It is recommended that you write to these agencies before you start your journey. Most of the major hotels have toll free numbers that can be obtained by calling 1-800-555 1212. For information about the National Parks and Monuments please write to the Department of Interior.

Denver and Colorado Convention & Visitors Bureau, 225 West Colfax Ave., Denver, CO 80202. 892-1112.
Idaho Travel Committee, Statehouse, Boise, ID 83720. 1-800-635-7820. In Idaho, 334-2470.
Montana Travel Promotion, Dept. of Commerce, Helena, MT 59620. 1-800-548-3390.
Salt Lake Valley Convention & Visitors Bureau, 180 South West Temple, Salt Lake City, UT 84101. 521-2822.
Wyoming Travel Commission, Cheyenne, WY 82002. 1-800-443-2784. In Wyoming, 777-7777.
United States Dept. of Interior, National Park Service, Washington D.C. 20240.

(For listing of accommodation, *see* appendix.)

COMMUNICATION

Postal Services

Post office hours can vary in different areas of the Rockies. Hotels and motels will be able to advise you about the post office hours in the area nearest to you. You can have letters sent to you in care of General Delivery at the main post office in the town you will be spending time in. This mail has to be picked up by you personally.

As of Feb. 1985 the postage rates are as follows: Letters within the United States, Mexico and Canada are 22 cents for the first ounce and 17 cents for each additional ounce.

Postcards are 14 cents within the United States, Mexico and Canada.

Surface mail letters to foreign countries are 37 cents for each ounce and 20 cents for each additional ounce.

Airmail letters to foreign countries are 44 cents for each half ounce.

The post office sells aerograms for 36 cents each. Vending machines at airports, shops, bus depots, train stations, hotel lobbies and drug stores sell stamps.

A 24-hour express mail is available within the United States.

Using the five digit zip code facilitates quick delivery.

Telegrams and Telex

Western Union and International Telephone and Telegraph (I.T.T.) will accept telex and telegram messages over the phone. Most major hotels have their own telex machines.

Western Union .... 1-800-325-6000.
I.T.T. .... 1-800-221-4064.

Telephones

Public phones are located in hotel lobbies, restaurants, street corners, drug stores, garages, gas stations, bus depots and other general locations. In the national parks and forests, phones are available at the ranger stations. The cost of making local calls vary from 10 to 25 cents. Have plenty of change if you are making a long distance call from a public phone. Long distance rates decrease considerably after 5 pm, and even still more after 11 pm. Overseas calls can be dialed direct from many areas in the Rockies. The operator will give you the code and dialing instructions.

Several hotels and state travel commissions have toll free numbers. To find these out call 1-800-555-1212. Each state in the Rockies has a different area code. These are Colorado-303, Idaho-208, Montana-406, Utah-801 and Wyoming-307.

NEW MEDIA

Newspapers and Magazines

The daily newspapers that are most widely read in Colorado are the **Rocky Mountain News** and the **Denver Post.** These along with national newspapers are available at most drug stores, grocery stores, bookstores and coin operated newspaper stands on street corners. Weekly newspapers in Denver are **Denver Sentinel Newspapers, City Edition** and **Denver Downtowner.** The **Rocky Mountain Business Journal** is devoted to the business community, and **Up the Creek** is for singles. Ethnic newspapers in Denver are **Intermountain Jewish News, Denver Catholic Register** and **Denver Rocky Mountain Jiho Times,** a Japanese English newspaper. There are a variety of monthly magazines published in Denver that are available in general stores in the city. The **Denver Magazine,** covers a variety of material about Colorado.

Most Rocky Mountain towns and cities have their own local newspapers. In Colorado, the **Boulder Daily Camera, Colorado Springs Gazette Telegraph, Colorado Springs Sun, Pueblo Chieftan-Pueblo Star Journal** and the **Grand Junction Daily Sentinel** have a wide circulation.

The major daily newspapers in Salt Lake City are the **Salt Lake Tribune** and the **Deseret News.** Most of the smaller towns in Utah have their own local newspapers. The **Standard Examiner** printed in Ogden has a wide circulation.

In Montana, some of the more well circulated newspapers are the **Billings Gazette,** the **Bozeman Daily Chronicle,** Helena's **Independent Record,**

Butte's **Montana Standard,** the **Great Falls Tribune** and the **Missoulian.**

The prominent daily newspapers in **Wyoming** are the **Casper Star Tribune, Cheyenne Wyoming Eagle** and the **Cheyenne Wyoming State Tribune.**

In Idaho the main newspapers are the **Idaho Statesman,** in Boise, the **Lewiston Morning Tribune,** the **Post Register,** in Idaho Falls, the **Idaho State Journal,** in Pocatello, and the **Twin Falls' Times News.**

Television

Most towns in the Rockies have their own local TV stations besides having the national networks and cable TV options. Complete listings appear in the daily newspapers. The **TV Guide** is a booklet available at most grocery and drug stores that list the week's programs in the area. In the Rockies area some of the major stations are:

Colorado

Channel 14 KTVJ Boulder
　　　　 11 KKTV Colorado Springs (CBS)
　　　　 13 KRDO Colorado Springs (ABC)
　　　　　9 KBTV Denver (ABC)
　　　　　4 KCNC-TV Denver (NBC)
　　　　 31 KDVR Denver
　　　　　7 KMGH-TV Denver (CBS)
　　　　　6 KRMA-TV Denver (PBS)
　　　　　2 KWGN-TV Denver
　　　　　6 KREZ-TV Durango

Idaho

Channel 4 KAID Boise (PBS)
　　　　 2 KBCI-TV Boise (CBS)
　　　　 6 KIVI Boise (ABC)
　　　　 6 KPVI Pocatello and Idaho Falls (ABC)
　　　　10 KIBU-TV Pocatello (PBS)
　　　　12 KUID-TV Moscow (PBS)

Montana

Channel 2 KTVO Billings (CBS)
　　　　 8 KULR-TV Billings (ABC)
　　　　 7 KCTZ Bozeman
　　　　 6 KTVM Butte (NBC)
　　　　 4 KXLF-TV Butte (ABC)
　　　　12 KTVG Helena (NBC)

Utah

Channel 30 KOOG-TV Ogden
　　　　 11 KBYU-TV Provo (PBS)
　　　　　5 KSL-TV Salt Lake City (CBS)
　　　　 20 KSTU Salt Lake City
　　　　　4 KTVX Salt Lake City (ABC)
　　　　　7 KUED Salt Lake City (PBS)
　　　　　2 KUTV Salt Lake City (NBC)

Wyoming

Channel 14 KCWY-TV Casper (CBS, ABC)
　　　　　2 KTWO-TV Casper (ABC)
　　　　 27 KLWY Cheyenne

5 KYCU-TV Cheyenne (CBS, ABC, NBC)
4 KCWC-TV Lander (PBS)
5 KOWY Lander (CBS, ABC)
13 KWWY Rock Springs (CBS)

Radio

Most American Radios (in cars, hotel rooms and transistors) pick up two frequencies; the AM and FM. The FM frequency has less commercials and a greater range of program. Most stations specialize in pop, classical, country, gospel or jazz music.

(For listing of radio stations, *see* Appendix pages 339-340.)

HEALTH AND EMERGENCIES

Being sick in America can be an expensive affair. Make sure you are covered by medical insurance while travelling in the Rockies. An ambulance can cost around $200, an emergency room treatment costs a minimum of $50, an average hospital room can cost approximately $300 per night.

If you need any medical assistance, turn to the Yellow Pages in the local directory for a doctor or pharmacy closest to you. In larger cities in the Rockies area there is usually a physician referral service whose number is listed in the directory.

Listed below are some of the facilities in Salt Lake City and Denver.

Hospitals

Salt Lake City

L.S.D. Hospital — 8th Ave and C St.
Holy Cross Hospital — 1045 E. 100 S.
St Marks Hospital — 1200 E. 3900 S.
University of Utah Hospital — 50 N. Medical Dr.
Cottonwood Hospital — 5770 S. 300 E. (Murray)
Primary Children's Hospital — 320 12th Ave.
InstaCare Medical Center — 1344 Foothill Blvd.

Denver

Children's Hospital, E. 19th and Downing, 861-8888.
Presbyterian/St. Lukes Medical Center, 719 E. 19th Ave. and Williams, 839-6000.
Denver General Hospital, 777 Bannock St. 893-6000.
St. Anthony's Hospital, 4231 W. 16th Ave. 629-3511.
(Flight for life-helicopter emergency service)

Pharmacies

Most modern drug stores stock a variety of medications and have a pharmacist on duty. Certain drugs can only be prescribed by a doctor. Chain drug stores like **Skaggs Drug Center** and **Walgreens** are located in many of the cities in the Rockies area. In these drug stores, most drugs and prescriptions are available. In Denver, King Soopers has over 25 stores all over town. This general supermarket has an excellent and moderately priced drug depart-

ment. The Yellow Pages will have the specific locations of these stores. **Jolley Pharmacy,** (900 E. 900 S.) in Salt Lake City is one of the primary pharmacies.

Clinics and Health Care

Rose Medical Center at One Denver Place, 999 18th St. (18th and Champa), Suite 250, 298-0891. Minor emergency care in downtown area. (8am to 4.30pm)
Professional Respite Care, 1776 Jackson, Suite 410, 757-4808. (Nursing/attendant care for disabled or seniors, in home, hotel or while travelling.)
Bryner Clinic, (and pharmacy) 745 E. 300 S.
Salt Lake Clinic, (and pharmacy) 900 E. 333 S.
Intermountain Clinic, 700 E. 350 S.

Health tips for your visit to the Rockies

Altitude: Give yourself time to get used to the new altitude. Some of the lower parts of the Rockies are a mile high and the ski areas can exceed 13,000 feet (4000 meters). Avoid over-exhaustion and heed early warning signs of shortness of breath, fatigue or headache, by resting or returning to a lower altitude. If you have heart or lung problems check with your doctor before making the trip.
Sun: The Rockies sun can be very intense. Use highly rated sun screens on all exposed areṣ of the skin and avoid the peak intensity sunshine. The direct sun rays reflecting off the snow can cause serious burns even on the coldest days. Wear sun glasses or ski goggles at all times specially when the ground is covered with snow.
Temperature: In the summer to avoid heat exhaustion, avoid strenuous activities during the mid-day hours and drink plenty of fluids. In the winter, frostbite is a potential hazard. It generally occurs in the fingers, toes or other exposed areas of skin. Keep all skin covered from brisk wind and cold.
Equipment: Take a variety of clothing, first aid kit, sunscreens, insect repellents, drinking water (if travelling in wilderness areas), protective eye gear, map of area, important.

Security and Crime

Many areas of the Rockies are best enjoyed on foot and it is generally very safe to walk the streets. However, it is recommended that you are cautious when sightseeing, shopping and moving around.

Whenever possible travel with another person, especially after dark. Avoid deserted areas. Never leave your luggage unattended, at the airport, at your hotel or anywhere else. Clutch on to your purse and important documents.

If not driving, always lock your car and don't leave luggage, cameras and other valuables in view. Lock them in the trunk. At night, park in lighted areas.

Never leave money or jewelry in your hotel room, even if it is only for a short time. Always turn in your room key at the desk when going out. Free storage service is provided by most hotels.

Don't carry around extra cash. Use credit cards and travellers checks whenever possible. When making purchases avoid making a display of large amount of cash.

Emergencies

In case of an emergency **dial 911** for police, fire, ambulance or any other emergency. If you dial the operator "O" and state the nature of the emergency you can receive some assistance. Another option, time permitting, is to check the inside cover of the local telephone directory for a list of emergency numbers.

The following numbers in Denver and Salt Lake City may come in handy.

Denver (area code 303)

Tourist Information	892-1505
Travelers Aid	832-8194
Weather Conditions	639-1515
Road Conditions (north, south, east)	639-1234
Road Conditions (west, mountains)	639-1111
Dial-4-Health	443-2584
Dental Referral Service	798-7451
Bus Information	778-6000

Salt Lake City (area code-801)

Weather	521-3650
F.B.I.	355-7521
Time	933-9122
Utah Transit (highway information)	263-3737
Highway Patrol	533-5621

DINING GUIDE

Whether a snack or a feast, eating in the Rockies can be exciting. The large cities, small towns, mountain resorts, and alpine villages have a diversity of restaurants and cuisines. The steakhouses have become a standard institution, serving some of the best beef in the West. French, Italian, Oriental and Latin American foods have proliferated and authentic cuisine from far away lands are easily available.

The Rockies provides the best mountain trout, which is served in season in local restaurants. Fast food places serving the traditional hamburgers, pizzas and tacos are plentiful. While more formal city restaurants require jackets and ties for men, the majority of eating places will welcome you in casual attire. Reservations are advisable for the popular restaurants. The Yellow Pages in each area gives a list of restaurants.

(For listing, *see* appendix.)

SHOPPING

Enormous shopping centers are a part of the suburban life in the United States. In the Rockies too, most of the towns and cities, resorts and mountain villages have their shopping malls. Shopping Centers can be quite an adventure as there are a variety of shops, stores, fast food restaurants, ample parking and sometimes beautiful landscaping, all under one roof. Specialty shops in America carry a wide range of products in a specific merchandise. Some shops specialize in books, jewelry, fabrics, cowboy clothing, crafts and other interesting items. You might have to venture off to find some these specialty shops.

Some of the typical souvenirs of the Rockies are Rocky Mountain jade jewelry, buckskin jackets, cowboy shirts, hats, belts and boots, Indian jewelry, baskets, weavings and crafts, pottery and other crafts.

In the Rockies area there are a variety of stores and shops. Chain stores, discount stores, factory outlets, drug and grocery stores, department stores and small shops are some of the different kind of stores accessible to you. The local newspapers usually advertise sales and discounts in the local shops.

Denver

The leading department stores in downtown Denver are **The Denver, Fashion Bar, Joslins** and **May D & F.** Nationally known department stores and discount stores like **Sears, Walgreens, J.C. Penneys, Target, Wards, Woolworth's** and **Skaggs** are also here. The world's largest sports store **Gart Brothers** is located on 10th and Broadway. Shopping in Denver has always been an attraction. **17th St. and 16th St. Mall** with its free shuttle bus presents a mile of excellent shopping. **Larimer Square,** offers interesting and quaint shopping in restored Victorian buildings. Antique shops are abundant on South Broadway, between 1300 and 1500 South. Every neighborhood has a shopping area and often a mall. **Cherry Creek North,** 2 miles (3.5 kms) southeast of downtown, centered around 3rd and Detroit has many intimate shops, restaurants and cafes. **Heritage Square** on Highway 40, near Golden, has wonderful arts and crafts for sale and a great amusement park for children.

An exciting shopping complex is **Tivoli,** which features shops through a restored brewery. This is located on 9th and Lawerence and specializes in high fashion shops, casual and elegant dining. A highlight of this area is a 12 screen cinema complex. **The Southweast Mall,** 8501 W. Bowles Ave. (Littleton) is the largest mall in the West having over 200 shops and 5 major department stores.

There are factory outlets that sell name brand items at bargain prices. Check the newspapers and the Yellow Pages for these, especially before buying your ski attire.

Salt Lake City

The **Z.C.M.I. Center,** in downtown Salt Lake City is one of the largest malls in the United States. The stores are open from Monday through Friday from 10am to 9pm, and on Saturdays from 10am to 6pm. This center is closed on Sundays. One of the features of this shopping center besides the variety of shops is the several levels of parking for the customers.

Four floors of shops, stores, boutiques and restaurants are in one of the largest covered shopping malls in the country, the **Crossroads Plaza.** The complex houses movie theatres, a sports complex, offices, and 8 levels of parking. The plaza is open Monday through Friday from 10am till 9pm, Saturday from 10am till 6pm and on Sundays from 12 noon till 5pm. The **Triad Center,** on South Temple and Third West has many exclusive shops, boutiques and Utah's first millionaire's restored mansion. Other attractions include an outdoor summer theatre, flowered terraces, fountains, ice skating and hot chestnuts in the winter. Triad Center and Theatre is opened from 10am to 6pm daily. Old street lights, Victorian mansions, restored trolley cars along with specialty shops, theatres and restaurants are what you will find at **Trolley Square.** Shops are open from Monday through Friday from 10am till 9pm, Saturdays from 10am to 6pm with a few shops and restaurants opened on Sunday afternoons. Restaurants and theaters are opened late during the week.

Other Shopping Areas

Most of the ski resorts in the Rockies area have excellent shopping. **Vail** has a beautiful mall with specialty shops and restaurants. **Aspen** has a variety of shops and crafts stores. **Colorado Springs** is a large city and has many shopping centers in different parts of the city. In Cheyenne, Wyoming, the **Frontier Mall** along Del Range Ave. is the primary shopping complex. Downtown Cheyenne has a variety of shops and stores. **The Wrangler** has an excellent selection of western styled clothing. The **Eastridge Mall** in Casper Wyoming has over 90 shops and stores. In Boise, Idaho, the **Westgate Shopping Mall** and the **Overland Park Shopping Mall** are the main shopping areas.

Some of the main malls in Montana are **Rimrock Mall** in Billings, **Main Mall** in Bozeman, **Southgate Mall** in Missoula and the **Holiday Village Shopping Mall** in Great Falls.

OUTDOOR GUIDE

(For a supplementary listing of outfitters and guides, refer to Appendix pages 338-339.)

Colorado

Ballooning

The San Luis Valley in Southern Colorado is America's first ballooning resort. This Balloon Ranch is open May 15th to Feb. 15th. Reservations are advised. Write to: Balloon Ranch, Box 41, Del Norte, CO 81132. 754-2533. Also check Balloons in the Yellow Pages.

Bicycling

Free publication "Road rules, equipment requirements and safety tips for bicyclists" write to: Colorado Dept. of Highways, 4201 E. Arkansas, Denver, CO 80222. Hike-Bike trails of Denver is available. Write to: Mountain Bicyclists Association, 1290 Williams St. #304, Denver, CO 80218. 333-2453. For information about the Coors Classic write to: Coors Bicycle Classic, 1540 Lehigh, Boulder, CO 80303.

Backpacking

Over two thirds of Colorado is National Forest land with more than 400 public campgrounds. Excellent backpacking areas include Rocky Mountain National Park, Pikes Peak, West of Denver in the Mt. Evans area, San Juan Mountain Range, North of Glenwood Springs, in the Flattops and the Rabbit Ears Pass area near Steamboat Springs, the Ten Mile Range South of Vail. For information write to: US Forest Service, National Park Service, Bureau of Land Management, US Geological Survey, Colorado Mountain Club. For renting and purchasing equipment check the Yellow Pages under "Mountain Climbing" and "Camping Equipment."

Boating

World's highest registered anchorage at Grand Lake, skiing at Bonnie Reservoir, Granby, Shadow Mountain, Blue Mesa and Dillon are also major boating areas for large craft. Water skiing is a sport in more than 40 lakes in Colorado. All boats with motor or sails must be registered and display registration numbers. Write to: Colorado Division of Parks and Recreation, National Park Service, US Forest Service, Colorado Division of Wildlife for more information and regulations.

Camping

Colorado is teeming with camping sites. Colorado's National Forests, Parks and Monuments, Recreation Areas, State and private campgrounds gives a wide choice of campsites. Most public campgrounds are equipped with water, tables, benches, fire grates, garbage containers, and simple toilet facilities (no showers). Private campgrounds offer electrical and plumbing hookups, showers, laundry facilities, and occasionally a swimming pool and clubhouse. Write to: US Forest Service, National Park Service, Bureau of Land Management, Colorado Division of Parks and Outdoor Recreation. Colorado Campgrounds Association. Also check "Campgrounds" in the Yellow Pages. Look for the "tree" symbol on the Colorado Highway Map.

Write for the "Roster of Rocky Mountain Summer Camps for Boys and Girls" which has a list of accredited camping facilities for young people. American Camping Association, Rocky Mountain Section, 2727 Bryant St., Denver, CO 80211. 778-8774.

Jeeping

The U.S. Forest Service recreational maps are excellent guides for 4-wheelers. These can be purchased for .50 cents from the U.S. Forest Service. Some resorts offer RV rentals for do-it-yourself jeepers or well guided jeep tours. Popular jeeping areas are Ouray, Montrose, Telluride, Crested Butte, Alamosa, Creede, Steamboat Springs, Estes Park, Aspen, Vail, Leadville. Dillion, Lake City, Salida, Grand Junction and Gunnison. Good information sources are US Forest Service, Colorado Division of Parks and Recreation, Chambers of Commerce. Check the Yellow Pages under "Automobile", "Truck", "Camper" and "Recreational Vehicle".

Rafting

More than 40 whitewater rafting companies are operating in Colorado. There are hundreds of miles of rivers in Colorado that can be rafted. Only the Yampa and Green Rivers in the Dinosaur National Monument requires a permit. Permits must be obtained before Jan. 15th of each year. For more information write to: Colorado River Outfitters Association, P.O. Box 1032 CR, Buena Vista, CO 81211. Dinosaur National Monument, Box 210, Dinosaur, CO 81610. 374-2216. Consult your travel agent and chambers of commerce. Check "Float trips" and "Boat-rentals" in the Yellow Pages.

Railroading

The Rio Grand Zephir a scenic train trip between Denver and Salt Lake City operates Mon, Thu and Sat with a return trip on Tue, Fri and Sun. Advanced bookings advised. Write to: Denver and Rio Grande RR, P.O. Box 5482, Denver, CO 80217. 595-2241.

Cripple Creek and Victor Narrow Gauge Railroad

Trains depart every 45 minutes starting at 10 am from Cripple Creek Museum from May 30th through first weekend in October. Call 689-2640.

Cumbres and Toltec Scenic Railroad

Passengers have a choice of two all-day sight seeing excursions originating from the terminal at Antonio, Colorado or terminal at Chama, New Mexico. Limited reservations are available for full length trip betwen Antonio and Chama with return trip by van. Both trains leave their terminals at 10 am and return at 5 pm. This train operates Fri through Tue from mid-June to mid-October. For information and reservations write to: C&TS RR, P.O. Box 789, Chama, New Mexico 87520. (505) 756-2151. C&TS RR, Box 668, Antonio, CO 81120. 376-5483.

Durango to Silverton Narrow Gauge

Passengers may ride the train round trip or ride the train one way (3 hours) and return on the Million Dollar Highway by motorcoach. Schedule is May 15th to Oct. 24th departure 8:30 daily, in the summer second departure 9:30 daily. Oct 25th to Nov 29th 9:00 daily, Now 30th to May 14th, 9:55 daily. Reservations advised at least one month in advance. Write to: Agent-Narrow Gauge Depot, Durango, CO 81301. 247-2733. Weather permitting this train operates through the year.

Georgetown Loop

Four mile trip from Silver Plume to the end of the track and back. Operates daily except Mondays. June through Labor Day. Departures from Georgetown and Silver Plume depots. 569-2403/279-6101.

Rodeo

For information about all the Rodeos in Colorado write to: Professional Rodeo Cowboys Associa-

tion, 101 Pro Rodeo Drive, Colorado Springs, CO 80219. 593-8840.

Winter Recreation

Skiing For up-to-date guide to Colorado ski areas write to: Colorado Ski Country USA, Brownleigh Court, Suite A201, 1410 Grant Street, Denver, CO 80203. 837-0793. For updated snow reports call 837-9907. For air travellers, check the Ski Information Booth at the Stapleton Airport in Denver.

Ski Touring/Cross Country Skiing

For Cross Country Skiing, see National Forest Service Maps for excellent trails. Many resort areas provide ski touring and have cross country ski centers at their resort.

(For ski directory, see listing in appendix pages 340-341.)

Snowmobiling

The Colorado Division of Parks and Outdoor Recreation is responsible for registering and having regulations for this sport. All vehicles must be registered and proper display of the registration number is required. For information on registration write to: Colorado Division of Parks and Outdoor Recreation. Write to: US Forest Service for a Forest Service map of the area you are interested in ($.50) which will show trails, and closure areas in the eleven National Forests in Colorado. For snowmobile sales and rentals, check Yellow Pages. Ask your travel agent for Ski/Winter Recreation Package. Write to local Chambers of Commerce. For club activity write to: Mile-Hi Snowmobile Club, Box 26368, Denver, CO 80226.

Package Tours

Contact your travel agent for special package tours that are available for sightseeing and activities. American Travel Brokers, 20 W. 84th Ave., Denver, CO 80221. 426-1981.
Mesa Verde Company, P.O. Box 277, Mancos, CO 81328. 529-4421.
Range Tours, 1540 S. Holly St., Denver, CO 80222. 759-1988.
Maupintour and Tauck Tours offer Colorado package tours. Ask your travel agent.
(For listing of Outdoor Guide, see appendix.)

Fishing

Colorado

Most of the 11,300 miles of streams and 2400 lakes of Colorado are open to public fishing. Best trout fishing spots are Grand Lake, Granby, Shadow Mountain, Green Mountain, Trappers Lake, Twin Lakes, Sweetwater Lake, Dillon Reservoir, Navajo Reservoir, Monument Lake, Vallecito Reservoir, Blue Mesa, and more than 200 other lakes on the Grand Mesa. A fishing license is required and is available at the numerous sporting good stores as well as the

Division of Wildlife. For more information write to: the Colorado Division of Wildlife, Colorado Division of Parks and Outdoor Recreation. For recorded message about fishing conditions call 292-3474.

The annual resident fishing license is $11, and for non-residents it costs $35. Two day fishing license costs $7 and a one day stamp is $3 (this stamp must be attached to a previously purchased short-term license of the same year).

General fishing statutes and regulations apply to all State waters. The fishing season in Colorado is through the year.

Idaho

A fishing license is essential for residents and non-residents in Idaho. Some waterways provide year round fishing. The licenses and copies of official fishing regulations can be obtained from vendors in most towns and the Department of Fish and Game.

Montana

The general fishing season in Montana is from mid-May to end-Nov. All fishermen have to purchase a $2 conservation license besides a fishing license. Those under 15 years in age only need the conservation license. The non-resident fishing license costs $30 for the season and $6 for two days. A resident fishing license for the season costs $8.

Montana like most of the Rockies area, boasts of thousands of miles of blue ribbon trout streams. Western Montana is famous for its rainbow, brown and cutthroat trout. In the Eastern part of Montara the waters are full of northern pike, channel catfish, large and small mouth bass, perch, walleye and sauger. The Yellowstone and Missouri Rivers offer a variety of fish including the rare paddlefish and shovelnose sturgeon. The Department of Fish, Wildlife and Parks will supply you with all the necessary information and a copy of the rules for fishing in Montana.

Utah

The Flaming Gorge in the northeast and Lake Powell in south-central Utah are two man-made lakes that furnish splendid fishing. Utah like most of the Rockies has an abundance of lakes and streams well stocked with fish ranging from rainbow trout to cutthroat, kokanee salmon, Mackinaw, grayling, bass and walleye pike.

The non-resident license fees are one-day-$5, five-day-$15, season-$35. Resident season license fees are $10.50 (16 to 64 years), $5 (over 65 years) and $4.50 (12 to 15 years). Utah also requires a trout stamp for all licenses except for the one and five day non-resident license. The cost of this stamp is $2.30 (12 to 16 years) and $3.30 (all adults). The regular fishing season is from end-May to end-Nov. Utah fishing regulations, limits and areas along with other information is available from Utah Division of Wildlife Resources.

Wyoming

The season non-resident license in Wyoming costs about $30 and a five-day tourist fishing license

costs $10. Non-resident children can fish without a license if accompanied by a licensed adult. Any fish caught by such a child will apply to the adult's legal daily limits. A $3 five-day tourist license can be purchased for the youth to have his own allocation.

Fishermen holding a valid Wyoming fishing license will have to purchase a $3 fishing stamp if he wants to fish in the Utah part of the Flaming Gorge National Recreational Area. A regular Montana fishing license is required to fish in the Montana part of the Bighorn Canyon National Recreational Area. A Wyoming license is not required to fish in the Yellowstone National Park but a free permit and package of regulations need to be collected from any park ranger station before you go fishing. Grand Teton National Park requires a Wyoming fishing license. The Wind River Reservation has special tribal regulations for fishing.

Fishing licenses could be purchased from selling agents, game and fish District offices and national recreation areas. For more information write to: the Wyoming Game and Fish Department.

Hunting

Big game and small game hunting are very popular sports in the Rocky Mountains. All the states have their own regulations and require that you have a paid license to participate in this activity. Hunters unfamiliar with the rugged mountains might be advised to hire the services of a hunting guide. Some states insist that you complete a hunter safety training course before you can purchase a firearms hunting license. It is also required that you wear a certain amount of fluorescent blaze orange while hunting. This amount differs in each state. Many of the more rugged hunting areas can be reached by 4-wheel drive vehicle but successful hunters do most of their hunting on foot. Check with the U.S. Forest Service for local road closures and restricted areas before you go on your hunting expedition.

It is your responsibility as a sportsmen to get permission from the landowner before you camp, hunt, fish or trap on his property. Some states have severe legal penalties for hunting, fishing or trapping on private land without written permission.

The unpredictable and varied climate of the Rockies requires that you bring a variety of clothing along with you. Some of the hunting grounds for deer and elk are in high altitude areas that require you to be in good physical condition.

A hunter needs to find out the specific dates, deadlines, application fees, hunter safety requirements, and other information before he takes off on a hunting trip. There are specific dates for receiving applications for certain animals. Most application fees are nonrefundable. For some animals there are only a few permits available and to ensure fairness, random computer selections are made for the species where the applications exceed the available permits. Some states provide party applications. Write to the wildlife agency in the state you plan to go hunting in for license applications, hunting maps, hunting information and regulations, and a list of guides and outfitters available.

Colorado

Big game hunting for elk, deer, antelope, bears, mountain lions, bighorn sheep and mountain goats is available in Colorado. Some of the big game seasons require limited licenses through, application and drawing, others have unlimited licenses that can be obtained at agencies or the Division of Wildlife offices in Colorado.

Deer and elk season are usually in October and November. Big horn sheep and mountain goat opens in late August, and antelope in September. Black bears are hunted in spring and also during the big game seasons. Mountain lions can be hunted during the big game season. Special archery, muzzle-loading and high country deer seasons are usually held prior to the regular deer and elk rifle season.

Non-resident hunting license for bighorn sheep and mountain goat are $500 each, and for elk and bear (during the regular season) are $210. Resident licenses for bighorn sheep and mountain goat are $100 each, and for elk and bear are $25. Deer and antelope licenses for non-residents are $120 each and for residents are $17 each. A trapping license for non-residents are $200 and for residents are $10. Small game license for non-residents are $32.50 (a separate turkey license costs $50) and for residents are $7.50, (turkey license is $7.50).

Most information and brochures can be obtained by writing to the Colorado Division of Wildlife.

Idaho

Idaho offers a great variety of animals and gamebirds with specific seasons. Like in the other Rockies States, the non-resident licenses are more expensive than the resident licenses. These are available from vendors all over the state and the Department of Fish and Game. Along with this, request a copy of hunting rules and regulations for Idaho.

Montana

The minimum age for hunting is 12 years. Hunters between the ages of 12 and 17 years have to go through a hunter education course before they can legally hunt. The Department of Fish, Wildlife and Parks will give you all the information about hunting requirements, licenses and seasons. A conservation license costing $2 is a requirement.

A combination big game hunting license can be purchased by non-residents for $300 ($35 for residents). This entitles a hunter to an elk, a deer, one black bear, a upland gamebird license and a fishing license. There are special tags for only deer that cost between $50 and $100. Animals hunted in Montana include black bears, grizzly bears, mountain lions, antelopes, mountain goats, moose, and big horn sheep. Some of these animal have limited tags and license are obtained on a drawing basis.

Utah

Utah has been known as one of the finest deer hunting areas in the country. Utah also has some excellent marshlands for waterfowl hunting. Other varities of game birds include pheasant, chukar,

Hungarian partridge, forest and sage grouse, quail, mourning dove and cottontail.

Predator shooting and hunting for non-game animals like coyote, red and gray fox, bobcat and rabbit, are also permitted in Utah.

Non-resident big game license costs $120 and small game costs $30. Resident license for big game is $10 and for small game is $8. Small game licenses for ages between 12 and 15 years costs $4. Minimum age for big game hunting is 16 and small game and waterfowl is 12 years. As hunting fees and regulations can change write for more complete information to Utah Division of Wildlife Resources.

Wyoming

Applications and fees must arrive at the Wyoming Game and Fish Department in Cheyenne by the last application date. Within 15 days they will inform the random number computer selection results. There is a non-refundable application fee of $5 for most of the animals in addition to the license fee. Write to the Wyoming Game and Fish Department regarding individual licenses, party licenses, hunting rules and regulations and for a list of guides and outfitters. The cost of licenses vary from $250 to $30 each, depending on the animal. If the person is successful in receiving a license the fee is nonrefundable.

Parks, Monuments and Forests

National Parks

There are ten national parks in the five Rocky Mountain states covered in this book. Each park has a variety of facilities, activities and regulations.

Entrance fees are charged at most of the parks varying from 50 cents per person to $3 per vehicle. A Golden Eagle Passport (an annual entrance to all parks costing $10) can be purchased at all parks. Auto camping is allowed only in designated campgrounds mostly on a first-come, first-serve basis. Campground fees range from $3 to $8 per night for an individual site. Most campgrounds have cold water restrooms and no hook-up for showers. In the summertime campgrounds get filled up early, and its advisable that you reach your campground by early afternoon to ensure a site. The Ranger Station at the entrance of the park will be able to advise you on what camp sites are available and also supply you with information on the park. Winter operation of the parks is often limited and some parks have no water during the off-season.

Backcountry use in most of the parks require free permits for overnight stays. Many parks require advanced reservations for overnight backcountry use as there are a limited quantity of permits available.

Most boats must meet state regulations on reservoirs, lakes and rivers in national parks. The use of motors is not allowed in some areas except in the case of emergencies.

Drinking water is available at most campgrounds. It is recommended that you check with the ranger responsible for the site regarding the drinking water as some areas of the Rockies may have contaminated water.

All plants and animals are protected in the national parks. It is against the law to molest them in any form. Most parks require that pets be kept on a leash or otherwise confined at all times. If you plan to bring your pet please consult the ranger responsible for the park ahead of time.

Off-road vehicle use is not allowed except on designated four-wheel-drive roads. Some parks offer National Park Service (N.P.S.) guided tours to organized groups that may require advanced reservations.

Colorado

Mesa Verde National Park, CO 81330.
Accommodations — Food, gasoline and lodging are available from mid-May to mid-Oct, no services are available rest of the year. Full interpretive services begin mid-June and continues through Labor Day. **Morefield Campground,** with single and group camp sites have six camp sites for physically impaired persons. Commercial campgrounds are located close to the Park entrance.
Recreational Facilities — N.P.S. Guided Tours, self-guiding tour, guides for hire, picnic area.
Other facilities — Museum, groceries, ice, Visitor Center, handicapped access, restrooms.
Rocky Mountain National Park, Estes Park, CO 80517.
Accommodations — Hotels, motels and lodges are available at Estes Park and Grand Lake, just outside the Park. The four campgrounds at Rocky Mountain National Park are all at an elevation above 8200 feet (2500 meter).
Moraine Park Campground, located 3 miles west of Head Quarters Visitors Center, on Bear Lake Rd. has 250 campsites, including walk-in camp sites, ranger station, sanitary dump station, public telephone and campfire amphitheater. Campsites can be reserved. The **Glacier Basin Campground** located 9 miles (15 km) west of Estes Park on Bear Lake Rd. has 152 campsites plus 18 group campsites. Facilities include a ranger station, sanitary dump station, comfort station, telephones and an amphitheater. Campsites can be reserved.
Longs Peak Campground is for tents only. It is 11 miles (18 km) south of Estes Park. There are 30 campsites, a ranger station and comfort stations. No reservations for this campground.
Timber Creek Campground, is on the west side of the Park and 10 miles (16 km) north of Grand Lake on Trail Ridge Rd. Facilities include 100 campsites, a ranger station, comfort stations, sanitary dump station and an amphitheater. Timber Creek is on a first-come basis.
Recreational Facilities — N.P.S. Guided Tour, self-guiding tour, picnic area, backcountry use permits, hiking, mountain climbing, horseback riding, fishing, snowmobile route, cross country ski trail.
Other facilities — Museum, restaurant, handicap access, restrooms and Visitor Center.

Montana

Glacier National Park, West Glacier, MT 59936. Glacier National Park is open from mid-June to mid-Sept and comprises of hundreds of miles of backcountry trails that lead to 50 living glaciers, many waterfalls and alpine gardens. Commercial

airlines Kalispell and Great Falls service the Park. Amtrack and regular bus travel are available to East and West Glacier. By car, use highways 2, 89 and 93. If you are travelling from Canada, use Alberta highways 2, 5 or 6.
Accommodations — Comfortable accommodations include two lodges, two hotels, two motor inns and cabins. The campgrounds have from 6 to 200 campsites. Write to the Park Superintendant for information.
Recreational facilities — N.P.S. Guided Tour, self-guided tour, backcountry use permits, mountain climbing, horseback riding, boating, fishing, picnic areas, cross country ski trail, float trips, boating.
Other facilities — Groceries, ice, restaurant, restrooms, handicap access, Visitor Center, boat rentals.

Utah

Arches National Park, 446 S. Main St., Moab, UT 84532. Depart from Moab and travel 5 miles (8 km) north via U.S. 191 to the Park. Driving time through the Park is 2 hours but allow additional time for hiking.
Accommodation — Devil's Garden Campground is located in the Park, 18 miles (33 km) from the Visitor Center. Motels and commercial campgrounds and other services are available in Moab.
Recreational Facilities — N.P.S. Guided Tour, self-guiding tour, picnic area, backcountry use permits, hiking.
Other facilities — Handicap access, restrooms, Visitor Center, Museum and exhibit.

Bryce Canyon National Park, Bryce Canyon, UT 84717. Allow three hours for the Park tour, with extra time for hiking. T.W.A. offers services in the Park from mid-May to Oct.
Accommodation — Services and accommodations are available just outside the Park, in the surrounding communities. Camping is available year-round in the Park but water is only available in the summer.
Recreational Facilities — N.P.S. Guided tour, self-guiding tour, hiking, backcountry use permits, picnic areas, cross country ski trail, horseback riding.
Other Facilities — Museum, exhibit, groceries, ice, restaurant, handicap access, restrooms and Visitor Center.
Canyonlands National Park, 446 S. Main St., Moab, UT 84532. The Park can be reached from Moab travelling 60 miles (96 km) via U.S. 191 and U-221. Allow 3 hours to tour the Needles section of Canyonlands. Hiking, jeeping, river running or scenic flights are some of the best ways to explore this Park.
Accommodations — There are primitive camp sites located in four-wheel drive areas of the Park. Piped water is available in the **Needles Campground** only. Anywhere else in the Park water must be carried in. Accommodations and services are available in Moab and Monticello.
Recreational Facilities — Self-guiding tour, guides for hire, hiking, picnic areas, backcountry use permits, boating.

Capitol Reef National Park, Torrey, UT 84775. This Park is accessible on U-24. Allow three hours to drive through the Park.

Accommodations — There are no commercial facilities in the Park. There are two campgrounds located within the Park boundaries. The main campground 1 mile south of the Visitor Center has 53 sites, comfort stations and fire places. Accommodations and services are available in Torrey, Bicknell and Loa.

Recreational Facilities — Hiking, mountain climbing, horseback riding, picnic areas, N.P.S. Guided Tour, self-guided tour, boating.

Other facilities — Exhibit, Visitor Center, handicap access.

Zion National Park, Springdale, UT 84767-1099. Depart from St. George and travel 46 miles (74 km) via I-15 and U-90. Allow 3 hours to tour the Park and the Visitor Center. T.W.A. Services Inc. operates accommodations and services to the Park from mid-May to mid-Oct.

Accommodations — Of the three campgrounds located within the Park, one is open year-round. Accommodations and services are available in communities just outside the Park and in St. George.

Recreational Facilities — N.P.S. Guided Tour, self-guiding tour, picnic area, hiking, horseback riding, mountain climbing, backcountry use permit.

Other facilities — Museum, exhibit, restaurant, handicap access, Visitor Center, restrooms.

Wyoming

Grand Teton National Park, P.O. Drawer 170, Moose, WY 83012.

Accommodations — Cabins, lodge facilities and rooms are available from 21 different concessionaires within the Park. Reservations are recommended for all facilities. A list of concessionaires and their addresses can be received by writing to the Park Superintendent. There are a number of campgrounds in the Park. **Colter Bay** (trailer village with hookups), **Lizard Creek, Jenny Lake** (no trailers), **Gros Ventre,** and **Signal Mountain.** The surrounding communities, specially Jackson Hole, are developed tourist areas with excellent accommodations and services. A maximum stay of 14 days is allowed in all the camp grounds except Jenny Lake which is limited to 10 days.

Food and lodging are offered at Colter bay, Jackons Lake, Jenny Lake and Signal Mountain Lodges in Moran. Signal Mountain has limited services in the winter.

Recreational Facilities — Boating, boat rides, bus tours, fishing, hiking, horseback riding, interpretive program, mountain climbing, skiing, snowmobiling, swimming, water skiing (allowed only on Jackson Lake), hiking, backcountry use permits, N.P.S. Guided Tour, self-guiding tour, guides for hire.

Other facilities — Museums, exhibit, amphitheaters with naturalist talks, general stores, self-service laundry, restaurants, service stations, Visitor Centers (Moose and Colter Bay), handicap access.

Yellowstone National Park, P.O. Box 168, WY 82190.

Acommodations — Within Yellowstone National Park are hotels, cabins, the Fishing Bridge Trailer Village and a number of campgrounds. These accommodations are open from mid-June through Labor Day. Limited accommodations are available off season with winter activities centering at Old Faithful. Reservations are advised specially during June and July. These can be made by writing to Yellowstone Park Co., Yellowstone National Park, 82190. Some of the lodges and hotels are **Roosevelt Lodge** (T.W.A. Services), **Canyon Village Lodge and Cabins** (588 units), **Lake Lodge and Cabins** (176 units), **Old Faithful Lodge/Cabins** (236 units), **Old Faithful Inn** (326 units) and **Old Faithful Snowlodge** (65 units). For information and reservations call (307) 344-7311.

Campgrounds are open from mid-June to mid-Sept, with limited camping during the rest of the year. The majority of campgrounds have been filled to capacity usually by noon during the summer. The ranger station at the entrance can inform you about which campgrounds have vacancies. When you arrive at a campground the ranger in charge will help you. Camping or overnight stopping is allowed only in designated areas. Your stay in the Park as a camper is limited to 14 days in the summer and 30 days during the rest of the year. Some campsites are restricted to hard-sided vehicles and some only for tents. Check with the ranger station for current information. Two campgrounds are available for organized groups and can be reserved ahead of time.

Recreational Facilities — Boating, driving, horseback riding, stagecoach rides, boat and bus tours, hiking, N.P.S. Guided Tours, self-guiding tour, backcountry use permits, mountain climbing, fishing, bicycle trail, snowmobile route, cross country ski trail.

Other facilities — Commercial airlines, railroad and bus lines provides service to Yellowstone National Park. Evening campfire programs, nature walks, Museums, exhibits, handicap access, restaurants, general stores, laundry facilities (self-service), Visitor Centers.

National Monuments, Historic Sites and Recreation Areas

(For listing, *see* appendix.)

National Forests
(For listing, *see* appendix.)

State Parks and Recreation Area
(For listing, *see* appendix.)

CULTURAL ACTIVITIES

Museums and Attractions

(For listing, *see* appendix.)

Libraries

Every city and town in the Rockies has a public library. The quality of each library can vary greatly depending on the location. Most of the larger cities have a library system consisting of the main library and several branch libraries in different parts of the city. The main library in Denver (1300 and Broadway) has the world's largest Western library. Across the street from here is the State Historical Society which has a good research library and a collection of 75,000 photographs of William Henry Jackson.

Salt Lake City has the world's largest genealogical library, located in the LDS Church Office Building at Temple Square.

The different universities in the Rockies area have excellent libraries.

Non-residents cannot borrow library books, but are welcomed to spend time in the libraries, reading material from newspapers, magazines to reference books. The use of all libraries is free.

Bookstores

Bookstores are prevalent in most neighborhood shopping areas in the Rockies. Larger drug stores, grocery shops and general stores have a department for books, cards, magazines, post cards and other stationery. In the major cities the largest chain bookstores, **B. Dalton** and **Waldenbooks** have stores in many locations. The Yellow Pages in the local directory give a list of the bookstores in the area. One of the best bookstores in the Rockies area is the **Tattered Cover Bookstore**, 2930 E. 2nd Ave., Denver, CO 80209. (303) 322-7727. This store is opened daily, and has over 150,000 books, maps and services.

EVENTS AND FESTIVALS

(For listing, *see* appendix.)

NIGHTLIFE

In the larger cities there is a variety of night time happenings. The problem isn't what to do but what to choose. A choice of music, theater, dance, cinema, disco, opera and more is yours. From famous performers to unknown talents, from Broadway performances to old time melodramas, the bigger cities in the Rockies offers something to suit your taste. Outside the big cities abundant entertainment awaits you. Rodeos and festivals have their own nightly entertainment of dances, singers, square dancing, fairs and carnivals. In the smaller towns entertainment is usually confined to the weekends. In some places the nightly entertainment is limited to a motel lounge and bar or sometimes a roadhouse with a local band in the corner. The hotel receptionist or local residents, local newspapers and magazines are usually your best source of information. Listed below are some of the popular nightly entertainment in the cities of Denver and Salt Lake City.

Denver

Boulder's Dinner Theater, 5501 Arapahoe, Boulder, CO 80303. 449-6000. Elegant atmosphere, gourmet dinner served by the performers along with an excellent Broadway musical.

Confetti, 350 S. Birch, Glendale, CO 80222. 320-0118. Denver's hottest night spot. Current music, video, lights and fashion.
Country Dinner Playhouse, 6875 S. Clinton, Englewood, CO 80110. 799-1410. Professional dinner theater from Tuesday through Sunday. Matinees during the weekends. 470 seats, buffet included.
Comedy Works, 1226 15th St., Denver, CO 80202. 595-3637. Denver's all comedy nighclub in Larimer Square. Open nightly, dinner/show package.
Heritage Square Opera House, Heritage Square, Box D-109, Golden, CO 80401. 279-7881. Great theater/restaurant specializing in unmatched comedy entertainment for 13 years. Reasonable prices, reservation required.
The Landmark Inn, 455 S. Colorado Blvd., Denver, CO. Folk music and 24 hour coffee shop.
"Turn of the Century" 8930 E. Hampden Ave, Denver CO. Nightclub with nationally known entertainers.
Downtown Denver —
Live music of all varieties can be found all over the downtown area. **Ivory Piano Bar,** 1620 Market St. is a quiet spot, and a popular jazz cantina **El Chapultepec** at 20th and Market St., provides good music. In the Larimer Square area are **Josephina's** for jazz, pop and wine, **Basin's Up** for local favorites and a 23 year old piano bar **Laffite.** An old jazz lounge is located in the Oxford Hotel on 1600 17th St. called **Sage Restaurant** and the **Corner Room.**
Glendale and Cherry Creek —
The **Bull and Bush,** 4700 Cherry Creek Dr. South, offers a variety of musical talents. **Aspen City Limits,** 4501 E. Virginia Ave. specializes in local blues and jazz.

Salt Lake City

Dead Goat, Arrow Press Square, a laid back beer bar decorated in Old Colorado has a full service grill with dancing to live music during the weekends.
The Bay, 1130 E. 2100 S. 466-3733. A disco.
Broadway Disco, 34 South Main, 532-9252. A disco.
Matt Limburg's Dance Entertainment and Light Show, 2983 W. 3500 S., 96709797. Disco and light show.
Thirteenth Floor, 161 W. 600 S., 364-7013. A disco.
Xenon, 909 E. 2100 S., 486-4261. A disco.
Cafe Viceuses Rumeurs, Salt Lake's new piano bar-cum-sushi bar. Decorated French bistro Style, good food.
The Green Parrot, 155 W. 200 S. A casual cafe style club with live music and dancing Thursday through Saturday.

SPORTS

Spectator Sports

The Rocky Mountain area is packed with spectator sporting events. In the summer and the winter each state has its own sports events. Professional sporting events are prominant in Denver and Salt Lake City.

Denver

Denver Zephyrs, professional baseball. Mile High Stadium. 433-8645.
Denver Broncos, professional NFL Football. Mile High Stadium, 433-7466.
Denver Gold, professional USFL Football. Mile High Stadium, 455-0234.
Denver Nuggets, professional NBA Basketball. McNichols Sports Arena, 1635 Clay. 893-6700.
University of Colorado Football, University of Colorado, Boulder. 492-5161.
Horse Racing, Arapahoe Park, 4100 S. Parker Rd. Aurora, CO 80114. 699-2900. (late May through early Nov.)
Dog Racing, Mile High Kennel Club, 6200 Dahlia, 288-1591. (Greyhound racing with pari-muteul wagering.) June-Aug. Year-round off-track betting from other Colorado dog tracks. Admission $.50 PFK.

Salt Lake City

The Central Hockey League's **Golden Eagles** and the National Basketball Association's **Utah Jazz** play at the Salt Palace. The minor league baseball team, **the Gulls,** have their games at Derk's Field. University of Utah, sports activities are played at the campus in Salt lake City.

A full range of athletic events occur at **Brigham Young University,** at Provo. The B.Y.U. Football team is usually one of the nation's top college teams. **Utah State University,** in Logan and **Weber State University** in Ogden have many spectator sporting events during the year.

SPECIALS

What Children Can Do

In most of the cities in the Rockies, public parks, zoos, amusement parks, children's museums are great places to take your kids to. These places often have special attractions for kids. **Elitch Gardens** and **Lakeside Amusement Park** in Denver, the **Lagoon Amusement Park** in Farmington, Utah, offer a lot of fun for kids and adults. The **Renaissance Festival** at Lakspur is specially entertaining for children.

The national parks, forests and monuments offer educational and exciting times for the entire family. The outdoor activities that the Rockies offers is something that children love to participate in. Conveniently located camping sites offer children the space and freedom not found in hotels and motels. Many hotels and motels have baby sitting services, playrooms, day care centers, cribs, strollers, high chairs....etc to make it more convenient for the family. Some of the ski resorts provide children's ski schools and day care centers for the very young.

Handicapped Travellers

One of the newest groups that are exploring the travel scene are the handicapped travellers. Today extensive measures have been taken in many areas to offer safe and comfortable travelling for the physically limited person. The wheelchair symbol is seen all over the Rockies area specifically demarking parking, toilets, ramps, camping.....etc. for the handicapped. **A travel Guide for the Handicapped** by Louise Weiss is an excellent book. The chambers of commerce, park services and other travel agencies will send special material for the handicapped traveller. The following will also supply you with material.
Rehabilitation International U.S.A. 20 W. 40th St., New York, N.Y. 10018. **Utah State Board for Vocational Education,** 250 E. 500 S., Salt Lake City, UT 84111. (They have a handicapped guide to the city.)

A special book written for the handicapped is **Guide to National Parks and Monuments.** The book **Barrier Free** lists 300 roadside rest areas that have facilities for the handicapped and is available through the Commission at Washington D.C. A list of tour operators who have tours for the handicapped could be obtained by writing to:
The Society for Advancement of Travel for the Handicapped, 26 Court St., Brooklyn, N.Y. 11242. T.W.A. publishes a special 12 page brochure named "Consumer information about Air Travel for the Handicapped." This book explains all special travel arrangements that are available. Greyhound Bus System and Amtrack put out such publications too.

Day trips from Denver

Central City

Restored gold mining town, a National Historic District. Pan for gold, tour gold mines, Teller Opera House and Hotel, restaurants, antiques, shops and saloons. Located 34 miles north west of Denver.

Georgetown

Elegant silver mining town with over 200 Victorian buildings. Shops, restaurants, Hotel de Paris, Hamil House, Georgetown Loop narrow gauge railroad, silver mining tour. Thirty four miles west of Denver.

Idaho Springs

Historic gold mining town. Shops, restaurants, attractions, 21 miles west of Denver on I-70. National Forest information center in town for information on camping. Gateway to Mount Evans Highway, highest paved road in North America for automobiles. Free 14 mile highway goes up to 14,260 feet. Open June through Labor Day.

Boulder

Location of beautiful University town at foot of Rockies. University of Colorado, historic Boulder Mall downtown, shops, Victorian Buildings, restaurants. 27 miles Northwest of Denver on highway 36.

Golden

Historic place just outside Denver. Coors tour, Colorado Railroad Museum, Heritage Square, Buffalo Bill Museum and grave site, Colorado School of Mines. On the way to Golden, detour a few miles and visit the beautiful Red Rocks Amphitheater.

Skiing

Many ski resorts are located within a few hours from Denver. Call your travel agent or write to the chambers of commerce for information.

Sightseeing Tours

Best Mountain Tours by Mountain Men, 11100 E. Dartmouth, #219 Aurora, CO 80014, 750-0090. One day and half day tours in 4-wheel drive vans to gold mines, mountains and ghost towns. Private charters also available.

Gray Line Bus Tours, Box 38667, Denver CO 80238, 289-2841. Two-hour to full day tours to mountain parks, Colorado Springs, Gold mining towns, Rocky Mountain National Park. Prices range from $8 to $25 for the day.

Historic Denver Tours, 1701 Wynkoop, #200 Denver CO 80202. 534-1858. Driving, walking, van tours of city's historic landmarks. Prices range from $4 to $10 per tour.

Tours by Arrangement, 623-1492. The Arrangers Inc. offer half day tours to small and large groups in the city and surrounding areas.

Charters Unlimited, 980-1922. Scenic tours, special tours in the city and surrounding areas.

Day Trips from Salt Lake City

City Creek Canyon
Enter the canyon off East Capitol Rd. Paved road extends five miles to Rotary Park. Great for picnicking and hiking. Canyon open from 8am to 8pm.

Parley's Canyon
Most of this canyon is in Wasatch National Forest. Golfing, hunting in the fall and hiking are some of the activities available here. Many historical markers and cafes and service stations are located at the summit and near the gold course.

Mill Creek Canyon
This box canyon offers picnicking, and hiking amidst oak, conifer and aspen. Picnic grounds and sports areas are available for families.

Emigration Canyon
Monument and Hogle Zoo are at the mouth of the canyon. Main entrance from Sunnyside Ave., Utah Hwy 85 connects with U.S. 40 and I-80. Hiking and picnicking.

Big Cottonwood Canyon
In the Wasatch National Forest. At the top of the canyon is Brighton Ski and Summer resort. Picnicking, hiking and beautiful vistas.

Little Cottonwood Canyon
Effects of glaciation can be seen in this U-shaped canyon. At the end of the canyon is Alta and Snowbird Ski Resorts. Excellent rock climbing, hiking, picnicking and some fishing.

How To Watch a Rodeo

The Rockies is Rodeo Country and every weekend in the summer, you can find a rodeo somewhere in this area. In 1880 for the first time the sport developed as a professional entertainment. Today most modern rodeos have a parade that precedes the event. Listed below are some of the major events in a rodeo.

Saddle Bronc Riding:

Saddle broncs are not trained to buck, but do so instinctively. The rider has to use a standard P.R.C.A. (Professional Rodeo Cowboys Association) saddle and buck rein which is a braided rope. The bronc rider is judged by the performance of his riding and the animal's bucking. Men are specially designated the job of helping the rider dismount from the horse when the riding time is up.

Bareback Riding:

This event does not allow the use of stirrups or reins. The horse has a stiff leather strap that goes around the horses belly and the cowboy has to hold on to this with one hand. The rider must spur the horse for eight seconds and is disqualified if his free hand touches the horse or if he misses spurring the horse on the first jump.

Calf Roping:

Within a given time limit the cowboy has to put the calf down and tie three of its legs together. The calf is given a ten foot (3 meter) lead before the cowboy starts chasing it. The horse's job is to bring the cowboy close to the running calf and stop, so he can rope it.

Steer Wrestling:

Here the cowboy grabs a 700 pound (320 kg) steer by its horns and wrestles it to the ground. The cowboy that performs this in the shortest time wins the event.

Bull Riding:

A contest between small man and huge beast. Here a 150 pound (70 kg) is pitted against a 1500 pound (700 kg) bull. The cowboy is required to ride one-handed with a loose rope, which is around the bull's belly. The other end of the rope is around the rider's hand. The ride is 8 minutes long and spurring is not required but will add to the score.

Barrel Racing:

This event allows women to show their rodeo skills. Women run well trained horses through a cloverleaf pattern at amazing speed. A fast horse and a good rider makes this an exciting event.

The Wild Horse Race:

Two men hold the wild horse long enough to saddle it and allow a third man to mount and ride it. This is an exciting event as there are many competitors.

Besides the professional rodeos, there are many special rodeos held in the Rockies area. These are all girl rodeos, all Indian rodeos, old times rodeos and college rodeos. If you write to the chambers of commerce a list of rodeos and dates will be sent to you.

SUGGESTED READINGS

General

Rich Cahill, *The Colorado Hot Springs Guide,* Pruett Publishing Co. 1983.
Irving Stone, *Men to Match My Mountains,* Berkley Books, New York, 1982.
Frank L. Wentworth, *Aspen the Roaring Fork,* Sundance Publications, Denver, 1976.
Virginia Hopkins, *The Colorado River: A Portrait,* Quatro Publications, London, 1985.
Dale Morgan, *The Great Salt Lake,* University of New Mexico Press, Albuquerque, 1973.
Works Project Administration, *Utah Guide to the State,* New Revised Edition, Ward J. Loyance, Utah Arts Council, Salt Lake City, 1982.
Peggy Clifford and John M. Smith, *Aspen/Dreams and Dilemas,* The Swallow Press In., Chicago, 1970.
Suzanne Lord, *America's Travel Treasury,* American's Discover America Series, William Morrow, N.Y. 1977.
Phillip Ashton Rollins, *The Cowboy,* University of New Mexico Press. 1979.
Howard R. Lamar (editor), *The Reader's Encyclopedia of the American West,* Crowell, 1977.
Fodor's Rockies and Plains, David McKay and Co., Inc., New York, 1979.
Wyoming, A Guide to its History, Highways, and People, compiled by the workers of the Writers Program of the Work Projects Administration, University of Nebraska Press, 1981.
Robin Hough, *The Friendly Native Guide Book to Utah,* Salt Lake City, n.p., 1979.
Peter Wiley and Robert Gottlieb, *Empires in the Sun: The Rise of New American West,* G.P. Putnam's Sons, 1982.
Neal R. Peirce, *The Mountain States of America: People, Politics and Power in the Eight Rocky Mountain States,* W.W. Norton and Co., 1972.
American Automobile Association, *Tour Book, AAA,* Falls Church, Va, 1984.
Harry Hansen, *Colorado, A Guide to the Highest State,* Hastings House, New York, 1970.
Royal B. Hassick, Cowboys, *The Real Story of Cowboys and Cattlemen,* Octopus Book Ltd., London, 1974.
Wallace Stegner, *The Gathering of Zion,* The Story of the Mormon Trail, Salt Lake City, Westwater Press, 1981.

Roderunner Travel Guide to Big Wyoming, Roderunner Travel Guide, Jackson Wyoming, 1983.
Frank Fosset, *Colorado, it's Gold and Silver Mines, Farms and Stock Ranges and Health and Pleasure Resorts,* Arno Press, New York, reprint 1973.
Tom and Sanse Sudduth, *Central Colorado Ski Tours,* Pruett Publishing Co., Boulder, 1977.
Bicidehaan, *Bike Rides of the Colorado Front Range,* Pruett Publishing Co., 1981.

History

C.W. Buckholtz, *Rocky Mountain National Park: A History,* Colorado Associated University Press, Boulder, 1983.
J Donald Hughes, *American Indians in Colorado,* Pruett Publishing Co., Boulder, 1984.
The American Heritage Book of Indians, American Heritage Publishing Co., 1961.
Eliott Coues, (editor) *The History of Lewis and Clark Expedition,* (3 volumes) Dover Publication, N.Y. 1965.
David Lavender, *The Rockies,* University of Nebraska Press, 1968.
J.R. Swanton, *Indian Tribes of North America,* 1953.
Wallace Atwood, *The Rocky Mountains,* New York, 1945.
David E. Miller, *Great Salt Lake: Past and Present,* Salt Lake City, Publishers Press, 1977.
Thomas E. Mails, *The Mystic Warriors of the Plains,* Garden City, N.Y. Doubleday, 1972.

Geography, Wildlife and Nature

Michael Robbins, *Along the Continental Divide,* National Geography, 1981.
Orrin H. Bonncy, Lorraine G. Bonney, *Guide to the Wyoming Mountains and Wilderness Areas,* (Climbing Routes and Back Country), Swallow Press Inc., Chicago, *Montana Wildlife,* Montana Magazine, Helena. Peter Matthiessen, *Wildlife in America,* 1959.
Robert Ormes, *Guide to the Colorado Mountains,* Chicago, Swallow Press Inc. 1977.
Ruth Ashton Nelson, *Plants of Rocky Mountain National Park,* Colorado Associated University Press, 1982.
Doug Wheat, *The Floater Guide to Colorado,* Falcon Press Publishing Co., Billings and Helena, MT. 1983.
Sierra Club Guides to the National Parks, Rocky Mountains and the Great Plains, Stewart, Tabori and Co., 1984.
Anne Zwinger and Beatrice Willard, *Land Above the Trees,* Farper and Row, New York, 1972.
Robert Schraff, *Exploring Yellowstone National Park,* The World Publishing Co., N.Y. 1969.
Frank Craighead, *Track of the Grizzly,* Sierra Club Books, San Francisco, 1979.
The Old West, (series) New York Time Life Books, 1974 to 1977.

Art and Photography

David Brownell and Nancy Tate (photography), John Sabella (text), *Aspen the 100 Year High,* Books in Focus, N.Y., 1981.
Clifford P. Westermeier, *Colorado's First Portrait,*

University of New Mexico Press, 1970.
William Albert Allard, *Vanishing Breed,* photographs of the Cowboy and the West, Little, Brown and Co., 1983.
Peter Hassick, *Frederic Remington,* Harry N. Abrams, Inc., 1973.
Peter H. Hassrick, *The Way West: Art of Frontier America,* N.Y. Abrams, 1977.
Mary Carroll Nelson, *Masters of Western Art,* New York, Watson Guptill, 1982.

APPENDIX

Accommodations

In Colorado:

Aspen:

Best Western Aspenalt Lodge, P.O. Box 428, Basalt, CO 81621. 927-3191. Located 16 miles from Aspen/Snowmass on Frying Pan River in Basalt. Moderate rates. AAA.
Continental Inn, 515 S. Galena, Aspen, CO 81611. 925-1150. Aspen's largest lodge with indoor/outdoor pool, overlooking Aspen Mountain. (Write for rates.)
The Gant, P.O. Box K-3 Aspen, CO 81611. 925-5000. 140 units, 2 heated pools, hot tubs, saunas, tennis.
Bavarian Inn, 801 W. Bleeker, Aspen, CO 81611. 925-7391. West side of town, economical. (Write for rates.)

Beaver Creek:

Beaver Creek Resort, P.O. Box 7, Vail, CO 81658. 1-800-525-9132. Spectacular mountain setting, 195 units.
The Charter at Beaver Creek, P.O. Box 5310, Avon, CO 81620. 1-800-824-3064. Luxury full service condominium hotel.

Boulder:

American Youth Hostels Inc, P.O. Box 2370, Boulder, CO 80306. 442-1166. Hostels all over Colorado. (Write for details.)
Best Western Boulder Inn, 770 28th St., Boulder, CO 80303. 449-3800. Across from campus, 98 units, pool, sauna.
The Hilton Harvest House, 1345 28th St., Boulder, CO 80302. 443-3850. Resort hotel at the base of the Rocky Mountains.
Holiday Inn Boulder, 800 28th St., Boulder, CO 80303. 443-3322. Holidome recreation center, close to campus.

Breckenridge:

Blue River Condominiums, P.O. Box 1942, Breckenridge, CO 80424. 453-2260. Completely furnished, 36 units.
Beaver Run Resort, 620 Village Rd., Breckenridge, CO 80424. 453-6000. Luxury resort with 329 rooms, and all facilities including its own ski lift.
The Village at Breckenridge Resort, P.O. Box 1979, Breckenridge, CO 80424. 453-2000. Luxury ski resort.
Summit Ridge Inc., 11072 Hwy 9, Breckenridge, CO 80424. 1-800-525-3882. Homes and condominiums at varying rates.

Central City:

Golden Rose Hotel, P.O. Box 8, Central City, CO 80427. 582-5060. Restored Victorian Hotel, hot tub and sauna.

Colorado Springs:

The Broadmoor, P.O. Box 1439, Colorado Springs, CO 80901. 634-7711. Pool, golf, tennis, alpine slide, 565 units.
Hilton Inn, 505 Popes Bluff Trail, Colorado Springs, CO 80909. 598-7656. Restaurant, pool, 222 units.
Palmer House Best Western, 3010 N. Chestnut, I-25 at Fillmore, Colorado Springs, CO 80907. 636-5201.

Cripple Creek:

Imperial Hotel of Cripple Creek, 123 N. 3rd St., Cripple Creek, CO 80813. 689-2922. Restored Victorian Hotel. Colorado's oldest melodrama, staged in the Gold Bar Room Theater.

Denver:

The Aapartel, 1221 Clarkson, Denver, CO 80218. 867-9630. Tasteful one bedroomed apartments, near downtown. Seven days minimum stay. $25-30.
The Brown Palace Hotel, 321 17th St., Denver, CO 80202. 297-3111. Historic downtown hotel 25 minutes from Stapleton Int'l Airport. Transportation provided, 460 rooms.
The Burnsley Hotel, 1000 Grant St., Denver, CO 80224. 830-1000. Small super luxury hotel. Located near State Capitol. Suites $85-135, penthouse suites $300.
Executive Tower Inn, 1405 Curtis, Denver, CO 80202. 571-0300. Athletic club, shopping, 337 rooms, $61-96.
Fairmont Hotel, 1750 Welton St., Denver, CO 80202. 295-1200. Mobil 4 star, AAA, 540 rooms with tennis, swimming, award winning restaurant, meeting facilities.
Holiday Chalet, 1820 E. Colfax Ave., Denver, CO 80218. 321-9975. Restored brownstone mansion, charming suites, $37.50-45. (Write for brochure.)
The Oxford, 1600 17th St., Denver, CO 80202. 628-5400. Elegant restored 82 roomed hotel, near Union Station.
El Camino Motel, 1576 S. Colorado Blvd., Denver, CO 80222. 756-9487. Quiet 14 family motel, 2 blocks north of I-25 on Colorado Blvd. $32-40. (Weekly rates available.)
Holiday Inn Denver Downtown, 1540 Glenarm Pl., Denver, CO 80202. 573-1450. Prime downtown location, 396 rooms, all amenities.
Holiday Inn, 1474 S. Colorado Blvd., Denver, CO 80222. 757-7731. Six miles from the airport, free transportation, 253 rooms, revolving roof top restaurant. $52-61. (There are other Holiday Inns on I-70 and East Chambers, 1975 Bryant St. and 9009 E. Arapahoe, Englewood. Call toll-free 1-800-HOLIDAY for information.)
Howard Johnson's Denver South, 6300 E. Hampden, Denver, CO 80222. 758-2211. Located at I-25 and Hampden. Close to shopping, restaurants, theaters and golf. $52-60.
Quality Inn South, 4760 E. Evans Ave., Denver, CO

80222. 757-7601. Exit 203 on I-25. Restaurant, lounge and 80 rooms. $40-55 per night.

Ramada Hotel Republic Park, 7007 S. Clinton, Englewood, CO 80112. 799-6200. Ten storied, 265 roomed hotel. Concierge Floor has glass ceilings. Teleconferencing, pool and lounge.

Denver Marriott Hotel, City Center 1701 California, Denver, CO 80202. 297-1300. Five restaurants, 612 luxury rooms with fitness center, convention facilities. (Other excellent Marriott Hotels are located on I-25 at Hampden Ave. and 1717 Denver West Blvd. Golden.)

The Denver Hilton, 1550 Court Place, Denver, CO 80202. 893-3333. Colorado's largest first class hotel. Downtown on the 16th St. Mall., 758 rooms, $78.

Airport Hilton, 4411 Peoria, Denver, CO 80239. 373-5730. A first class, 200 rooms. Full amenities, airport shuttle, children free. $66-102.

The Westin Hotel Tabor Center, 1672 Lawerence St., Denver, CO 80202. 572-9100. New luxury hotel, downtown, on 17th St. Mall, 430 rooms.

Writers Manor Hotel, 1730 S. Colorado Blvd., Denver, CO 80222. 756-8877. Athletic club, nightly entertainment, 325 rooms.

Clarion Hotel Denver Airport, 3203 Quebec St., Denver, CO 80207. 1-800-325-6064. First class hotel, ten minutes from downtown, all amenities, free limousine to airport, 588 rooms.

Sheraton Graystone Castle, 83 E. 120th Ave., Thornton, CO 80233. 451-1002. Unique castle architecture, large rooms, jacuzzi, mountain views, suites. (Other Sheraton Hotel are **Sheraton Denver Tech,** 4900 DTC Parkway, Denver, CO 80237; and **Sheraton Denver Airport,** 3535 Quebec St., Denver, CO 80207. 333-7711)

Rodeway Inn, Denver Airport, 4590 Quebec St., Denver, CO 80216. 320-0260. Restaurant, lounge with weekend entertainment. Therma-sol rooms available. $57-66.

Stapleton Plaza Hotel and Athletic Center, 3333 Quebec St., Denver, CO 80207. 321-3500. Two minutes from airport, 300 rooms, special week rate, athletic center.

Regency Hotel, 3900 Elati St., Denver, CO 80216. 458-0808. Metro hotel, 405 rooms, all amenities, free shuttle downtown.

Best Western Capri Hotel Plaza, 11 E. 84th Ave., Denver, CO 80221. 428-5041. Located on I-25 and 84th Ave. Close to Mercahdise Mart, 107 rooms.

Brock Residence Inn, Downtown, 2777 North Zuni, Denver, CO 80211. Aspen-like setting, free continental breakfast, evening cocktail party, 156 suites, downtown shuttle.

Days Inn, 36 E. 120th Ave., Northglenn, CO 80233. 1-800-325-2525. Rates $36-43.

(Days Inn West is located in Golden.)

Chalet Motel, 6051 W. Alameda Ave., Lakewood, CO 80226. 237-7775. A small place with excellent service. French, Italian, German and English speaking staff. $32-46. (Write for a brochure.)

Bar X Motel, 5001 W. Colfax, Denver, CO 80204. 1-800-528-1100. All suite hotel. Units have two rooms, kitchenette and all amenities. Free breakfast and evening cocktail party.

Condominium Short Term Rentals, 1190 S. Birch, Suite #101, Denver, CO 80220. 320-4823. (Write for brochure.)

Condo Inn Summit, 10651 E. Bethany, #140, Aurora,

CO 80014. 671-7401. Luxury condos for short term rentals. All facilities provided.

Denver East KOA, P.O. Box 579, Strasburg, CO 80316. 622-9274. Large shady pull thru' sites, camping, cabins, playground, game room, cafe, easy access to I-70.

Dillion:

Dillion Super 8 Motel, P.O. Box B, Dillion, CO 80435. 468-8888. Economical lodging, 5 minutes from ski area.

Best Western Ptarmigan Lodge, 625 Colorow St., CO 80435. 468-2341. Located on the lake, central location for summer and winter activities.

Holiday Inn — Lake Dillion, P.O. Box 669, Dillion, CO 80435. 668-5000. Located on the lake, 15 minutes from Copper, Keystone, A-Basin and Breckenridge Ski Areas.

Season Extraordinaire, P.O. Box 1526, Golden, CO 80402. 839-0333. Luxury, exclusive accommodations with full amenities. (Rates available on request.)

Durango:

Best Western Durango Inn, 21382 Hwy 160 W., P.O. Box 3099, Durango, CO 81301. Beautiful location, close to Mesa Verde and Purgatory Ski Area.

Four Winds Motel, 20797 W. Hwy 160, Durango, CO 81301. 247-4512. Near Durango-Silverton train, on the way to Mesa Verde.

Quality Inn Summit, 1700 Country Rd. 203, Durango, CO 81301. 1-800-228-5151. Pool, sauna, jacuzzis, 95 units.

Strater Hotel, 699 Main Ave., Durango, CO 81301. 247-4431. Restored Victorian Hotel located downtown.

Estes Park:

The Crags Lodge, P.O. Box 480 Estes Park, CO 80517. 586-6100. Historic hotel with magnificent view.

Holiday Inn Resort, P.O. Box 1468, Estes Park, CO 80517. 586-2332. Deluxe accommodations, pool, sauna, whirlpool.

The Stanley Hotel, P.O. Box 1767, Estes Park, CO 80517. 586-3371. Historic hotel, elegant, children under 17 free.

Glenwood Springs:

Glenwood Hot Springs Lodge and Pool, Box 308, Glenwood Springs, CO 81601. 945-6571. World's largest mineral hot springs pool, athletic club, open all year.

Hotel Colorado, 526 Pine, Glenwood Springs, CO 81601. 945-6511. Restored historic hotel. Outdoor activities.

Idaho Springs:

Historic Indian Springs Resort, P.O. Box 1990, Idaho Springs, CO 80452. 825-6513. Hot mineral baths, deluxe accommodations.

Leadville:

Mountain Mansion, 129 W. 8th St., Leadville, CO 80461. 486-0655, Historic hotel, 8 units, group rates.

Ouray:

Best Western Twin Peaks, P.O. Box 320, Ouray, CO 81427. 325-4427. Hot springs, whirlpool, luxury units.

Pueblo:

Ramada Inn, 2001 N. Hudson, Pueblo, CO 81001. 542-3750. 180 units, pool, live entertainment, group rates.

Snowmass Resort:

The Snowmass Club, P.O. Box Drawer G-2, Snowmass Village, CO 81615. 923-5600. Luxury resort, athletic club, tennis, golf, very exclusive.
Timberline Condominiums, P.O. Box 1-2, Snowmass Village, CO 81615. 923-4000. 96 condominiums, pool, sauna.
Woodrun Place, P.O. Box 6077. Snowmass Village, CO 81615. 923-5392. 55 units, steam shower, whirlpool, all facilities.

Steamboat Springs:

Sheraton at Steamboat, P.O. Box 774808, Steamboat Springs, CO 80477. 879-2220. 450 rooms, luxury hotel, pools, ski-in/ski out, sauna, live entertainment.
Storm Meadows Resort, P.O. Box AAA, Steamboat Springs, CO 80477. 879-1035. 260 units, pool, athletic club.

Telluride:

New Sheridan Hotel, P.O. Box 980, Telluride, CO 81435. 728-4351. Victorian gem, 30 units, close to ski area.

Vail:

Best Western Inn at Vail, 2211 N. Frontage Rd., Vail, CO 81657. 476-3890. Resort hotel, shuttle bus to ski area.
Marriott's Mark Resort, 715 Lionhead Cir., Vail, CO 81657. 476-4444. 350 units, full service resort hotel.
Westin Hotel Vail, 1300, Westhaven Dr., Vail, CO 81657. 476-7111. 185 units, resort hotel next to forest.
Vail Home Rentals, 143 E. Meadow Dr., Vail, CO 81657. 1-800-525-9803. Offers an extensive list of condominiums and private homes. Many homes have pools and saunas.

Bed and Breakfast and Hostels

American Youth Hostels, Box 2370, Boulder, CO 80303, 442-1166. Inexpensive accommodations in 21 Colorado cities and towns.
Bed and Breakfast Colorado, Box 20596, Denver, CO 80220. 333-3340. Statewide reservations for private homes, ranches, farms and inns. All selected and include breakfast. Rates vary from $25 to $50 per couple. ($3 for the directory.)
Bed and Breakfast Rocky Mountains, P.O. Box 804, Colorado Springs, CO 80901. 499-9343. Nearly 100 homes and inns. In the city and the mountains, statewide reservations. Mansions, ski homes and ranches. Budget-$25, luxury-$95. (Directory available.)

Colorado Campground Association (C.C.A.) 5101 Pennsylvania Ave., Boulder, CO 80303. 449-9343. (Camping information, Colorado Directory free at visitors centers. By mail send $2.)

Guest Ranches

Aspen's T-Lazy Guest and Horse Ranch, P.O. Box 240, Aspen, CO 81612. 925-4614. 500 acre ranch in the heart of Marron Primitive Wilderness Area, 18 units, pool, lodges and cabins. (Write for details.)
Lost Valley Ranch, Rt 2 Sedalia, CO 80135. 647-2311. Authentic horse-cattle ranch with cabins. Sixty miles (96 kms) north of Colorado Springs, children's discount.
Ah Wilderness Guest Ranch, P.O. Box 997, Durango, CO 81301. 247-4121. Modern cabins, horses, overnight pack trips.
The Aspen Lodge and Guest Ranch, Longs Peak Route, Estes Park, CO 80517. 586-4241. Rustic mountain lodges with a great view. Outdoor activities. (Write for details.)
Wilderness Trails Ranch, Box V, Bayfield, CO 81122. 247-0722. Open end-May to mid-Sept, and hunting season. Close to Durango, western lodge with log cabins.
Double JK Ranch, Box V, Estes Park, CO 80517. 586-3537. Family ranch, 9 miles (15 kms) south of Estes Park. Home cooked meals, hay rides. (Write for details.)
YMCA of the Rockies — Estes Park Center, P.O. Box 578, Association Camp, CO 80511. 586-3341. Adjoining Rocky Mountain National Park, activities for all ages.
YMCA of the Rockies — Snow Mountain Ranch, Box 558, Granby, CO 80446. 887-2152. Variety of summer and winter recreational activities for the family.
Arapaho Valley Ranch, P.O. Box 142DC, Granby, CO 80446. 887-3495. Open mid-May to end-Sept. Great fishing.
Sylvan Dale Ranch, 2939 N. County Rd, 31 D, Loveland, CO 80537. 667-3915. Authentic working ranch resort.
S Bar S Ranch, Clark Rt, Steamboat Springs, CO 80487. 879-0788. Working cattle ranch, trout stream, ski, ride, open year round. (Write for details.)
Skyline Guest Ranch, Box 67, Telluride, CO 81435. 728-3757. View of San Miguel Range, hiking and fishing.

For more information write to:
Colorado Dude/Guest Ranch Association, Box 300, Tabernash, CO 80478. 887-3128.

In Idaho:

Boise:

Best Western Safari Motor Inn Inc. 1070 Grove St., 344-6556. 105 rooms, pool, free car to airport, downtown.
Boisean Motel, 1300 S. Capitol Blvd., 1-800-645-3645. 135 rooms, pool, free car to airport, close to museum, parks and shops.
Holiday Inn Boise, 3300 Vista Ave., 344-8365. 265 rooms, pool, recreation center.
Red Lion Inn Downtowner, 1800 Fairview Ave.,

344-7691. 182 rooms, suites, pool, entertainment.
Red Lion Motor Inn Riverside, 2900 Chinden Blvd., 343-1871. 308 rooms and suites, located on Boise River, restaurant, dancing, pool.

Idaho Falls:

Best Western Stardust, 700 Lindsay Blvd., 522-2910. 254 rooms, pool, live entertainment.
Quality Inn West Bank, 475 River Parkway, 523-8000. 198 rooms, reasonably priced, pool, overlooks falls.
Weston Lamplighter Motel, 850 Lindsay Blvd. 523-6260. 130 rooms, pool, electrical truck hook-up. (Weekly rates.)

Lewiston:

Pony Soldier Motor Inn, 1716 Main, 1-800-635-2062. 66 rooms, pool.
Sacajawea Lodge, 1824 Main, 746-1393. 95 rooms, pool.
Sundance Motor Inn, 1021 Main, 743-4501. 62 rooms, pool, satellite T.V., spa, senior citizen's rates.
Tapadera Motor Inn, 1325 E. Main, 746-3311. 81 rooms, pool, entertainment, cable T.V.

Moscow:

Best Western University Inn, 1516 Pullman, 882-0550. 122 rooms, pool, sauna, putting green, entertainment.
Motel 6, 101 Baker St., 882-6639. 110 rooms, economical.

Pocatello:

Best Western Cotton Tree Inn, 1415 Beach Rd., 237-7650. 150 rooms, pool, racquet ball, tennis.
Holiday Inn, 1399 Bench Rd., 237-1400. 206 rooms, pool.
Little Tree Inn, 133 W. Burnside, 237-0020. 120 rooms, sauna, jacuzzi, complimentary breakfast.
Oxbow Motor Inn, 4333 Yellowstone, 237-3100. Reasonably priced, 184 rooms, pool, coffee shop.
Motel 6, 291 W. Burnside, 237-6667. Reasonably priced.
Quality Inn Pocatello, 1555 Pocatello Creek, 233-2200. 152 rooms, pool, whirlpool, sauna, entertainment.

Twin Falls:

Best Western Canyon Springs Inn, 1357 Blue Lakes Blvd. N., 734-5000. 112 rooms, pool, senior citizen's discount.
Motel 6, 1472 Blue Lakes Blvd. N., 733-6663. 157 rooms, reasonably priced, pool.
Holiday Inn, 1350 Blue Lakes Blvd., 735-0650. Pool, 204 rooms, live entertainment, inroom movies, babysitting.

Guest Ranches and Resorts

Grandview Lodge and Resort, Star Rt., Box 48, Nordman, ID. 83848. 443-2433. Reeder Bay on Priest Lake. 28 units, restaurant, sea plane tours, snowmobile. (Write for details.)

Hill's Resort, Rt 5, Box 162-A. Priest Lake, ID 83864. 443-2551. Located at Luby Bay on Priest Lake, fully equipped cabins, condos, beach location. (Write for details.)
Whitewater Ranch, Cascade, ID 83611. 382-4336. 90 miles east of Grangeville, cabins, hunting, float boats, fishing, horseback riding. (Write for details.)
Cook Ranch, 5727 Hill Rd., Boise, ID 83703. 344-0951. 50 miles south of Elk City. Lodge, family style meals, snowmobile, hunting, horseback riding. (Write for details.)
Sawtooth Lodge, 1403 E. Bannock St., Boise, ID 83702. 344-6685. Located in Grandjean, cabins, RV facilities, hunt, fish, backpack, pack trips. (Write for details.)
Sulphur Creek Ranch, 7153 W. Emerald St., Boise, ID. 83704. 377-1188. Middle fork of Salmon River. Lodge, cabins, 5 acre trout reservoir, ski, climb. (Write for details.)
Clark Miller Guest Ranch, Star Route, Ketchum, ID. 83340. 774-3535. 12 miles south of Redfish Lake. Six primitive fully equipped cabins, located on 300 acres of land, fishing streams. (Write for details.)
Sun Valley Resort, Sun Valley Lodge, Sun Valley, ID. 83353. 622-4111. 550 units, pool, golf, tennis, ski.
Elk Creek Ranch, Island Park, ID. 83429. 558-7404. Rustic luxury cabins 25 miles north of Ashton. (Write for details.)

In Montana:

Billings:

Best Western Northern Hotel, Broadway at First Ave. North., 1-800-528-1234. Located downtown, lounge, live entertainment, children under 16 free.
Billings Plaza Holiday Inn, 5500 Midland Rd., 1-800-HOLIDAY. Under 18 years free. Pool, indoor recreation center, electronic games, restaurant.
Billings Sheraton Hotel, 27, N. 27th St., 1-800-325-3535. Pool, Nautilus center, 300 luxury rooms, downtown.

Bozeman:

Best Western City Center Motor Inn, 507 W. Main, 1-800-528-1234. Sauna, pool, Bridger Bowl Ski Area 15 miles (24 kms).

Holiday Inn of Bozeman, 5 Baxter Lane, 1-800-HOLIDAY. Pool, airport limousine service, full service restaurant.
Thrifty Scot Motel, 1321 N. 7th Ave., 1-800-228-3222. Economical, free continental breakfast, 8 miles to airport.

Butte:

Best Western Copper King Inn, 4655, Harrison, 1-800-548-6008. 151 luxury rooms, pool, sauna, live music and dancing, coffee shop, dining.
Best Western War Bonnet Inn, 2100 Cornell Ave., 1-800-528-1234. Pool, jogging track, 134 rooms.
Thrift Inn, 2900 Harrison, 494-3500. Full service budget motel, pool, live entertainment, steakhouse.

Great Falls:

Best Western Heritage Inn, 1700 Fox Farm Rd., 1-800-528-1234. Indoor recreation center, 2 pools, sauna, whirlpool, 250 rooms.
Fox Hollow Residence Inn, 1700 10th St., SW., 727-0702.
Sheraton Great Falls, 400 10th Ave. South., 1-800-325-3535. Luxury hotel, pool, full service.

Helena:

Best Western Colonial Inn, 2301 Colonial Dr., 1-800-528-1234. Pool, sauna, truck parking.
Coach House East, 2101 E. 11th Ave., 1-800-521-2743. Restaurant, pool, lounge, full service.
Park Plaza Hotel, 22 N. Last Chance Gulch, 1-800-322-2290. Downtown in historic mall.

Kalispell:

Best Western Outlaw Inn, 1701 Hwy 93 S., 1-800-528-1234. 250 luxury rooms, 2 pools, sauna, spa, live music.
Red Lion Motor Inn, 1330 Hwy 2 W., 1-800-547-8010. Full service hotel, pool.

Missoula:

Comfort Inn, 744 E. Broadway, 1-800-228-5150. Pool, 89 luxury rooms, fishing, tennis, full service.
Red Lion Motel, 700 W. Broadway, 1-800-547-8010.
Village Red Lion Motel Inn, 100 Madison, 1-800-547-8010.

West Yellowstone:

Best Western Executive Inn, Corner of Gibbon and Dunraven, 1-800-528-1234. Beautiful location, pool, fish, snowmobile.
Quality Inn Ambassador, 315 Yellowstone Ave., 1-800-228-5151. Close to Yellowstone Nat. Park. Pool, whirlpool, restaurant.
Stagecoach Inn Travelodge, Madison and Dunraven, 1-800-255-3050.

Whitefish:

Grouse Mountain Lodge, 1205 Hwy 93 W., 1-800-321-8822. Luxury Lodge, pool.
Bay Point Estates, 300 Bay Point Dr., 862-2331. Ski & gold packages, family retreat, pool.
Viking Lakeshore Inn, 1360 Wisconsin, 862-3547.
Ptarmigan Village, Big Mountain Rd., 862-3547. Pools, sauna, tennis, fireplaces.

Ranches & Resorts, Hostels & Hot Springs

Birchwood Hostel, 600 S. Orange, Missoula, MT 59801. 728-9799. 22 bed dorm with bunk beds, fully equipped, bring your food and sleeping bags. Rates $4.25 and up. (Reservations advised.)
Crystal Lakes Resort, Fortine, MT 59918. 882-4455. Forty condominiums, pool, tennis, cross country skiing, hiking. $43 to $75 for two.
Dolezal Home Hostel, Rt 2, Box 65, Ronan, MT 59864. 676-2154. Six bedroom home, bring food. $5 per night. (Guests must have youth pass and reservations.)

Flathead Lake Lodge, Box 248, Bigfork, MT 59911. 837-4391. Dude ranch on Flathead Lake, riding, sailing, water-skiing, tennis, cottages. $698/adult for a week.
Circle 8 Ranch, Box 729, Choteau, MT 59422. 466-5964. Modern cabins, family meals, riding, swimming, wilderness pack trips, hunting. $75/day each.
7 Lazy P Ranch, Box P, Choteau, MT 59422. 466-2044 Pack trips, hunting and fishing in Bob Marshell Wilderness. Cabins and home style cooking. $60/day each.
Jackson Snyder Ranch, Box 1099, Lewistown, MT 59468. 538-3571. 2000 acre mountain ranch. Includes two meals. $30/day each.
Bar Y Seven Ranch, Brusett, MT 59318. 557-6150. 5000-acre working cattle ranch, fishing hunting, snowmobile, cabins, family style meals. (Write for rates.)
Sleeping Buffalo Resort, Star Rt 3, Box 13, Saco, MT 59621. 527-3370. Hot springs resort, golf, fishing, hunting, pools. Rates $20/night for two and up. Large cabins $60.
Bill Sweet Hostel, Box 16, Darby, MT 59829. 821-3792. Pitch your tent or rent a tipi. Camping $1.50/night. Tipi $2/night. Shower $1 each.
CB Cattle and Guest Ranch, Box 604, Cameron; MT 50720. 682-4954. Working ranch, riding, cabins, $50 to 80/day. No children under 13 years.
Diamond J Ranch, Ennis, MT 59729. 682-4867. Cabins, riding, pool, fishing on Madison River. $630/adult for a week.
Burnt Leather Ranch, McLeod, MT 59052. 222-6795. Working ranch bordering national forest. (Write for rates.)
Lazy K Bar Ranch, Melville Rt., Big Timber, MT 59011. 537-4404. 20,000 acre working cattle and horse ranch. One week minimum stay. $400 to 500/week for an adult.
BYXBE Ranch, Pompey's Pillar, MT 59064. 987-2377. Hiking, rock hunting in 640 acre working cattle ranch. $70/adult for a week, $50/child for a week.
Rooney Ranches, Tongue River Stage, Miles City, MT 59301. 784-2770. Two working ranches, hiking, skiing and riding. Camper hookups, family lodging in home, $50/day each.

In Utah:

Alta:

Rustler Lodge, 742-2200. 54 units, heated pool, saunas, skiing, suite available.
Alta Lodge, 742-3500. Ski lodge. (Call for details.)

Beaver:

Best Western Piace Motel, 161 S. Main, 438-2438. AAA, 24 units, pool, golf, close to Holly Ski Resort.
Country Inn Restaurant and Fuel Stop, N. off-ramp interchange, 438-2484. 38 units, pool.

Castle Dale:

Best Western El Roy Inn, 80 S. Main, 586-6528. Pool, sauna, whirlpool, 75 units.
Meadeau View Lodge, (Bed and Breakfast) 30 miles (48 kms) E. of Cedar City, on Nordic Ski Center, near Cedar Breaks.

Delta:

Best Western Pendray Plaza, 527 E. Topaz Blvd., 864-3882. 83 units, restaurant, pool.

Green River:

Best Western River Terrace, 564-3401. 51 units, pool.
Motel 6, east of Green River, 564-3266.

Heber City:

Green Acres Lodge, 989 S. Main, 654-2202. 36 family units, playground.
Wasatch Motel, 875 S. Main, 654-2123. 20 units, pool.

Kanab:

Best Western Red Hills, 124 W. Center, 644-2675. 55 units.
Treasure Trail Motel, 140 W. Center, 644-2687. 28 units, pool, airport service.

Minersville:

Apache Motel Friendship Inn, 166 S. 400 E., 259-5755. AAA 2 room units, pool.
Ramada Inn, 182 S. Main, 1-800-228-2828. Pool, hot-tub/jacuzzi, AAA.

Ogden:

Best Western Flying J Motel, 1206 W., 21st, 393-8644. Pool, game room.
Holiday Inn, 3306 Washington Blvd. 399 5671. 109 units, pool, restaurant, airport service.
Ogden Hilton, 247 24th St., 627-1190. 288 units, indoor pool, 2 restaurants, game room.

Panguich:

Color Country Motel, 500 N. Main, 676-2386. 26 units, pool, AAA, close to five National Parks.
New Western Motel, 180 E. Main, 676-8876. Pool, 26 units.

Park City:
(Ski Country)

The Blue Church Lodge, 424 Park Ave., 649-8009. Units with kitchen, golf, tennis, skiing, horses.
Deer Valley Lodging, Deer Valley Rd., 649-4040. Family units.
The Yarrow/a Holiday Inn Resort, 1800 Park Ave., 649-7000. 179 units, pool, restaurant.
Edelweiss Haus, P.O. Box 495, 649-9342.
Resort Property Management and Lodging, 592 Main, 649-6613. 25 units, condos, kitchen, playground.
Snowflower, 400 Silver King Dr., 1-800-852-3101. 90 units, fully equipped, 2 pools, hot tubs, skiing.

Price:

Carriage House Inn, 590 E. Main, 637-5660. Pool and spa, restaurant.

Provo:

Best Western Columbian, 79 E. 300 S., 373-8973. AAA, 28 family units, pool.
Best Western Cotton Tree Inn, 2230 No. University Pkwy., 373-7044. 80 units, peaceful setting, pool, spa.
Budget Host University Western Inn, 40 W. 300 S., 1-800-368-4400. 29 family units, pool, playground.
The Provo Excelsior, 101 W. 100 N., 377-4700. Pool, 250 units, 2 restaurants, sauna, whirlpool.

Richfield:

Best Western High Country Inn, 145 S. Main, 896-5481. AAA, 65 units, airport service.

St. George:

Best Western Thunderbird, 1000 E. 150 N., 673-6123. Family units, pool, sauna.
Hilton Inn, 1450 S. Hilton Dr., 628-0463. Pool, sauna, whirlpool, golf, tennis, 100 units.
Regency Inn, 770 E. St. George Blvd., 673-6119. 49 units, pool, sauna, whirlpool.

Snowbird (Ski Country):

Snowbird Ski and Summer Resort, 1-800-453-3000. 571 units, kitchen, restaurants, pools, shopping.

Salt Lake City:

Hilton Hotel of Salt Lake, 150 W. 500 S., 1-800-528-0313. 352 rooms, outdoor pool.
Holiday Inn & Holidome Downtown, 230 W. 600 S., 1-800-238-8000. 160 rooms, indoor pool, children's recreational facilities.
Hotel Utah, Main and S. Temple. 1 800-453-3820. Children under 14 free, 500 rooms, restaurant.
Little America Hotel, 500 S. Main, 1-800-453-9450. 850 rooms, 2 pools, all facilities.
Marriott Hotel, 75 South West Temple, 1-800-228-9290. Pool, handicapped facilities, children's recreation.
Quality Inn City Center, 154 W. 600 S., 1-800-228-5151. 250 rooms, outdoor pool, sauna.
Salt Lake Sheraton, 255 S. West Temple, 1-800-325-3535. Pool, 502 rooms, children under 18 free when accompanied by adults.
Town House Motel, 245 W. North Temple, 1-800-453-4511. AAA, 66 rooms, reasonably priced, pool, children under 13 free.
Holiday Inn Airport, 1659 W. North Temple, 1-800-238-8000. 91 rooms, no charge for children under 18 years, pool.
Salt Lake Airport Hilton, 5151 Wiley Post Way, 1-800-528-0313. Tennis, paddle boats, pool, putting green, children free.
Motel 6, 1990 W. North Temple, 322-3061. Outdoor pool, reasonably priced. (No credit cards.)
Se Rancho Motel, 640 W. North Temple, 532-3300. 97 rooms, reasonably priced, outdoor pool, tennis.

Bed and Breakfast

Bed N Breakfast Association of Utah, P.O. Box 16465, Salt Lake City, UT 84116. 532-7076. Reservations. (Write for listings.)

Brigham Street Inn, 1135 E. S. Temple, Salt Lake City, UT 84102. 364-4461. National historic site, private baths, fireplace, continental breakfast.
Eller Bed & Breakfast, 164 S. 900 E., Salt Lake City, UT 84012. 533-8184. State historical site, full breakfast, sauna. (No credit cards.)

Vernal:

Antlers Motel Best Western, 423 W. Main, 789-1202. Pool, playground, 53 units, AAA.
Flaming Gorge Motel, 486, E. Main, 789-1365. Kitchen, family units, boat parking.

Guest Ranches/Resorts/Cabins:

Diamond Valley Guest Ranch, P.O. Box 712, St. George, UT 84770. 574-2281.
Manning Meadow Ranch, 2052 E. 4500 South, Salt Lake City, UT 84117. 277-6928.
Rock Creek Ranch, P.O. Box 409, Duchesne, UT 84021. 353-4744.
Bryce Canyon National Park Lodge, T.W.A. Services, 451 N. Main, Cedar City, UT 84720. 586-7686.
Goulding's Lodge, Box 1, Monument Valley. UT 84536. 727-3231.
Zion National Park Lodge, T.W.A. Services, 451 N. Main, Cedar City, UT 84720. 586-7686.
Bullfrog Resort and Marina, Del E. Webb Recreational Properties Inc. Hanksville, UT 84734. 1-800-528-6154.
Hilton Inn, 1450 S. Hilton Dr., St. George, UT 84770. 1-800-662-2525.
Prospector Square and Conference Center, P.O. Box 1698, Park City, UT 84060. 1-800-453-3812.
Snowbird Ski and Summer Resort, Snowbird, UT 84092. 1-800-453-3000.
Brian Head Ski and Summer Resort, P.O. Box 8, Brian Head, UT 84719. 677-2035.
Sundance, P.O. Box 837, Provo, UT 84602. 225-4107.
Nordic Valley Resort, P.O. Box 178, Eden, UT 84310. 745-3511.
Mt. Majestic Lodge, Brigton, UT 84121. 364-3382.

In Wyoming

Casper:

Ramada Inn, I-25 & Center, 123 W. E. St., 235-5713. Swimming pool, full facility hotel. AAA.
Holiday Inn, 300 W. F St., Box 3500, 235-2531. 200 units, swimming pool, full facility hotel. AAA.

Cheyenne:

Hitching Post Inn, 1700 W. Lincolnway, 1-800-221-0125. Full service hotel, pool, 250 units, AAA.
Holiday Inn, 204 W. Fox Farm Rd., 638-4466. Full service hotel, pool, 246 units.
Holding's Little America, P.O. Box 1529, 634-2771. Full service hotel, 190 units, pool.

Cody:

Holiday Inn Convention Center, 1701 Sheridan Ave., 587-5555. Full service hotel, pool, 132 units.
Irma Hotel, 1192 Sheridan, 587-4221. Historic hotel built by Buffalo Bill named after his daughter Irma.

Douglas:

Plains Motel, 841 S. 6th St., 358-4484. Economical motel, 47 units, pool.
Holiday Inn, 1450 Riverband Drive, 358-9790. Full service hotel, pool, 117 units.

Evanston:

Best Western Dunmar Inn, Box 768, 789-3770. Full service hotel, 200 units, pool.
Travel Center Inn, 1936 Highway 30 E., 789-2810. 115 units, pool.

Gillette:

Holiday Inn, 2009 S. Douglas Highway, 686-3000. Full service hotel, pool, 161 units.

Jackson:

American Snow King Resort, Box SKI, 733-5200. Full service resort, pool, 200 units.
Jackson Hole Racquet Club Resort, Star Rt. 362A, 733-3990. Full service resort, pool, 95 units.
Virginian Lodge, 750 W. Broadway, 733-8247. 149 units, full service lodge, pool.
Executive Inn-Best Western, 325 W. Pearl St., 1-800-528-1234. Full service hotel, pool 59 units.
Wort Hotel, Broadway and Glenwood, 733-2190.

Laramie:

Holiday Inn, Box 1065, 742-6611. Full service hotel, 100 units, pool.
Ramada Inn, 1503 S. 3rd., 742-3721. Full service, pool.

Little America:

Holding's Little America, Box 1, 875-2400. 150 units, pool, full service.

Rawlings:

Quality Inn, 2222 E. Cedar, 324-6615. Full service, pool.
Holiday Inn, 1801 E. Cedar, 324-2783. Full service hotel, pool, 132 units.

Rock Springs:

Rock Spring Hilton Inn, 2518 Foothill Blvd., 362-9600. 150 units, pool, full facility hotel, AAA.
Outlaw Inn, 1630 Elk St., 362-6623. Full service hotel.

Saratoga:

Saratoga Inn, Box 869, 326-5261. Full service hotel, 60 units.

Sheridan:

Sheridan Center Motor Inn, Box 4008, 612 N. Main, 674-7421. Full service hotel, pool, 142 units.
Trails End Motel, 2125 N. Main, 672-2477. Full service motel, pool, 83 units.

Teton Village:
(Adjoining Teton National Park)

Alpenhof, Box 228, 1-800-733-3244. 40 units, pool.
Inn at Jackson Hole, Box 328, 1-800-842-7666. 70 units, pool, full service.
The Sojourner Inn, Box 348, 1-800-842-7600. 100 units, pool, AAA.

Thermopolis:

Holiday Inn, Hot Springs State Park, 864-3131. Full service hotel, pool, 80 units.

Dude Ranches and Resorts

Crossed Sabres Ranch, Box WTC Wapiti, WY 82450. 587-3750. Located 9 miles (15 kms) east of Yellowstone National Park, weekly guest ranch, pack trips, Park tours, rodeo, cookouts.
4-Bear Outfitters, 1297 Ln 10, Rt 1, Powell, WY 82435. Fishing, hiking, hunting, wilderness horseback trips, special services for the handicapped. Historic trips to Cody.
Goff Creek Lodge, Box 155TC Cody, WY 82414. 587-3753. Located 10 miles (16 kms) from east entrance of Yellowstone National Park, deluxe cabins, trail rides, campfire get-togethers.
Bill Cody's Ranch Resort, P.O. Box 1390-T, Cody, WY 82414. 1-800-621-2114. Modern mountain cottages, lounge, heated pool, whirlpool. Operated by Buffalo Bill Cody's grandson.
Flagg Ranch, P.O. Box 187, Moran, WY 83013. 543-2861. Located between Grand Teton and Yellowstone National Park, cabins, float trips, horse, cookout rides.
Triangle X Ranch, Moose, WY 83012-733-5500. Located 26 miles (40 kms) northeast of Jackson, float trips, pack trips, hikes, ranch activities.
Jackson Hole Ski Area, P.O. Box 220, Teton Village, WY 83025. 1-800-443-6931. Located 12 miles (19 kms) northeast of Jackson Hotel, centrally situated.
Heart Six Guest Ranch, Moran, WY 83013. 543-2477. Located at the northeast end of Jackson Hole, modern cabins, pack trips, float trips on the Snake River.

Airlines

Airlines that serve Denver

American, Stapleton Int'l Airport, CO 80207. 595-9304.
Braniff, Stapleton Int'l Airport, CO 80207. 398-6012.
Continental, 9000 E. Smith Rd. Suite 210, Denver, CO 80207. 398-3000.
Delta, 7555 E. Hampden #605 Denver, CO 80231. 695-8180.
Eastern, 443 Stapleton Int'l Airport, CO 80207. 623-4800.
Frontier, 8250 Smith Rd., Denver, CO 80207. 399-0808.
Frontier Horizon, 3333 Quebec, Denver, CO 80207. 398-3741.
Mexicana, Stapleton Int'l Airport, CO 80207. 832-5454.

Northwest, 707 17th St. #120, Denver, CO 80207. 293-2376.
Ozark, 4685 Peoria #111, Denver, CO 80239. 573-6541.
Piedmont, 2260 S. Xanadu Way, #375 Aurora, CO 80014. 893-3567.
People's Express, Stapleton Int'l Airport, CO 80207. 623-0060.
Pioneer, Stapleton Int'l Airport, CO 80207. 398-2195.
Republic, 3333 Quebec St. Denver, CO 80207. 398-5572.
Southwest, 950 S. Cherry, #218, Denver, CO 80222. 759-9220.
Trans World Airlines (TWA), 7200 E. Hampden, Denver, CO 80237. 753-6318.
United, 7700 Smith Rd., Denver, CO 80207. 398-4181.
Western, 8080 Smith Rd. Denver, CO 80207. 398-3400.
Wein Air Alaska, Stapleton Int'l Airport, CO 80207. 592-1727.

Regional Carriers

Aspen Airways, Stapleton Int'l Airport, CO 80207. 1-800-322-1332.
Rocky Mountain Airways, Stapleton Int'l Airport, CO 80207. 398-3896.

Air Travel to Colorado

The following airlines serve Colorado with regularly scheduled flights.
Alamosa, Rocky Mountain Airways, Pioneer.
Aspen, Aspen Airways, Rocky Mountain Airways.
Avon, Rocky Mountain Airways.
Colorado Springs, Frontier, Continental, T.W.A., Western, America West, Rocky Mountain Airways, Aspen Airways, Trans-Colorado.
Cortez, Pioneer, Trans-Colorado.
Durango, America West, Aspen Airways, Trans-Colorado.
Grand Junction, Frontier, Continental, Pioneer, Sky West, American West.
Gunnison, Trans-Colorado, (all year)
Lar Mar, Air Midwest.
Montrose, Trans-Colorado.
Pueblo, Rocky Mountain Airways.
Steamboat Springs — Rocky Mountain Airways.

Air Travel to Idaho

The following air carriers service the Idaho gateway cities.
Boise, United, Wein Air Alaska, Frontier, Western, Cascade, Horizon.
Pocatello, Cascade, Trans-Western, Horizon.
Sun Valley, Horizon.
Idaho Falls, Horizon, Western, Frontier, Cascade.
Twin Falls, Cascade, Western (Dec-April).

Air Travel to Montana

The following airlines serve Montana with scheduled flights.
Billings, Northwest Orient, Western, Frontier, Big Sky, United.
Bozeman, Northwest Orient, Frontier, Western.
Butte, Western
Great Falls, Northwest Orient, Western, Frontier

Helena, Northwest Orient, Frontier, Western.
Kalispell, Frontier, Western, Cascade.
Lewiston, Big Sky.
Missoula, Northwest Orient, Frontier, Western.
West Yellowstone, Frontier, Western.

Air Travel to Wyoming

The following airlines serve Wyoming.
Cheyenne, Rocky Mountain Airways.
Casper, United, Frontier, Continental.
Jackson, Western, Frontier.

Air Travel in Utah
Salt Lake City

Most major commercial airlines arrive and depart from **Salt Lake City International Airport**, located on 4000 West, 900 North. For information write to A.M.F., Box 2204, Salt Lake City, UT 84122. (801)539-2205.

Commuter connections are available from Salt Lake City to cities in Utah and other Rocky Mountain States. Airlines that serve Salt Lake City are American, Delta, Eastern, Continental, Frontier, Republic, Trans-World Airlines (T.W.A.), United Airlines, Western, Sky West, Alpine and Wein Air Alaska.

There are many smaller airports located in Utah which have flights to the resorts, national parks and some cities. For information write to — **Utah State Div. of Aeronautical Operations**, Salt Lake City International Airport, 135 N. 2400 W., Salt Lake City, UT 84116. (801)328-2066.
St George — Sky West, Alpine Aviation Inc.
Moab — Alpine Aviation Inc.
Price — Alpine Aviation Inc.

Chambers of Commerce

In Colorado (Area Code — 303)

Adams County Chamber of Commerce, 7100 Broadway, Bldg. 1, Unit B, Denver, CO 80221. 426-1570.
Alamosa Chamber of Commerce, P.O. Box 120, Alamosa, CO 81101. 589-6531.
Arvada Chamber of Commerce, 7305 Grandview Ave., Arvada, CO 80015. 424-0313.
Aspen Chamber of Commerce, 328 E. Hyman Avenue, Aspen, CO 81611. 925-1940.
Aurora Chamber of Commerce, 13799 E. Colfax Avenue, Aurora, CO 80011. 366-2676.
Boulder Chamber of Commerce, 1001 Canyon Blvd., Boulder, CO 80302. 442-1044.
Breckenridge Resort Association, 325 S. Main, Breckenridge, CO 80424. 453-2918.
Broomfield Chamber of Commerce, 1380 Midway Blvd., Broomfield, CO 80020. 466-1775
Buena Vista Chamber of Commerce, 343 US Highway 24 S., Buena Vista, CO 81211. 395-6612.
Burlington Chamber of Commerce, 410 — 14th, Burlington, CO 80807. 346-8070.
Brighton Chamber of Commerce, 1401 E. Bridge, Brighton, CO 80601. 659-0223.
Brush Chamber of Commerce, 301 Edison, Brush, CO 80723. 842-2666.

Canon City Chamber of Commerce, P.O. Box 366, Canon City, CO 81212. 275-2331.
Central City Chamber of Commerce, City Hall, Central City, CO 80427. 582-5251.
Colorado Springs Chamber of Commerce, P.O. Drawer B, Colorado Springs, CO 80901. 635-1551.
Copper Mountain Resort Association, P.O. Box 1, Copper Mountain, CO 80443. 668-2882.
Cortez Chamber of Commerce, P.O. Box 968, Cortez, CO 81321. 565-3414.
Craig Chamber of Commerce, 341 E. Victory Wy., Craig, CO 81625. 824-5689.
Crested Butte Resort Association, P.O. Box 565, Crested Butte, CO 81224. 349-5100.
Cripple Creek Two Mile High Club, 347 E. Bennett, Cripple Creek, CO 80813. 689-2594.
Delta Chamber of Commerce, 224 Main, Delta, CO 81416. 874-3801.
Denver Chamber of Commerce, 1301 Welton, Denver, CO 80202. 534-3211.
Denver Convention & Visitors' Bureau, 225 West Colfax Ave., Denver, CO 80202. 892-1112.
Dillon Chamber of Commerce, 50 Chief Colorow, Dillon, CO 80435. 468-6222.
Durango Chamber of Commerce, 2301 N. Main, P.O. Box 1311, Durango, CO 81301. 247-0312.
Englewood Chamber of Commerce, 180 W. Girard Ave., Englewood, CO. 781-7838.
Estes Park Chamber of Commerce, 125 E. Elkhorn Ave., Estes Park, CO 80517. 586-4431.
Evergreen Chamber of Commerce, Evergreen, CO 80439. 674-3412.
Fort Collins Chamber of Commerce, P.O. Box D, Fort Collins, CO 80521. 482-3746.
Fort Lupton Chamber of Commerce, 330 Park Ave., Fort Lupton, CO 80621. 857-4474.
Fort Morgan Chamber of Commerce, 407 Main, Fort Morgan, CO 80701. 867-6702.
Georgetown Chamber of Commerce, 600 Rose, Georgetown, CO 80444. 569-3150.
Glenwood Springs Chamber of Commerce, P.O. Box 97, Glenwood Springs, CO 81601. 945-6589.
Golden Chamber of Commerce, 911 — 10th St., Golden, CO 80401. 279-3113.
Granby Chamber of Commerce, 200 Agate Ave., Granby, CO 80446. 887-2311.
Grand Junction Chamber of Commerce, P.O. Box 1330, Grand Junction, CO 81501. 242-3214.
Grand Lake Chamber of Commerce, P.O. Box 57, Grand Lake, CO 80447. 627-3402.
Greeley Chamber of Commerce, 1407 — 8th Ave., Greeley, CO 80631. 352-3566.
Gunnison Chamber of Commerce, 500 East Tomichi Ave., Gunnison, CO 81230. 641-1501.
Idaho Springs Chamber of Commerce, P.O. Box 1045, Idaho Springs, CO 80452.
La Junta Chamber of Commerce, P.O. Box 408, La Junta, CO 81050. 384-7411.
Lake City Chamber of Commerce, Lake City, CO 81235.
Lakewood Chamber of Commerce, 55 Wadsworth Blvd., Lakewood, CO 80226. 233-5555.
Las Animas Chamber of Commerce, 205 N. Bent Ave., Las Animas, CO 81054. 456-0453.
Leadville Chamber of Commerce, 116 E. 9th, Leadville, CO 80461. 486-0418.
Littleton Chamber of Commerce, 5600 S. Sante Fe Drive, Littleton, CO 80120. 795-8014.

Longmont Chamber of Commerce, 455 Kimbark, Longmont, CO 80501. 776-5295.

Loveland Chamber of Commerce, 114 Fifth St., Loveland, CO 80537. 667-6311.

Manitou Springs Chamber of Commerce, 354 Manitou Ave., Manitou Springs, CO 80829. 685-5089.

Meeker Chamber of Commerce, 286 Main, Meeker, CO 81641. 878-5510.

Monte Vista Chamber of Commerce, 924 — 1st Ave., Monte Vista, CO 81144. 852-2731.

Montrose Chamber of Commerce, North 6th & Townsend Ave., Montrose, CO 81401. 249-5515.

Ouray Chamber of Commerce, P.O. Box 145, Ouray, CO 81427. 325-4746.

Pueblo, Chamber of Commerce, P.O. Box 697, Pueblo, CO 81002. 542-1704.

Rifle Chamber of Commerce, 108 W. 3rd, Rifle, CO 81650. 625-2085.

Rocky Ford Chamber of Commerce, 908 Elm Ave., Rocky Ford, CO 81067. 254-7483.

Salida-Heart of Rockies Chamber of Commerce, 123 E. 3rd St., Salida, CO 81201. 539-2068.

Silverton Chamber of Commerce, 1233 Empire, Silverton, CO 81433. 387-5429.

Steamboat Springs Chamber of Commerce, 1201 Lincoln Ave., Steamboat Springs, CO 80477. 879-0880.

Sterling & Logan County Chamber of Commerce, 131 North 2nd St., Sterling, CO 80751. 522-5070.

Telluride Chamber of Commerce, 323 W. Colorado Ave., Telluride, CO 81435. 728-3614.

Trinidad-Las Animas County Chamber of Commerce, 212 Nevada Ave., Trinidad, CO 81082. 846-9285.

Vail Resort Association, P.O. Box 1368, Vail, CO 81657. 476-5677.

Westminster Chamber of Commerce, 3489 W. 72nd Ave., Westminster, CO 80030. 428-6597.

Wheatridge Chamber of Commerce, 6470 W. 44th Ave., Wheatridge, CO 80033. 423-3800.

Winter Park Resort Association, P.O. Box 5, Winter Park, CO 80482. 726-5588.

Woodland Park Chamber of Commerce, 221 Midland Ave., Woodland Park, CO 80863. 687-9885.

In Idaho (Area Code — 208)

Aberdeen Chamber of Commerce, P.O. Box 276, Aberdeen, ID 83210. 397-4148.

American Falls Chamber of Commerce, P.O. Box 207, American Falls, ID 83211. 226-7214.

Arco Chamber of Commerce, P.O. Box 837, Arco, ID 83213.

Ashton Chamber of Commerce, P.O. Box 624, Ashton, ID 83420.

Bayview Chamber of Commerce, P.O. Box 122, Bayview, ID 83803.

Bellevue Chamber of Commerce, P.O. Box 406, Bellevue, ID 83318.

Blackfoot Chamber of Commerce, P.O. Box 801, Blackfoot, ID 83221. 785-0510.

Bliss Chamber of Commerce, P.O. Box 65, Bliss, ID 83314. 352-9985.

Boise Chamber of Commerce, P.O. Box 2368, Boise, ID 83701. 344-5515.

Boise Convention Center, P.O. Box 2106, Boise, ID 83701. 344-7777.

Bonners Ferry Chamber of Commerce, P.O. Box 3, Bonners Ferry, ID 83805. 267-3156.

Buhl Chamber of Commerce, P.O. Box 28, Buhl, ID 83316. 543-6682.

Burley Chamber of Commerce, 1401 Overland, Burley, ID 83318. 678-7230.

Caldwell Chamber of Commerce, 404 S. 10th, Caldwell, ID 83605. 459-7493.

Cambridge Commercial Club, P.O. Box 56, Cambridge, ID 83610.

Cascade Chamber of Commerce, P.O. Box 26, Cascade, ID 83611. 382-4132.

Coeur d'Alene Chamber of Commerce, P.O. Box 850, Coeur d'Alene, ID 83814. 664-3194.

Cottonwood Chamber of Commerce, P.O. Box 15, Cottonwood, ID 83522. 962-3281.

Council Chamber of Commerce, P.O. Box 1550, Council, ID 83612. 253-4423.

Craigmont Chamber of Commerce, P.O. Box 365, Craigmont, ID 83523. 924-5567.

Driggs Chamber of Commerce, P.O. Box 92, Driggs, ID 83422. 354-2337.

Emmett Chamber of Commerce, 917 S. Washington, Emmett, ID 83617. 365-3485.

Fruitland Chamber of Commerce, P.O. Box 408, Fruitland, ID 83619. 452-4350.

Glenns Ferry Chamber of Commerce, P.O. Box 317, Glenns Ferry, ID 83623. 366-2910.

Gooding Chamber of Commerce, P.O. Box 177, Gooding, ID 83330. 934-4402.

Grangeville Chamber of Commerce, P.O. Box 212, Grangeville, ID 83830. 983-0460.

Hagerman Chamber of Commerce, Route 1, Hagerman, ID 83332. 837-4822.

Hailey Chamber of Commerce, P.O. Box 100, Hailey, ID 83333. 788-3444.

Harrison Chamber of Commerce, P.O. Box 24, Harrison, ID 83833.

Hayden Lake Chamber of Commerce, P.O. Box 122, Hayden Lake, ID 83835.

Hope-Clark Fork-Trestle Creek Chamber of Commerce, P.O. Box 515, Clark Fork, ID 83811. 266-1477.

Homedale Chamber of Commerce, Homedale, ID 83628.

Idaho Falls Chamber of Commerce, P.O. Box 498, Idaho Falls, ID 83402. 523-1010.

Jerome Chamber of Commerce, 112 S. Lincoln #3, Jerome, ID 83338. 324-2711.

Kamiah Chamber of Commerce, P.O. Box 451, Kamiah, ID 83536. 935-0347.

Kellogg Chamber of Commerce, 712 W. Cameron, Kellogg, ID 83837. 784-0821.

Ketchum-Sun Valley Chamber of Commerce, P.O. Box 2420, Ketchum, ID 83340. 726-4471.

Kuna Chamber of Commerce, P.O. Box 123, Kuna, ID 83634. 922-4238.

Kimberly Chamber of Commerce, Route 2, P.O. Box 629, Kimberly, ID 83341. 423-5360.

Lava Hot Springs Chamber of Commerce, P.O. Box 668, Lava Hot Springs, ID 83246. 776-5221.

Lewiston Chamber of Commerce, 1030 F Street, Lewiston, ID 83501. 743-3531.

Lowman Chamber of Commerce, S. Fork Lodge, Lowman, ID 83637. 259-3322.

Mackay Chamber of Commerce, P.O. Box 207, Mackay, ID 83251. 766-2300.

McCall Chamber of Commerce, P.O. Box E, McCall, ID 83638. 634-7631.

Meridian Chamber of Commerce, P.O. Box 557, Meridian, ID 83642. 888-2817.

Montpelier Chamber of Commerce, P.O. Box 265, Montpelier, ID 83254.

Moscow Chamber of Commerce, P.O. Box 8936, Moscow, ID 83843. 882-3581.

Mountain Home Chamber of Commerce, Mountain Home, ID 83647.

Nampa Chamber of Commerce, P.O. Drawer A, Nampa, ID 83651. 466-4641.

New Plymouth Chamber of Commerce, Route 2, P.O. Box 2143-B, New Plymouth, ID 83655. 278-5556.

Nez Perce Chamber of Commerce, P.O. Box 278, Nez Perce, ID 83543. 937-0347.

Orofino Chamber of Commerce, P.O. Box 2221, Orofino, ID 83544. 476-4335.

Parma Chamber of Commerce, P.O. Drawer B, Parma, ID 83660. 733-4644.

Payette Chamber of Commerce, 700 Center Ave., Payette, ID 83661. 642-2362.

Pierce Chamber of Commerce, P.O. Drawer B, Pierce, ID 83546. 464-2323.

Pocatello Chamber of Commerce, P.O. Box 626, Pocatello, ID 83204. 233-1525.

Post Falls Chamber of Commerce, P.O. Box 909, Post Falls, ID 83854.

Preston Chamber of Commerce, P.O. Box 289, Preston, ID 83263. 852-0533.

Priest Lake Chamber of Commerce, Route 5, P.O. Box 206-E, Priest Lake, ID 83856. 443-2049.

Paul Chamber of Commerce, P.O. Box 756, Paul, ID 83347. 438-5332.

Rexburg Chamber of Commerce, 51 North Center St., Rexburg, ID 83440. 356-5066.

Rigby Chamber of Commerce, P.O. Box 217, Rigby, ID 83442. 745-6677.

Riggins Chamber of Commerce, P.O. Box 289, Riggins, ID 83549. 628-3613.

Rupert Chamber of Commerce, P.O. Box 452, Rupert, ID 83350. 436-4793.

St. Anthony Chamber of Commerce, P.O. Box 18, St. Anthony, ID 83445. 624-3479.

St. Maries Chamber of Commerce, 724 Main St., St. Maries, ID 83861. 245-5106.

Salmon Chamber of Commerce, P.O. Box 657, Salmon, ID 83867. 756-4935.

Sandpoint Chamber of Commerce, P.O. Box 928, Sandpoint, ID 83864. 263-2161.

Shelley Chamber of Commerce, 152 S. State, Shelley, ID 83274. 357-7437.

Shoshone Chamber of Commerce, P.O. Box 575, Shoshone, ID 83354. 886-2451.

Spirit Lake Chamber of Commerce, P.O. Box 68, Spirit Lake, ID 83869. 623-4452.

Stanley-Sawtooth Chamber of Commerce, P.O. Box 45, Stanley, ID 83278. 744-2279.

Sun Valley-Ketchum Chamber of Commerce, P.O. Box 2420, Sun Valley, ID 83353. 726-4471.

Twin Falls Chamber of Commerce, 323 Shoshone St. N., Twin Falls, ID 83301. 733-3974.

Victor Chamber of Commerce, P.O. Box 110, Victor, ID 83455. 522-1349.

Wallace Chamber of Commerce, P.O. Box 1167, Wallace, ID 83873. 753-7151.

Soda Springs Chamber of Commerce, P.O. Box 697, Soda Springs, ID 83276. 547-3331.

Weiser Chamber of Commerce, 8 East Idaho, Weiser, ID 83672. 549-0452.

In Montana (Area Code — 406)

Anaconda Chamber of Commerce, P.O. Box 757, Anaconda, MT 59711. 563-2400.

Baker Chamber of Commerce, P.O. Box 849, Baker, MT 59313. 778-3317.

Belgrade Chamber of Commerce, P.O. Box 1126, Belgrade, MT 59714. 388-4871.

Big Fork Chamber of Commerce, P.O. Box 237, Big Fork, MT 59911. 837-5611.

Big Sandy Chamber of Commerce, P.O. Box 511, Big Sandy, MT 59520. 378-2247.

Big Timber Chamber of Commerce, P.O. Box 1012, Big Timber, MT 59011. 932-2217.

Billings Chamber of Commerce, P.O. Box 2519, Billings, MT 59103. 245-4111.

Bitterroot Valley Chamber of Commerce, 105 E. Main, Hamilton, MT 59840. 363-2400.

Bozeman Chamber of Commerce, P.O. Box B, Bozeman, MT 59715. 586-5421.

Broadus Chamber of Commerce, Powder River Commercial Club, Broadus, MT 59317. 436-2834.

Butte-Silver Bow Chamber of Commerce, 2950 Harrison Avenue, Butte, MT 59701. 494-5595.

Chester Chamber of Commerce, P.O. Box 632, Chester, MT 59522.

Chinook Chamber of Commerce, P.O. Box 575, Chinook, MT 59523. 357-2264.

Choteau Chamber of Commerce, P.O. Box 1241, Choteau, MT 59422. 466-2005.

Circle Chamber of Commerce, Circle, MT 59215. 485-2414.

Columbia Falls Chamber of Commerce, P.O. Box 312, Columbia Falls, MT 59912. 892-2072.

Columbus Chamber of Commerce, P.O. Box 783, Columbus, MT 59019. 322-4778.

Conrad Chamber of Commerce, 406½ South Main, Conrad, MT 59425. 278-7791.

Culbertson Chamber of Commerce, P.O. Box 633, Culbertson, MT 59218. 787-5821.

Cut Bank Chamber of Commerce, P.O. Box 1243, Cut Bank, MT 59427. 873-4041.

Deer Lodge Chamber of Commerce, 300 Main, Deer Lodge, MT 59722. 846-2094.

Dillon Chamber of Commerce, Beaverhead Chamber, P.O. Box 830, Dillon, MT 59725. 683-5511.

Ekalaka Chamber of Commerce, P.O. Box 297, Ekalaka, MT 59324. 775-6658.

Ennis Chamber of Commerce, P.O. Box 291, Ennis, MT 59729.

Tobacco Valley Chamber of Commerce, P.O. Box 186, Eureka, MT 59917. 296-2674.

Fairfield Chamber of Commerce, Booster Club, P.O. Box 282, Fairfield, MT 59436. 467-2323.

Fairview Chamber of Commerce, P.O. Box 374, Fairview, MT 59221. 747-5226.

Forsyth Chamber of Commerce, P.O. Box 448, Forsyth, MT 59327. 356-2115.

Community Improvement Association, P.O. Box 313, Fort Benton, MT 59442. 622-5254.

Gardiner Chamber of Commerce, P.O. Box 81, Gardiner, MT 59030. 848-7681.

Glasgow Chamber of Commerce, P.O. Box 832, Glasgow, MT 59230. 228-2222.

Glendive Chamber of Commerce, P.O. Box 930, Glendive, MT 59330. 365-5601.

Great Falls Chamber of Commerce, P.O. Box 2127, Great Falls, MT 59403. 761-4434.

Hardin Chamber of Commerce, Route 1, P.O. Box 1206A, Hardin, MT 59034. 665-1672.

Harlowton Chamber of Commerce, P.O. Box 694, Harlowton, MT 59036. 632-4652.

Havre Chamber of Commerce, P.O. Box 308, Havre, MT 59501. 265-4383.

Helena Chamber of Commerce, 201 E. Lyndale, Helena, MT 59601. 442-4120.

Hinsdale Chamber of Commerce, Hinsdale, MT 59241. 364-2221.

Hot Springs Chamber of Commerce, P.O. Box 580, Hot Springs, MT 59845. 741-2652.

Jordan Chamber of Commerce, Jordan, MT 59337. 557-2480.

Kalispell Chamber of Commerce, 15 Depot Loop, Kalispell, MT 59901. 755-6166.

Lakeside Chamber of Commerce, Westshore Chamber, P.O. Box 181, Lakeside, MT 59922. 844-3809.

Laurel Chamber of Commerce, P.O. Box 395, Laurel, MT 59044. 628-8105.

Lewistown Chamber of Commerce, P.O. Box 818, Lewistown, MT 59457. 538-5436.

Libby Chamber of Commerce, P.O. Box 704, Libby, MT 59923. 293-3832.

Lincoln Chamber of Commerce, P.O. Box 399, Lincoln, MT 59639. 362-4223.

Livingston Chamber of Commerce, P.O. Box 660, Livingston, MT 59047. 222-0850.

Malta Chamber of Commerce, P.O. Box 716, Malta, MT 59538. 654-2145.

Miles City Chamber of Commerce, P.O. Box 730, Miles City, MT 59301. 232-2890.

Missoula Chamber of Commerce, P.O. Box 7577, Missoula, MT 59807. 543-6623.

Montana Chamber of Commerce, P.O. Box 1730, Helena, MT 59624. 442-2405.

Philipsburg Chamber of Commerce, P.O. Drawer Q, Philipsburg, MT 59858. 859-3215.

Plains-Paradise Chamber of Commerce, P.O. Box 714, Plains, MT 59859. 826-3831.

Plentywood Chamber of Commerce, P.O. Box 4, Plentywood, MT 59254. 765-2340.

Polson Chamber of Commerce, P.O. Box 677, Polson, MT 59860. 883-5969.

Poplar Chamber of Commerce, P.O. Box 313, Poplar, MT 59255. 768-3323.

Red Lodge Chamber of Commerce, P.O. Box 998, Red Lodge, MT 59068. 446-1718.

Richey Chamber of Commerce, P.O. Box 279, Richey, MT 59259. 773-5887.

Ronan Chamber of Commerce, P.O. Box 254, Ronan, MT 59864. 676-4600.

Roundup Chamber of Commerce, P.O. Box 751, Roundup, MT 59072. 323-1966.

Saco Chamber of Commerce, Saco, MT 59261. 527-3361.

Scobey Chamber of Commerce, P.O. Box 91, Scobey, MT 59263. 487-5311.

Seeley Lake-Condon Chamber of Commerce, P.O. Box 516, Seeley Lake, MT 59868. 677-2775.

Shelby Chamber of Commerce, P.O. Box 488, Shelby, MT 59474. 434-2031.

Sidney Chamber of Commerce, 909 S. Central Ave., Sidney, MT 59270. 482-1916.

St. Ignatius Chamber of Commerce, P.O. Box 216, St. Ignatius, MT 59865. 745-2166.

Stanford Chamber of Commerce, Commercial Club, P.O. Box 386, Stanford, MT 59479. 566-2596.

Superior Chamber of Commerce, P.O. Box 483, Superior, MT 59872. 822-4643.

Swan Lake Chamber of Commerce, Highway 83, Swan Lake, MT 59911. 886-2324.

Terry Chamber of Commerce, P.O. Box 677, Terry, MT 69349. 637-5782.

Thompson Falls-Trout Creek-Noxon Chamber of Commerce, P.O. Box 493, Thompson Falls, MT 59873. 827-4722.

Three Forks Chamber of Commerce, P.O. Box 1143, Three Forks, MT 59752. 285-3674.

Townsend Chamber of Commerce, P.O. Box 947, Townsend, MT 59644. 266-3176.

Troy Chamber of Commerce, P.O. Box 161, Troy, MT 59935. 295-4693.

Virginia City Chamber of Commerce, Vigilance Club, P.O. Box 295, Virginia City, MT 59755.

West Yellowstone Chamber of Commerce, P.O. Box 458, W. Yellowstone, MT 59758. 646-7701.

Whitefish Chamber of Commerce, P.O. Box 1309, Whitefish, MT 59937. 862-3501.

Whitehall Chamber of Commerce, P.O. Box 667, Whitehall, MT 59759. 287-3343.

White Sulphur Springs Chamber of Commerce, P.O. Box 356, White Sulphur Springs, MT 59645. 547-3331.

Wibaux Chamber of Commerce, P.O. Box 260, Wibaux, MT 59353. 795-2429.

Wolf Point Chamber of Commerce, P.O. Box 237, Wolf Point, MT 59201. 653-2012.

In Utah (Area Code — 801)

Edge of the Cedars, 660 West 4th N. Blanding, UT 84511. 678-2238.

Brigham City Chamber of Commerce, 6 N. Main, Brigham City, UT 84302. 723-3931.

Bryce Canyon National Park, Visitor Center, Bryce Canyon, UT 84717. 834-5322.

Cedar City Chamber of Commerce, 286 N. Main, Cedar City, UT 84720. 586-4484.

Duchesne Chamber of Commerce, 175 W. Main St., Duchesne, UT 84021. 738-2501.

Green River Chamber of Commerce, 165 S. K.O.A. River Blvd., Green River, UT 84525. 364-3651.

Wasatch County Chamber of Commerce, Red Caboose, 33 N. Main, Heber City, UT 84032. 654-3666.

Dinosaur National Monument, Visitor Center and Quarry, P.O. Box 128, Jensen, UT 84035. 789-2115.

Kanab Chamber of Commerce, Information Center, 48 S. 100 East, Kanab, UT 84741. 644-5229.

Cache Chamber of Commerce, 52 W. 2nd North, Logan, UT 84321. 752-2161.

Grand County Travel Council, 805 N. Main, Moah, UT 84532. 259-8825.

Monticello Visitor Center, 117 S. Main St. Monticello, UT 84535. 587-2231.

Monument Valley Information Center, Monument Valley, UT 84536.

Golden Spike Empire, Union Station, Ogden, UT 84404. 399-8288.
Orem City Chamber of Commerce, 777 S. State, Orem, UT 84601. 224-3636.
Information Center, City Park, Panguitch, UT 84759.
Park City Chamber/Bureau, 528 Main St., Park City, UT 84060. 649-6100.
Carbon County Chamber of Commerce, Municipal Building, 200 E. Main, Price, UT 84501. 637-2788.
Provo City Chamber of Commerce, 10 E. 300 N., Provo, UT 84601. 373-6770.
Richfield Chamber of Commerce, 220 N. 600 West, Richfield, UT 84701. 896-4241.
Roosevelt Chamber of Commerce, 332 South 200 E., Roosevelt, UT 84066. 722-4598.
Salt Lake Area Chamber of Commerce, 19 E. 200 S., Salt Lake City, UT 84111. 364-3631.
Springville Chamber of Commerce, 175 S. Main, Springville, UT 84663. 489-4681.
St. George Chamber of Commerce and Information Center, 97 E. St. George Blvd., St. George, UT 84770. 628-1658.
Tooele County Chamber of Commerce, 90 N. Main, Tooele, UT 84074. 882-0690.
Vernal Chamber of Commerce, 120 E. Main, Vernal, UT 84078. 789-1352.

In Wyoming (Area Code — 307)

Afton Chamber of Commerce, P.O. Box 1107, Afton, WY 83110. 886-5297.
Buffalo Chamber of Commerce, P.O. Box 927, 55 N. Main, Buffalo, WY 82834. 684-5544.
Casper Chamber of Commerce, P.O. Box 399, 500 N. Center, Casper, WY 82601. 234-5311.
Cheyenne Chamber of Commerce, P.O. Box 1147, 301 W. 16th, Cheyenne, WY 82001. 638-3388.
Cody Chamber of Commerce, P.O. Box 2777, 836 Sheridan, Cody, WY 82414. 587-2297.
Douglas Chamber of Commerce, 318 — 1st St. W., Douglas, WY 82633. 358-2950.
Dubois Chamber of Commerce, P.O. Box 632, Dubois, WY 82513. 455-2556.
Evanston Chamber of Commerce, P.O. Box 365, 946 Front St., Evanston, WY 82930. 789-2757.
Gillette Chamber of Commerce, P.O. Box 1006, 314 S. Gillette, Gillette, WY 82716. 682-3673.
Glenrock Chamber of Commerce, P.O. Box 411, 506 W. Birch, Glenrock, WY 82637. 436-2754.
Green River Chamber of Commerce, 1450 Uinta Dr., Green River, WY 82935. 875-5711.
Greybull Chamber of Commerce, 613 Greybull Ave., Greybull, WY 82426. 765-2100.
Jackson Hole Chamber of Commerce, P.O. Box E, 532 N. Cache, Jackson Hole, WY 83001. 733-3316.
Kemmerer Chamber of Commerce, P.O. Box 1100, 700 Cedar Ave., Kemmerer, WY 83101. 877-9761.
Lander Chamber of Commerce, 160 North 1st, Lander, WY 82520. 332-3892.
Laramie Chamber of Commerce, 401 Garfield, Laramie, WY 82070. 745-7339.
Lovell Chamber of Commerce, 184 E. Main, Lovell, WY 82431. 548-7552.
Lusk Chamber of Commerce, P.O. Box 180, 257 S. Main, Lusk, WY 82225. 334-2773.
Medicine Bow Chamber of Commerce, P.O. Box 456, Medicine Bow, WY 82329. 379-2255.

Meeteetse Chamber of Commerce, P.O. Box 38, Meeteetse, WY 82433. 868-2278.
Newcastle Chamber of Commerce, 113 W. Main St., Newcastle, WY 82701. 746-2739.
Pinedale Chamber of Commerce, P.O. Box 176, 187 W. Pine, Pinedale, WY 82941. 367-2242.
Powell Chamber of Commerce, P.O. Box 814, 111 S. Day, Powell, WY 82435. 754-3494.
Rawlins Chamber of Commerce, P.O. Box 1331, 511 W. Spruce, Rawlins, WY 82301. 324-4111.
Riverton Chamber of Commerce, P.O. Box 469, 1st & Main, Riverton, WY 82501. 856-4801.
Rock Springs Chamber of Commerce, 1897 Dewar Dr., Rock Springs, WY 82901. 362-3771.
Saratoga Chamber of Commerce, P.O. Box 1095, 102 W. Bridge, Saratoga, WY 82331. 326-8855.
Sheridan Chamber of Commerce, P.O. Box 707, 5th & I-90, Sheridan, WY 82801. 672-2485.
Shoshoni Chamber of Commerce, P.O. Box 324, Shoshoni, WY 82649. 876-2389.
Thermopolis Chamber of Commerce, 220 Park St., Thermopolis, WY 82443. 864-2636.
Torrington Chamber of Commerce, 350 W. 21st Ave., Torrington, WY 82240. 532-3879.
Wheatland Chamber of Commerce, P.O. Box 427, 600 — 9th, Wheatland, WY 82201. 322-2322.
Worland Chamber of Commerce, 120 N. 10th St., Worland, WY 82401. 347-3226.

Dining Guide

Colorado

Colorado Springs:

Dale Street Cafe, 115 E. Dale, 578-9898. (Wholesome eating.)
Edelweiss, 34 E. Romona Ave., 633-2220. (German and Continental cuisine, in a Bavarian setting.)
Pepe's, 2427 N. Academy Blvd., 574-5801. (Fine Mexican food.)
The Rose Room, 1318 W. Colorado Ave., 578-9018. (American specialities served in a Victorian setting, excellent menu.)

Durango:

L'Entrepoint Restaurant and Bar, 1769 Main Ave., 247-3751. (Gourmet French cuisine, Creole dishes, desserts, a variety of wines.)
The Ore House, 147 6th St., 247-5707. (One of Durango's oldest restaurants, seafood and steaks.)
Mr Rosewater, 522 Main St., 247-8788. (A deli serving a variety of soups, pastries, wines, juices, egg dishes.)
The Strater Hotel, 699 Main Ave., 247-4431. (Live ragtime music, all you can eat fish fry on Friday nights, luncheon buffet specials.)
Yesterday's, 800 Camino del Rio in Holiday Inn, 247-5393. (Rocky Mountain trout, prime rib.)

Aspen and Snowmass:

Aurthur's, 132 W. Main, 925-7931. (Szechuan and Mandarin cuisine.)
Country Road Ltd., Bar and Restaurant, 400 E. Main, 925-6556. (Fresh trout, sea food delicacies. Reservations advised.)

Crystal Palace, 300 E. Hyman Ave., 925-1455. (Large collection of stained glass. Gourmet food and music daily.)

Eastern Winds, 520 East Copper, 925-5160. (Szechuan and Mandarin specialities including Peking Duck.)

The Grand Finale, 312 E. Hyman, 925-6328. (Dinner theater serving Continental cuisine. Reservations advised.)

The Greenhouse Restaurant, 315 E. Hyman, 925-6328. (Intimate atmosphere, Italian and Continental cuisine with daily seafood entrees.)

Parlour Car, 615 W. Hopkins, 925-7601. (French cuisine and wine served in a restored 1887 railway car.)

Steak Pit, City Market Bldg., 925-3459. (Excellent steaks, prime rib, loster, fresh fish, salad bar.)

Denver

Baby Doe's Matchless Mine, 2520 W. 23rd Ave., Near Mile High Stadium, 433-3386. (Features chicken, steaks and nightly dancing, grand view of Denver's skyline.)

Bay Wolf, 231 Milawakee, 388-9221. (Specializes in veal and fish, live jazz music.)

Berardi and Sons, 1525 Blake St., 623-5155. (Underground hideaway in Larimer Square, wide selection of wines, beers, sandwiches, hamburgers.)

Brendles, 1624 Market St., 893-3588. (New American cuisine with entrees like grilled duck breast, fetticini with goat cheese.)

The Broker Restaurants, 821 17th St., 893-5065. (Good steaks, prime rib and trout.)

Buckhorn Exchange, 1000 Osage, 534-9505. (Historic eating and drinking emporium.)

Cafe Kandahar, 2709 W. Main Littleton, 798-9075. (Continental cuisine with a ski museum.)

The Chrysler, 2955 E. First Ave., 355-2955. (Home made entrees and seafood served till 1 am.)

Churchill's Restaurant, 1730 S. Colorado Blvd. and I-25., 756-8877. (Nouvelle cuisine, nightly entertainment.)

Dudley's, 1120 E. 6th Ave., 744-8634. (Pate, duck and veal specialities. Menu changes daily.)

Fins Oyster Bar and Restaurant, 1401 Larimer St., 571-1150. (Fresh seafood and other specialities. Downtown location.)

Fresh Fish Company, 7600 E. Hampden Ave, (Specializes in seafood.)

Gasho of Japan, Downtown at 1627 Curtis, 892-5625 and 5701 S. Syracuse St. (DTC), 773-3277. (Japanese steak house.)

H. Brinkers, 7209 S. Clinton, I-25 and Arapahoe Rd., 771-0285. (Seafood, steaks, live entertainment.)

Hudson's, 1800 Glenarm Pl., 595-0448. (Red snapper, veal, lamb, prime rib, excellent desserts, entertainment.)

The Harvest, 430 S. Colorado Blvd. (Natural goodies.)

Hoffbran Steaks, 13th and Santa Fe., 629-1778. (Good steaks.)

The Library Restaurant, 800 S. Colorado Blvd., 757-7868. (Fine food, cozy atmosphere.)

Ming Dynasty, 4251 E. Missippi, Glendale, 757-4923. (Mandarin, Szechuan and Oriental cuisine.)

Maxwells, 435 S. Cherry St., (Thick Sicillian pizza.)

Manhattan Cafe, 1620 Market St., (New York style atmosphere.)

Magic Pan Creperie, 1465 Larimer St., 534-5140. (Fluffy crepes, souffles, delicacies.)

The Old Spagetti Factory, 1215 18th St., 295-1865. (Variety of sauces and spagetti.)

Pierres Quorum Restaurant, East Colfax at Grant. 861-8686. Twenty five years of award winning French cuisine.

Paradise Bar and Grill, 100 E. 9th Ave., 861-8694. (Excellent seafood.)

Rich's Cafe, 80 S. Madison St., (Specialities are salads, sandwiches, Mexican food. Opens late.)

Red Apple Restaurant and Lounge, Rodeway Inn, 4590 Quebec St., 320-0260. (Steaks, seafood, salad bar.)

Sky Chef's, Stapleton International Airport, 398-3767. (Airline catering, restaurants, bar.)

Soren's, 315 Detroit, 322-8155. (Good eating, meat, fish and vegetarian food.)

Sushi Koi, 1626 Market St., (Japanese delicacies.)

Tanre Louise, 4900 E. Colfax Ave., 355-4488. (Culinary treats, French country style restaurant.)

Wellshire Inn, 3333 S. Colorado, 759-3333. (Lunch, dinner, Sunday brunch, full Continental service.)

Wilscam Restaurant, 1735 Arapahoe St., 296-0142. (Elegant Restaurant, Continental cuisine.)

Zang Brewing Co., 2301 7th St., (Fun, casual with a Denver sports tradition before and after games.)

Idaho

Boise:

The Gamekeeper, located in the Owyhee Plaza Hotel. (Top quality steaks, seafood, wines.)

The Boarding House, (Moderately priced, Basque-style restaurant.)

The Royal, Located downtown. (Good food served, turn-of-the-century decor.)

Pengilly's, (Unusual lunches, served in an unique atmosphere.)

Coeur D'Alene:

The Cedars, (Excellent food, floating restaurant on Lake Coeur D'Alene.)

North Shore Plaza Restaurants, Located in the Lakeshore complex with plush roof top dining. (Shore Restaurant offers casual atmosphere, Templin's has excellent chicken-to-go.)

Lewiston:

Cedars III, (Moderately priced, hand cut steaks, salad bar.)

Helm, (Excellent cooking, prime rib, shrimp, steaks. Children's menu.)

Twin Falls:

Morgan's Rogerson Restaurant, (Family dining, casual atmosphere, warm hospitality moderate prices.)

Sandpoint:

Garden Restaurant, (Moderately priced, outdoor dining, Oriental food, fresh seafood, roast duck.)

Montana

Bozeman:

New Asia Kitchen, 1533 W. Babcock, 586-6362. (Chinese cuisine. Take-out orders accepted.)
John's Pork Chop, 209 E. Main, 586-0029. (Original pork chop sandwich.)
Gene's Cartwheel Supper Club, located 7 miles (11 km) W. on Hwy 191. (Full menu, steak, seafood.)
Jordans Restaurant, 1104 E. Main, 586-9791. (Family meals, full menu.)

Utah

Cedar City:

Sugar Loaf Cafe, excellent chicken and steak, moderate.

Logan:

Country Kitchen, good family eating, moderately priced.

Ogden:

Olde Country Bar, Family style American food.

Park City:

Adolph's, Exclusive continental dining, expensive.

Provo:

Jedediah's Famous Dining, at the Rodeway Inn, 1292 University Ave. Moderately priced good family meals.

St. George:

Atkin's Sugar Loaf Cafe, great chicken and steak, moderately priced.

Salt Lake City:

Argentina Beef House, Trolley Square, 600 S. 700 E. 322-3732. Argentina steak, seafood, prime rib.
Bratten's Seafood Grotto, 644 E. 400 S. 364-6547. Seafood.
Chuck-A-Rama Buffet, 744 E. 400 S. 531-1123. Smorgasbord.
Hibachi Teppan-Yaki, Suki-Yaki House, 238 E. South Temple. 364-5456. Japanese cuisine.
New Orleans Cafe, 307 W. 200 South, 363-6573. Creole, Cajun, seafood.
Pasta Mulino, 859 E. 900 S. 364-5000. Deli, Italian.
Peppers, 249 S. 400 East. 532-1425. Mexican food.
R. J. Wheatfields, Trolley Square, 500 S. 700 E. 364-8963. Natural foods, seafood, steak.
Sizzler Family Steak House, 371 E. 400 S. 532-1339. American steak.
Szechuan Restaurant, 542 E. 400 S. 359-2652. Chinese (Szechuan and Mandarin cuisine.)
Temple Family Restaurant, 320 N. Temple, 355-7799. American, Oriental, Korean.
Zaccheo's Hansom House, 280 E. 800 S. 322-0815. Italian, American.

Beefeaters, 2160 S. 700 E. 466-0689. Large steaks.
Cowboy Grub Restaurant, 2350 Foothill Drive, 466-8334. American, barbeque.
Ho Ho Gourmet, 1504 So State, 487-7709. Chinese, American.
Paprika Restaurant, 2302 Parley's Way, 484-0901. International.
Balkan Village, 1500 N. Temple, 531-7762. Greek, American.
Dee's Family Restaurant, 855 W. North Temple, 359-3916. American coffee shop.
Gallo's Italian Restaurant, 1447 W. 1000 N. 364-6052. Italian, seafood.
Amber Restaurant, 217 E. 3300 S. 484-3222. American.
Bamboo Garden, 1142 E. 3900 S. 268-9631. Chinese, American.
Francesco's Italian Restaurant, 7200 So State, 561-2203. Italian, American.
Prestwich Farms, 1250 E. 3300 S. 485-6301. American steak, salad bar.
Shaleemar, 3298 Highland Dr. 467-6912. East Indian.
Tijuana Tilly's, 6351 So State, 268-2549. Mexican, American.
Far West Cafe, 3572 W. 3500 S. 966-9001, Vietnamese, Chinese, American.
Golden Corral, 3810 W. 5400 S. 969-3263. American steak.
Western Sizzling Steak House, 2222 W. 3500 S. 972-0800. Steak, American.
Belgian Waffle & Omelette Inn, 7331 So 900 E. 566-5731. American.
Copper Rim Cafe, 305 State Highway, 934-8871. Coffee shop.
La Caille at Quail Run, 9565 Wasatch Blvd. 942-1751. French, International.
Ming's Dynasty, 9400 So 6500 E. 571-5073. Chinese.
Union Station, Union Square, 685 E. 9450 S. 571-8051. American.

Wyoming

Casper:

Benham's, steaks and businessmen's lunch.

Cody:

Green Gables, Smorgasbord, excellent food.

Irma Grill, moderately priced steaks and ribs. Buffalo Bill's cherrywood bar.

Jackson:

Alpenhof Garden Room, in Teton Village, European gourmet restaurant. Veal, seafood and homemade pastries.
Anthony's Italian Restaurant, 50 S. Glenwood, Jackson. Authentic Italian cuisine.
Lame Duck, in Jackson, featuring a variety of Oriental dishes at reasonable prices.
Soup Kitchen, in Jackson. Fast food, deli sandwiches, soups, salads, yoghurt, desserts.

Laramie:

Diamond Horseshoe, moderately priced American and Chinese cuisine.

Lander:

Miner's Delight, An exclusive restaurant in Atlantic ghost town serving Continental food.
Calvaryman, an excellent prime rib restaurant.

Embassies and Consular Services

Belgium

Mr. Anderson, (Rep) 231 Edison, Salt Lake City, UT. 335-2135. (Consulate Gen. in Los Angeles)

Chile

Mario Melendez, (Cons) 1110 S. 150 W., Orem, UT. 225-3768. (Consultate Gen. in Los Angeles)

Costa Rica

Consulate Gen, 2045 Franklin, Denver, CO. 839-5522.

Denmark

Danish Consulate, 3100 S. Sheridan Blvd., Denver, CO. 922-4545.
Julius Anderson, (Cons) 231 Edison St., Salt Lake City, UT. 355-2135.

Dominican Republic

Dominican Republic Consulate, 8515 Pearl, Denver, CO. 289-2110.

Finland

M. W. Smith, (Rep) Deseret Plaza, 4th Fl., Salt Lake City, UT. 350-5262.
Finnish Consulate, 2315 E. 7th Ave., Denver, CO. 377-5529.

France

French Honorary Consul, Western Federal Savings Bldg., Denver, CO. 573-5629.
French Trade Offices, 1840 Willow Ln., Denver, CO. 233-7484.
French Consul, University of Utah, Salt Lake City, UT. 581-6807. (Consulate General in San Francisco)

Germany

German Honorary Consul, 1801 Jackson Golden, Denver, CO, 279-5383.
Herwig Galnder, (Cons), 455 E. 4th S., Suite 404A, Salt Lake City, UT. 364-9573.

Italy

Henry N. Aloia, (Cons) 2895 S. 800 E., Salt Lake City, UT. 466-7615. (Consulate Gen. in San Francisco)

Korea

Korean Consulate, Equitable Bldg., Denver, CO. 629-1761.

Mexico

Mexican Consulate, 1670 Broadway, Denver, CO. 832-2621.
Enrique Vazquez, (Cons), 182 S. 600 E., Suite 202, Salt Lake City, UT. 521-8503.

Netherlands

Netherlands Consulate, Suite 700, 910 16th, Denver, CO. 825-6109.
J. Leland Teerlink, (Vice Cons) 314 E. 1st S. Salt Lake City, UT. 364-7916.

Norway

John Langeland, (Cons) Zion First National Bank, Salt Lake City, UT. 524-4711.
Norwegian Consulate, 1600 Sherman, Denver, CO, 861-4065.

Peru

Jorge J. Arce-Larreta, (Cons) 1801 Yuma Ave., Denver, CO. 467-6355.

Senegal

Louis S. Leathem, 546 DeSoto, Denver, CO. 328-3055.

South Africa

Harlem W. Clark, (Cons) 61 S. Main, Salt Lake City, UT. 531-8300.

Sweden

Swedish Consulate, Denver, CO. 578-0999.

Switzerland

Swiss Consulate, 430 S. Newland, Denver, CO. 935-1666.
Gottlieb L. Schneebeli, Consul, 617 8th Ave., Salt Lake City, UT. 532-1874.

Events and Festivals

In Colorado

January:

National Western Stock Show and Rodeo, Denver. **Annual Cowboy Downhill/Torchlight Parade,** Steamboat Springs. **Winterskol,** Snowmass. **Breckenridge World Freestyle Invitational/Ullr-Fest,** Breckenridge.

February:

U.S. Alpine Championships, Copper Mountain. **Dog Sled Races,** Granby. **American Ski Classic,** Vail and Beaver Creek.

March:

World Cup, Aspen. St Patrick's Day Parade, Denver.

April:

Spring Splash/Closing Day, Winter Park.

May:

Annual Music and Blossom Festival, Canon City. People's Fair, East Highschool, Denver. Bolder Boulder Race, Boulder.

June:

Renaissance Festival, Lakspur. Colorado Music Festival, Boulder. Annual Aspen Music Festival, Aspen. Madam Lou Bunch Day: "Original Bed Race", Central City. Colorado Music Festival, Chautauqua Park, Boulder. Donkey Derby Days, Cripple Creek. Annual Bluegrass and Country Music Festival, Telluride. "The Way it Wuz" Celebration, Steamboat Springs. Independence Stampede, (Rodeo, Parade, Dance,) Greely. Twilight PRCA Rodeo, Alamosa. Yatch Club Races, Grand Lake.

July:

Colorado Shakespeare Festival, (Weekends) Boulder. The Ballet/Aspen Summer Dance Festival, Aspen. Central City Opera Festival, Central City. Pike's Peak Hill Climb, Cascade. Coors Bike Classic, Boulder, Vail, Aspen, Fruita, Grand Junction. Invitational Snowmass Hot Air Balloon Races, Snowmass. "World Famous Rooftop Rodeo", Estes Park. Pow Wow Parade, Fairgrounds, Boulder. Arts Festival, Durango. Tennis Classic, Beaver Creek. Cool Water Revival, (Windsurfing) Winterpark.

August:

Boom Days Celebration, Burro Race, Leadville. Pike's Peak or Bust Rodeo, Colorado Springs. Jerry Ford Invitational Golf Tournament/Concert, Vail. Buena Vista Pack Burro Race: Parade, Crafts, Buena Vista. Telluride Jazz Festival, Telluride. Annual Telluride Film Festival, Telluride. Festival of Mountain and Plain, Denver. Colorado Springs Balloon Race, Memorial Park, Colorado Springs.

September:

Annual Scottish Highland Festival, Estes Park. World Hang Gliding Championships, Telluride. Annual German Harvest Festival; Octoberfest, Larimer Square, Denver. Snowmass Old Car Classic, Snowmass. Crested Butte Marathon, Crested Butte. Annual Trathlon, Aspen. Annual Potato Day Festival, Carbondale. Vailfest Weekend, Vail.

October:

Larimer Square Halloween Bash, Denver. United Bank's Annual Denver Film Festival, Denver.

November:

Veteran's Day Parade, Denver. Larimer Square Christmas Walk, Denver.

December:

Georgetown Christmas Market, Georgetown. Parade of Lights, Denver. Snow Sculpture Contest, Beaver Creek. All-Cal Ski Week, Vail. Decemberfest, Denver. Aspen Winter Concert Series, Aspen.

In Idaho

January:

Winter Carnival, Schweitzer, Sandpoint.

February:

Winter Carnival, McCall.

March:

Idaho State Champion Cutter and Chariot Races, Pocatello.

May:

Salmon River Rodeo, Riggins. Locust Blossom Festival, Kendrick. Lake Coeur D'Alene Days Festival, Coeur D'Alene. Kamloops and Kokannee Week, (fishing derby) Sandpoint. Priest Lake Spring Festival and Flotilla, Priest Lake.

June:

National Old Time Fiddlers Contest, Weiser. State High School Rodeo Championship, Jerome.

July:

Snake River Stampede and Festival, Nampa. Kootenai River Days, (parade, rodeo, lumberjack competition, pancake breakfast,) Bonners Ferry.

August:

Huckleberry Festival, (parade, firemen's water fight, huckleberry judging contest,) Priest River. Pilgrimage to Old Mission, (Indian Pageant including performance, encampent, traditional dinner,) Cataldo. Western Idaho State Fair, Boise. Shoshone Bannock Indian Festival and Rodeo, Fort Hall. Pierre's Hole Rendevous BBQ, (parade and rodeo).

September:

Bunyan Days, (lumberjack competition, antique auto show, parade, dances, games, carnival). St Maries. Lewiston Round up, (cowboy breakfast rodeo and breakfast,) Lewiston. Wagon Days, (pancake breakfast, vintage wagon parade, buggies, trappings,) Ketchum. Shoshone Bannock Indian Day, Fort Hall.

October:

Four Nations Pow Wow, Lapwai. **Fiddlers Jamboree,** (jam sessions and Salmon River Art Annual,) Riggins.

December:

Traditional Basque Shepherder's Ball, Lamb Auction, Boise.

In Montana

January:

P.R.C.A. Rodeo Finals, Great Falls. **H.C.I.A. Carnival,** Hardin. **Montana Winter Fair,** Bozeman. **Winter Carnival,** Big Sky. **Nashua Winterfest,** Nashua. **Cabin Fever Days,** Hungry Horse and Environs.

February:

Sno Fest, Anaconda. **Winter Carnival,** Bozeman and Whitefish. **Boat Show,** Kalispell.

March:

Annual Gun Show, Kalispell. **Charles Russell Art Auction,** Great Falls. **Great American Ski Chase,** West Yellowstone. **Red Lodge Winter Carnival,** Red Lodge. **Oly Days,** Big Sky. **St. Patrick's Day Parade,** Butte. **Doug Betters Winter Classic,** The Big Mountain.

April:

M.S.U. Rodeo, Bozeman. **Gem and Mineral Show,** Billings. **Northern International Livestock Exposition and Spring Show,** Billings. **Peak to Prairie Triathalon,** Red Lodge. **Science Fair,** Missoula. **Libby Arts Festival,** Libby Memorial Gymnasium. **North American Skiing/Yachting Championship,** The Big Mountain.

May:

Stump Town Follies, Whitefish. **Bluebay Regatta,** Polson. **Cherry Festival,** Polson. **U. of M. Rodeo,** Missoula. **Veterans Memorial Powwow,** Fort Belknap. **Roosevelt County Range Tour,** Wolf Point. **Memorial Day Powwow,** Lame Deer. **Horse Racing and Bucking Horse Sale,** Miles City. **Western Heritage Art Classic,** Billings. **Vigilante Parade,** Helena.

June:

Governor's Cup Marathon, Helena. **US Open Fiddlers Contest,** Dillon. **College National Finals Rodeo,** Bozeman. **Midland Empire Horse Show,** Billings. **Western Days Parade,** Billings. **Red Lodge International Ski Race Camp/Music Festival/Run to the sun,** Red Lodge. **VFW Rodeo,** Hardin. **Demolition Derby,** Hardin. **Wild West Days,** Poplar. **Match Bronco,** Wolf Point. **Jaycee Rodeo,** Chinook. **Heritage Gun Show,** Libby. **Viking Boat Regatta,** Whitefish. **Big Sky Logging Championships,**

Kalispell. **Homestead Days,** Hot Springs. **Jazz Festival,** Helena.

July:

Glacier International Horse Show/Quarter Horse Show, Kalispell. **Whitefish Cup Regatta/Lake to Lake Canoe Race,** Whitefish. **Montana State Fiddlers Championship/Wagon Burner Regatta/Independence Cup Regatta,** Polson. **Great Western Montana River Race,** Missoula. **Arlee Powwow,** Arlee. **State Fair Rodeo and Horse Races,** Great Falls. **Central Horse Show, Fair and Rodeo,** Lewiston. **Fort Belknap Indian Days,** Fort Belknap. **Opeta-Ye-Teca Indian Days/Wild Horse Stampede,** Wolf Point. **Annual Northern Cheyenne Powwow,** Lame Deer. **4th and 5th East Fork Roping Club Rodeo/Old Timers Rodeo,** Broadus. **Youth Rodeo,** Hardin. **Carbon County Fair/Rodeo/Beartooth Run,** Red Lodge. **Billings Railroad Days,** Billings. **Yellowstone Boat Float,** Livingston. **Last Chance Stampede and Fair,** Helena. **4th of July Parade,** Butte. **Daly Days,** Hamilton. **North American Indian Days,** Browning. **Lewis & Clark Expedition Festival,** Cut Bank.

August:

Festival of Nations/Silver Bow County Fair, Butte. **Raft Race and River Remedy/Western Rendezvous of Art/Governor's Cup All Breeds Horse Show,** Helena. **All Girl Rodeo,** Dillon. **Bannack Days,** Bannack. **Mile High Lake Catamaran Regatta,** Georgetown Lake. **Sweet Pea Festival,** Bozeman. **Eastern Montana Fair,** Miles City. **Sun Dance,** Lame Deer. **Crow Fair Celebration and Powwow,** Crow Agency. **Miller's IGA Sanction Barrel Race/Madden's 4 State Roping/Espy Team Roping,** Broadus. **White River Cheyenne Powwow,** Busby **Rocky Boys Powwow,** Box Elder. **Western Montana Fair/Rodeo and Horse Races,** Missoula. **Festival of Nations,** Red Lodge. **Yellowstone Exhibition,** Billings. **Western Rendezvous of Art,** Helena Civic Center.

September:

Missoula Gun Show, Missoula. **Harve Festival Days,** Harve. **All Indian Rodeo,** Wolf Point. **Jaycees Demolition Derby,** Wolf Point. **Harvest Festival,** Glasgow. **Yellowstone Exhibition Fall Race Meet/Montana State Chili Cook Off,** Billings. **McIntosh Apple Days/Ravalli County Fair, Rodeo and Horse Races,** Hamilton. **Whitefish Summer Games,** Whitefish. **Kalispell Art Show and Auction,** Kalispell. **Montana State Draft Horse Show,** Bozeman Fairgrounds. **Threshing Bee and Antique Show,** Culbertson.

October:

Electrum, Helena. **Northern International Stock Show and Rodeo,** Billings. **Octoberfest,** Glendive. **Art-in-the-Park,** Great Falls, C.M. Russell High School.

November:

International Snafflebit Futurity, Malta.

December:

Good Neighbor Days, Anaconda. **Christmas Stroll,** Bozeman Main Street.

Late October — Mid November

Bald Eagle Gathering, Glacier Park, Apgar. An extraordinary event which occurs each fall as migrating eagles stop to feed on spawning Kokanee salmon in lower McDonald Creek. Park rangers are on hand each day to answer questions.

Early January — Late March

Camera Safaris, Yellowstone National Park. Exciting guided tours through the northern section of the park, led by park naturalists. Car caravans are escorted, using CB radios. The three to four hour tours include information on wildlife, geology, and history.

In Utah

January:

U.S. Film and Video Festival, Park City.

February:

Annual Winter Carnival, Park City. **Winterskol Annual Winter Festival,** Snowbird. **Park City Snow Sculpture Contest,** Park City.

March:

Mormon Festival of the Arts, Provo.

April:

Park City Ski and Sail Race, Park City.

May:

Utah Heritage Foundation Historic House Tour, Salt Lake City. **Spring State Square Dance Festival,** Salt Lake City. **Annual Indian Arts and Crafts Exhibit and Sale,** Salt Lake City. **Annual Sand Castle/Sculpture Contest,** Salt Lake City.

June:

Utah Arts Festival, Salt Lake City. **Utah Scottish Association Highland Games,** Salt Lake City. **Utah Pageant of the Arts,** American Fork. **Annual Golden Spike, National Old Time Fiddle and Blue Grass Festival,** Ogden.

July:

"Days of '47", Salt Lake City. **Murray Fun Day,** Murray. **Annual Festival of the American West,** Logan.

August:

Salt Lake County Fair, Murray. **Annual Park City Arts Festival,** Park City. **Railroaders Folk Festival,** Promontory.

September:

Annual Greek Festival, Salt Lake City. **Annual Oktoberfest,** Snowbird. **Utah State Fair,** Salt Lake City. **Ice Capades,** Salt Lake City. **Fall State Square Dance Festival,** Salt Lake City. **Swiss Days Celebration,** Midway. **Bonneville National Speed Trials,** Bonneville Salt Flats. **Ringling Bros Circus,** Salt Lake City. **"Viva la Fiesta",** Salt Lake City.

October:

Utah Symphony/Ballet West/Reportory Dance Theater & Utah Opera Co, Salt Lake City.

November:

Performing arts season begins for **Ririe-Woodbury Dance Company,** Salt Lake City. **Utah Chorale,** Salt Lake City.

December:

Tabernacle Choir Performances, Salt Lake City. **Ethnic Festival, Utah Museum of Fine Arts,** Salt Lake City. **"Festival of Lights",** Salt Palace, Salt Lake City. **Christmas Eve Torchlight Parades on Skis,** Snowbird, Alta and Park City.

In Wyoming

January:

Wyoming State Winter Fair, Lander. **All American Cutters Races — Melody Ranch,** Jackson.

February:

Wyoming State Snowmobile Association Races, Riverton. **Snowsation,** Saratoga. **Winter Carnival — Sheridan Creek Snow Oval,** Dubois. **Five Shot Rabbit Hunt,** Shoshoni. **Winter Carnival,** Main Street, Pinedale.

March:

White Pine Ski Open, Pinedale. **Coors Rocky Mountain Speed Run Snowmobile Race Championship,** Evanston. **Para Ski Championship,** Jackson Hole Ski Area, Teton Village. **Boat, Sports and Travel Show,** Events Center Casper. **Wyoming State Cross Country Ski Championships,** Togwotee Mountain Lodge. **World Championship Snow King Hill Climb,** Snow King Ski Area, Jackson.

April:

Pole, Paddle, Paddle Race, Jackson. **Togwotee Spring Fling 10 km Nordic Race,** Togwotee Mountain Lodge.

May:

Annual State Championship & Old Time Fiddle Contest, Shoshoni. **Old West Days,** Jackson. **Rodeo Days,** Thermopolis.

June:

Woodchoppers Jamboree, Encampment.

July:

Indian Tribal Powwow, Sundance, Ft Washakie. **Laramie Jubilee Days Rodeo,** Laramie. **Sheridan WYO Rodeo,** Sheridan. **Boysen Pike Fishing Derby,** Shoshoni. **Grand Teton Music Festival,** Teton Village. **Green River Rendezvous,** Pinedale. **Cheyenne Frontier Days,** Cheyenne. **Cody Stampede,** (parade and rodeo,) Cody. **Lander Pioneer Days,** (rodeo and parade,) Lander.

August:

Gift of the Waters Pageant, Thermopolis. **Wyoming State Fair,** Douglas.

September:

Fort Bridger Mountain Man Rendezvous and Black Powder Shoot, Fort Bridger. **Cowboy Days,** Evanston. Oktoberfest, Worland. **One Shot Antelope Hunt,** Lander.

Museums and Attractions

Colorado

Aspen:

The Aspen Art Museum, 590 N. Mill St. Exhibitions of art, photography, sculpture of local and international artists.
Aspen Historical Society Museum, 620 W. Bleeker St. History of silver mining, skiing, and ranching. (Walking tour of five or more can be arranged by reservation.) Open Tue-Sun 1pm-4pm. Closed holidays and 6 weeks in spring and fall.
Aspen Mountain Gallery, 555 E. Durant Ave. Graphics, painting, sculpture and jewelry.
Aspen Potters Guild, 107 S. Mill St. A unique shop selling porcelain, stoneware handcrafted by locals.
Bryne-Getz Gallery, 520 E. Durant Ave. Contemporary Southwest art, American Indian jewelry, pottery.
Heather Gallery, 555 E. Durant Ave. Contemporary American art, crafts and woodworking.
Joanne Lyon Gallery, 525 E. Cooper Ave. Art Gallery.
The Thundercloud Corporation, American Indian Art.

Boulder:

University of Colorado Museum, Henderson Bldg. Prehistoric life from the Plains and Southwest. Geological exhibits, art gallery, other displays. Open Mon-Fri 9am-5pm. Free.
Pioneer Museum, 1655 Broadway. Open daily in the summer 2pm-5pm and weekend rest of the year. Small admission charged.
Friske Planetarium, University of Colorado, Boulder Campus. Call 492-5001 for show times.

Canon City:

Canon City Municipal Museum, 612 Royal Gorge Blvd. Exhibits on the history of the area. Open Mon-Sat 9am-5pm, Sun 1pm-5pm. Free.
Robinson Mansion, 12 Riverside Dr. Restored 1884 home with period furnishings. Open mid-April to mid-Nov. Tues-Sun 9am-6pm, mid-Nov to mid-April weekends only 1pm-5pm.

Central City:

Central Gold Mine and Museum, 126 Spring St. Open daily May-Sept. 9am-5pm. Mine tour given. Admission charged.
Central City Opera House and **Teller House,** Eureka St. Both are restored historic buildings.

Colorado Springs:

Pioneers' Museum, 25 W. Kiowa St. Artifacts from Pikes Peak area, Indian displays. Open Tue-Sat 10am-5pm, Sun 2pm-5pm. Free.
El Pomar Carriage House Museum, Lake Ave. Vehicles, saddles, riding accessories of 1890's. Open Tue-Sun 10am-5pm. Free.
Colorado Springs Fine Arts Center, 30 W. Dale St. Prehistoric art of the Southwest, other collections. Open Tue-Sat 9am-5pm, Sun 1.30pm-5pm. Free.
Manitou Cliff Dwellings Museum, U.S. 24 Bypass. Open daily in the summer 9am-5pm (except Fri.), closed Oct-mid-May. Small admission charged.
Hall of Presidents, 1050 S. 21st St. 100. Wax figures of America's greatest and historical figures. Open 10am-5pm daily.
National Carvers Museum, 14960 Woodcarver Rd, 10 miles (16 kms) N. on I-25. Woodcarving exhibits and demonstrations. Open Mon-Sat 9am-5pm, Sun 10.30am-5pm. Admission charged.
Clock Museum, 21st St. at Bott Ave. Over 100 clocks. Open summers 9am-sunset. Admission charged.
Colorado Car Museum, 137 Manitou Ave. Cars of 1900 and custom built cars belonging to celebrities. Open May-Sept. Mon-Sat. 9am-5pm, Sun 10.30am-5pm. Oct-Apr. Sat & Sun 1pm-5pm. Admission charged.
May Natural History Museum of the Tropics, 8 miles (13 kms) SW on SR 115. Tropical invertebrates from all over the world. Open May-Sept. 8am-9pm. Admission charged.
U.S. Airforce Academy, 10 miles (16 kms) N. on I-25. Visitor Center has films, displays, self guided auto tour. Open daily 8am-5pm. Free.

Cripple Creek:

Cripple Creek Museum, on SR 67. Relics from this old gold town. Open end-May to early-Oct. Daily 10am-5.30pm., weekends only in the winter. Small admission charged.
The Imperial Hotel, Restored historic hotel.

Denver:

Celebrity Sports Center, 888 South Colorado Blvd. 755-3312. Family Recreation: Bowling, swimming, year round water-slides, arcades, restaurants, bar, free childcare.
Colorado Renaissance Festival, 2660 S. Monaco, Denver, CO 80222. 756-1501. In Larkspur, a re-creation of a 16th Century European marketplace.

Weekends — June and July.

Civic Center Park, Fountains, monuments, outdoor Greek Theater, pleasant center of the city.

Colorado State Capitol, 30 Broadway and Colfax. Panoramic view of Denver and mountains. Free tours weekdays 9-3.

Confluence Park, 15th St. and South Platte River. Man made river, spot where Denver started in 1858.

Coors Brewery, 12th and East St., Golden, CO. 12 miles west of Denver. Free tours and samples at one of the nation's largest breweries.

Denver Botanic Gardens, 1005 York St. Over 800 species of native and exotic plants. Open 9am-4.45pm. Admission free.

Denver's Zoo, at City Park off 23rd Ave. Modern Zoo with over 1500 specimens, beautiful setting. Open 10am-5pm winter, 10am-6pm summer. Admission free.

Elitch Gardens Amusement Park, W. 38th at Tennyson, 455-4771. Top rated roller coaster, flower gardens, log flume and amusement park rides and games. Open weekends in May, at noon June-Labor Day. Admission free.

Heritage Square, South of Golden on US Hwy 40. Reconstructed Colorado City from 1870's with crafts shops, restaurants, alpine slides and amusement rides. Open year round. Admission free.

Hyland Hills Water World, 90th Ave and Pecos St., Federal Heights, CO 80221, 427-SURF. One of America's largest water theme Parks. Open Memorial Day-Labor Day. Features 5 foot waves and 14 water slides.

Lakeside Amusement Park, W. 44th Ave. and Sheridan Blvd. Forty major rides, games, speedway for stock cars. Open weekends in May, June-Labor Day. Admission free.

Larimer Square, 1400 block of Larimer St. Restored section of Denver's oldest street with courtyards, gas lamps, Victorian buildings, shops, outdoor cafes, nightclubs, restaurants, special events. Shops open in the evening. Free walking tour brochure available in shops.

Molly Brown House, 1340 Pennsylvania. Unusual Victorian House that belonged to the "Unsinkable Molly Brown" heroine of the Titanic disaster. Closed Mon. in the winter. Admission free.

Red Rocks Amphitheater, North of Morrison on Hogback Rd. 12 miles West of Denver. An amphitheater that accommodates 8,000 set between 400 foot high red sandstone rocks. Panoramic views. Summer concerts. Free admisson except when there is a performance.

Sakura Square, 19th St. and Lawrence. An entire block of oriental shops and restaurants surrounded by authentic Japanese gardens.

16th Street Mall, 16th St. from Broadway to Market St. Mile-long, tree-lined pedestrian path with stores, shops, restaurants and cafes. Twelve fountains, special events, free shuttle bus rides.

United States Mint, W. Colfax and Cherokee St. Largest Depository of gold outside Fort Knox. The Mint produces 5 billion coins annually. Free 20 minute tours. 8am-5pm weekdays, 9am-1pm Sun in summer, 9am-5pm Sat.

Denver Art Museum, 100 W. 14th St. 10-storey, 28-sided structure covered with a million sparkling tiles, contains the world's greatest collection of American Indian artworks, and 35000 art objects in seven curatorial departments. Open Tue-Sat 9am-5pm, Wed 9am-8pm, Sun noon-5pm. Closed Mon. 575-2793. Admission free.

Museum of Western Art, 1727 Tremont Pl. 296-1880. Located in a one time gambling den and brothel, this new museum has over 125 classical paintings and bronzes by artists like Remmington, Russel, Moran, Bierstadt and Georgia O'Keeffe. Tue-Fri 10am-6pm, Sat 10am-5pm, Sun-Mon 1pm-5pm. Admission free.

Trianan Art Museum and Gallery, 335 14th St. 623-0739. European Masterpieces and Oriental art treasures. Fine selection in sales gallery. Mon-Sat 10am-4pm. Admission free.

Buffalo Bill's Grave and Museum, Top of Lookout Mountain exit 256 off I-70 West of Denver. Panoramic View from grave site. Summer 8am-5pm, Winter 9am-5pm. Closed Mon. Admission free.

The Children's Museum, 2121, Crescent Dr. New and modern museum for kids of all ages. TV Station, "hands-on" exhibits, super market, and 80,000 plastic balls. Call for hours. 571-5198. Admission free.

Colorado Historical Society, 1300 Broadway. A fabulous $22 million facility traces the colorful history of the Indians, goldminers and settlers of the Rockies. Exhibits, graphics, and dioramas. Tue-Sat 10am-4.30pm, Sun 12pm-4.30pm. Closed Mon. Admission free.

Colorado Railroad Museum, 17155 W. 44th. 279-4591. Largest Railroad Museum in the Rockies. Open daily year round, 9am-5pm.

Denver Firefighters Museum and Restaurant, 1326 Tremont Pl. 892-1436. Collection of antique firefighting equipment. Open for tours, lunch and private parties. Mon-Fri 11am-2pm.

Denver Museum of Natural History, City Park. Seventh largest museum in USA and one of the great natural history museums of the world. Over 70 dioramas of international animals and hundreds of exhibits. Also includes the **Imax Theater** using the world's largest movie projection equipment on a 4.5x6.5 story screen: and **Charles C. Gates Planetarium** which offers a variety of changing shows. Open 9am-5pm daily. Call 370-6300 for show times. Admission free for all three.

Forney Transportation Museum, 1416 Platte. 433-3643. Excellent collection of 300 cars, carriages, cycles, steam engines, rail coaches and "Big Boy" locomotive. Take I-25 to exit 211, 5 blocks East. Mon-Sat 10am-5pm, Sun 11am-5.30pm. Admission free.

Four Mile Historic Park, 715 S. Forest St. 399-1859. Restoration of this former stage coach stop on the Cherokee Trail. Oldest home in Denver, working farm.

Grant Humphrey's Mansion, 770 Pennsylvania St. 866-3507. Turn-of-the-century mansion built by former Governor Grant. Mon-Fri 9am-3pm. Can be rented for private receptions. Admission free.

Pearce McAllister Cottage, 1880 Gaylord St. 1899 Dutch Colonial Revival Architecture and original interior furnishings, historical.

Arvada Center for the Arts and Humanities, 6901 Wadsworth Blvd. 422-8050. Nationally known artists perform in this beautiful arts center. Symphony, dance, theater, historical museum, art gallery and special events. Call for schedule.

Central City Opera Festival, Historic opera house in gold mining town of Central City offers great performances. Runs July and Aug. Call 571-4435 for schedule.

Colorado Shakespeare Festival, University of Colorado, Boulder. Outdoor theater. July and Aug. Call 492-8181 for schedule.

Denver Center for the Performing Arts, 14th and Curtis. A four-square block complex larger than the Lincoln Center in New York. Includes **Denver Center Theater Company,** the largest resident acting company in the West. Produces a season of eight plays on three stages. **Denver Center Cinema** screening 500 films a year, and hosts performances by **Opera Colorado and Colorado Ballet.**

Center Attractions, brings touring Broadway shows to the Auditorium Theater. Free tours of the complex on weekdays at 12.15pm. Box office 893-4100.

Turner Museum, 773 Downing St. 832-0924. Prints by British artist J.M.W. Turner and American artist Thomas Moran. Open Sun 1pm to 6pm., and by appointment.

Durango:

Joy Cabin, 23rd St. and Main. 247-0312. First home built in Durango furnished with antiques. Call for a guided tour.

Southwest Studies Center, Library Bldg., Fort Lewis College, 247-7928. Museum and study materials from the Southwestern United States. Mon-Fri 8am to 5pm.

Top Atin Gallery, 145 W. 9th St. Large collection of Indian modern art, jewelery, pottery and Navajo rugs and weavings.

Estes Park:

Estes Park Museum, 200 4th St., Estes Park, 586-6256. Exhibits of local authors, artists and musicians. Call for tour or research.

Eureka:

Clarke Memorial Museum, 240 E. St. Fossils, minerals, Indian artifacts, local historical materials. Open Tue-Sat 10am to 4pm. Closed holidays, free admission.

Fort Collins:

Pioneer Museum, 219 Peterson St. Prehistoric & contemporary Indian displays. Local historic items. Open Tue-Sat 1pm-5pm. Free.

Grand Junction:

Historical Museum and Institute of Western Colorado, 4th and Ute St. Geological, anthropological and historical displays. Open June-Nov. Tues-Sat 10am-5pm, Sun 2pm-5pm. Free.

Greeley:

Meeker Memorial Museum, 1324 9th Ave. Meeker's home containing personal and historical belongings.

Open Mon-Fri 9am-noon, and 1pm-5pm. Free.

Municipal Museum, new city complex. Local history. Open 9am-5pm, Mon-Fri. (closed noon-1pm for lunch).

Leadville:

Tabor Home, 116 E. 5th St. Restored historical home. Open daily Memorial Day-Labor Day, 8.30am-8pm. Rest of the year 9.30am-5.30pm. Small admission.

Tabor Opera House, 308 Harrison Ave. Guided tours. Memorial Day-Oct, Sun-Fri 9am-5.30pm. Small admission.

Healy House and Dexter Cabin, 912 Harrison Ave. Restored historical buildings. Open June-mid-Oct, daily 9am-4.30pm. Free.

Heritage Museum and Gallery, 9th & Harrison. Period costumes, Leadville's history in dioramas, mining, geological and other displays. Contemporary Western artists. Open Memorial Day-early Sept daily, 10am-9pm. Admission charged.

Longmont:

Pioneer Museum, 302 Kimbark. Open Mon-Sat 9am-5pm, Sun 1pm-5pm. Free.

Montrose:

Ute Indian Museum, 2 miles S. (3.5 kms) on U.S. 550. History of Ute Indians in dioramas, photos, prehistoric material and Indian artifacts. Open May-mid-Oct daily 9am-5pm. Free.

Pueblo:

El Pueblo State Historical Museum, 905 S. Praire Ave. Local history, iron and steel industry. Open Tue-Fri 9am-5pm. Sun and some holidays 10am-5pm.

Pueblo Metropolitan Museum, 419 W. 14th St. 37 roomed brick mansion of 1891. Open June-Sept 1st, Tue-Sat 9am-5pm. Sun and holidays 2pm-5pm. Sept-June 1st, Tue-Sun 1pm-4pm. Admission charged.

Sterling:

Overland Trail Museum, 1.5 miles (2.4 kms) E. on U.S.6. Local pioneer exhibits. Open late-Apr to late-Sept. Mon-Sat 9.30am-5pm. Sun 10.30am-5pm. Free.

Snowmass:

Anderson Ranch Arts Museum, 5263 Owl Creek Rd. Art, photography, ceramics, ... Open Mon-Sun from 9am-5pm.

Vail:

Colorado Ski Museum and Ski Hall of Fame Inc., 15 Vail Rd, Vail. History of skiing from 1800 to today. Includes Ski Hall of Fame, ski exhibits and equipment.

Idaho

Boise:

Boise State Capitol, 8th and Jefferson St. Houses changing exhibits. Open 8am-6pm daily. Admission free.
Boise Art Gallery, Julia Davis Park. Idaho artists, European, Oriental and American painting and sculpture. Open Tue-Sun, 10am-5pm. Admission free.
Idaho State Historical Society, 610 N. Julia Davis Dr. Pioneer and Indian life, outdoor display. Open Mon-Fri 9am-5pm; Sat, Sun 1pm-5pm. Admission free.

Franklin:

Pioneer Relic Hall, Contains early artifacts, a steam engine Brigham Young shipped up the Missouri River. Open Mon-Fri 9am-5pm. Admission free.

Idaho City:

Boise Basin Museum, Montgomery and Wall St. Small gold rush museum. Open Memorial Day — Sept. Free.

Kellogg:

Catalado Mission, 11 m W. off US 10 to Catalado Mission of the Sacred Heart 1848. Indian murals and handprints. Hand carved altar. Open mid-April-Sept. 9am-dark. Small admission. Will open on request.

Montpelier:

Daughters of Utah Pioneers Historical Museum, 430 Clay St. Open June-Aug, Mon-Sat 4pm-9pm. Admission free.

Moscow:

Latah County Museum, 110 S. Adams. 1880 Victorian mansion, houses, dioramas, and artifacts illustrating local history. Open Wed and Sun 2pm-5pm. Sat 10am-noon. Admission charged.
Appaloosa Horse Museum, Pullman Highway. Saddles and cowboy gear, Nez Perce artifacts. Open Mon-Fri 8am-5pm. Admission free.

Pocatello:

Bannock County Historical Society, Center St. and Garfield Ave. Early railroad, fur trade and Shoshone artifacts. Open Mon-Sat 2pm-5pm. Admission free.

Old Fort Hall Replica, Ross Park, 3 m S. at 2nd Ave. Historic displays of houses, shops and buildings in the Fort. Open June-mid-Sept daily 9am-8pm. April and May Wed-Sun 9am-1pm. Admission free.
Idaho State University houses a **Museum** and **Art Gallery.**

Twin Falls:

Twin Falls County Historical Museum, 3 m W. on US 30. Pioneer life exhibits. Open Mon-Fri 10am-5pm, Sun 2pm-5pm. Small admission.
Herret Arts and Science, 1220 Kimberly Rd. Open Mon-Sat 9am-6pm. Museum, planetarium and observatory open on request.

Wallace:

Coeur d'Alene District Mining Museum, 509 Bank St. Open Mon-Fri 10am-4pm, June-Aug Mon-Sat 9am-6pm. Mine tours and Ghost town tours available nearby.

Weiser:

Historical Museum and National Fiddlers' Hall of Fame, 44 W. Commercial St. contains local historic and folk music exhibits. Open June-Labor Day Thur-Sat 10-noon and 1pm-4pm. Admission free.

Montana

Billings:

Yellowstone County Museum, On SR3 at Logan Int. Airport. Pioneer and Indian artifacts, old vehicles. Western Heritage Center. 2822 Montana Ave., Billings. Collection of Western History and Indian artifacts. Open Tue-Sat 10.30-noon. 1pm-5pm on Sun 2pm-5pm. Free admission.

Bozeman:

Museum of the Rockies, Montana State University. S. 7th and Kagy Blvd. Bozeman. Physical and social heritage of Northern Rockies. Open Mon-Fri 8am-5pm. Sat-Sun 1pm-5pm. Admission free. Closed hols and school vacation.

Browning:

Blackfeet Indian Reservation Museum of Plains Indian and Crafts Center (headquarters), Half mile W. at Jct US2 89: Displays costumes, beadwork, carvings and other Blackfeet artifacts. Crafts for sale. Nearby is the **Museum of Montana Wildlife,** Dioramas, paintings and sculptures. Open early May-Sept daily 7am-5pm. Admission charged.

Butte:

World Museum of Mining, W. Park Rd., Butte. Mining displays, reconstructed mining camp, saloon, other buildings. Open June-Sept. daily 9am-9pm. Oct-May 10am-5pm. Admission free.
Copper King Mansion, 219 W. Granite St., Butte. Victorian home.

Dillon:

Beaverhead County Museum, 15 S. Montana St., Dillon. Indian and Pioneer artifacts, gold mining relics. Open mid June-Aug daily 9am-5pm. Sept-mid-June, Mon-Fri 9am-5pm.

Glaslow:

Pioneer Museum, half mile W. on US2. Indian artifacts and Pioneer Displays. Open June thru Labor Day Mon-Sat, 9am-9pm. Admission free.

Great Falls:

Charles M. Russell Museum and Original Studio, 1201 4th Ave. N., Great Falls. Home of famous cowboy artist. Excellent collection of Russell paintings. Log studio, Indian and cowboy artifacts. Open mid-May thru mid-Sept Mon-Sat 10am-5pm. Sun 1pm-5pm. Rest of the year open Tue-Sat 10am-5pm Sun 1pm-5pm. Small admission.

Havre:

H. Earl Clack Memorial Museum, On US 2 in Hill County Fairgrounds. Indian exhibits, archeological and geological displays, frontier life, buffalo era. Open Memorial Day-Labor Day, daily 9am-10pm. Admission free.
Glacier National Park Museum, W. Glacier. History of Glacier National Park.

Helena:

Montana Historical Museum and C.M. Russell Gallery, 225 N. Roberts Rd., Helena, across from the Capitol. Montana prehistory to now. Charlie Russell collection. Historical library. Open Mon-Fri 8am-5pm (8am-8pm summer), Sat, Sun and hols noon-5pm. Admission free.
Last Chance Train Tour, Runs daily from here in the summer to major points of interest.
Canyon Ferry Arms Museum, 10 ml E. on US 12, then 9 ml N. on SR 284 to Canyon Ferry Rec. Area. Indian and military artifacts. Open May-mid-Oct daily 9am-9pm. Admission free.
In Helena other interesting buildings are **Governor's Mansion, St. Helena Cathedral, Northwestern Bank Pioneer Cabin** and **Kluge House.** Nearby Ghost town Marysville.

Kalispell:

Hockaday Art Center, 3rd St. and 2nd Ave. Open Mon-Sat noon-5pm. Admission free. Travelling exhibits. **Conrad Mansion,** Woodland Ave. Restored 1895 mansion.

Miles City:

Range Riders Museum, W. on US 10, 12. Westward expansion and ranching memorabilia. Open daily June-Aug 8am-8pm. Apr-May and Sept-Oct 8am-6pm. Small Admission.

Missoula:

Gallery of Visual Arts, Turner Hall on Unversity of Montana campus. Exhibits local work. Open Mon-Fri 10am-5pm. Sat and Sun 2pm-5pm. Admission free.
Missoula Museum of the Arts, 335 N. Patte, Missoula.
Fort Missoula Historical Museum, Fort Missoula

Bldg. 322 W. of S. Ave. Displays of Missoula timber industry, military commerce and agriculture.

Red Lodge:

Big Sky Historical Museum, S. of town on US 212. Indian and Pioneer artifacts, gun display. Open June-mid-Sept daily 8am-9pm. Admission free.

Virginia City:

Thompson Hickman Memorial Museum, Wallace St. Relics of Gold Days. **Virginia City-Madison County Historical Museum,** Wallace St. Exhibits on area history. Open daily 8am-6pm May-Sept.

Wolf Point:

Wolf Point Historical Museum, 220 S. 2nd Ave. Indian and ranching exhibits. Open mid May thru Sept. Mon-Fri 10am-6pm. Admission free.
Poplar Museum, 21 miles E. on US2 in Poplar. A former jail. Displays Indian artifacts, arts and crafts. Open June-Aug daily, small admission.

Utah

Brigham City:

Railroad Museum, located 7 miles (11 kms) W. on SR 83 in Corinne. Railroad cars, caboose, locomotives, photos and memorabilia, blacksmith shop. Open May thru' Sept. Tue-Sat 9am-5pm, Sun 2pm-5pm. Admission fee.
Golden Spike National Historic Site, 30 miles (48 kms) W. via SR 83 & unnumbered road to Promontory. Visitor Center with exhibits, film, self guided tour. Open daily June-Aug 8am-6pm, Sept-May 8am-4.30pm.

Cedar City:

Palmer Memorial Museum, 75 N. 300 W. Piute basketry, beadwork, other artifacts. Open 8am-5pm Mon-Fri. (closed holidays) Free.
Museum of Southern Utah, W. of Main St. on Center St. (College Campus). Indian and pioneer artifacts. Open Mon-Sat 9am-5pm. Closed hols.

Logan:

Daughters of Utah Pioneers Museum, 52 W. 2nd North St. Displays of Mormon pioneers. Open early-June to late-Sept. Mon-Fri 1pm-5pm or by appointment. Free.
Man and His Bread & Historical Farm, 5 miles (8 kms) S. on U.S.89,91. Illustrates development of agriculture. Open daily in the summer.

Ogden:

Daughters of Utah Pioneer Relic Hall, Tabernacle Sq. 2150 Grant Ave. Pioneer furnishings and relics. Open June-Sept. Mon-Fri 1pm-4.30pm. Free.
John M. Browning Gun Collection, 4 miles (7 kms) south on U.S. 89 at 450 E. 5100 S. Past and current models of Browning firearms. Open Mon-Sat 8am-5pm, closed holidays. Free.

Price:

Prehistoric Museum, City Hall, Main & E. St. Open June-Aug. Mon-Sat 8.30am-9pm, Sept-May Mon-Fri 9am-5pm. Free.

Provo:

Pioneer Museum, 500 N. 500 W. Pioneer artifacts of the region, pioneer village. Open June-mid-Sept daily 9am-5pm. Free.
Fairview Museum of History and Art, 46 miles (74 kms) S. on U.S. 89 in Fairview. Pioneer relics, old vehicles, Indian artifacts, paintings, sculptures, carvings. Open April-Oct. Tues-Sat 10am-5pm, Sun 2pm-5pm. Free.

St. George:

Daughters of Utah Pioneers Museum, McQuarrie Memorial Bldg. 145 N. 100 E. Photos and relics of pioneers, who lived in primitive dwellings attempting to start a cotton industry. Free. Open June-Aug. Mon-Sat 7pm-9pm. Rest of the year by appointment.

Salt Lake City:

All attractions are downtown within 1.5 mile (2 km) area.
Salt Lake Art Center, Northeast entrance on West Temple. Changing art exhibits, sculpture court, art, photography, weekend films and lectures. Open Mon-Sat 10am-5pm. Sun 1pm-5pm.
Symphony Hall, home of Utah symphony, interesting architecture. Free tours. Call 533-5626 for schedule. Box office 533-6407.
Museum of Church History and Art, Paintings, sculpture, historical memorabilia, open April-Dec. 9am-9pm; 10am-7pm. 531-3310. Admission free.
Temple Square, center of Salt Lake City. Free tours of the Tabernacle, North and South Visitors Centers, daily every 15 minutes between 8am-8.30pm (in summer) and 9am-7.30pm (in winter). Mormon Tabernacle Choir rehearsals Thursday 8pm, Sunday morning broadcasts are open to the public. (Be in your seat at 9.20am.)
Beehive House, Brigham Young's official family residence, a National Historic Landmark, beautifully restored home with artifacts of the period. Open Mon-Sat 9.30am-4.30pm, Sun mid-day tours. Admission free.
LDS Church Office Building, extensive library for genealogical researchers. Open Mon 7.30am-6pm, Tuesday-Fri 7.30am-10pm, Sat 7.30am-5pm. Tours of building, including 26th floor observation deck are available free. Call for details. 531-2190.
Hansen Planetarium, one of the finest planetariums in the world, largest of its kind between Denver and the West Coast. Facility has a space science library and museum. Open Mon-Sat. Admission charged.
Promised Valley Playhouse, multi million dollar restoration of a famous 19th century theatre. Playhouse has a full season of live music and dramatic productions from Sept to May. Summer offers a production of a family oriented musical Tue-Sat at 7.30pm free of charge. Tickets at Temple Square Visitor's Center. Box Office 364-5678. Tours

of the restored theater can be arranged, call 364-5697.
Liberty Park, from 900 to 1300 South, from 500 to 700 East, beautifully landscaped grounds, swimming, tennis, playground, and children's amusement park. Close to the Chase Mill, Brigham Young Home and the **Tracy Aviary.** This 11 acre (4.5 ha) aviary is the home of hundreds of birds including the rare Andean condor and many waterfowl specimens. Open at 9.30am daily. Closes at 8.30pm-summer; 6pm fall and spring; 4.50pm-winter. Admission free.
Hogle Zoological Gardens, this zoo is the home of over 1000 animals from all over the world. Open daily at 9am. Closes at 6pm-summer; 4.30pm-winter.
Utah Museum of Fine Arts, public general art gallery. Special collections include Navajo textiles, Southeast Asian sculptures, Japanese screens and prints, ceramics. Open Mon-Fri 10am-5pm, weekends 2pm-5pm. Admission free. 581-7332.
Utah Museum of Natural History, on the University of Utah campus. Halls of minerals, biology, geology and earth science. Open Mon-Sat 9.30am-5.30pm. Sun noon-5pm. Sun noon-5pm. 581-6827.
Utah State Capitol, an attractive building, Corinthian style of marble and granite capped with a huge copper covered dome. Open Mon-Fri 8.30am-5pm and summer weekends 9.30am-6pm. Tour available. Admission free. 533-5900.
Pioneer Memorial Museum, thirty seven exhibit rooms. Dolls, handmade textiles, period furniture, artifacts. Open Mon-Sat 9am-5pm, and Sun afternoons from May-Oct. Admission free. 533-5759.

Vernal:

Utah Field House of Natural History, 235 E. Main St. Outstanding museum with life size models of dinosaurs. Displays on basketmaking, prehistoric cultures, fossils, minerals, pioneer artifacts, regional wildlife. Open daily 9am-6pm. Summer hours 8am-9pm. Admission free.
Thorne's Photo Studio, 18 W. Main St. Tools and prehistoric artifacts of Utah. Open Tue-Sat 9am to 6pm. Closed holidays, admission free.

Wyoming

Wyoming Pioneer Memorial Museum, Wyoming State Fair Grounds, Douglas, WY 82633. Indian and artifacts, firearms, photos, antique cars. Open Mon-Fri 9am-5pm., Sat and Sun 1pm-5pm. April through Nov., Mon-Fri 9am-5pm Dec-March. Admission free.

Fort Bridger:

Fort Bridger State Historic site, Fort Bridger, WY 82933. State Historic Site. Military and Indian artifacts. Open mid-May to mid-Oct daily 9am-6pm. Weekends only mid-Oct to mid-May. Admission free.

Fort Laramie:

Fort Laramie National Historic Site, Fort Laramie, WY 82212. 15,000 item museum of military artifacts, Indian artifacts and a 3000 book Western Library. Open Memorial Day thru Labor Day 8am-8pm. Labor Day thru Memorial Day 8am-4.30pm. Admission free.

Grand Teton National Park, Moose Visitor Center, Jenny Lake Visitor Center, Colter Bay Visitor Center Indian Arts Museum.

Jackson:

Jackson Hole Historical Museum, 105 N. Glenwood, P.O. Box 1005, Jackson, WY 83001. Artifacts of mountainmen and Indians. Open daily 9am-9pm. Admission adults $1.75, children under 6 free.

Lander:

Pioneer Museum, 630 Lincoln St., Lander, WY 82520. Old West artifacts. Mon-Sat 9am-6pm., Sun 3pm-6pm. June thru Oct 1pm-4pm. Oct-June (except Mon and holidays).

South Pass City State Historic Site, Route 62, Box 164, Lander, WY 82520. Historic mining town. Open daily 9am-6pm mid-May thru mid-Oct. Admission free.

Laramie:

Laramie Plains Museum, 603 Ivinson Ave., Laramie, WY 82070. Historical and cultural collection, photographs and manuscripts. Open 9am-noon and 1pm-4pm (summer) 2pm-4pm Feb-Dec. Admission adults $1.50, 6-16 years 50¢.

Rocky Mountain Herbarium, Third Floor, Aven Nelson Bldg., University of Wyoming, Laramie, WY 82070. 350000 plant specimens. Open 8am-5pm (Academic year) Mon-Fri 7.30am-4.30pm (summers) Mon-Fri. Admission free. Guided tours on request.

Lusk:

Stage Coach Museum, 342 S. Main, Lusk, WY 82225. Relics of Pioneer Days. Concord Stage Coach from Cheyenne-Dreadwood run. Indian artifacts. Call (307) 334-3444 for hours. Admission adults 50¢.

Buffalo:

Johnson County Jim Gatchelle Memorial Museum, 110 Fort St., Buffalo, WY 82834. Dioramas of Johnson County Cattle War of 1892, Indian artifacts, pictures. Open 9am to 9pm. June to Labor Day. Admission free.

Casper:

Old Fort Casper Museum, 14 Fort Casper Rd., Casper, WY 82601. Historic site, Artifacts relating to Fort Casper, Central Wyoming, reconstructed log structures. Open all year, 10am to 5pm. Admission free.

Nicolaysen Art Museum, 104 Rancho Rd., Casper, WY 82601. Tue-Sat 11.30am-4.30pm.

Cheyenne:

Warren Military Museum, Bldg. 210, F.E. Warren AFB, WY 82001. Memorial Day-Labor Day 1pm-4pm Mon, Wed, Fri and Sun. Open all year on Sun 1pm to 4pm. Admission free. Military Uniforms, 19th century artifacts.

Wyoming State Museum, Barret Bldg., 24th and Central. Cheyenne, WY 82002. Art, Ethnographic material, historical material, gift shop. Open Mon-Fri 8am-5pm. Sat 1pm-5pm. Sun (summer only). Admission free.

National First Day Cover Museum, 702 Randall Blvd., Cheyenne, WY 82001. Rare first day covers, stamps, flags of 50 States. Open Mon-Sat 9am-5pm. Admission free.

Wyoming State Capitol, Cheyenne, WY 82001. Open Mon-Sat 8am-5pm. Guided tours every 30 minutes in the summer. Admission free.

Cody:

Buffalo Bill Historical Center, P.O. Box 1000, Cody, WY 82414. (307) 587-4771. Fire arms, Indian art and artifacts, Buffalo Bill memorabilia, Western art and sculpture...one of the best museums in the world. Call for hours. Admission adults $4.50, 6-12 years $2. Under 6 years free.

Old West Trail Town, One mile West of Cody. Frontier era buildings, cabins and horse drawn vehicles.

Douglas:

Fort Fetterman State Historic Site, Route 3, P.O. Box 6, Douglas, WY 82633. State Historic Site. Open mid-May — Labour Day 9am-6pm. Admission free.

Riverton:

Riverton Museum, 700 East Park, Riverton, WY 82501. Shoshone and Arapaho relics. Homestead cabin. Open daily June thru Sept 11am-6pm. Oct thru May 10am-4pm. Admission free.

Sheridan:

The Sheridan Inn, Box 781, 5th and Broadway. Sheridan, WY 82801. Historic Site. Antiques and Art gallery. Open daily 10am-10pm year round. Admission free.

Medicine Wheel, on US 14A in Big Horn National Forest. Amazing construction in stone of almost perfect circle 70 feet (20 meters) across 28 stone spokes radiate like a wheel. Unknown origin.

Wyoming National Guard Museum, Buffalo Star Route, Box 57, Sheridan, WY 82801. National Guard artifacts, flags, uniforms, museum education. Open Mon-Fri 8am-5pm. Admission free.

Sundance:

Crook County Museum, Sundance, WY 82442. General Wyoming history, Art Gallery. Open Mon-Fri 9am-5pm. Admission free.

Thermopolis:

Hot Springs County Museum, 700 Broadway. Thermopolis, WY 82443. Indian relics, fossils, minerals. Open Mon-Sat 10am-8pm, Sun 1pm-5pm (June thru Labor Day). Daily 1pm-5pm (Labor Day thru

May 31). Admission free.
Yellowstone National Park, Albright Visitor Center, Canyon Visitor Center, Fishing Bridger Museum, Madison Explorer's Museum, Norris Museum, Grant Village, Mammoth Hot Springs Visitor Center. Admission free.

National Forest

Idaho

Clearwater National Forest, Orofino, ID 83544.
Coeur d'Alene National Forest, Coeur d'Alene, ID 83814.
Kaniksu National Forest, Coeur d'Alene, ID 83814.
St. Joe National Forest, Coeur d'Alene, ID 83814.
Nezperce National Forest, Grangeville, ID 83530.
Boise National Forest, Boise, ID 83702.
Caribou National Forest, Pocatello, ID 83201.
Challis National Forest, Challis, ID 83226.
Payette National Forest, McCall, ID 83638.
Salmon National Forest, Salmon, ID 83467.
Sawtooth National Forest, Twin Falls, ID 83301.
Targhee National Forest, St. Anthony, ID 83445.

Montana

Beaverhead National Forest, Dillon, MT 59725.
Bitterroot National Forest, Hamilton, MT 59840.
Custer National Forest, Billings, MT 59103.
Deerlodge National Forest, Butte, MT 59703.
Flathead National Forest, Kalispell, MT 59901.
Gallatin National Forest, Bozeman, MT 59715.
Helena National Forest, Helena, MT 59626.
Kootenai National Forest, Libby, MT 59923.
Lewis & Clark National Forest, Great Falls, MT 59403.
Lolo National Forest, Missoula, MT 59801.

Colorado

Arapahoe National Forest, Ft. Collins, CO 80526.
Roosevelt National Forest, Ft. Collins, CO 80526.
Grand Mesa National Forest, Delta, CO 81416.
Uncompahgre National Forest, Delta, CO 81416.
Gunnison National Forest, Delta, CO 81416.
Pike National Forest, Pueblo, CO 81008.
San Isabel National Forest, Pueblo, CO 81008.
Rio Grande National Forest, Monte Vista, CO 81144.
Routt National Forest, Steamboat Springs, CO 80477.
San Juan National Forest, Durango, CO 81301.
White River National Forest, Glenwood Springs, CO 81602.

Wyoming

Bighorn National Forest, Sheridan, WY 82801.
Medicine Bow National Forest, Laramie, WY 82070.
Shoshone National Forest, Cody, WY 82414.
Bridger National Forest, Jackson, WY 83001.
Teton National Forest, Jackson, WY 83001.

Utah

Ashley National Forest, Vernal, UT 84078.
Dixie National Forest, Cedar City, UT 84720.
Fishlake National Forest, Richfield, UT 84701.

Manti National Forest, Price, UT 84501.
LaSal National Forest, Price, UT 84501.
Uinta National Forest, Provo, UT 84603.
Wasatch National Forest, Salt Lake City, UT 84138.
Cache National Forest, Salt Lake City, UT 84138.

National Monuments, Historic Sites and Recreation Areas

Colorado

Bent's Old Fort National Historic Site, 35110 Hwy. 194 East, La Junita, CO 81050-0523.
Black Canyon of the Gunnison National Monument, P.O. Box 1648, Montrose, CO 81402.
Colorado National Monument, Fruita, CO 81521.
Curicanti National Recreation Area, P.O. Box 1040, Gunnison, CO 81230.
Dinosaur National Monument, (Colorado and Utah) Box 210, Dinosaur, CO 81610.
Florissant Fossil Beds National Monument, P.O. Box 185, Florissant, CO 80816.
Great Sand Dunes National Monument, Mosca, CO 81146.
Hovenweep National Monument (Colorado and Utah) c/o Mesa Verde National Park, CO 81330.

Idaho

Craters of the Moon National Monument, P.O. Box 29, Arco, ID 83213.
Nez Perce National Historical Park, P.O. Box 93, Spalding, ID 83551.
Atomic Energy National Historic Landmark, West of Idaho Falls. (The world's first Breeder Reactor #1.)
Hells Canyon Recreation Area, Hellsgate State Park, Information Center, Lewiston. (Best viewed via jet or float boat.)
Sawtooth National Recreational Area, Stanley, ID. (Over half a million acres of recreational paradise.)

Montana

Big Hole National Battlefield, P.O. Box 237, Wisdom, MT 59761-0237.
Big Horn Canyon National Recreation Area, (Montana and Wyoming) P.O. Box 458, Fort Smith, MT 59035.
Custer Battlefield National Monument, P.O. Box 39, Crow Agency, MT 59022.
Grant-Kohrs Ranch National Historic Site, P.O. Box 790, Deer Lodge, MT 59722. (216 acre historic ranch with demonstrations and tours.)

Utah

Cedar Breaks National Monument, P.O. Box 749, Cedar City, UT 84720.
Glen Canyon National Recreation Area, (Utah and Arizona) P.O. Box 1507, Page, AZ 86040.
Golden Spike National Historic Site, P.O. Box 394, Brigham City, UT 84302.
Natural Bridges National Monument, c/o Canyonlands National Park, 446 S. Main St., Moab, UT 84532.

Rainbow Bridge National Monument, c/o Glen
Canyon National Recreation Area, P.O. Box 1507,
Page, AZ 86040.
Timpanogos Cave National Monument, R.R.3 Box
200, American Fork, UT 84003.
Flaming Gorge National Recreation Area, P.O. Box
278, Manilla, UT 84046.

Wyoming

Devil's Tower National Monument, Devil's Tower,
WY 82714.
Fossil Butte National Monument, P.O. Box 527,
Kemmerer, WY 83101.
John D. Rockerfeller Jr Memorial Parkway, c/o
Grand Teton National Park, P.O. Box Drawer 170,
Moose, WY 83012.
Fort Laramie National Historic Site, Fort Laramie,
WY 82212.

Outdoor Guide

In Idaho

Outfitters and Guides

Agalpah River Trips, P.O. Box 425, Salmon, ID
83467. 756-4167. (Backpacking, river running.)
Chamberlain Divide Outfitters, 205 E. 40th St.,
Boise, ID 83704. 343-8504. (Fishing, trail riding.)
Grizzly Mountain Outfitters, P.O. Box 809, North
Fork, ID 83466. 865-2164. (Snowmobiling, guest
ranch, big game hunting, bird hunting.)
Indian Creek Ranch, Rt 2, Box 105, North Fork, ID
83466. Dial Operators, Give #208-05-7121 ask
Salmon operator for 24F211. (Trail riding, bird
hunting, big game, snowmobiling.)
Lazy J Outfitters, Rt 1, Kuna ID 83634, 922-5648.
(Snowmobile, river/lake fishing.)
Salmon River Experience, 812 Truman, Moscow, ID
83843. 882-2385. (River running, fishing, kayaking.)
Sun Valley Treking Company, P.O. Box 2200, Sun
Valley ID 83353. 726-9595. (Kayaking, X-C skiing,
technical mountaineering.)
Sun Valley Helicopter Ski Guides, P.O. Box 978, Sun
Valley, ID 83353.
Teton Experience, P.O. Box 218, Rigby, ID 83442.
523-4951. (Trail riding, river running, fishing.)
Teton Mountain Touring, P.O. Box 514, Driggs, ID.
83422. 354-2768. (X-C skiing.)
Whitewater Outfitters, Salmon River Air Rt.,
Cascade, ID 83611. 382-4336. (Jet boating, fishing,
trail riding.)
Wilderness Learning, P.O. Box 431, Ammon, ID
83401, 524-1874. (Survival training.)

In Montana

Outdoor Activities

Crazy Mountain Company, Chico Hot Springs,
Pray, MT 59065. 333-4779. (Whitewater scenic float
and fishing trips on the Yellowstone River.) Guided
hikes and ski trips. Group rates available.
Mountain Whitewater, P.O. Box 486, Bozemen, MT
59717. 995-4613. (Whitewater scenic float and
fishing trips on the Gallatin and Madison Rivers.)

Group rates available.
Venture Yellowstone, Box 846, Canyon Route,
Gallatin Gateway, MT 59730. 995-4841. Scenic and
whitewater trips down the Yellowstone and Gallatin
Rivers. Group rates available.
Yellowstone Raft Company, Box 46, Gardiner, MT
59030. 848-7777. Rafting headquarters for south-
west Montana and Yellowstone National Park. (Ex-
clusive whitewater trip through the Bear Trap
Canyon Wilderness Area on the Madison River.)
Other half day and full day trips are available.
Group rates.
**Guided Outdoor Activities offered by T.W.A. Ser-
vices Inc. Stagecoach Rides,** (The authentic Concord Stagecoach has exciting 45 minute rides
through the rolling sagebrush country. Rides depart
from Roosevelt Corrals.) Between June 10th and
Sept 9th.
Old West Cookouts, Cook a delicious meal outdoors at a site reached by a horse-drawn wagon near
Roosevelt Corrals. Departs at 4.30pm and 5.30pm,
and returns by 7.30pm. June 10th to Sept 9th.
Sceniccruiser Rides, Boats depart several times daily
from the Bridge Bay Marina for a leisurely cruise on
Yellowstone Lake. This is conducted by T.W.A. Services Inc, Yellowstone Park Divison, Yellowstone
National Park, WY 82190. 344-7901. June 15 to Sept
23.

In Utah

Recreational Tour Operators

Aerial Tours:

Arrowhead Helicopters, P.O. Box 1343, Moab, UT
84532. 259-5956.
Park City Balloon Adventures, 2040 Sunnside Ave.,
Salt Lake, UT. 84108. 583-3120.
SkyWest Aviation, P.O. Box T, St. George Municipal
Airport, St George. UT 84770. 1-800-453-9417.

Backpacking and Hiking:

Ken Sleight Expeditions, P.O. Box 81185. Salt Lake
City, UT 84108. 564-3656 (summer); 583-6255
(winter).

Excursion Train:

Heber Creeper, Deer Creek Scenic Railroad, 600 W.
100 South, Salt Lake City, UT 84032. 654-3229.
Old Salty Railroad Inc, 549 W. 500 South, Salt Lake
City, UT 84101. 359-8800.

Fly/Drive Tours:

Mountain Tours, 1380 West North Temple, Salt Lake
City, UT 84116. 359-9996. Telex: 381.022

Horse Packing:

Calvin-Alpine Outfitters, 2567 E. Pringle Circle,
Ogden, UT 84403, 479-6977.
Rell Enterprises, P.O. Box 14, St. George, UT 84770.
574-2266.
High Country Adventure, Rt. #1 Box 118, Roosevelt,
UT 84066. 722-3065.

Wild & Scenic Inc, P.O. Box 401, Moab, UT 84532. 259-8625.

Hunting and Fishing:

Hatt's Ranch, Box 275, Green River, UT 84525. 564-3238.
Tavaputs Plateau Ranch, P.O. Box 786, Price, UT 84501. 564-3463.
United Sportsmen, P.O. Box 21141, Salt Lake City, UT 84121. 268-9557.

Jeep/4 wheel Drive Tours:

Adrift Adventures in Canyonlands Inc, 5620 S. Waterbury, Suite 203-A, Salt Lake City, UT 84121. 272-3442.
Tag-A-Long Tours, 452 N. Main St., Moab, UT 84532. 1-800-453-3292.

National Park Tours:

Allwest Leisure Tours, 451 E. Broadway, Salt Lake City, UT 84111. 532-2113.
Western River Expeditions, 7258 Racquet Club Dr., Salt Lake City, UT 84121. 942-6669.
Color Country Tours, 281 S. Main St., Cedar City, UT. 84720. 586-9916.

River Runners:

Colorado River and Trail Expeditions Inc. P.O. Box 7575, Salt Lake City, UT 84107. 261-1789.
Moki Mac River Expeditions, P.O. Box 21242, Salt Lake City, UT 84121. 943-6707.
Mountain River Guides, 3325 Fowler, Ogden, UT 84403. 399-1297.
Tex's River Expeditions. P.O. Box 67, Moab, UT 84532. 259-5101.

Salt Lake City and Vicinity Tours:

Allwest Leisure Tours, 451 E. Broadway, Salt Lake City, UT 84111. 532-2113.
Gray Line of Salt Lake City, 158 N. 400 West, Salt Lake City, UT 84103. 521-7060.
Mountain Tours, 1380 W. North Temple, Salt Lake City, UT 84116. 359-8677. Telex: 381.022.

In Wyoming

Special Camps and Wilderness Schools

Wind River Wilderness Camp, Box W.T.C. 6878 S. Arapahoe Dr., Littleton, CO 80120. (303) 794-9518. Camp located in Bridger-Teton National Forest. (Wilderness and outdoor activities for teenagers. Back packing, technical climbing, kayaking, glacier climbing, wilderness survival.....)
Sodergreen Horsemanship School, Buford, WY 82052. (307) 632-7954. (Ten day, live-in, intensive riding school.)
Western Wheels, Box W.T.C., 6878 S. Arapahoe Dr., Littleton, CO 80120. (303) 794-9518. (Offers bicycle tours to all ages through Teton and Yellowstone National Parks. Equipment furnished, bicycles can be rented.)
Jackson Hole Mountain Guides, Teton Village, WY

83025, (307) 733-4979. (Personal climbing instruction and guiding service.)
Rawhide Ranch Camps, 916 S. 11th St., Laramie, WY 82070. (307) 472-6115. (winter) Box 1810, Cody, WY 82414. (307) 587-2061. (summer) Camp for girls and boys ages 9 thru' 16 near Yellowstone National Park. (Horseback riding, fishing, archery, crafts, rodeos....)
Audubon Ecology Camp in the West, 4150 Darley, Boulder, CO 80303. (303) 499-5409. (Naturalists lead adults for two week sessions of ecosystem studies in Wind River Mountains.) University credit available. June thru' mid-Aug.
Girls Scouts National Center West, Box 95, Ten Sleep, WY 82442. (The 14,134 acre center offers troop camping, special programs for girl scouts and their families.)
Siggins Triangle X Camp, Southfork Route, Cody, WY 82414, (307) 587-2031. Camp for 25 young people (ages 10-17). (Horse riding, fishing, tennis, dance, swimming, hiking, 8-day wilderness packtrip.....) June 25 to July 24.
Teton Valley Ranch Camps, Box 8, Kelly, WY 83011. (307) 733-2958. Located in Jackson Hole. Five week camps for boys and girls. (Activities include photography, pack trips, riflery, crafts, archery, fly tying and rodeos.)
Yellowstone-Grand Teton Photographic Expeditions, Box 3238, Jackson, WY 83001. (307) 733-5298. One and two day guided tours for naturalists, photographers, film makers in Grand Tetons and Yellowstone National Parks.
Skinner Brothers Guides and Outfitters, Box B, Pinedale, WY 82941. (307) 367-4675. (Family and adult, group pack trips and fishing trips.)

Radio Stations

Colorado

AM

1280	KBRQ	Denver (Country and Western)
1340	KHOW	Denver News (NBC)
950	KIMN	Denver (Top 40, easy listening)
1390	KJJZ	Denver (Easy Listening)
1090	KKBB	Denver (Easy Listening)
560	KLZ	Denver (Country and Western)
850	KOA	Denver (News and Talk)
910	KPOF	Denver (Classical)
930	KUIP	Durango (Easy Listening)
1470	KSIR	Estes Park (Easy Listening)
600	KIIX	Fort Collins (Country and Western)
1230	KEXO	Grand Junction (Contemporary)
1100	KREX	Grand Junction (Easy Listening)
620	KSTR	Grand Junction (Easy Listening)
1310	KFKA	Greeley (Farm news, easy listening)
1450	KYOU	Greeley (Country and Western)
1490	KQUC	Gunnison (Easy Listening)

FM

90.1	KCFR	Denver (Classical)
950	KYGO	Denver (Country and Western)
100.3	KLIR	Denver (Adult Contemporary)
103.5	KOAQ	Denver (Contemporary hits)
95.7	KPKE	Denver (Contemporary hits)
99.5	KVOD	Denver (Classical)

101.3	KIQX	Durango (Rock)
100.5	KRSJ	Durango (Country and Western)
93.3	KTCL	Fort Collins (Rock)
90.9	KCSU	Fort Collins (Educational)
99.9	KEKB	Grand Junction (Country)
90.3	KJOL	Grand Junction (Religious and Educational)
93.1	KQIX	Grand Junction (Easy Listening)
91.3	KUNC	Greeley (Easy Listening, news)
102.3	KVLE	Gunnison (Easy Listening)
97.7	KSPN	Aspen
90.5	KEPC	Colorado Springs

Idaho

AM

670	KBOI	Boise
630	KIDO	Boise
103.1	KVNI	Coeur D'Alene
930	KSEI	Pocatello

FM

92.3	KBBK	Boise
103.1	KCDA	Coeur D'Alene
104.9		Pocatello

Montana

AM

730	KURL	Billings (Religious, specials)
970	KOOK	Billings (Contemporary)
1230	KBMN	Bozeman (Easy Listening)
1090	KBOZ	Bozeman (Country)
550	KBOW	Butte (Country and Western)
1370	KXLF	Butte (Contemporary)
1400	KARR	Great Falls (Top 40, rock)
1310	KEIN	Great Falls (Country and Western)
1240	KBLL	Helena

FM

88.9	KRER	Billings (Educational)
93.3	KYYA	Billings (Contemporary)
93.7	KBOZ	Bozeman (Contemporary)
95.5	KQUY	Butte (Adult Contemporary)
98.9	KAAK	Great Falls (Adult Contemporary)
92.9	KLFM	Great Falls (Modern Country)

Utah

AM

1230	KOAL	Price (Easy Listening)
960	KDOT	Provo (Easy Listening)
1400	KFTN	Provo (Modern Country)
910	KALL	Salt Lake City (Adult Contemporary)
1320	KBUG	Salt Lake City (Adult Contemporary)
1280	KDYL	Salt Lake City (News)
570	KLUB	Salt Lake City (Nostalgia)
630	KZJO	Salt Lake City (Talk)
860	KWHO	Salt Lake City (Classical)

FM

98.3	KARB	Price (Country and Western)
88.9	KBYU	Provo (Classical)
94.9	KLRZ	Provo (Contemporary)
99.3	KRDC	St. George (Variety)
94.1	KLCY	Salt Lake City (Contemporary)
98.7	KCPX	Salt Lake City (Contemporary)
104.3	KSOP	Salt Lake City (Country and Western)
90.1	KUER	Salt Lake City (Classical and jazz)

Wyoming

AM

1240	KFBC	Cheyenne (Easy Listening)
1030	KTWO	Casper (Easy Listening)
1230	KVOC	Casper (Modern Country and Western)
1340	KSGT	Jackson (Easy Listening)
1330	KOVE	Lander (Country and Western)
1490	KOJO	Laramie (Easy Listening)

FM

95.5	KTRS	Casper (Top 40)
94.5	KAWY	Casper (Rock and jazz)
97.9	KFBQ	Cheyenne
100.7	KKAZ	Cheyenne (Adult Contemporary)
97.9	KTAG	Cody (Top 40)
96.9	KMTN	Jackson (Adult Contemporary)
97.5	KDLY	Lander (Adult Contemporary)
102.9	KIOZ	Laramie (Top 40)
96.5	KLWD	Sheridan

Ski Directory

Colorado

Breckenridge, Breckenridge Resort Chamber, P.O. Box 1909, Breckenridge, CO 80424. 1-800-221-1091. Open mid-Nov to mid-April.

Keystone, Keystone Ski Resort, Box 38, Keystone, CO 80435. (303) 468-4242. Open from Oct to April.

Steamboat Springs, Steamboat Springs, Box 774408, Steamboat Springs, CO 80477. (303) 879-0740. Open late-Nov to mid-April.

Vail Resorts, Vail Resorts Association, 421 E. Meadow Dr., Vail, CO 81657. 1-800-525-3875. (For Beaver Creek and Vail ski areas.) Open Nov to April.

Aspen Resorts, Aspen Resorts, 700 S. Aspen St., Aspen, CO 81611. (303) 925-9000. (For Aspen Mountain Ski Area, Snowmass Ski Area & Buttermilk Ski Area.) Open late-Nov to mid-April.

Copper Mountain Resort, Copper Mountain Resort, P.O. Box 3001, Copper Mountain, CO 80443. (303) 968-2882. Open Nov to April.

Idaho

Bogus Basin, 16 miles (25 km) north of Boise via the Bogus Basin Rd. For reservations and information: 2405 Bogus Basin Rd., Boise, ID 83702. 1-800-367-4397. Open Dec to April.

Schweitzer, 11 miles (17 km) NW of Sandpoint, 88

miles (140 km) NE of Spokane. Schweitzer Reservations, P.O. Box 815, Sandpoint, ID 83864. (202) 263-9555. Open late-Nov to mid-April.
Sun Valley, 80 miles (128 km) north of Twin Falls. Sun Valley Co. Sun Valley ID 83353. 1-800-635-8261. Open end-Nov to mid-April.
Grand Targee, 78 miles (125 km) NE of Idaho Falls. Grand Targee Reservations, Driggs, ID 83422. 1-800-443-8146. Open mid-Nov to mid-April.

Montana

Bridger Bowl, Bridger Bowl, 15795 Bridger Canyon Rd., Bozeman, MT 59715. 1-800-223-9609. Open daily mid-Dec to mid-April.
Red Lodge, Red Lodge Ski Area, Post Office Drawer R, Red Lodge, MT 59068. 1-800-468-8977. Open daily mid-Nov to mid-April.
Big Mountain, Big Mountain, Box 1215, Whitefish, MT 59937. (406) 862-3511. Open daily Nov to mid-April.
Big Sky, Big Sky Ski Area, Box 1, Big Sky, MT 59716. 1-800-548-4486. Open daily mid-Nov to mid-April.

Utah

Park City, 27 miles (43 km) east of Salt Lake City, via interstate 80. Park City Ski Corp. P.O. Box 39-UP84, Park City, UT 84060. 1-800-222-PARK. Open mid-Nov to end April.
Snowbird, 24 miles (38 km) southeast of Salt Lake City. Snowbird Ski and Summer Resort, Snowbird, UT 84092. 1-800-453-3000. Open mid-Nov to early-May.
Alta, 33 miles (55 km) southeast of Salt Lake City. Alta Reservations, Alta, UT 84092. (801) 742-2040. Open mid-Nov to May.
Deer Valley, 27 miles (43 km) east of Salt Lake City. Deer Valley Resort, P.O. Box 1525, Park City, UT 84060. 1-800-543-3833. Open Dec 8 to April 7.

Wyoming

Teton Village, Jackson Hole Ski Corp. Box 290, Teton Village, WY 83025. (307) 733-2292. Ski area open mid-Dec to mid-April.
Jackson, Snow King Inc. Box 1137, 400 Snow King, Jackson, WY 83001. Night skiing possible. (307) 733-2042. Operates from mid-Dec to mid-April.
Pinedale, White Pine Lodge Ski Area, Box 833, Pinedale, WY 82941. (307) 367-4142. Open mid-Dec to mid-April. (Fri-Sun) In Jan and Feb open Thursday too.
Casper, Hogadon Basin, Hogadon Basin, 1715 E. 4th St., Casper, WY 82601. (307) 266-1600. Open mid-Dec to mid-April, Wed thru' Sun.
Cody, near Yellowstone National Park. Open mid-Dec to mid-April, Wed thru' Sun.
Sleeping Giant, P.O. Box 790, Cody WY 82414. (307) 587-4044.
Centennial, Medicine Bow area. Open mid-Dec to mid-April, Wed thru' Sun.
Medicine Bow/Snowy Range, Box 138, Centennial, WY 82055. (307) 745-5750.

State Parks and Recreation Area

Colorado

Barbour Ponds State Recreation Area, 7 miles (11 km) east of Longmont, (Camping, sailboarding.)
Barr Lake State Park, 18 miles (29 km) northeast of Denver. (Picnic sites, sailboarding, hunting.)
Bonny State Recreation Area, 22 miles (35 km) north of Burlington. (Camping, water sports, hunting.)
Boyd Lake State Recreation Area, 1 mile (1.6 km) east of Loveland. (Camping, water sports, hunting.)
Castlewood Canyon State Park, 3 miles (5 km) south of Franktown. (Picnic sites, cross country skiing.)
Chatfield State Recreation Area, 8 miles (13 km) southwest of Denver. (Camping, water sports, riding.)
Cherry Creek State Recreation Area, adjacent to southeast Denver. (Water sports, camping, snowmobiling.)
Crawford State Recreation Area, 1 mile (1.6 km) south of Crawford. (Camping boating, cycling.)
Eldorado Canyon State Park, 8 miles (13 km) southwest of Boulder. (Picnic sites, rock climbing.)
Eleven Mile State Recreation Area, 8 miles (13 km) southwest of Lake George. (Camping, snowmobiling, hunting.)
Golden Gate Canyon State Park, 15 miles (24 km) west of Golden. (Camping, horseback riding, hunting.)
Highline State Recreation Area, 7 miles (11 km) northwest of Loma. (Camping, water sports, ice skating.)
Island Acres State Recreation Area, 15 miles (24 km) east of Grand Junction. (Camping, ice skating, sailboarding.)
Jackson Lake State Recreation Area, 22 miles (35 km) northwest of Fort Morgan. (Camping, water sports, hunting, cross country skiing.)
Lanthrop State Park, 3 miles (5 km) west of Walsenburg. (Hunting, camping, water sports.)
Lory State Park, 5 miles (8 km) west of Ft Collins.
Mueller State Park, (closed) 3 miles (5 km) south of Divide.
Navajo State Recreation Area, 1 mile (1.6 km) south of Arboles. (Camping, hunting, water sports.)
Paonia State Recreation Area, 6 miles (10 km) west of Pueblo. (Picnic sites, water sports.)
Rifle Gap/Falls State Recreation Area, 7 miles (11 km) north of Rifle. (Camping, hunting.)
Roxborough State Park, (open by tour only) 15 miles (24 km) southwest of Denver.
State Forest, 21 miles (34 km) southeast of Walden. (Camping, cross country skiing, snowmobiling.)
Steamboat Lake State Park, 26 miles (42 km) north of Steamboat Springs. (Camping, snowmobiling.)
Sweitzer Lake State Recreation Area, 3 miles (5 km) south of Denver. (Picnic sites, water sports.)
Trinided State Recreation Area, 3 miles (5 km) west of Trinidad. (Camping, hunting, horseback riding.)
Vega State Recreation Area, 12 miles (19 km) east of Collbran. (Camping, hunting, snowmobiling, cross country skiing, water sports.)

Idaho

Priest Lake State Park, located 35 miles (53 km) north of Priest River on Priest Lake.

Round Lake State Park, 10 miles (16 km) south of Sand Point on U.S. 95.

Farragut State Park, located 4 miles (6 km) east of U.S. 95 at Athol.

Old Mission State Park, east of Cataldo, exit 39 off I-90.

Mowry State Park, only accessible by boat from Coeur D'Alene or Harrison to Grasser Point.

Heyburn State Park, located between Plummer and St Maries on Highway 5.

Hells Gates State Park, 4 miles (6 km) south of Lewiston on Snake River Ave.

Winchester Lake State Park, 1 mile (1.6 km) southwest of Winchester on U.S. 95.

McCroskey State Park, 26 miles (42 km) north of Moscow on U.S. 95.

Packer John State Park, 9 miles (15 km) northwest of McCall on Highway 55.

Ponderosa State Park, located just north of McCall on Payette Lake.

Eagle Island State Park, west of Eagle, off Hwy 44.

Veteran's Memorial State Park, located west of Boise at 36th and State St.

Lucky Peak State Park, (3 units) located 8 miles (13 km) east of Boise on Hwy 21.

Three Island State Park, 1 mile (1.6 km) west of Glenns Ferry.

Malad Gorge State Park, east of Bliss on I-84 exit 147.

Massacre Rocks State Park, 12 miles (19 km) west of American Falls.

Indian Rocks State Park, 25 miles (40 km) southeast from junction I-25 and I-86 at Pocatello.

Bear Lake State Park, 18 miles (29 km) south of Montpelier on Hwy 89.

Harriman State Park, 18 miles (29 km) north of Ashton, 33 miles (53 km) southwest of West Yellowstone.

Henry's Lake State Park, 17 miles (27 km) southwest of West Yellowstone.

Montana

Bannack State Park, 5 miles (8 km) south of Dillon on I-15, then 21 miles (33 km) west on Secondary 278, and four miles south on County Rd.

Makoshika State Park, 2 miles (3.5 km) south of Glendive on Snyder Ave.

Medicine Rocks State Park, 25 miles (40 km) south of Baker on Montana 7, milepost 10, then 1 mile (1.6 km) west on County Rd.

Missouri Headwaters State Park, 3 miles (5 km) east of Three Forks on US 10, then 3 miles (5 km) north on Secondary 286.

West Shore State Park, 20 miles (32 km) south of Kalespell, on US 93 milepost 93.

Wild Horse Island State Park, Access from Big Arm State Recreational Area, via boat to Little Sheeko Bay (NW side of island).

Giant Springs, edge of Great Falls on River Drive, N. (One of the fresh water springs in the world.)

Ulm Pishkun, off I-15, 12 miles (20 km) west of Great Falls. (A picturesque buffalo kill site.)

Lewis and Clark Caverns, just off I-90, 47 miles (75 km) east of Butte. (One of the largest known limestone caverns in the Northwest.)

Lost Creek, 9 miles (15 km) north of Anaconda, on Montana 273.

Utah

Bear Lake Marina State Park, in Garden City, 1 mile (1.6 km) north on U.S. 89.

Hyrum Lake State Park, in Hyrum, Utah.

Bear Lake Rendezvous Beach, Laketown, 3 miles (5 km) NW on Hwy 30.

Goosenecks of the San Juans, Mexican Hat, 4 miles (6.5 km) off Hwy 261.

Dead Horse Point State Park, Moab, 34 miles (55 km) west on Hwy 313.

Millsite Lake State Park, Ferron, 4 miles (6.5 km) off Hwy 10.

Green River State Park, Green River, 2 miles (3.5 km) south of I-70.

Goblin Valley State Park, Hanksville, 35 miles (57 km) NW of Hwy 24.

Huntington Lake State Park, Huntington, 2 miles (3.5 km) NW of Hwy 155.

Scofield Lake State Park, Soldier Summit, 17 miles (27 km) west of U.S. 6.

Minersville Lake State Park, Beaver, 12 miles (19 km) west of Hwy 21.

Kodachrome Basin, Cannoville, 4 miles (6.5 km) south of Hwy 2.

Escalante Petrified Forest, Escalante, 5 miles (8 km) west off Hwy 12.

Coral Pink Sand Dunes State Park, Kanab, 35 miles (57 km) NW of U.S. 89.

Gunlock Lake State Park, St. George, 16 miles (26 km) NW of Hwy 56.

Snow Canyon State Park, St. George, 5 miles (8 km) NW of Hwy 18.

Starvation Lake State Park, Duchesne, 3 miles (5 km) west off U.S. 40.

Steinaker Lake State Park, Vernal, 6 miles (10 km) north of Hwy 44.

Great Salt Lake, Saltair Beach, Salt Lake City, 15 miles (24 km) west off I-80.

Deer Creek Lake State Park, Heber City, 5 miles (8 km) SW on US 189.

Wasatch Mountain State Park, Midway, off U.S. 40, 189 or Hwy 113.

Utah Lake State Park, Provo, 4 miles (6.5 km) west off I-15.

Rockport Lake State Park, Wanship, 2 miles (3.5 km) south on U.S. Alt. 189.

Otter Creek Lake State Park, Antimony, 4 miles (6.5 km) north on Hwy 22.

Piute Lake State Park, Junction, 5 miles (8 km) north on U.S. 89.

Yuba Lake State Park, Nephi, 25 miles (40 km) south off U.S. 91.

Paradise Lake State Park, Sterling, 3 miles (5 km) east off U.S. 89.

Wyoming

Buffalo Bill State Park, located a few miles west of Cody. (Offers picnicking and minimum camping facilities. The adjacent reservoir features excellent trout fishing.)

Sinks Canyon State Park, 10 miles (16 km) southwest of Lander is in a spectacular mountain canyon. (Limited camping facilities, hiking trails, scenic overlooks, trout-filled pools are a part of this park.)

Boysen State Park, in central Wyoming. (Surrounded by the Wind River Reservation. Good for overnight camping, fishing and water sports.)

Hot Springs State Park, at Thermopolis is centered around the world's largest mineral hot springs. (Indoor and outdoor swimming pools, lodging accommodations and bath house are on the grounds.)

Seminoe State Park, located 34 miles (54 km) north of Sinclair, is surrounded by giant white sand dunes, antelope, sage grouse and sagebrush. (Fishing and camping.)

Edness Kimball Wilkins State Park, east of Casper, along the North Platte River is currently under development.

Curt Gowdy State Park, is reached by taking the road (Wyo 210) west out of Cheyenne, and is midway between Cheyenne and Laramie. (Two reservoirs offer excellent fishing and water.)

Glendo State Park, is located at Glendo. (Overnight camping, commercial concession, cabin and trailer court facilities and marina operation. Good for fishing and boating.)

Guernsey State Park, is 3 miles (5 km) from the rown of Guernsey. (This is Oregon Trail country, offering a museum and some camping.)

Keyhole State Park, is four miles (6 km) north of I-90, between Sundance and Moorcraft. Antelope, deer and wild turkey inhabit this western Black Hills area. The park is located along the shores of Keyhole reservoir and is a popular spot for fishing. The Devil's Tower National Monument can be seen from here.

ART/PHOTO CREDITS

155	Hara Photographics	217	Tom Tidball
156	Vautier-de Nanxe	219	Tom Tidball
157	Joseph F Viesti	220-221	Tom Tidball
158	Vautier-de Nanxe	222	Vautier-de Nanxe
159	Vautier-de Nanxe	223	Robert Michael
160L	Joseph F Viesti	225	Lee Foster
160R	Tom Tidball	226	Robert Michael
161	Tom Tidball	227	Tom Tidball
163	Tom Tidball	228-229	Rick McIntyre
164	Rick McIntyre	230	Tom Tidball
165	Tom Tidball	231	Joseph F Viesti
166-167	Tom Tidball	232	Lee Foster
168	Tom Tidball	233	Tom Tidball
169	Tom Tidball	234	Tom Tidball
171	Tom Tidball	235	Lee Foster
172	Tom Tidball	236-237	Vautier-de Nanxe
173	Ricardo Ferro	238	Tom Tidball
175	Ricardo Ferro	239	Tom Tidball
176	Tom Tidball	240	C M Russell Museum, Great Falls, Montana
177	Ricardo Ferro	241	Vautier-de Nanxe
178	Tom Tidball	242	Vautier-de Nanxe
179	Tom Tidball	243	Vautier-de Nanxe
180	Joseph F Viesti	244-245	Vautier-de Nanxe
181	Tom Tidball	246	Tom Tidball
182	Tom Tidball	247	Tom Tidball
183	Tom Tidball	248	Tom Tidball
184	Pat Canova	249	Tom Tidball
185	Tom Tidball	250	Tom Tidball
186-187	Joseph F Viesti	251	Vautier-de Nanxe
189	Joseph F Viesti	252	Vautier-de Nanxe
190	Tom Tidball	253	Vautier-de Nanxe
191	Tom Tidball	254-255	Tom Tidball
192	Ricardo Ferro	256	Lee Foster
193	Joseph F Viesti	257	Hara Photographics
194	Lee Foster	258	Lee Foster
195	Robert Michael	260	Tom Tidball
196	Tom Tidball	261	Tom Tidball
197	Joseph F Viesti	262-263	Tom Tidball
198-199	Joseph F Viesti	264	Tom Tidball
200	Joseph F Viesti	267	Tom Tidball
201	Joseph F Viesti	268	Courtesy of the Salt Lake Valley Convention & Visitors Bureau
202L	Edgar Boyles	269	Tom Tidball
202R	Joseph F Viesti	270	Joseph F Viesti
204	Tom Tidball	271	Vautier-de Nanxe
205	Joseph F Viesti	272L	Tom Tidball
206-207	Tom Tidball	272R	Tom Tidball
208	Tom Tidball	273	Vautier-de Nanxe
210	Tom Tidball	274	Vautier-de Nanxe
211	Tom Tidball	275	Bruce Bernstein Collection, Courtesy of
212	Tom Tidball		
213	Tom Tidball		
214-215	Tom Tidball		
216	Tom Tidball		

	Princeton Library, NJ.
276	Bruce Bernstein Collection, Courtesy of Princeton Library, NJ.
277	Bruce Bernstein Collection, Courtesy of Princeton Library, NJ.
278	Vautier-de Nanxe
279	Courtesy of the Salt Lake Valley Convention & Visitors Bureau
280	Bruce Bernstein Collection, Courtesy of Princeton Library, NJ.
281	Bruce Bernstein Collection, Courtesy of Princeton Library, NJ.
283	Joseph F Viesti
284	Tom Tidball
285	Vautier-de Nanxe
286	Tom Tidball
287	Tom Tidball
288	Vautier-de Nanxe
289	Tom Tidball
290	Tom Tidball
Backcover	Tom Tidball (Hospitality) Tony Stone Worldwide (Indian) Bruce Bernstein Collection, Courtesy of Princeton Library, NJ (History) Rick McIntyre (Majesty) Vautier-de Nanxe (Motion) Michael H Francis (Grizzly) Michael H Francis (Encounters) Lee Foster (Geysers) Christine Faucher (Landscapes) Vautier-de Nanxe (Journey) Joseph F Viesti (Fun) Tom Tidball (City) Tom Tidball (Sports)
Spine (from top to bottom)	Rick McIntyre Tom Tidball Joseph F Viesti Rick McIntyre Tom Tidball